CONFOUNDING
THE REICH

CONFOUNDING THE REICH

The RAF's Secret War of Electronic Countermeasures in WWII

The Story of 100 (Special Duties) Group RAF
Bomber Command 1943–1945

Martin W. Bowman
and
Tom Cushing

Pen & Sword
AVIATION

A newly delivered NFXXX of No 85 Squadron taxies out at Swannington at the start of a Night
Intruder *over Germany. The unit started swapping its NFX VIIs and XIXs for definitive NFXXXs
in September 1944. (IWM)*

First published in
Great Britain in 2004
By Pen and Sword Aviation
an imprint of Pen and Sword Books Ltd
47 Church Street, Barnsley,
South Yorkshire, S70 2AS, England

ISBN 1 84415 124 7

A CIP catalogue record for this book
is available from the British Library

Typeset in Times New Roman 10 on 12 point by
Mac Style Ltd, Scarborough, N. Yorkshire

Printed and bound in England by
CPI UK

Pen & Sword Books Ltd incorporates the Imprints of
Pen & Sword Aviation, Pen & Sword Maritime,
Pen & Sword Military, Wharncliffe Local History,
Pen & Sword Select, Pen & Sword Military Classics
and Leo Cooper.

For a complete list of Pen & Sword titles, please contact
Pen & Sword Books Limited
47 Church Street, Barnsley, South Yorkshire
S70 2AS, England
Email: enquiries @ pen-and-sword.co.uk
Website: www.pen-and-sword.co.uk

Contents

The time will come when thou
Shall lift thine eyes
To watch a long drawn battle
In the skies
While aged peasants, too amazed
For words
Stare at the flying fleets
Of wondrous birds
England, so long mistress of the sea
Where wind and waves confess
Her sovereignty
Her ancient triumphs yet on high
Shall bear
And reign, the sovereign of
The conquered air

'Luna Habitalis' By Thomas Gray, 1737

NFIIs first equipped 157 Squadron on 13 December 1941. DD750, which served with 157, 25, 239 and 264 Squadrons, is fitted with AI Mk.IV 'arrowhead', and wing-mounted azimuth aerials. All four machine guns were deleted to make room for Serrate apparatus. The all-black scheme could slow the aircraft by up to 23 mph (37 kph). When NFIIs began equipping 100 Group in December 1943, the extended operational service had begun to tell and the Merlin 21s were well used. Finally, in February 1944, all reconditioned engines were called in and while stocks lasted, only Merlin 22s were installed. (via Philip Birtles).

Acknowledgements

I am enormously grateful to the following people for making it possible to include detailed information in this book. Don F. Aris very kindly allowed me to quote from his superb unpublished three-volume history of 141 Squadron, which has taken him a lifetime to compile. His fellow armourer, Johnny Claxton, kindly made these available for a long period of time. Dr Theo Boiten provided enormous expertise on victories and details of German crews. As always, I am most grateful to Mike Bailey for his guidance, proofing and kind loan of much-needed books for research purposes. Bob Collis unstintingly provided his customary expertise and furnished much valuable information on aircraft and crews, often in very detailed and painstaking correspondence. Last but not least I would like to pay tribute to Tom Cushing for his most marvellous assistance, and for so very graciously giving me free rein to use his vast historical collection of memorabilia, documents and photographs at Little Snoring. Time spent at his house on Snoring airfield, served with plentiful cups of tea from his lovely wife Wendy, have been some of the most enjoyable interludes during the preparation of this book.

Jerry Scutts and Philip J. Birtles provided many superb photographs. Steve Jefferson worked wonders making prints from glass negatives. I am no less grateful to the following for their help and support throughout: The late Michael Allen DFC**; Jim Avis; Captain 'Buddy' Badley; Len Bartram; Tim Bates; Derek 'Taffy' Bellis DFC*; Frank Bocock; Eileen Boorman; Les Bostock; Bill Bridgeman; Lewis Brandon DSO, DFC*; Jean Bunting; Peter Celis; Squadron Leader Joe Cooper AFC; Andrew Crotch; the late Squadron Leader John Crotch DFC; Henry 'Hank' Cooper; Hans-Peter Dabrowski; Squadron Leader Mike Daniels; Bob Davies AFC; Ernie Frohloff; *Legion Magazine;* Richard T. Goucher; Peter B. Gunn, author of *RAF Great Massingham;* Terry Groves; Alan Hague, Curator, Norfolk & Suffolk Aviation Museum; Lewis Heath; Gerhard Heilig; Raymond Hicks; Leslie 'Dutch' Holland; George Honeyman; Stephen Hutton; Harry Jeffries; Wing Commander Howard C. Kelsey DSO DFC*; Geoff Liles; Ron Mackay; Sister Laurence May; Neville Miller; W. H. Miller DFC; Mosquito Aircrew Association; Simon Parry, Murray Peden DFC QC; Eric Phillips; Don Prutton; Barbara and John Rayson G.Av.A; Harry Reed DFC; Alf Rogers; Group Captain J. K. 'Sport' Rogers OBE FBIM RAF (Retd); Squadron Leader Derek Rothery RAF (Retd); Walter Rowley; Wing Commander Philip Russell DFC; Group Captain J. A. V. Short MBIM; Group Captain E. M. Smith DFC* DFM; Martin Staunton; Robert 'Bob' Symon; Harry Welham DFC; Graham 'Chalky' White; Squadron Leader R. G. 'Tim' Woodman DSO DFC; Johnny Wynne DFC and finally the City of Norwich Aviation Museum.

Introduction

On 8 November 1943, 100 (Special Duties) Group of RAF Bomber Command was formed. The object was to consolidate the various squadrons and units that had been fighting a secret war of electronics and radar countermeasures, attempting to reduce the losses of the heavy bombers – and their hard-pressed crews – in Bomber Command. This secret war involved the use of air and ground radars, homing and jamming equipment, special radio and navigational aids, and intruding night-fighters to seek out and destroy their opposite numbers, the Ju 88s and Bf 110s of the *Nachtjägdgeschwader* now defending the vivid night skies of the *Third Reich* with ever-increasing success.

While there were various radar counter-measures that could be activated from the ground, the airborne operations took two distinct forms. One was a force of heavy bomber aircraft flying over Germany and occupied Europe, carrying a variety of radar and radio jamming equipment, sometimes on spoofing operations; the other was provided from the home defence night-fighter squadrons. Since June 1943 these had been carrying out high-level, freelance Intruder sorties specifically against the German night-fighters.

These activities, conducted by specialist bomber and night-fighter crews, and the equipment they used, were cloaked under some weird and strange-sounding code-names such as *Serrate*, *Mandrel*, *Jostle*, *Monica* and *Airborne Cigar*. The night-fighter crews who completed a first tour on one of seven fighter squadrons in 100 Group could expect to go for their 'rest' of six months either to the Bomber Support Training Unit (BSTU), or the Bomber Support Development Unit (BSDU). In the latter, they were still expected to continue flying on operations because the new equipment could only be tested adequately on the job. In those halcyon days that meant 'over the other side'.

The losses among the Lancasters, Halifaxes, Stirlings and Wellingtons were many times greater than among the *Serrate* Mosquitoes. The task of trying to reduce those losses was a rewarding challenge for all British night-fighter crews. It had to be pursued to the very limit and beyond. Sometimes they saw the bombers being shot down in flames around them. Sometimes they could return to base and tell their welcoming and faithful ground crews that they had 'got one' which meant that one German night-fighter would not be returning to its base that night, nor taking off the following night to hit the 'bomber boys'.

Glossary

Abschuss   Confirmed victory in air combat

AI   Airborne Interception (radar)

AI Mk IV   1.5 metre fixed dipole aerials working on the 'floodlighting' principle

AI Mk V   as Mk IV but with pilot indication

AI Mk VI   as Mk V but installed in single-seat fighter

AI Mk VII   10 cm radar with spirally rotating scanner; max. range 5–6 miles (8–10 km)

AI Mk VIII   as Mk VII but with beacon and IFF facilities; max. range 7–8 miles (11–13 km)

AI Mk IX   10 cm radar having spiral scanner with facility to lock onto target; max. range 10 miles (16 km)

AI Mk X   10 cm radar with fully rotating scanner; max. range 10 miles (16 km)

AI Mk XV   (ASH) 3 cm radar with horizontal scanner; max. range 8 miles (13 km)

ADGB   Air Defence of Great Britain

ASH   air-surface homer

ASR   air-sea rescue

blip   radar echo or response

bogey   unidentified aircraft

Bordfunker or *Funker*   German wireless/radar operator

Bordschütze   air gunner

BSDU   Bomber Support Development Unit

Bull'seye   training aircraft engaged by sector searchlights and subjected to dummy attacks by night-fighters

Canary   IFF used by radar and anti-aircraft sites to identify friendly aircraft

CRT   cathode ray tube

C-scope   CRT showing front elevation of target

Diver   V–1

Düppel   German code-name for *Window*, after a town near the Danish border where RAF metal foil strips were first found

Emil-Emil   German code-name for *Lichtenstein AI*

Fähnrich   German rank. RAF equivalent: flight sergeant

Feldwebel   German rank. RAF equivalent: sergeant

Flensburg   German device to enable their night-fighters to home on to *Monica*

Flieger   German rank. Private second class

Flower   low-level night Intruder patrol over German airfields

Freelance   patrol with the object of picking up a chance radar contact or visual sighting of the enemy

Gefreiter   German rank. Private first class

Gee   British navigational device

General der Flieger   German rank. RAF equivalent: air marshal

Generalfeldmarschall   German rank. RAF equivalent: marshal of the RAF

Generalleutnant   German rank. RAF equivalent: air vice marshal

Generalmajor   German rank. RAF equivalent: air commodore

Generaloberst   German rank. RAF equivalent: air chief marshal

H2S   British 10 cm radar

Hauptmann   German rank. RAF equivalent: flight lieutenant

HCU   heavy conversion unit

Helle Nachtjägd   light (or bright) night chase; night interception in searchlight-illuminated zones

Horrido!   German for 'Tallyho!'

IAS   indicated air speed

IFF   identification friend or foe

Instep   patrol seeking air activity in Bay of Biscay

Leutnant   German rank. RAF equivalent: pilot officer

Lichtenstein   first form of German AI

Mahmoud   high-level bomber support sortie

Major   German rank. RAF equivalent: squadron leader

Mandrel   airborne radar-jamming device

Monica   tail-mounted warning radar device

Nachtjägdgeschwader (*NJG*)   night-fighter wing

NFT   night-flying training/test

Oberfähnrich　German rank. RAF equivalent: warrant officer

Oberfeldwebel　German rank. RAF equivalent: flight sergeant

Oberleutnant　German rank. RAF equivalent: flying officer

Oberst　German rank. RAF equivalent: group captain

Oberstleutnant　German rank. RAF equivalent: wing commander

op.　operation

OTU　operational training unit

Out step　patrol seeking enemy air activity off Norway

Pauke! Pauke!　German for 'Kettledrums! Kettledrums!' (meaning 'Going in to attack!')

PFF　Pathfinder Force

R/T　radio telephony

RCM　radio countermeasures

resin　aircraft identification light

Rhubarb　low-level daylight fighter sweep

Ritterkreuz(träger)　Knight's Cross (holder)

Schräge musik　slanting music; German night-fighter's guns that fire upwards at 70 degrees

Serrate　British equipment designed to home in on Lichtenstein radar

Stab　Staff flight

TI　target indicator

Unteroffizier　German rank. RAF equivalent: corporal

V–1　jet-engined flying bomb

Vapour　airborne directing of night-fighters from a specially equipped Wellington

Viermot　Four-engined bomber

WOP　wireless operator

WOP-AG　wireless operator/air gunner

Wilde Sau　German single-engined night-fighters operating over the RAF's target, relying on freelance interceptions from a running commentary, aided by the light from fires and searchlights

Zahme Sau　German single-engined and twin-engined fighters fed into the bomber stream on the way to the target as soon as its track was properly established

* indicates a bar to an existing award

FBVI RS566 of 515 Squadron at dispersal at Little Snoring in late 1944. Issued to the unit almost straight from the Hatfield factory, this aircraft later served briefly with 141 Squadron until it transitioned to NFXXXs in April 1945. Following a brief spell in storage, R5566 was one of around fifty-seven FBVIs sold to the Armée de L'air *in August 1947.* (Tom Cushing Collection)

CHAPTER I

Serrate Squadron

Ist die Lufischlacht in der Steige
Und die Nacht, die dröhnt und lämt wie dumm.
Pauke! Pauke! *Rums die Geige!*
'Das Lied von der, "Wilden Sau"' by Peter Holm

'**M**arie-5,' sounded in the earphones of the *Bordfunker* crouched in the cockpit of the Bf 110G-4a night-fighter. The code word, sent from the ground controller, indicated that the *Nachtjägdgeschwader* night predator was only 5 km (3 miles) behind a British bomber. It had been picked up on German ground-radar, fixed on the Seeburg plotting table and transmitted to the *Leutnant* and his *Unteroffizier* stalking the bomber on their *Helle Nachtjägd* (night chase). As soon as the *Bordfunker* picked up contact on his Lichtenstein C-1 wide-angle radar, he transmitted 'Emil-Emil' to alert his controller.

'*Pauke! Pauke!*' The *Leutnant* had visual contact of his target. It was a Lancaster, crossing gently from port to starboard. His *Bordfunker* immediately transmitted '*Ich beruhe.*' Then they closed in rapidly for the kill – 300, 200, 150 metres, finally opening fire from 100 metres. Strikes peppered the fuselage and danced along the wing root. Another two-second burst and the four-engined bomber burst into flames. Doomed, it fell away to port in a flaming death dive, impacting in a German forest. Gouts of fuel from ruptured tanks ignited and lit up the night sky with a reddish hue. The engines buried themselves deep into the earth. '*Sieg Heil!*' said the pilot over the R/T to ground control. The British bomber-crew had unwittingly been 'homed in' on: its H2S set had been picked up by the night-fighter's Naxos Z FuG 250, while its Flensburg FuG 227/1 homed in on the bomber's Monica tail-warning device.

On another night it would be the turn of the *Leutnant* and his *Unteroffizier* to be the preyed-upon. It was all part of a deadly and sophisticated electronic game in which the RAF and the *Nachtjägdgeshwader*, aided by the scientists, pitted their wits in an ethereal, nocturnal battleground. One side gained the ascendancy until the inevitable countermeasure was found.

When a British listening station monitoring German R/T traffic picked up the code-word 'Emil-Emil', and special operators aboard aircraft of 1473 Flight subsequently detected transmissions on the 490 Mhz band on *Ferret* flights over occupied Europe, proof was needed that they came from enemy night-fighters. On 3 December 1942 a Wellington IC of 1473 Flight, flown by Pilot Officer Edwin Paulton RCAF, went with the bomber stream to Frankfurt to pinpoint the source of the transmissions. If they did in fact come from German night-fighters, the crew were to allow the enemy aircraft to close in to attack and to follow his radar transmissions throughout. Pilot Officer Harold Jordan RAF, the special wireless operator, picked up a signal, which came closer until it was so loud that it nearly deafened him. It was a Ju 88.

Jordan warned the crew that an attack was imminent and Flight Sergeant Bill Bigoray RCAF, the wireless operator, sent out signals to base. The 'Wimpy' took evasive action as the Ju 88 made ten to twelve attacks. Four of the crew were wounded. Jordan was hit in the arm and jaw in the first two attacks but continued to work his set. In the third attack, he was wounded again, this time in the eye. Almost blind, he explained the operation of the wireless set to the navigator. Bigoray, although badly wounded in both legs, had persisted in passing on the messages from Jordan. Edwin Paulton managed to fly the badly damaged Wellington to England and ditched off Walmer Beach near Deal. Jordan was awarded an immediate DSO, and Paulton and Bigoray received the DFC and DFM respectively.

The courage of the crew enabled information to be pieced together on the new radar. As a result, a new, lighter *Window* was produced. Also, the Telecommunications Research Establishment (TRE) at Malvern, Worcestershire, developed a homer using a receiver known as *Serrate,* which actually homed in on the radar impulses emitted by the Lichtenstein (Emil-Emil) interception radar. *Serrate* got its name from the picture on the cathode ray tube (CRT). When within range of a German night-fighter, the CRT displayed a herringbone pattern either side of the time trace, which had a serrated edge. *Serrate* came to be the code name for the high-level Bomber Support operations.

The TRE, and its airfield at Defford nearby, was the centre of all wartime RAF radar research. In 1941, it had begun work on jammers to counter the German Freya early-warning ground radar, which was first discovered at Auderville on Cap de La Hague in February. After the famous raid on Bruneval on 27/28 February 1942 in which British paratroopers and an RAF radar technician dismantled a complete Würzburg radar installation and removed it to England along with one of its operators, TRE developed jammers for the Würzburg also.

During 1942, some RAF night-fighter squadrons had re-equipped with the de Havilland Mosquito – 'a lethal brute with no vices' – and in October of the same year Air Chief Marshal Arthur 'Bomber' Harris, the AOC RAF Bomber Command, advocated that Mosquito fighters should be used in the bomber stream for raids on Germany. Air Chief Marshal Sir W. Sholto Douglas, AOC Fighter Command, loath to lose his Mosquito fighters, argued that the few available Mosquitoes were needed for home defence should the *Luftwaffe* renew its attacks on Britain. However, on 5/6 March 1943 the Battle of the Ruhr began with an attack by 442 bombers on Essen. Between the beginning of March and the end of July, 872 bombers were lost and 2,126 were either badly damaged or crash-landed in England. Something equally dramatic had to be done to curb the *Nachtjägd.*

Back in late 1941, a joint services committee had been established to study the future application of radio countermeasures (RCM). It had been mooted by TRE that such countermeasures could be effectively carried out in support of main force operations over Germany. Now one of the first steps was to transfer a squadron, No. 141, from Fighter Command to Bomber Support using the new *Serrate* homer. No. 141 Squadron, a long-established night-fighter home-defence squadron which had been stationed at Predannack since February, was a natural choice for the task, although it was equipped

AI Mk IV radar installation in the Beaufighter Mk IF, showing the nose-mounted dipole transmitter aerial and wing-mounted receiver aerials. (BAe)

with the Beaufighter IF which had neither the range nor the performance of the Mosquito.

On 19 June 1940, 141 Squadron had lost ten aircrew with two injured when six Defiants were destroyed and one damaged, all by Bf 109s. The Defiants were switched to night fighting and 141 destroyed its first enemy aircraft at night on 16 September 1940. At Ayr on 26 June 1941, the first Beaufighter IF equipped with Mk IV AI radar was delivered to the squadron. The first operational patrol by a Beaufighter IF of 141 Squadron took place on 25 August 1941. On 4/5 June 1942, 141 used Mk VII AI radar operationally in a Beaufighter IF for the first time when a Dornier 217 was damaged.

In December 1942, Wing Commander John Randall Daniel 'Bob' Braham, DSO, DFC*, not yet twenty-three, assumed command of the squadron. An outspoken individualist, unsurpassed in his sheer aggressive fighting spirit and relentless determination, Bob Braham was already a living legend, having shot down twelve enemy aircraft, eleven of them at night. The son of a First World War RFC pilot, Braham shot down his first aircraft during the Battle of Britain and at twenty-three had become the youngest wing commander in the RAF. 'The Night Destroyer', as he was dubbed in the press, had an overdeveloped sense of modesty and could see no reason for the press having an interest in him. It is perhaps because he shunned publicity wherever possible, that he is not as well known as some other aces of the Second World War.

Posted with Braham to 141 Squadron from 29 Squadron was Flying Officer William J. 'Sticks' Gregory DFC DFM his navigator and radio/radar operator, who had partnered Braham in seven kills. Gregory earned his nickname as a result of having been a drummer in Debroy Somer's band. Another inspired appointment was Flight Lieutenant Bernard 'Dickie' Sparrowe who arrived in November 1942 as Adjutant. Flying Officer Cedric 'Buster' Reynolds, the Intelligence Officer and Flying Officer (later Flight Lieutenant)

Wing Commander 'Bob' Braham DSO DFC* and Flying Officer W. J. 'Sticks' Gregory DFC in four of his eight victories in 141 Squadron, 14 June 1943–29 September 1943 (Flight Lieutenant Jacko Jacobs partnered him in the other four). Braham finished the war with 29 victories. (IWM)

James Dougall MD BCh. completed a superb team under Braham. It was not unusual for Reynolds and 'Doc' Dougall – who was known as 'the Mad Irishman' because of his wild antics – to fly on operations with their commanding officer!

Lack of enemy air activity over England saw fighters, including Beaufighters during the moon period, employed in incursion missions in France and the Low Countries. On 13 March 1943 141 flew the first *Ranger* patrol by night in Beaufighter IFs over south-west France. A *Ranger* was a deep penetration flight into enemy territory with the object of engaging any target of opportunity on the ground or in the air. (*Rangers* were normally patrols by single aircraft while *Intruders* were normally flown in pairs.) Aircraft fitted with Mk VII or Mk VIII AI radar equipment were not permitted to fly over enemy territory lest their highly secret apparatus should fall into German hands. Those with Mk IV AI had to have their equipment taken out, or at least major parts of it removed. On 23 March they flew their first *Instep* patrol, by day, over the Bay of Biscay. *Insteps* were long-range fighter-protection operations to intercept attacking enemy aircraft or to report on aircraft or shipping in the Western Approaches and the Bay of Biscay.

Only a few such operations had been flown when, on 15 April, Braham and Reynolds were summoned to HQ Fighter Command at Bentley Priory near Stanmore. The top-level meeting was attended by a number of staff officers and two civilians from the TRE. Air Marshal Sir Trafford L. Leigh-Mallory, who had taken over Fighter Command in November 1942, was obviously impressed with the aggressive spirit Braham had instilled in his squadron in so short a time. He informed him that 141 Squadron had been selected as the first *Serrate* squadron for bomber support operations over enemy territory. On 30 April, 141 Squadron at Predannack flew north-east to Wittering, their new station. *Ranger* and home-defence duties continued while Beaufighter Mk VIs arrived and *Serrate* and the *Gee* radio navigation aid equipment were installed. New crews arrived from 51 Operational Training Unit (OTU) at Cranfield to fly the Beaufighters. Then, on 12 May the first six 141 Squadron crews flew to Drem in Scotland to begin *Serrate* training.

A few days before, on 9 May a Ju 88R-1 of IV/NJG3 was flown from Kristiansund/Kjevik in Norway to Dyce, near Aberdeen, after its crew defected during an aborted interception of a Courier Service Mosquito off Denmark. The fiancée of the pilot, *Flugzeugführer Oberleutnant* Herbert Schmidt, was Jewish and had been arrested and transported to a concentration camp, while his *Bordfunker, Oberfeldwebel* Paul Rosenberger, was of Jewish descent. *Bordschütze Oberfeldwebel* Erich Kantvill, a Nazi, went along with the defection. This aircraft was equipped with the *FuG 202 Lichtenstein BC* AI. Examination by TRE scientists enabled them to confirm that the *Serrate* device operated on the correct frequencies to home in on the FuG 202 Lichtenstein BC and Lichtenstein FuG 212 radars. *Serrate* could only home in on Lichtenstein AI radar and then only if it was turned on. The Beaufighters would also be equipped with Mk IV AI radar, which would be used in the closing stages of a *Serrate* interception because *Serrate* could not positively indicate range. The Mk IV was also needed to obtain contacts on enemy night-fighters that were not using their radar.

On 14 June 141 Squadron flew its first bomber support operation. Late in the afternoon, five Beaufighter FVIs equipped with *Serrate* and Mk IV AI radar flew to their forward airfield at Coltishall, Norfolk and took off again shortly before midnight for operations over Holland and Germany. Meanwhile, 197 Lancasters and six Mosquitoes of the main force were *en route* to Oberhausen in the Ruhr. Squadron Leader Charles V 'Winnie' Winn DFC – an old friend of Braham in 29 Squadron – and R. A. W. Scott, with Braham and Gregory took off at 2335 hours. Braham headed for the German night-fighter airfield at Deelen near Arnhem in Holland. The flight over the North Sea was uneventful and they patrolled Deelen in wide orbits, sometimes flying as far as Venlo – another German night-fighter airfield in Holland – and Wesel in Germany in their search

On 9 May 1943 a Ju 88R-1 of IV/NJG3 *flown by* Flugzeugführer *Oberleutnant Herbert Schmidt, Oberfeldwebel Paul Rosenberger and bordschütze Oberfeldwebel Erich Kantvill, and equipped with* Flensburg FuG 202 Lichtenstein BC *AI radar, landed at Dyce, near Aberdeen. The aircraft is now on permanent display at the RAF Museum, Hendon.* (Author)

for 'trade'. They found nothing and so, at 0151 hours Braham and Gregory set course for the coast again.

At 10,000 ft (3,050 metres) over Staveren on the north-east coast of the Zuider Zee, Gregory saw an enemy aircraft coming up behind them to attack from the port side. Braham orbited hard left to get behind him but as he did so the enemy pilot also turned to port. A dogfight ensued as each pilot tried to get the upper hand. Finally Braham got on to the enemy's port beam and from 400 yd (366 metres) opened fire with cannon and machine guns. He finished with a five-second burst from astern at 200 yd (183 metres). The enemy machine, a Bf 110, was raked along the fuselage from tail to cockpit and the port engine caught fire. Braham throttled back to attack again but it was unnecessary The Bf 110 went into a vertical dive and crashed in flames 8 miles (13 km) north of Staveren. Low on fuel, the victorious RAF crew set course for home and landed at Wittering at 0315 hours.

Squadron Leader Winn and R. A. W. Scott had landed thirty-five minutes earlier, having encountered no trade at Eindhoven. At 0325 hours Flying Officer R. C. MacAndrew and Pilot Officer F. Wilk landed at Wittering, having seen no activity at Gilze Rijen in Holland. The fourth Beaufighter, crewed by Flying Officer B. J. Brachi and his navigator/radio operator Pilot Officer A. P. MacLeod, had returned early with technical problems. Despite 141 Squadron's efforts, seventeen Lancasters were lost on that night's raid.

On 14/15 June the 44-year old Belgian pilot, Flight Lieutenant Lucien J. G. Leboutte, and his navigator/radio operator, Pilot Officer Harry Parrott, had an equally uneventful trip to Holland. Leboutte had joined the *Aviation Militaire* in April 1919. In 1924 he joined the *Militaire Vliegwezen* (the air component of the Belgian Army). LeBoutte had a successful career, rising to *Capitaine Aviateur* (Captain-Flyer) and commander of the III Group of the 2nd Regiment by 1930. As CO of this unit, he became the first leader of a Belgian aerobatic team. In June 1935, he became a major and CO of a group of the 1st Luchtvaartregiment based at Evere. This unit was equipped with Fairey Foxes and later, Fairey Battles. In January 1940 LeBoutte was sent to the Belgian Congo on an assignment to form three squadrons at Leopoldville, Stanleyville and Elizabethville. Having successfully completed his mission there, he left this Belgian colony on 16 May 1940 but the war and the rapid advance of the German armed forces in the west interrupted his voyage home and he became stranded in Algiers. On 1 June his diplomatic passport enabled him to embark on a ship heading for Marseilles, where he visited the Belgian government in exile then residing in Poitiers. Belgian officials there ordered him to return to Belgium, together with a group of Belgian pilots. Very reluctantly, LeBoutte obeyed the order.

He went into hiding in Belgium but the Germans tracked him down. However he told them that he was an official state photographer and they believed him! This incident convinced Leboutte that he should try and escape to England. On 3 January 1941 he began a long journey via France and Spain to Gibraltar, but Franco's soldiers captured him and he was thrown into jail. Living conditions were very harsh and Leboutte lost a lot of weight. Almost every day fellow prisoners were executed. After ten weeks he was transferred to the notorious prison at Miranda. He survived the ordeal and after four months he was released. Five days later he reached Liverpool. When he finally arrived in England, he was greeted with bad news. – aged forty-three and wearing glasses, he was declared unfit for flying duties by the RAF medical board. Disillusioned, he sought advice from Belgian friends who had successfully joined the British armed forces. While visiting one of them, LeBoutte stole his identity card and set off for the recruiting centre for night-fighter aircrew at Uxbridge. The interviewing board was impressed by his flying career, hardly glancing at 'his' identity card, and the medical board declared him 'perfectly fit'. He immediately joined the RAF as a pilot officer. He did not care about his rank, as he only wanted fly! His training on Oxfords and Blenheims was soon successfully completed and at OTU he crewed up with young Sergeant Harry Parrott, who wanted to improve his French. Despite his age and the fact that he wore glasses, LeBoutte was finally commissioned into the RAF as a pilot officer in January 1942 and that summer he and Parrot were posted to 141 Squadron.

On 15 June Bob Braham was awarded a second Bar to his DFC. Bad weather that night meant no main force and therefore no *Serrate* operations, so 141 Squadron was stood down. On 16/17 June Bomber Command dispatched 202 Lancasters and ten Halifaxes to Cologne while six Beaufighters of 141 Squadron again attempted to draw the enemy fighter force away from the main stream with patrols over German airfields in Holland. Winnie Winn and R. A. W. Scott patrolled Gilze Rijen but were forced to return early after taking a hit by a flak burst, which knocked out all their instruments. Flying Officer R. C. MacAndrew and Pilot Officer F. Wilk damaged a Bf 110 while on patrol near Eindhoven before icing caused the pilot's guns to jam. Braham and Gregory had headed for the German night-fighter airfield at Venlo where they damaged a Ju 88. Braham got in a two-second burst from astern before his guns also jammed. LeBoutte and Parrott saw a Ju 88 west of Eindhoven but lost it in cloud. Flying Officer Leonard Florent Alexandre Louis Renson, another Belgian pilot in the squadron, and his navigator/radio operator, Pilot Officer J. A. Pouptis, returned early before reaching the Dutch coast with a valve failure in their AI radar. (Renson was killed on 18/19 November 1943 with Flying Officer Ken Baldwin during an *Intruder* patrol to Hoya, Germany). A sixth Beaufighter, piloted by Flying Officer Douglas Sawyer and his navigator/radio operator, Sergeant Albert Smith, failed to return following a patrol over Gilze Rijen. Fourteen Lancasters also failed to return.

There was a two-night lull in Bomber Command operations until 19/20 June when 290 bombers raided the Schneider armaments factory and the Breuil steelworks at Le Creusot in France. Five Beaufighters of 141 Squadron flew Bomber Support operations over Holland again, this time using Ford in Hampshire as a forward base. Bob Braham and Flying Officer Howard Kelsey's Beaufighters were fired at by flak batteries but returned safely. The Beaufighters were again called upon for bomber support on 21/22 June when Krefeld was attacked by just over 700 bombers. Seven Beaufighters flew to Coltishall and flew patrols over German fighter airfields in Holland but LeBoutte's and Flying Officer Thornton's Beaufighters remained at the Norfolk base, grounded with technical troubles. Squadron Leader Charles Winn and R. A. W. Scott destroyed a Ju 88 while on patrol to Deelen but forty-four bombers were shot down, most of them by German night-fighters.

On 22/23 June 557 bombers attacked Mülheim. New tactics were employed whereby four Beaufighters were ordered to patrol 6–8 miles (10–13 km) north of the bomber stream and the other four patrolled to the south. Eight Beaufighters were duly dispatched to the forward base at Coltishall, from where they took off again late that night for *Intruder* operations over Holland. One Beaufighter, flown by Howard Kelsey and his navigator/radio operator, Sergeant Edward M. Smith, destroyed their first enemy aircraft, a Bf 110, during a patrol to Soesterberg. Smith's *Serrate* and AI sets became unserviceable after Kelsey had fired his guns. Flight Lieutenant D. C. Maltby and Flying

Officer J. E. Watts had to return early when their AI set also became unserviceable. On this and recent Bomber Support operations, Beaufighter crews reported interference from their Grocer equipment which made homing 'almost impossible'. Equipment problems could, in time, be corrected, but infinitely more worrying to the air force chiefs of staff was the loss of thirty-five bombers.

The situation was almost as bad on 24/25 June when thirty-four bombers were lost in a raid on Wüppertal by 630 RAF heavies. Five Beaufighters were flown to Coltishall but Winn burst a tyre and his place on the operation was quickly taken by the ever-eager Bob Braham, who flew to Coltishall with Sticks Gregory in the navigator's seat. They took off from Coltishall at 2345 hours and headed for Gilze Rijen. At Antwerp, a cone of about thirty searchlights pierced the sky, accompanied by a heavy flak barrage. At Gilze, Braham and Gregory found to their satisfaction that the flarepath and visual Lorenz south-east–north-west runways were lit up like beacons. After a few minutes, the lights were doused, to be replaced with a decoy set of lights to the south-west. Braham and Gregory were not diverted from their task, however. They could see the exhausts of twin-engined German night-fighters orbiting the area and Gregory spotted a Bf 110 chasing a Beaufighter. Braham allowed the pursuer to get almost within firing range before coming up 1,000 ft (300 metres) behind it. At 600 ft (180 metres) dead ahead, he pumped a three-second burst of cannon and machine-gun fire into the aeroplane. There was a white glow and it burst into flames. Braham followed it down and pumped another two-second burst into the doomed aeroplane before it hit the ground and exploded.

On 25/26 June six Beaufighters were employed on bomber support operations as 473 bombers bombed Gelsenkirchen. Winnie Winn and R. A. W. Scott, and Kelsey and Smith, set out from Coltishall to patrol the German night-fighter airfield at Rheine in Germany while the other four Beaufighters were to head for the airfields at Deelen, Twenthe and Venlo in Holland. Ninety miles out to sea, Winn suffered an engine failure and was forced to return to Coltishall on one engine. LeBoutte and Parrott, and Flying Officer R. J. Dix and Sergeant A. J. Salmon, aborted with radio malfunctions soon after leaving the English coast and returned to Wittering. Kelsey and Edward Smith caught a Bf 110 flying east in a gentle curve to the south and gave chase before the enemy crew could creep up on them. For ten minutes both aircraft tried to outmanoeuvre each other. Finally Kelsey got behind his adversary and from 900 ft (275 metres) gave him a three-second burst of cannon and machine-gun fire. First the enemy's port engine caught fire and there were strikes on his fuselage and starboard engine. Then, as Kelsey overshot him, he lifted his right wing to avoid collision and a shower of large burning pieces flew off the enemy aircraft and struck

The enemy. Messerschmitt BF 110G-4/R1 night-fighter of NJG3 equipped with early type FuG 202 Lichtenstein BC radar. The equipment worked on 490 MHz and could operate as far as $2\frac{1}{2}$ miles (4 km).

the Beaufighter, fortunately doing no more than make some dents and scratches under the wings and fuselage. The enemy machine went down over Hardenburgh in a ball of flame. On the debit side, Bomber Command lost thirty aircraft this night.

In an attempt to rack up more losses in the bomber streams, *Oberleutnant* Hans-Joachim 'Hajo' *Herrmann*, a bomber pilot, began forming a *Kommando* on 27 June using Fw 190A fighters fitted with 300 litre (66 gal) drop tanks for *Wilde Sau* attacks on heavy bombers over Germany. *Herrmann* reasoned that enemy bombers could easily be identified over a German city by the light of the massed searchlights, Pathfinder flares and the flames of the burning target below. By putting a mass concentration of mainly single-seat night-fighters over the target, his pilots could, without need of ground control, visually identify the bombers and shoot them down. Three *Geschwader, JG300, JG301* and *JG302*, which formed *30 Jägddivision*, were raised to carry out *Wilde Sau* tactics. These units were equipped with the Focke Wulf 190F-5/U2 and the Bf 109G-6/U4N. Additional FuG 25a and FuG l6zy radio equipment and the FuG 350 Naxos Z radar-receiving set were installed. The *30 Jägddivision* operated until March 1944, picking up H2S radar emissions from up to 30 miles (50 km) away.

Meanwhile, on 28/29 June, when Harris sent 608 bombers to Cologne, twenty-five failed to return. Six Beaufighters of 141 Squadron operated but without success. Bob

Oberleutnant *Fritz Krause,* Staffelkapitän I/NJGr.10, *(later* Kommandeur III./NJG2*) stands beside his Fw190A-5 of the* Wilde Sau Staffel, *one of the* Luftwaffe Nachtjagd *units used mainly to hunt Mosquitoes at night at high altitude. The Fw is fitted with FuG 217 Neptun J radar and a long-range belly tank. Over Berlin on the night of 20/21 April 1944 Krause shot down a 239 Squadron Mosquito crewed by Squadron Leader E. W. Kinchin and Flight Lieutenant D. Sellars. Surviving the war with a score of twenty-eight night victories, Krause was awarded the* Ritterkreuz (Knight's Cross) on 7 February 1945. (via Hans Peter Debrowski)

As one of 100 Group's most successful pilots, Harry White had joined the RAF as a 17-year-old in 1940, having lied about his age. On 4 August 1941 he crewed up with 18-year-old Mike Seamer Allen at 54 OTU at Church Fenton. The following month the two of them were posted to 29 Squadron at West Malling, where they started defensive night patrols in Beaufighters. White was eventually commissioned as a pilot officer on 26 March 1942 and, after scoring three kills and two damaged in July/August 1943, both he and Allen were awarded DFC – bars followed in April and October 1944. White and Allen's first Mosquito victory came on 27/28 January 1944 when they destroyed an Bf 109 near Berlin. On 15/16 February they claimed a He 177 Beleuchter (Illuminator), which was being used in conjunction with single-engined fighters conducting Wilde and Zähme Sau tactics against RAF bombers. The pair continued to score until their lengthy tour with 141 Squadron came to an end in July 1944, by which time their tally had risen to twelve destroyed and three damaged. Their final claim was for a Ju 88 damaged whilst flying an NFXXX with the BSDU in January 1945. (Mike Allen)

Braham and Sticks Gregory had a close encounter with two Ju 88s at 18,000 ft (5,500 metres) near Beverloo during their Intruder patrol near Venlo. One of the Junkers attacked from behind while the other approached the Beaufighter from straight ahead. At a range of 1,000 ft (300 metres) the under gun opened up, firing three quick bursts of red tracer and continuing until the Beaufighter passed underneath. Braham's left engine burst into flames and continued burning for some minutes until he switched it off. He managed to elude his adversaries by diving and weaving hard to starboard into cloud.

In all, 141 Squadron flew forty-six *Serrate* sorties during June, destroying five enemy aircraft for the loss of one Beaufighter. On ten occasions, aircraft were forced to return with failures of radar equipment, instruments or an engine. It was obvious that despite its impressive firepower and rugged airframe, which could absorb great punishment, the Beaufighter was not going to be the answer for successful *Serrate* operations. Enemy aircraft picked up more than 4 to 5 miles (6–8 km) away on *Serrate* were out of range for the Beaufighter VIF which did not have sufficient speed to chase and close at this distance. Its lack of manoeuvrability in combat was a worrying factor and the aircraft's reduced time on patrol cut down the opportunities for interception. The much vaunted Mosquito, however, was not available for *Serrate* operations and 141 Squadron was forced to continue using the Beaufighter, at least for a few more months.

In July the squadron flew sixty-six *Serrate* bomber support operations on ten nights. Flying Officer H. E. 'Harry' White and his navigator/radio operator Flying Officer Mike Seamer Allen damaged a Bf 110 near Aachen while on patrol to the German airfield at Eindhoven on 3/4 July when 653 bombers went to Cologne. White blasted the night-fighter at 200 yd (183 metres) dead astern in a two-second burst and then gave the enemy a second burst of cannon and machine-gun fire before diving violently away to port to avoid collision. The enemy aircraft was not seen again and they could only claim a 'damaged'. Thirty RAF bombers failed to return; twelve of them were shot down by Hajo Herrmann's Fw 190A-4s employing *Wilde Sau* tactics.

Harry White had enlisted in the RAF as a 17-year-old, in 1940, having lied about his age. On 4 August 1941, Sergeant White, as he then was, crewed up with 18-year-old AC2 Allen at 54 OTU Church Fenton. In September 1941, they were posted to 29 Squadron at West Malling, where they started defensive night patrols in Beaufighters. Harry White was then only eighteen and a half. After only six weeks, they were posted to 1455 Flight (later renumbered 534 Squadron) at Tangmere, a Havoc and Boston Turbinlite squadron. Young Harry was commissioned as a pilot officer on 26 March 1942. They operated on Turbinlites on home defence until 19 January 1943 with no success at all, but before he was twenty-one Harry White's bravery had earned him a DFC and Bar. When the Turbinlite units were disbanded, he and his navigator were posted back to a Beaufighter squadron, 141 at Ford. Much to their disappointment, they were attached to a ferry unit at Lyneham and spent four frustrating months ferrying new Beaufighters from Britain to Egypt, eventually rejoining 141 at Wittering on 15 June 1943.

The only enemy aircraft destroyed in July – on 15/16 July – fell to White and Allen, their first victory. The two men took off from the forward base at West Malling on an Intruder patrol to Juvincourt, one of six Beaufighters providing bomber support for the main force of 165 Halifaxes whose target was the Peugeot Motor Works at Montbelliard, a suburb of Sochaux. Eight miles (13 km) south-east of Rheims, Harry White and Mike Allen saw a Bf 110 flying straight and level at 10,000 ft (3,050 metres). The Beaufighter, which was 2,000 ft (610 metres) above the enemy machine, flown by *Major* Herbert Rauth of *II/NJG4*, a thirty-one victory *Ritterkreuzträger*, dived and got dead astern and slightly below before White opened fire from 750 ft (230 metres), closing to 600 ft (180 metres). The two-second burst of cannon and machine-gun fire hit both engines and the fuselage. A moment later, the aircraft exploded in flames, broke in two and struck the ground. Michael Allen recalls:

> As it went down in flames we started to congratulate ourselves and for the next ten minutes the Beau flew itself, whilst we continued to tell each other what clever chaps we were and how easy it was to shoot down enemy aircraft … and how many more we were going to get! [White and Allen would become the most successful fighter team 141 Squadron ever had]. After all, we had been flying together for two years with 'NO JOY' at all, so a little celebration was justified! But as usual, we overdid it and nearly got ourselves shot down in the process!
>
> In our exuberance (shooting down an enemy aircraft was just like scoring a try in rugby … the feeling was just the same!) we flew over Dreux. 'A searchlight came on and tried unsuccessfully to pick us up and there was a good deal of heavy flak, far too accurate for comfort …' (so reads our combat report). We managed to extricate ourselves from the mess into which our carelessness had led us and 'recrossed the coast at Ouistreham at 0245 hours

...' On landing back at Wittering, the excitement of our ground-crew matched ours of earlier in the night which had nearly cost us so dear! As the immortal Group Captain Cheshire said 'The moment you think everything is all right and I'm clear ... that is the time to watch out for trouble ...'

Losses to the main force had reached such proportions (275 were shot down in June) that Bomber Command was at last given permission to use *Window*. This was the code-name for strips of black paper with aluminium foil stuck to one side, cut to a length equivalent to half the wavelength of the *Würzburg* ground and *Lichtenstein* airborne radars, and dropped by aircraft one bundle a minute to 'snow' the tubes. Although it had been devised in 1942, its use by Bomber Command had been forbidden until now for fear that the Luftwaffe would use it in a new blitz on Great Britain. When 'Bomber' Harris launched the first of four raids, code-named *Gomorrah*, on the port of Hamburg on 24/25 July, *Window* was carried in the 791 bombers for the first time. Led by H2S PFF aircraft, the bombing force rained down 2,284 tons of HE and incendiaries on the dockyards and city districts, creating a firestorm which rose to a height of $2^1/_2$ miles (4 km). The *Himmelbett* (literally translated, 'bed of heavenly bliss', or 'four-poster bed' because of the four night-fighter control zones) GCI control system and the German night-fighters had no answer to the British countermeasures. Only twelve bombers, just 1.5 per cent of the force, were lost. Hamburg had been destroyed once before by fire, in 1842. Over four nights in July–August 1943 3,000 bombers dropped 10,000 tons of HE and incendiary bombs to totally devastate the city and kill 50,000 of its inhabitants.

No. 141 Squadron's Beaufighters did not participate in the Hamburg operation on 24/25 July but five were used on the night of the second raid on 27/28 July, when only seventeen aircraft from the force of 787 aircraft were lost. And eight took part on 29/30 July when twenty-eight out of 777 bombers were shot down. Seven Beaufighters flew *Intruder* patrols on the fourth and final night of the raids on Hamburg on 2/3 August when thirty out of 740 bombers were lost.

By the late summer of 1943, the majority of the German night-fighter force was in complete disarray. *Window* rendered useless the *Würzburg* ground radar, the *Lichtenstein* AI airborne radar in the night-fighters, and the radar-predicted AA guns and searchlights. Crews took advantage of this ascendancy. On 9/10 August Bob Braham notched his fourth victory since joining 141 Squadron, and his sixteenth overall, when he destroyed a Bf 110 on a patrol to the German fighter airfield at St Trond in Belgium. Sticks Gregory, who as usual flew as his navigator and operated the radar, was then rested and replaced by Flight Lieutenant H. 'Jacko' Jacobs DFC, who had been instructing at 51 OTU, Cranfield. On 12/13 August, when Bomber Command attacked Turin with 656 aircraft, 141 Squadron flew *Serrate* sorties over France. Squadron Leader F. P. Davis and Flying Officer J. R. Wheldon destroyed a Ju 88 about 30 miles (50 km) south-west of Paris. Three nights later Winnie Winn and Flying Officer R. A. W. Scott's Beaufighter was hit by machine-gun fire from a Wellington over France but Winn was able to belly-land at Ford, without flaps or undercarriage. One other crew was intercepted by a Mosquito and fired on by AA gunners near Chichester. Flight Sergeants M. M. 'Robbie' Robertson and Douglas J. Gillam were shot down by return fire from a He 177 over France and were taken prisoner.

On 16 August 141 Squadron began receiving the first of a few, rather war-weary Mosquito Mk II aircraft fitted with Mk IV AI radar. The first *Serrate*-equipped

Mosquitoes did not arrive until 16 October and even these were 'clapped out'. It was on 16/17 August that Howard Kelsey DFC and Edward Smith notched their third victory. They destroyed a Ju 88, claimed a Bf 110 as a 'probable' and damaged another Ju 88 when they jumped a formation of two Ju 88s and a Bf 110 near Etampes flying at 17,000 ft (5,100 metres) during an *Intruder* patrol to Châteaudun.

No. 141 Squadron's greatest operation so far, however, came on 17/18 August when Bomber Command attacked the secret experimental research establishment at Peenemünde on the Baltic, which was developing the V-1 pilotless flying bomb and the V-2 rocket. Some 597 bombers were dispatched and the bombing, carried out in moonlight to aid accuracy, was orchestrated for the first time by a master bomber, Group Captain John H. Searby. The German night-fighter force operated in large numbers employing large-scale *Zahme Sau* (Tame Boar) tactics for the first time. *Zahme Sau* had been developed by *Oberst* Victor von Lossberg of the *Luftwaffe*'s Staff College in Berlin. The *Himmelbett* ground network provided a running commentary for its night-fighters, directing them to where the *Window* concentration was at its most dense. Although the ground controllers were fooled into thinking the bombers were headed for Stettin and a further Spoof by Mosquitoes aiming for Berlin drew more fighters away from the Peenemünde force, some forty Lancasters, Halifaxes and Stirlings, or 6.7 per cent of the force, were shot down.

Ten of 141 Squadron's Beaufighters patrolled German night-fighter bases in Germany and Holland that night. Bob Braham and Jacko Jacobs destroyed two Bf 110s of *IV/NJG1* from Leeuwarden. Four Bf 110s of this unit under *Leutnant* Heinz-Wolfgang Schnaufer had taken off to intercept what they thought were heavy bombers. (Schnaufer and *Oberfeldwebel* Scherfling aborted after engine failure.) Braham's first victim was *Feldwebel* George Kraft, a night-fighter ace with fourteen victories. He and his *bordfunker*, *Unteroffizier* Rudolf Dunger, bailed out into the sea. Dunger was rescued two hours later but Kraft's body was washed ashore in Denmark four weeks later.

Braham's second victim was the Bf 110 flown by *Feldwebel* Heinz Vinke, a night-fighter ace with over twenty victories. In his book *Scramble,* Bob Braham related how he nearly collided with the Bf 110.

> Above me in a tight turn was another Me 110 and, at the speed we were travelling, looked as if we were going to ram him. I eased back the stick, put the sights on him and fired at the point blank range of about fifty yards. There was a blinding flash as the Me exploded in my face. Our Beau rocked violently, threatening to flick over on its back. My windscreen was flecked with oil from the exploding wreckage, which hurtled seawards.

'God that was close' was all Bob Braham could say. Then, by the light of the moon, he saw a parachute floating down.

> Something made my blood boil. Perhaps it was the narrow escape from the collision that angered me, or maybe it was because I was exhausted. I called Jacko on the intercom. 'One of the bastards must have been blown clear. I'm going to finish him off.' I had turned towards the parachute when Jacko said, 'Bob, let the poor blighter alone.' This brought me to my senses, and I felt ashamed of what I had intended to do. As we flew past the forlorn figure

dangling on the end of the chute and falling towards the sea, I wished I could call out to him that his life had been spared because of the compassion of my AI operator – a Jew like many of those the Nazis had slaughtered in the ghettos and concentration camps of Europe.

The *bordfunker, Feldwebel* Karl Schodl, and the gunner, *Unteroffizier* Johann Gaa – both of whom were wounded – and Vinke bailed out into the sea. Only Vinke, who was picked up after eighteen hours in the water, survived. He and Rudolf Dunger later formed a crew. Vinke had scored fifty-four victories when they were shot down by Spitfires on 26 February 1944 and he and Dunger were killed.

Harry White and Mike Allen had a close shave when, during their first contact, the enemy aircraft, a Bf 110, got on their tail and gave them a short burst of tracer, which fortunately passed just over the top of them. Twenty minutes later the Beaufighter crew got on the tail of a Bf 110 and Allen gave it brief burst. Strikes were recorded before it dived away but they could only claim a 'damaged'. (Their total number of victories was increased by one in the postwar years when Martin Middlebrook's research for his book *The Peenemünde Raid* revealed that the Bf 110 Wrk Nr 6228 of *III/NJG1,* flown by *Hauptmann* Wilhelm Dormann, a pre-war Lufthansa pilot and former *Wilde Sau* pilot with fourteen victories, had been destroyed. The *bordfunker, Oberfeldwebel* Friedrich Schmalscheidt was killed when his parachute did not open fully. Dormann also bailed out and suffered severe head injuries and burns, and a farm worker found him the following morning. |(Dormann never flew operationally again.) There was no mistake with the third contact, which was exploded by Harry White's raking fire, but the two men identified it as a Ju 88. It was actually a Bf 110 of *IV/NJG1* flown by *Leutnant* Gerhard Dittmann and *Unteroffizier* Theophil Bundschuh, both twenty years old, who were killed. The Bf 110 crashed into the sea near Leeuwarden.

Signs were that the German night-fighter force was beginning to overcome the RAF radar countermeasures, for on 23/24 August, when 719 bombers attacked Berlin, sixty-two aircraft were shot down, fifty-six of them by German night-fighters of *JG300* employing *Wilde Sau* tactics. This represented a loss rate of 8.6 per cent, the heaviest loss suffered by Bomber Command thus far. No. 141 Squadron put up ten Beaufighters, which patrolled bases in Holland and Germany, but to no avail.

At the end of August, Wittering became a little crowded with the influx of American personnel of the 20th Fighter Group, whose 77th and 79th Squadrons moved into the satellite airfield at King's Cliffe. The 55th Fighter Squadron was to be based at Wittering. The 20th was equipped with the P-38 Lightning. The Commanding Officer, Major D. R. McGovern from Providence, Rhode Island, had served in the Pacific flying P-39 Airacobras and had destroyed five Japanese aircraft. He and Bob Braham became friends. On 20 September Braham and Jacko Jacobs in a Mosquito engaged in a local friendly dogfight with a P-38. Braham found that even though the Mosquito was worn out and meant for training, and even though he was inexperienced with the aircraft, it was superior to the Lightning.

During September 141 Squadron flew fifty-six *Serrate* sorties on eleven nights. Flying Officers Harry White and Mike Allen scored their fourth kill when they destroyed a Ju 88 on 6/7 September. On 15/16 September 141 Squadron dispatched seven Beaufighters to Ford to provide support for the raid by 369 aircraft on the Dunlop rubber factory at Montluçon. A Beaufighter crewed by Flight Lieutenant Robert W. Ferguson and Flying Officer R. W. Osborn developed engine trouble on an *Intruder* patrol to the airfield at Chartres and had to ditch in the sea. Ferguson's body was never found. Osborn was found after thirty-six hours in a dinghy by a Walrus and returned to Wittering.

The month closed with two more memorable sorties by Bob Braham. On 27/28 September, during an *Intruder* patrol to the Bremen area, he and Jacko Jacobs chased a Do 217 10 miles (16 km) west of Hanover. The Dornier stood no chance and was quickly dispatched in flames. Braham recorded in his logbook that this operation was 'bags of fun'. He also stated that they received a hit on their aircraft by flak as they crossed from Holland over the island of Texel. Braham's twentieth victory, and the eighth while with 141 Squadron, occurred on 29/30 September when Major McGovern flew as a passenger with Braham and Jacobs on what was Braham's last operation with 141 Squadron. They set off from Coltishall at 1920 hours and carried out an *Intruder* patrol to Twenthe in Holland. Over the Zuider Zee they saw an enemy aircraft and shortly thereafter recognized it as a Bf 110. It took Braham ten minutes of fierce manoeuvering before he could finally out-turn the enemy aircraft and 5 miles (8 km) west of Elburg give him a three-second burst from astern. Although he did not know it, his adversary was *Hauptmann* August Geiger of *VII/NJG1* who had fifty-three victories. Geiger received hits all over his aircraft before it exploded into a mass of flames and dived straight into the Zuider Zee.

After a few minutes, Braham and Jacobs got a visual on a Ju 88 about 3 miles (5 km) south of Zwolle, which was also turning and climbing for a position to attack, just as Geiger had tried to do. He was no more successful than Geiger had been. Braham gave the Junkers a two-second burst of cannon and machine-gun fire from 150 yd (137 metres) astern before his cannons infuriatingly jammed. Strikes were observed on both wing roots and there was an explosion in the fuselage, which burned for one or two seconds before the Ju 88 dived away sharply to the right and disappeared from sight. he could only claim a 'damaged'. Much to his chagrin, after this operation Braham had to take a rest at the insistence of AOC 12 Group, Air Vice Marshal Roderic Hill. Wing Commander K. C. Roberts, late of 151 Squadron, arrived at Wittering to take command. Braham left the squadron as the top ace night-fighter pilot. That 141 Squadron had been selected as the first *Serrate* squadron was down to this exceptional pilot, who was a magnificent example to his men.

A convivial evening was held at the George Hotel, Stamford, to celebrate the squadron's victories. By the end of the evening, everyone except Doc Dougall, who was left behind, drove back to Wittering. The Mad Irishman did not fancy a long walk back to the airfield and so looked around for alternative transport. At the back of the hotel, he saw three bicycles, a man's, a woman's and one meant for a very small child, all belonging to the landlord. For a wheeze Dougall, with great difficulty rode the child's cycle all the way back to the station, and during the next few days proceeded to cycle around the camp on it. Unfortunately, the landlord did not see the funny side of what was just a high-spirited prank, and made an official complaint. At his subsequent court martial Dougall was accused of actually stealing the cycle! He was acquitted but posted to Balloon Command within days. He had the whole squadron's respect for his medical expertise and also for his courage in flying on some operations with Braham.

During October 141 Squadron flew forty-nine *Serrate* bomber support operations on nine nights. It was a very disappointing month for the squadron, with a large number of early returns (fifteen) caused by problems with radar, engines and the weather. One Beaufighter was lost. Operationally, November proved equally disappointing. Bad weather prevented Bomber Command flying any operations from 12 to 17 November. On the 18th it was announced that with effect from the 15th, Wittering had come under the command of the Air Defence of Great Britain (ADGB) on the reorganization of Fighter Command into ADGB and the Tactical Air Force. *Night Intruder* operations using Mosquitoes had begun in April–May 1943, when five squadrons had begun operations, and three more had begun *Day Rangers* (daylight cloud-cover patrols). In May 60 OTU at High Ercall had been expanded and made responsible for all *Intruder* training. Beginning in June, Mosquitoes of 605 Squadron began successful, albeit small-scale, bomber support *Flower* attacks on German night-fighter airfields during raids by main force bombers. *Flowers* supported bombers by disrupting the *Himmelbett* chain. Long-range *Intruder* aircraft fitted with limited radar equipment were used and these proceeded to the target at high altitude, diving down whenever they saw airfields illuminated. This type of operation, if correctly timed, prevented the enemy night-fighters, already short of petrol, from landing at their bases.

In August Mosquitoes of 25 and 410 Squadrons began *Mahmoud* sorties (single Mosquitoes employed as bait for enemy night-fighters in their known assembly areas) over enemy territory. The enemy fighter would be allowed to stalk its prey, picked up by *Monica* radar built into the tail of the Mosquito, then its crew would circle and shoot down the unsuspecting German crew using AI Mk IV for direction. Mosquito operations were extended to include loose escort duties for the main force. On 18/19 November Bomber Command began the main phase of the Battle of Berlin and for the next four and a half months, Air Chief Marshal Sir Arthur Harris attempted to destroy the German capital. A new RAF group would figure largely in the bombing campaign and the role of 141 Squadron was expanded.

NFII DD737, the type which began to equip 141 Squadron in October 1943. The first three received were elderly machines, which had seen extensive operational service with other squadrons, and the Merlin 21s were well used. There were also troubles with the Mk IV AI radar and Serrate *installed in the Mosquitoes.* (de Havilland)

CHAPTER II

The Battle of Berlin

Mitten in dem stärksten Feuer
Swischen Fliegern, Flak und Mordsradau,
Ja, das wird dem Tommy teuer:
Die Horridos der „Wilden Sau"1

'Das Lied von der "Wilden Sau"' by Peter Holm

Over Germany the battle cries *'Pauke! Pauke!'* and *'Horrido!'* ('Tallyho!' – St Horridus was the patron saint of German fighter pilots), were still being heard all too often as the *Nachtjägdgruppen* infiltrated the bomber streams and wreaked havoc among the heavy bombers, despite extensive countermeasures and Day and Night *Ranger* and *Intruder* patrols. The introduction of *Window* had changed the whole method of German night defence and the manner in which their night-fighters operated. *Zahme Sau* tactics in particular had reduced the chances of successful interceptions by the *Serrate*-equipped Beaufighters of 141 Squadron, especially when the target was as far away as Berlin where the Beaufighter's short range proved a severe handicap. The Mosquito could reach Berlin but re-equipment for the Wittering-based squadron was slow.

In October 1943 141 Squadron had only received three elderly Mk IIs, each of which had seen extended operational service with other squadrons before being issued to 141. One had been badly damaged on operations and a second had twice been involved in flying accidents. The Merlin 21s were also well used and over the next few weeks maintenance problems were the bane of the fitters' lives as they struggled to keep airworthy the few Mosquitoes in their charge. Finally, in February 1944, all reconditioned engines were called in, and while stocks lasted, only Merlin 22s were installed. There were also troubles with the Mk IV AI radar and Serrate installed in the Mosquitoes. Flying Officer MacKenzie of the TRE at Malvern was attached to 141 Squadron on 13 November to assist in locating the trouble with the radar equipment in the Mosquitoes.

One of the first Mosquitoes and crew were written off on 13 November during a practice flight and camera-gun exercise with a Stirling. Flying Officer I. D. Bridge and Flight Sergeant L. J. W. Cullen had just made a camera-gun attack on the bomber and had broken away when the Mosquito appeared to go into a vertical dive. Pieces of the aircraft were seen to break away and it finally hit the ground near Polebrook and exploded. Two days later a second Mosquito was lost during a test flight. Engine failure was blamed as the cause of the crash, which killed Flying Officers D. E. A. Welsh and W. C. Ripley. On 18/19 November Bomber Command attacked Berlin with 440 aircraft and Mannheim/Ludwigshafen with 395 aircraft. Thirty-two bombers failed to return. The next night, 141 dispatched two Beaufighters and a single Mosquito flown by Squadron Leader Winn DFC and Flight Lieutenant R. A. W. Scott. All returned safely. On 22/23 November 764 bombers attacked Berlin again and 141 Squadron dispatched three Mosquitoes and two Beaufighters. Two of the Mosquitoes and the two Beaufighters returned early with various equipment failures and only one Mosquito reached its patrol area at Salzwedel.

Despite the early problems, the Mosquito became the main offensive weapon in 100 Group (Bomber Support Group), which was created on 8 November under the command of Air Commodore (later Air Vice Marshal) E. B. Addison, at Radlett, Hertfordshire. It had become obvious that the RAF needed a specialized bomber support force to integrate RCM and electronic intelligence (ELINT), and a long-range fighter force. The primary duty of 100 Group was to reduce the escalating losses being suffered by the heavy bomber force over Germany. Addison had previously commanded 80 Wing RAF, which, as a wing commander, he had established at Garston in June 1940. At that time, the Air Ministry had a complete picture of the main blind bombing and navigation aids used by the *Luftwaffe*. Between June 1940 and the winter of 1941 the *X-Gerat* (X-equipment) blind-bombing aid (of which it had first been aware in 1939) and *Knickebein* (Bent Leg), which could be used by bombers equipped with the *Lorenz* blind-approach aid, were successfully jammed and rendered useless. The *Y-Gerat,* used only in the He 111H-4s of *III/KG26*, was also jammed effectively before this unit took part in *Barbarossa*, the invasion of the Soviet Union.

The first unit to move to 100 Group, from 3 Group at Gransden Lodge was 192 Squadron. Its Blind Approach Training Development Unit had started to fly on the German *Ruffian* and *Knickebein* beams. No. 192 had been formed at Gransden Lodge on 4 January 1943 from 1474 Flight for the ELINT role with three Mosquito Mk IVs, two Halifax Mk Ifs and eleven Wellington Mk Xs to monitor German radio and radar. The squadron had always been part of the Y-Service and, as such, its primary object had been a complete and detailed analysis from the air of the enemy signals organization. It arrived at Foulsham in Norfolk on 7 December.

Addison's HQ did not move to Norfolk until 3 December, when it was established at RAF West Raynham, 8 miles (13 km) from Fakenham. A permanent HQ at Bylaugh Hall, near Swanton Morley, was not ready for occupation on 18 January 1944, when 2 Group HQ moved to Mongewell Park, near Wallingford in Berkshire, becoming part of 2nd Tactical Air Force. Late in November Wing Commander Roberts was informed that West Raynham would also be the new home for 141 Squadron, which would become the first operational squadron in 100 Group, and that the squadron would be moving to Raynham on 3 December. There, 141 Squadron really got down to conversion from Beaufighter VIs to Mosquitoes. The squadron diarist reported:

> TRE were sublimely happy with their *Serrate* aerial design for the Mosquitoes. Everybody knew the design was perfect – except the aircrew who were troublesome enough to find it almost impossible to direction-find in a turn. This resulted in the squadron having to operate half Beaus and half-inadequate Mosquitoes and consequently many opportunities were lost. Spirits flagged. Despondency set in among the overworked Radar

mechanics. Perhaps the one thing which served to restore confidence more than anything was an informal chat in the Mess between Flying Officer Pollard (Squadron Radar Officer) and the AOC, which resulted in a Mosquito being placed exclusively at Pollard's disposal for experimental purposes. Within a fortnight this cutting of red tape bore fruit and a new and satisfactory aerial system was designed.

The fitting of these new aerials was a difficult and tedious operation. TRE were worried. De Havilland's representative was worried. In fact everyone was worried except Pollard, who proceeded to get on with the job slowly but surely with many a strip of tinfoil over the leading edges and vast quantities of Bostik. (Who in the squadron will ever forget Bostik night in the Mess? One Wing Commander at Group still wears his neatly parted hair as if it were rubberized.) Eventually, the job was done – and well done – and the squadron were completely converted to Mosquito II.

In the meantime, on 6 December, the advance party of 239 Squadron, which had been training at Ayr and Drem for *Serrate* bomber support operations, joined 141 Squadron at West Raynham. No. 239 had been reformed at Ayr in September 1943. Its previous function had been army co-operation, so that all aircrew for its new role of the offensive night fighting had to be posted in. With Wing Commander P. M. J. Evans DFC as squadron commander, Squadron Leaders Black and E. W. Kinchin as flight commanders and Flight Lieutenants Carpenter and 'Jacko' Jacobs DFC* as navigational/radar leader and navigation officer respectively the eighteen crews began their training. The squadron diarist recorded:

> They were all anxious to press on but a deplorable absence of aircraft made practice flying a very great rarity. It was not until well into October that a dual-controlled Mosquito became available, and as late as the last week in November Form 540 contained the pathetic entry: 'Training was carried out in the Mosquito.' Most of the flying personnel were experienced AI from Fighter Command, and their enthusiasm on being posted to a squadron destined for offensive work was somewhat lessened as week after week dragged by with the operational goal seemingly as far away as ever.

On 9 December 239 Squadron moved to West Raynham and on 11 December two operational Mosquito IIs equipped with Mk IV AI forward-looking and backward-looking *Serrate* equipment and the *Gee* navigational aid arrived. The squadron trained at every available opportunity when the weather allowed. Meanwhile, 169 Squadron, the third equipped with *Serrate,* moved from Ayr to Little Snoring on 7 and 8 December. The squadron had been reformed at Ayr on 15 September under the command of Wing Commander Edward John "Jumbo" Gracie DFC. Gracie was described as 'a little fire-eater' who, as a flight commander flying Hurricanes in 56 Squadron in the Battle of Britain, was credited with five enemy aircraft destroyed, two 'probables' and 'two damaged' before he was shot down and sustained a broken neck. He recovered and added to his score in 1941. The idea of using the Hurricane as a night-intruder aircraft probably originated with Gracie. As a flight commander with 23 Squadron in April 1941, he made a few sorties in a Hurricane I from Manston to the Lille and Merville areas. He did not have any actual successes then but he saw enemy aircraft on at least one occasion and showed the possibilities of single-engined intrusion. The experiment was copied by other squadrons. Later, in 1942, in the Mediterranean, Gracie flew Spitfires from the carriers *Eagle* and *Wasp* to reinforce units on Malta. He finally commanded a wing at Takali before returning to England to command 169 Squadron. The groundcrew were all retained from the old Mustang squadron and aircrew were posted in, mostly made up of volunteers from night-fighter squadrons. A Mosquito II and a Beaufighter were delivered towards the end of October, followed by further Beaufighters. All aircrew underwent a course with 1692 Flight at Drem and all pilots went on to the Rolls Royce engine handling course.

For twelve nights from 4 December, not one heavy bomber had operated because of a full moon and bad weather. When Bomber Command resumed operations on 16/17 December with an attack on Berlin by 483 Lancasters and fifteen Mosquitoes, two Beaufighters and two Mosquitoes of 141 Squadron took off from West Raynham on 100 Group's first offensive night-fighter patrols in support of the heavies. It was hardly an auspicious occasion and became known as 'Black Thursday'. Bomber Command lost twenty-five Lancasters and a further thirty-four were lost on their return to England owing to very bad weather causing collisions, crashes and some bale-outs after aircraft ran out of fuel. One of the Mosquitoes was flown by Squadron Leader (later Wing Commander) Freddie 'Cordite' Lambert and his navigator/radio operator, Flying Officer Ken Dear. Lambert had picked up the nickname while flying Westland Wapitis policing the North West Frontier. Later, he had commanded 110 Squadron in India, flying Vultee Vengeances against the Japanese. The two Beaufighters and Lambert and Dear patrolled the airfield at Hoya. One of the Beaufighters was forced to return to base early after *Serrate* and AI both failed near the German border, while the second Mosquito aborted with engine trouble on the way over the Dutch coast. Flight Sergeants Coles and J. A. Carter reached Hoya but had to abort the operation when their back hatch blew open during a hard turn to port. They turned for home and were chased for about twenty minutes by what was presumed to be an enemy night-fighter.

Lambert and Dear pressed on in their Mosquito II. From 30 miles (48 km) within the Dutch coast and all along the route they received indications of some eighteen to twenty aircraft, all about 10 miles (16 km) distant. Nevertheless, they proceeded as ordered to Hoya where, at 1920 hours, Dear picked up a *Serrate* contact 10 miles ahead and 25 degrees to port. The enemy aircraft was flying at about their height of 21,000 ft (6,400 metres). It had clearly picked up the Mosquito because the next indication they had was when the bogey closed, and some five minutes later an AI back blip at a range of 2,000 ft (610 metres) was picked up slightly to port. Lambert peeled off to port and lost height. He levelled off at 10,000 ft (3,050 metres) hoping that the enemy would reappear in front or allow him to turn and get behind it. The blip split into two and Dear suspected that there were two enemy night-fighters tailing them. A violent dogfight ensued and the enemy aircraft fired a long burst from close range and two more bursts from within 2,000 ft (610 metres) but without doing any damage. Throughout the fight the enemy aircraft clung on like a leech. Finally it overshot beneath the Mosquito as both turned hard to starboard. The enemy aircraft was close enough to be identified as a Bf 110. Lambert immediately gave it a burst of forty rounds from his cannons, lasting about two seconds, opening at 900 ft (275 metres) and ceasing fire at 1,200 ft (370 metres) from slightly above and with 1½ rings of deflection. Several strikes were observed and Lambert claimed a 'damaged'. He tried to follow up the attack but the Bf 110 was now lost to view and the AI set had packed up. Lambert and Dear returned to Norfolk and put down at Downham Market before returning to West Raynham.

The next heavy raid by the main force took place on 20/21 December when 650 bombers attacked Frankfurt. Again, losses were high. Some forty-one bombers were lost, despite a diversionary raid on Mannheim by fifty-four aircraft. No. 141 dispatched two Beaufighters, one of which returned almost immediately because of intercom trouble. On 23/24 December 390 bombers returned to Berlin. No. 141 Squadron was still going it alone on the *Serrate* beat and managed only three Beaufighters for the night's operation. One was forced to abort on reaching their patrol area at Hassalt when the *Serrate* equipment became inoperative. The 21-year-old pilot, Flying Officer Bernard Gunnill and 22-year-old Flight Sergeant Harry Hanson, his navigator/radar operator, took off from West Raynham at 0035 hours on Christmas Eve and were never seen again. Both these young men are buried in the Schoonselhof Cemetery at Antwerp in Belgium.

The third Beaufighter, flown by Howard Kelsey DFC and Edward 'Smithy' Smith, had taken off at the same time as Gunnill and Hanson. They stooged around for some time on their patrol track at Uckerath, picking up numerous weak *Serrate* contacts. At 0155 hours at 20,000 ft (6,100 metres) two *Serrate* contacts were made hard to starboard at 10 miles' (16 km) range but they were above them and as the Beaufighter was already at 20,000 ft (6,100 metres), Kelsey declined the chase. He patrolled Uckerath to no avail and then turned towards Duren. At 0215 hours at 23,000 ft (7,010 metres) Smith picked up a *Serrate* contact slightly below them and 10 miles (16 km) to the north. Kelsey turned the Beaufighter and chased the contact at 300 mph (480 kph) IAS, which was flying south very fast. At 5 miles' (8 km) range the enemy turned east. Smith obtained contact on the AI at a range of 14,000 ft (4,300 metres). Visual contact was obtained some minutes later. It was a Ju 88 burning green and white resins and though they did not know it, was a *IV/NJG1* machine piloted by *Oberleutnant* Finster. Kelsey had the impression the Junkers was drawing away so he let fly with a burst of cannon and machine-gun fire from 1,000 ft (300 metres). The Ju 88 slowed and Kelsey pumped another seven-second burst into it, closing to 300 ft (90 metres). Strikes were seen all over the aircraft, which turned steeply to port and dived straight down with flames streaming from both engines and the fuselage. It exploded on the ground where the glow of the burning pyre could be seen through the 10/10ths cloud. Finster was killed, the radio operator wounded and the gunner bailed out.

Immediately afterwards, Kelsey and Smith's Beaufighter was hit by flak at 19,000 ft (5,800 metres). The port engine began to run very roughly and various parts of the leading edges and wings were damaged. Smith picked up more *Serrate* contacts but Kelsey was unable to give chase because of the damage to the aircraft. However, when a contact was picked up just 5 degrees below and 5 degrees to starboard, Kelsey turned head-on into the enemy's path. It passed 300 ft (90 metres) to starboard and the RAF crew set off in pursuit. Disappointingly the enemy aircraft managed to lose them through its sheer speed and disappeared in the Moll area. Kelsey got back on course for home and recrossed Schouwen at 0310 hours at 15,000 ft (4,600 metres) in a dive. He gave out

Flight Lieutenant Howard Kelsey and Pilot Officer E. M. Smith in front of their Beaufighter VIF V8744 of 141 Squadron at RAF Wittering. On 23/24 December 1943 they scored the first 100 Group victory when they shot down a Ju 88 of IV/NJG1 *based at St. Trond. It crashed near Bergisch-Gladbach, near Cologne.* Oberleutnant *Finster, pilot and* Staffelkapitan *was killed.* Feldwebel *S. E. Beugel was wounded but managed to bale out.* s(Tom Cushing Collection)

a mayday signal but he managed to land back at West Raynham at 0400 hours without further mishap. This victory was their fourth since joining the squadron.

On Christmas Day 1943 there were no operations flown and RAF personnel enjoyed themselves with football matches between teams of officers and NCOs and an excellent Christmas lunch served to the men by the officers in the Airmen's Mess. In spite of the festivities, 141 Squadron was suffering its most dispirited period since it had suffered such tragic losses to its Defiants during the Battle of Britain. The main reason was the failure of its Mosquito aircraft. The squadron had continued to receive old models. Engines and radar were in such poor condition that on Boxing Day all Mosquitoes were temporarily grounded until modifications were completed by de Havilland engineers. The squadron diarist noted: 'Experimental work is still proceeding with the Mosquito aircraft and most difficulties have or are being solved.'

Despite this optimism engine and radar problems still grounded the Mosquitoes when on 29/30 December Bomber Command went to the 'Big City' again with a force of 712 bombers. Most of the Beaufighters had been transferred to other units in anticipation of converting completely to the Mosquito, so the squadron could only operate two Beaufighters at night. Diversionary Spoof raids on Düsseldorf, Leipzig and Magdeburg by Mosquitoes succeeded in drawing away a large percentage of the German night-fighters and helped keep losses down to twenty heavy bombers. In the hands of the long-range fighter squadrons in 100 Group, and cured of all its operating problems, the Mosquito would ultimately provide much of the support Bomber Command needed.

CHAPTER III

They Slay by Night

Denn – munter 1st die, Wilde Sau'!
Und wenn es runst und kracht, dann weiß er es genau:
Das war em Flugzeugführer von der,,Wilden Sau "!
'Das Lied von der "Wilden Sau"' by Peter Holm

On 1/2 January 1944 Bomber Command returned to the 'Big City' with a force of 421 Lancasters. Twenty-eight failed to return. The following night, 383 Lancasters returned to Berlin and twenty-seven were shot down. Throughout the two nights of sustained operations, 141 Squadron (motto 'We slay by night') was only able to put up two Beaufighters and none at all on the first night of the New Year. On 5/6 January, when 358 bombers raided Stettin, with the loss of sixteen, it mounted its last Beaufighter *Serrate* sortie of the war when Flight Lieutenant D. V. Anderson and Pilot Officer Johnson took off in a Beaufighter VIF for a bomber support patrol to the Friesian Islands. They landed back at West Raynham without incident.

On 7 January the first Mosquito fitted with new modifications was flown to Hatfield from West Raynham for final approval by de Havilland, while Wing Commander Roberts drove to Radlett to expedite the delivery of new equipment. Three days later, a completed Mosquito went to each of the three *Serrate* squadrons. Nos 239 and 169 were still under training but two Mosquitoes in 141 Squadron were aloft on *Serrate* duty on 14/15 January when 498 bombers hit Brunswick, of which a staggering total of thirty-eight failed to return. Almost predictably there were problems with the *Serrate* Mosquitoes. The Mk II crewed by Squadron Leader Freddie Lambert and Flying Officer Ken Dear suffered a port engine failure 20 miles (32 km) inland of the Dutch coast and was forced to land on one engine at Coltishall. Squadron Leader F. P. Davis and Flying Officer J. R. Wheldon developed faulty intercommunications, which forced them to abandon an AI contact chase in the Hoya area. They also had to contend with ominous orange-coloured flashes along the length of the cockpit for fifteen minutes on the return flight before they landed at 2150 hours without further mishap.

All three *Serrate* squadrons operated for the first time on 20/21 January when 769 aircraft attacked Berlin. Once again, the war-weary Mosquitoes posed problems for overworked ground staff. At West Raynham six Mosquito IIs were prepared for operation but heavy mist and fog delayed night-flying tests until 1600 hours. These revealed that four were unserviceable, mostly with AI radar and *Serrate* problems. By this late stage, only two Mosquitoes, crewed by Squadron Leader J. W. Murray DFC DFM and Flight Lieutenant G. S. Bliss, on their 'freshman' trip, and Flight Sergeant Ivan

D. 'Doug' Gregory and Flight Sergeant Derek H. 'Steve' Stephens, were cleared for flying. Doug Gregory recalls:

I had joined 141 Squadron in February 1943 as a very lowly member with very little idea of what I was doing as far as night fighting was concerned. I remained on the squadron for twenty-two months with my navigator D. H. Stephens, who I considered a better navigator than I was a pilot. We started in defensive night fighting from an aerodrome in Cornwall where almost no activity from the Germans occurred. After a while we moved to the east of England and I flew my first *Serrate* operation on 24 June 1943 in a Beaufighter. I continued with Beaufighters until 20 January 1944 when I flew a Mosquito on 'Ops' for the first time and continued with them until I left the squadron in October 1944.

We, that is the squadron, were perfectly certain that we would win the war, not from just a patriotic view but by measuring the activities of the *Luftwaffe*, which was becoming more and more defensive, the advances of the British Army in Africa, the massing of American aircraft and troops in England, the general build-up for the invasion of Europe, the successes of the Russians, the slow gaining of the upper hand in the U-boat war, and the RAF bomber offensive. Although this seemed pretty obvious to us the great 'powers that be' were most reluctant to put into being a maximum effort on the radar front, still assuming that so-called secret materials and apparatus would be of more use to the Germans than to ourselves. Hence, when we, in 141 Squadron could have been tremendously detrimental to the German night-fighter force, we were plodding around in slow Beaufighters, second-hand Mosquitoes using a radar which was the first operational type which had been obsolete for quite some time. As far as letting the 'Bomber boys' down, I felt, we were the ones to be let down because of a lack of determination and foresight at the top. Had someone in the higher echelons of power believed the passive experiments with *Serrate*, gone 100 per cent for it, provided us with suitable aircraft and the latest radar (after all, the country was awash with defensive night-fighter squadrons), we would have been much more successful.

The difficulties encountered at the 'sharp end' were twofold. Firstly, the poor quality of the aircraft and especially their engines, which suffered from acute surging when the second-stage superchargers engaged. Secondly, unenlightened boffins were allowed to tamper with the aircraft structures. Holes were drilled through spars to fit aerials, which necessitated splicing the spars to repair the damaged sections. I spent time scraping tinfoil from the tops of Mosquito wings when the reflective qualities did not work as intended. I did not carry out any operational flights during December 1943.

We often considered our operations to be a failure, when in fact, as we learned afterwards, the *Luftwaffe* night-fighter force was well aware of our existence so that every chase we made, whether a shooting match or not, not only lowered the morale of the German pilots but also distracted them from their main purpose. We did the job we were asked to do, probably better than expected, but we could have done so much more if the 'powers' had believed and supported us to a greater extent.

At Little Snoring on 20/21 January Wing Commander Edward John "Jumbo" Gracie DFC, Commanding Officer of 169 Squadron and his navigator, Flight Lieutenant Wilton W. Todd, climbed aboard the only squadron Mosquito Mk II fit for duty. No. 239 Squadron also could only muster one Mosquito; Flight Lieutenants Jackson S. Booth DFC and Tommy Carpenter flew the sortie. 'What did you get?' they were asked on their return to West Raynham. 'Back!' they said. A number of contacts with bogeys were made but no enemy aircraft fell to the guns of the Mosquitoes. Thirty-five bombers however, were shot down by the German defences, which operated the *Zahme Sau* tactics to excellent effect.

Window seemed to have been rendered counterproductive by the German night-fighter force. The following night, 21/22 January, when 648 bombers attacked Magdeburg, 20-year old Flight Sergeant Desmond Byrne Snape RAAF and Flying Officer I. H. Fowler RCAF of 141 Squadron, one of five Mosquito II crews airborne that night (the fifth was from 239 Squadron), tussled with a Ju 88 during their patrol in the Brandenburg area. German night-fighters shot down fifty-seven bombers in the raids on Magdeburg, Berlin and flying-bomb sites in France. These were the heaviest losses in any night of the war so far. *Major* Prinz zu Sayn Wittgenstein, *Kommodore* of *NJG4* and a night-fighter ace with eighty-three or eighty-four victories, shot down four or five of the bombers flying a Ju 88G that night and was then shot down and killed by the rear gunner of a Lancaster. *Hauptmann* Meurer, Commanding Officer of *I/NJG1*, was also killed when his He 219 *Uhu* (Owl) was accidentally rammed by a Bf 110.

The 169 Squadron B Flight commander, Squadron Leader Joseph Aloysius Hayes 'Joe' Cooper, and his navigator were flying their freshman *Serrate* op after having been posted from 141 Squadron. Cooper had been one of Bob Braham's flight commanders at West Raynham where he had crewed up with Flight Lieutenant Ralph D. Connolly, an income tax inspector from Dulwich, London. They went to the Dutch islands, 'to get flak up their arse' on the 21st. Joe Cooper's favourite mount was HJ711 'VI-P', as it was significantly coded. 'Mount' is the operative word. In the early 1930s Lance Corporal Joe Cooper or 'Trooper Cooper', had been a cavalryman in the 4th Hussars. When it mechanized in 1936, he decided he did not want to drive tanks – he wanted to fly aeroplanes. So he borrowed £25 from a friend and bought his discharge from the army. He applied for, and surprisingly got, a short-service commission in the RAF. 'I'd left school at fourteen without the School Certificate but to their credit, the RAF took me in,' he recalls. Apart from being a keen horseman, Cooper was an accomplished boxer and he became Lightweight Boxing Champion of the RAF in 1938–39.

Cooper soloed on the Tiger Moth and went on to fly Audaxes and Harts, Blenheim night-fighters and then Beaufighters in 141 Squadron, where he was B Flight commander. 'The Beaufighter was for men not boys,' he fondly recalls. 'I could out-turn the Mosquito in a Beau.' Flying a Beaufighter he and Connolly damaged a Ju 88 on the night of 18 January 1943. In 169 Squadron, Cooper had no problems converting to the new steed, which he christened *P-Pluto*. he recorded in his logbook: 'Two *Serrate* contacts. Chased one. No luck. One AI contact. Behind. Turned on it. Everything blew up. Jinked my way home very startled.'

The next major raid by Bomber Command took place on 27/28 January when a force of 515 bombers attacked Berlin. Again, losses were high: thirty-three Lancasters were shot down. No. 141 Squadron dispatched seven Serrate Mosquitoes and 239 and 169 Squadrons sent off three and two Mosquitoes respectively. However, none recorded any successes, mainly because five crews experienced engine failure and had to abort, while two other aircraft suffered AI failure. On 28/29 January seven Mosquitoes were dispatched from West Raynham. One returned early with equipment failure and 22-year-old Flight Lieutenant Basil 'Johnny' Brachi and his navigator, 37-year-old Flying Officer Angus P. MacLeod of 239 Squadron, failed to return. During a patrol to Berlin their Mosquito lost its starboard engine over enemy territory and then the port engine started cutting out and finally quit over the North Sea. Crews in 239 and 141 Squadrons conducted an extensive sea search but the two crewmen were never found. (MacLeod's body was later washed ashore in Holland, where he is buried.)

Joining the search between 1710 and 2120 hours were Harry White and Mike Allen, who had only just returned from their successful sortie at 0600 hours. Both men had joined 141 Squadron at the same time as Brachi and MacLeod. White and Allen had picked up AI contacts on an enemy aircraft, which turned out to be a single-engined machine, probably a Bf 109. White had dispatched it with a five-second burst of 20-mm cannon fire from astern and below. The enemy aircraft burst into flames and exploded, diving through haze. The other success of the night went to Flying Officers Munro and Hurley of 239 Squadron – the first squadron victory using *Serrate*.

On 30/31 January Berlin was attacked again, this time by a force of 534 aircraft. Thirty-three bombers were shot down. Two Mosquitoes were put up by 169 Squadron, including *P-Pluto*. Squadron Leader Joe Cooper and Flight Lieutenant Ralph Connolly went all the way to Berlin in VI-P. Joe Cooper recalls:

> I had to orbit 50 miles [80 km] from Berlin on one of the German beacons. We tootled along and just got into position when I picked up a blip in front of me. He was orbiting slowly. Turning down the gunsight I could see the shape. There was no moon and it was very, very dark. I got into position, slightly below, and astern, went up to him and gave him the treatment; cannon – a lot of cannon. We were at about 25,000 ft [7,600 metres]. He was a complete flamer. Actually I gave him a bit more. 'That's for Coventry,' I said. But I got in too close. I was mesmerized by it all. Rafe said, 'Look out Joe, you're going to hit the bastard.' I pulled the 'pole' back hard and the result was I stalled and went into a spin. We were not allowed to spin or acrobat the Mosquito because of our long-range belly tanks, which moved the centre of gravity of the aircraft. I put on the usual drill: full opposite rudder, stick forward. I'd done this before but never in a Mossie. Went straight into a spin the other way! I went into the spin about five times, heading for the ground all the while. During the spins I could see this 110 out of the corner of my eye; most extraordinary!
>
> One's thoughts were, what a bloody shame. This is going to be the first Hun the squadron's got and I won't be there to tell the boys. I wonder who's going to hit the ground first, him or me? What a bloody shame the boys aren't going to know. I told Rafe, 'Bail out. We've had it!' He had an

observer-type parachute under his seat. In the spin he couldn't bend down to pick it up! He took his helmet off and put it on again. I said, 'Get out!' Rafe replied, 'If you can get us out of this spin, I could!'

I thought, 'I'll try something else.' I centralized the pole and the rudder and eased it out of the dive. At 7,000 ft [2,100 metres] I straightened up. I had not been frightened but boy was I frightened now. Our radar blew up in the spin. I said to Ralph, 'You can kneel and look backwards and keep an eye out for the Huns!' We had light flak all the way back to the coast. Approaching Snoring I called up the tower, 'Is Squadron Leader Ted Thorne in the tower?' I asked. 'Yes,' they said. I said, 'Tell him he owes me ten bob.' (I had bet Ted ten shillings I would get a Hun before him!) Ted took the camp Tannoy – it was one in the morning – and announced, 'For your information everybody Squadron Leader Cooper is coming into land and he's got the first Hun!' When I landed there were 300 airmen and WAAFs around P-Pluto! Most extraordinary! I gave them a little talk and off we went.

Cooper and Connolly's victim was Bf 110G-4 Wrk Nr 740081 D5+LB of *Stab III/NJG3,* which crashed at Werneuchen, 12 miles (20 km) east of Berlin. *Oberleutnant* Karl Loeffelmaan, the pilot, was killed and *Feldwebel* Karl Bareiss, the radar operator*,* and *Oberfeldwebel* Oscar Bickert, the *bordschütze,* who were both wounded baled out.

On 30/31 January five Mosquitoes of 141 Squadron also were on patrol and one of the crews, Flight Lieutenant Graham J. Rice and Flying Officer Jimmie G. Rogerson, destroyed a Bf 110. Two aircraft returned early with engine trouble while Flight Lieutenant John C. N. Forshaw and Pilot Officer Frank Folley discovered to their dismay that the cannons would not fire when Forshaw had a Bf 110 in his sights at a range of 900 ft (275 metres). Howard Kelsey and 'Smithy' Smith chased six or seven *Serrate* contacts at heights varying from 22,000 to 6,000 ft (6,700–1,800 metres) but failed to get close to their prey to open fire. After thirty minutes over the target their AI began to develop a 'squint' so they turned for home.

There were no major raids by Bomber Command during the first two weeks of February 1944 but the Serrate squadrons were tasked to support a raid by small forces of Mosquitoes on Berlin, Aachen and Krefeld on 1/2 February. Flight Sergeant Snape and Flying Officer I. H. Fowler returned early after their oxygen supply failed. Just after taking off from West Raynham for practice night flying, a Mosquito flown by Squadron Leader A. Black of 239 Squadron crashed at Hill Farm, Great Dunham. Black and his navigator, Warrant Officer J. K. Houston, were both killed. Four enemy aircraft were shot down in February. Three of them were accredited to crews in 169 and 239 Squadrons but the first kill that month came on 15/16 February when 891 bombers resumed the attack on Berlin in the biggest raid on the capital so far.

Harry White DFC and Mike Allen DFC took off from West Raynham at 1920 hours and flew to Berlin. Although the city was covered by 10/10ths cloud they could see the city from 78 miles (125 km) away, illuminated by a concentration of red and green skymarkers dropped by the Pathfinders. As the Mosquito approached, the attack began in earnest. Clouds of *Window* cascaded down like sleet, searchlights illuminated the cloud-top and fighter flares could be seen. There were a few enemy *Serrate* fighters abroad too as the bombers approached from the north, over Denmark. After bombing they turned onto a westerly heading. *Window* added to the general confusion on the AI tubes and several chases that were initiated were soon broken off again because of *Window* identification or contacts turning out to be friendly aircraft.

After patrolling the target area for seven minutes a white light was observed ahead, crossing on the same level and moving gently to starboard. White and Allen followed it through a gentle turn and closed the range using full throttle because the enemy aircraft seemed to be drawing away from them. Mike Allen, meanwhile, had obtained contact on an aircraft closing from 7,000 ft (2,100 metres) distance. The Mosquito was closing much too fast to open fire, so White throttled back, turned hard starboard 45 degree and hard port until contact was regained at a range of 3,000 ft (900 metres). White gently closed the range to 800 ft (240 metres) and opened fire from dead astern with a three-second burst, placing in the centre of his sight the only part of the enemy aircraft that was visible, the tail light. Mike Allen read out the range. Strikes were observed on the fuselage and starboard engine, and the enemy aircraft caught fire. Harry White fired a second burst as the enemy aircraft turned gently to starboard. More flames appeared and in the illuminated sky they could quite easily make out the doomed machine to be an He 177. This special *Beleuchter* (illuminator) was dropping flares in an attempt to reveal targets to the *Wilde Sau* night-fighters. It spiralled down on fire followed to 12,000 ft (3,650 metres) by the Mosquito before disappearing in cloud. Harry White had fired 306 rounds of 20 mm cannon shells, ninety-two from each of three guns, and thirty from the fourth cannon (which then jammed). It was the sixth enemy aircraft destroyed by the White-Allen partnership.

Forty-three bombers were lost on 15/16 February and Wing Commander Jumbo Gracie and his navigator, Flight Lieutenant Wilton W. Todd were shot down in the Hanover area. Six weeks later news was received that Gracie had been killed and Todd was a prisoner in *Stalag Luft III*. (He later designed the memorial to the fifty airmen murdered by the *Gestapo*.)

On 19/20 February *Zahme Sau* tactics were the cause of the very heavy loss of seventy-eight bombers on the operation to Leipzig. The German night-fighters attacked the main force stream all the way into and out of the target area and the *Serrate* Mosquitoes were hard pressed to ward them off. It was clear to Harris that Berlin was becoming too costly a prize and he abandoned operations there. On 21 February, Wing Commander K. C. Roberts was replaced as Commanding Officer of 141 Squadron by Wing Commander F. P. Davis, promoted from squadron leader, the B Flight Commander. On 20/21 February the bomber force went to Stuttgart. Only four of the 598 bombers were lost. Flying Officers E. A. 'Tex' Knight and D. P. 'Paddy' Doyle of 239 Squadron shot down a Bf 110. On 23/24 February a 141 Squadron crew was shot down while supporting the Bomber Command raid on Schweinfurt. Pilot Officer Desmond Snape was killed and his navigator Flying Officer I. H. Fowler was captured and sent to *Stalag Luft III*. Snape is buried at Loppersum General Cemetery in Holland. On 24/25 February Harry White and Mike Allen had a lucky escape during their patrol in the Heligoland-Freyburg area, as Allen recalls:

> We were chasing something which we presumed was a hostile aircraft when the
> port engine failed (141 had been re-equipped with old Mosquitoes and had been

experiencing a number of engine failures and several crews had gone 'missing' without any trace; we suspected with engine failure). This meant we had lost the chance of making an attack on a German night-fighter and that we were faced with a long journey home on one engine (about 390 miles [625 km]) during which we would be unable to maintain our height. (We were between 20,000 and 23,000 ft [6,100–7,000 metres] when the engine failed.) We turned round onto 270 degrees (we had been heading east when chasing our target) and set course for home, steadily losing height down to 12,000 ft [3,650 metres] as we flew over the Danish peninsula, skirted the island of Sylt, on across the North Sea, and leaving the Dutch islands well away on our port side.

We were about level with the islands of Ameland and Terschelling and I had already picked up the radar beacon (known as 'Mother') at West Raynham when Harry managed to pick up R/T contact with Sector Control. We were still cross at having to abandon our chase so when Harry got hold of the ground controller he showed the poor little WAAF on the other end no mercy and let fly (he never had much patience with the controllers anyway). The girl answered our 'mayday' call and asked if we needed any help. Harry called back and without any preamble, said, 'Creeper 24 here. Returning on one … and tell the box it wasn't any f***ing flak or bastard fighters that got us … Listening out!'

They still had about 150 miles (240 km) to go. Harry White made a single-engined landing at night without incident. A Ju 88 was claimed damaged by Flight Lieutenant John Forshaw and Pilot Officer Frank Folley.

On 28 February, night-fighter ace and A&AEE test pilot Wing Commander R. Gordon Slade arrived to take command of 169 Squadron. With him came his navigator, Philip Truscott. Truscott, who hailed from Canterbury, had been Slade's observer on 22/23 August 1942 when they notched the first blood to 157 Squadron by shooting down a Do 217 of *KG2* over Suffolk. London-born Slade had joined the RAF in 1933 and had learned the deadly art of night fighting in 604 Squadron at West Malling under Wing Commander John Cunningham. His tenure at 169 was short – just under three months – but Truscott remained with the squadron until he was killed flying with Wing Commander Neil Bromley, Slade's successor. (Group Captain Slade OBE FRAeS left the RAF in July 1946 and took the post of Chief Test Pilot for Fairey Aviation, retiring as Chairman of Fairey Hydraulics in 1977.)

On 25/26 February Flying Officers N. Munro and A. R. Hurley, who had scored the first *Serrate* 239 Squadron victory on 28/29 January, crashed at Manor House, Tittleshall, Norfolk on returning from operations. Munro was killed in the crash and Hurley died in No. 53 Mobile Field Hospital at Weasenham a few hours later. February had proved a bad month for the three *Serrate* squadrons and to compound it, seventeen Mosquitoes had returned early with engine failure. On 27 February Wing Commander F. P. Davis, Commanding Officer of 141 Squadron, went to 100 Group HQ at Bylaugh Hall and he returned with the very good news that all reconditioned Merlin 22 engines in the Mosquitoes were to be returned. In future and while stocks lasted, only new engines were to be fitted when replacements were required. Ground staff worked from 0800 until 2200 hours for days on end in order to give the squadrons a fresh lease of life.

In March 1944, the *Serrate* Mosquito squadrons destroyed six aircraft while a seventh, He 177A-3 Wrk Nr 332214 5J+RL of *III/KG100*, was destroyed by Wing Commander Freddie Lambert and Flight Lieutenant E. W. M. Morgan DFM of 515 Squadron on 5 March. It crashed near Chateaudun, France, killing *Leutnant* Wilhelm Werner, pilot and *Unteroffizers* Kolemann Schoegl, *bordfunker,* Gustav Birkebmaier, flight engineer, Alfred Zwieselsberger and Josef Kerres, *bordschütze*. Four of the victories went to 141 Squadron crews. On 18/19 March Harry White and Mike Allen destroyed two Ju 88s during a patrol in the Frankfurt area which was the target for 846 bombers. Flying Officer John Forshaw and Pilot Officer Frank Folley also bagged a Ju 88. One of these three was Ju 88C-6 Wrk Nr 750014 R4+CS of *VIII/NJG2,* which crashed at Arheilgen near Darmstadt, 15 miles (25 km) south of Frankfurt. *Oberfeldwebel* Otto Müller, pilot, *Obergefreiter* Erhard Schimsal, *bordfunker* and *Gefreiter* Gunter Hanke, *bordschütz*, were killed.

On 19 March Harry White and Mike Allen went to 100 Group HQ at Bylaugh Hall to receive congratulations for their double victory from Group Captain Rory Chisholm, the Senior Air Staff Officer. Chisholm said that they would be sent to 51 OTU at Cranfield on 23 March to give a talk on the squadron's operations in a mission to try and garner volunteers for new *Serrate* crews, particularly from among the flying instructors on the completion of their rests.

On 22/23 March, when Bomber Command again dispatched 816 aircraft to Frankfurt, Squadron Leader F. W. Kinchin and Flight Lieutenant D. Sellars of 239 Squadron destroyed a Bf 110. (Both failed to return from operations on 20/21 April.) The following night Flight Lieutenant Butler and Flight Sergeant Robertson of 239 Squadron were added to the grim reaper's total following a support operation for Mosquitoes bombing Dortmund. The night of 24/25 March was one of mixed fortunes. Bomber Command dispatched 811 bombers to the 'Big City' in a finale to the Battle of Berlin; seventy-two failed to return. The Berlin offensive cost 625 bombers shot down, 2,690 crew killed and 987 crew taken prisoner. To these cold, harsh statistics can be added the loss of the *Serrate* crews who supported them. Flight Lieutenant Armstrong and Flying Officer Mold of 239 Squadron were posted missing, later to be declared POWS. Flight Lieutenant Howard C. Kelsey DFC* and Flying Officer Edward M. Smith DFC DFM were credited with the destruction of an Fw 190 over Berlin.

On 25/26 March the marshalling yards at Aulnoye in northern France were the target for 192 bombers. A 141 Squadron crew, Flying Officer Francois Emile D. Vandenplassche, a Belgian, and his navigator, 20-year-old Flying Officer George Mamoutoff, the son of Russians living in London, lost their port engine when it caught fire during a patrol to Aulnoye. Mamoutoff bailed out at 1,400 ft (425 metres) and the Belgian followed. Vandenplassche evaded capture and made a remarkable home run via the Pyrenees, Spain and Gibraltar. He arrived back in Britain on 2 May. Mamoutoff is buried at Choloy War Cemetery. (Vandenplassche was killed in May 1953 flying a Belgian jet.)

On the afternoon of 30 March Mosquito crews in 100 Group were briefed for the part they would play in the raid that night on Nuremberg. Flight Lieutenant R. G. 'Tim' Woodman, who had previously flown Beaufighters in 96 Squadron at Honiley before joining 169 Squadron, recalls:

Briefing showed the bombers' track going south across France, then turning east to a point north of Nuremberg where the bombers turned again on to their target. They were to leave the target in a south-westerly direction, then out west and north and back to England. We immediately protested that as the bombers entered Germany between Mannheim and Frankfurt they would be passing between two German marker beacons which would be heavily stacked by German night-fighters waiting to pounce. And having established the track of the bombers other night-fighters would be vectored in from the north and up from the Munich area. Only a month earlier I had shot down a 110 which was orbiting, along with other night-fighters, the south one of these two beacons. We knew from a captured map sent to us by the Resistance the positions of twenty-two of these German night-fighter marker beacons. Our request that the track of the bombers be changed was passed to the SASO, Air Commodore Rory Chisholm DSO DFC at 100 Group, who passed it on to Bomber Command. But they refused to change.

At the next briefing our escort countermeasures patrol lines were on the map, planned by Group. I saw that my route and patrol was at 20,000 ft [6,100 metres], from the North Sea down over the Netherlands, then west of the Ruhr and to cross ahead of the bomber stream as it entered Germany, to take up a patrol on its south side at 10 miles [16 km] range. I was to engage any German night-fighters approaching from that direction. We were informed that the main bomber formation would have climbed to 15,000–20,000 ft [4,600–6,100 metres] and that it would he some 5 miles [8 km] wide. To me it was utterly incomprehensible: I was being treated like a destroyer escorting a convoy. At 10 miles [16 km] range I would only have some two minutes to try and intercept on a dark night before a German night-fighter entered the bomber stream, where contact would be lost. I begged Group to let me get ahead of the bombers (fly in low down undetected) and go straight to one of those marker beacons, with another crew flying to the other one, and shoot at least one down and scare off the rest. Again the Group SASO tried with Bomber Command and again our request was turned down. We foresaw a night of heavy casualties, possibly as great as some recent ones, which had reached seventy-plus bombers shot down. The Station Commander Group Captain Rupert Leigh (he had done a couple of *Serrate* operations himself), enjoined us all to press on even if we had radar failure, which in the past had been an acceptable excuse for abandoning an operation and returning to base. Even one Mosquito's presence might save a bomber or two.

I took off and climbed out over the North Sea. It was a dark night; the moon would rise after the raid was over. At 18,000 ft [5,500 metres] flames and sparks burst out from the inner side of the starboard engine and back across the wing. This was a disaster. I throttled back the engine, cut my speed almost to stalling, but did not stop the engine. The fire died down and I now had to make a possibly fatal decision. The engine instruments were OK. Go on or go back? The golden rule was: never open again an engine which had been on fire. But I did. I had lost height to 13,000 ft [4,000 metres], carefully

I opened up the throttle and the engine roared away smoothly. No sign of fire so I decided to press on. Over the Netherlands my observer, Pat Kemmis DFC, spotted on radar another aircraft coming up behind me. I guessed, rightly, that it was Flying Officer Harry Reed from my squadron who had caught up with me. He was indeed trying to intercept me, thinking I was much farther ahead. I put the nose down and at full throttle lost him but ran into flak over Aachen, which I had to avoid. Back at 20,000 ft [6,100 metres] again and expecting shortly to cross ahead of the bomber stream Pat started picking up radar contacts coming from the right. It was the bombers. We had lost time getting there and they were being carried along on a wind which was much stronger than forecast. There was nothing for it but to cross through the stream. This required skilful monitoring of the CR screens by Pat as he could see a dozen or more blips at the same time, whilst I saw the dark shapes of the Lancs and Halifaxes crossing below, ahead and above me. And instead of the bomber stream being 5 miles [8 km] wide it was more like 50. Some had already been shot down and before I reached the far side of the stream they were being shot down on my left.

On the south side of the stream Pat immediately picked up *Serrate* contacts but before I could intercept these Hun night-fighters they had entered the bomber stream. I went back in among the bombers and told Pat to get me a *Serrate* contact dead ahead. But for the final interception it was necessary to switch over to Mk IV AI radar and each time Pat did so he had a dozen or more blips on his screens – bombers, plus among them the German night-fighter. Masses of *Window* were also being tossed out of the bombers which jammed our radar. We tried three times but each time came up below a bomber, the rear gunner spotting us the third time, his tracer coming uncomfortably close whilst his pilot did a corkscrew. It was hopeless, we were doing more harm than good. Ahead bombers were being shot down one after another, some going all the way down in flames, some blowing up in the air, the rest blowing up as they hit the ground. I counted forty-four shot down on this leg to Nuremberg. What was happening behind I could only guess.

I flew on to Nuremberg and saw that the bombing had been widespread, a number of fires in the city, with a separate area where bombs and incendiaries had obviously landed in the countryside. I prowled around until the last of the bombers had gone but got no more *Serrate* contacts. Then I saw the odd bomber still being shot down to the south-west as they were making their way home. I flew down that way towards Stuttgart, then ahead and low down I saw a bomber on fire. I went down to his height, 8,000 ft [2,400 metres] and it was a Halifax with its rear turret on fire. I kept formation with him but far enough away for the crew not to see me until the fire died down and went out. Silently wishing the crew best of luck (they did in fact make it back) I turned and went back to Nuremberg. I was inwardly raging at the incompetence of the top brass at Bomber Command.

Back at 20,000 ft [6,000 metres] again I prowled over the city again hoping the odd German might still be around. Pat picked up a contact on radar. I intercepted it but it was another Mosquito. I called them up and told them I was on their tail but got no reply. Later I discovered there were two other Mosquitoes over Nuremberg at that time: Flying Officer Mellows from my own Squadron and a Mosquito from 192 Squadron, also from 100 Group. [Flight Sergeants J. Campbell DFM and R. Phillips of 239 Squadron shot down Ju 88C-6 Wrk Nr 360272 D5+? of *IV/NJG3*, which crashed 6 miles (10 km) south-west of Bayreuth]. *Oberleutnant* Ruprecht Panzer, pilot, who was wounded, *bordfunker* and *bordschütze*, all baled out safely.

It was time to start the long haul back with the moon already up and the clouds closing in. Near Frankfurt my starboard engine caught fire again and this time I had to shut it down and feather the prop. We could maintain a height of 7,500 ft [2,300 metres], just above the clouds, with Pat keeping a lookout to the rear for anyone on our tail. But all the Huns had landed, sated with kills. Back at base they discovered that the engine exhaust gasket had been blown, doing a lot of damage from the intense heat inside the cowling. But for the delay of the earlier fire I am sure I would have ignored orders, got ahead of the bombers and tackled those German night-fighters on one of those beacons. For the next couple of raids on Germany I was invited to Group by Air Commodore Rory Chisholm DSO DFC to help plan *Serrate* operations, and on my future operations I was permitted to freelance.

A staggering total of 95 bombers (11.9 per cent) were lost from a force of 795 dispatched to Nuremberg, Bomber Command's worst night of the war.

CHAPTER IV

The Offensive Spirit

Mossies they don't worry me,
Mossies they don't worry me,
If you get jumped by a One-nine-O,
I'll show you how to get free.
Keep calm and sedate,
Don't let your British blood boil.
Don't hesitate,
Just go right through the gate,
And drown the poor bastard in oil!

As we have seen, there were a few men with the offensive spirit in 100 Group, including those at West Raynham. On 11/12 April Squadron Leader Nevil Everard Reeves DFC* and Warrant Officer A. A. O'Leary DFM DFC* of 239 Squadron destroyed a Do 217. It was Reeves and O'Leary's tenth victory of the war, the previous nine having been shot down in the Mediterranean with 89 Squadron. On 18/19 April Harry White (promoted Flight Lieutenant on 14 April) and Mike Allen of 141 Squadron gave chase during a *Serrate* patrol to Swinemunde and the western Baltic but their intended victim escaped. Their ninth kill would have to wait just a little longer. Altogether, eighteen Mosquitoes operated from West Raynham at night, including ten from 141 Squadron, its best effort so far. On 20/21 April when the main force went to Cologne, Harry White and Mike Allen were one of eight 141 Squadron Mosquitoes dispatched to patrol over France. (Five B-17s of 214 Squadron, including one captained by the Commanding Officer, Wing Commander McGlinn, flew their first jamming operation at night. No. 214 Squadron's role was to jam enemy R/T communication between the Freya radar and the German night-fighters. Among other counter measures, they also jammed the *FuG 216 Neptun* tail warning system.) Harry White wrote:

> We took off and set course over base at 6,000 ft [1,800 metres] at 2252 hours and continued uneventfully on course until 2350 hours when our first *Serrate* contact was obtained to starboard and below, crossing starboard to port. We gave chase going downhill and obtained an AI contact at 12,000 ft [3,650 metres] range, which was found to be jinking considerably. Height was decreased to 12,000 ft [3,650 metres] and range closed to 1,500 ft [460 metres] when *Serrate* and AI contacts faded. We turned starboard and back to port hoping to regain contact – no joy. Enemy aircraft switched off *Serrate* as we broke away. Throughout this attempted interception our

elevation was behaving most erratically and it is believed that the enemy aircraft was directly below us at 1,500 ft [460 metres] when contact faded, the usual reason for fading blips.

The gyro having spun during the interception, I had little idea of where this interception had taken me, so set course towards the estimated position of Paris, which I hoped shortly to see illuminated and fix my position. At 0020 hours various contacts were obtained on the bomber stream leaving the Paris area. *Window* was much in evidence. At 0025 hours an AI contact at 15,000 ft [4,600 metres] to port and below was obtained a few miles west of stream and chased. We decreased height and followed contact through gentle port and starboard orbits reducing height to 12,000 ft [3,650 metres] and eventually closing range to 600 ft [180 metres] where I obtained a visual on four blue-white exhausts, later positively identified at 300 ft [90 metres] as a Ju 88. For five minutes I followed the enemy aircraft patiently through gentle port and starboard orbits at 200 indicated air speed, eventually opening fire, still turning, at 500 ft [150 metres] with a one-second burst allowing 5° deflection; no results. Enemy aircraft, completely clueless, continued to orbit. Apparently clueless also, I tried again with a one-second burst. Again no results. A third burst was fired as enemy aircraft peeled off to starboard and disappeared from view. I have no idea why I continually missed enemy aircraft and can only attribute it to the dot dimmed out from the gunsight and gremlin interference.

At 0100 hours, being in the proximity of the bomber stream second attack on Paris, we obtained another *Serrate* contact starboard and below which we followed for three minutes. This *Serrate* momentarily faded and enemy aircraft was presumed to be orbiting, at least turning. This was confirmed within a few seconds by a head-on AI contact at 15,000 ft [4,600 metres] range well below. We turned behind and closed rapidly to 600 ft [180 metres], and there obtained a visual on four quite bright blue exhausts, identified from 300 ft [90 metres] as a Do 217 now flying at 10,000 ft [3,000 metres]. Enemy aircraft was now turning very gently port and was followed for five minutes not wishing to repeat above. At 450 ft [135 metres] only exhausts could be seen, though these, unlike the Ju 88, showed quite clearly. Not wishing to approach closer I opened fire at this range with a two-second burst and was gratified to see the enemy aircraft explode with a blinding flash and disintegrate. Several pieces were flung back at us and I instinctively ducked as they splattered over the windscreen and fuselage. Apart from two broken Perspex panels, which were causing more noise than worry, we appeared to be OK but visions of damaged radiators caused some concern for the first minutes. We had no trouble in that respect and returned uneventfully to base.

White and Allen's victim was either Do 217N-1 Wrk Nr 51517 of *V/NJG4*, which crashed near Meulan, north of Paris. *Oberfeldwebel* Karl Kaiser, pilot, and *Unteroffizier* Johannes Nagel, *bordfunker*, both wounded, bailed out. *Gefreiter* Sigmund Zinser, *bordschütze* was missing. Or it was Do 217E-5 Wrk Nr 5558 6N+EP of *VI/KG100*, with the loss of *Feldwebel* Heinz Fernau, pilot, *Hauptmann* Willi Scholl observer, *Unteroffizier* Josef Bach, *bordfunker,* and *Oberfeldwebel* Fritz Wagner, flight engineer. The Mosquitoes had done their work well. Only eight bombers were lost on the attacks on the French railway yards. The other confirmed victory at night went to Flight Lieutenant Gordon D. Cremer and Flying Officer R. W. 'Dick' O'Farrell of 169 Squadron, who flew a *Serrate* patrol in support of the bombers targeting Cologne. Their report was as follows:

> Airborne at 0110 hours and except for intense enemy activity over this country, the first patrol point was reached uneventfully, both searchlight and flak activity were non-existent. After patrolling a beacon for ten minutes without incident we headed towards Cologne along a line from the NW which we did for five minutes, afterwards turning starboard to a westerly course. Shortly after making this turn at approximately 0234 hours obtained an AI contact at maximum range ... we closed to 9,000 ft [2,750 metres] astern of (enemy) aircraft. He took evasive action consisting of climbing and diving turns to port and starboard. However with good AI interception and full throttle the range was reduced rapidly and seven minutes after original contact a visual was obtained ahead and above. Despite navigator's early warning to throttle back I was approaching much too fast. I saw the aircraft silhouetted slightly above against cirrus cloud and instantly recognized it as an Me 110 by its tail fins. To avoid overshooting I pulled up to port, losing visual momentarily, and then turned starboard and regained visual. As the (enemy) aircraft was diving away to starboard I closed astern and gave a short burst at about 100–50 yd range from slightly above. Strikes were seen instantaneously inboard of the port engine followed by a large flash of flame which clearly illuminated the cockpit, fuselage and tailplane. We then overshot, but in passing both my observer and I were easily able to recognize the enemy aircraft as an Me 110 in the glare of the flames. I turned first to port and then to starboard and my next visual of the aircraft was its vertical descent in flames. It disappeared through the clouds whose tips were at 10,000 ft [3,000 metres] and a few seconds later there was the reflection of an explosion, followed by a red glow on the clouds. No return fire experienced. When last seen the cockpit was enveloped in flames as the enemy aircraft dived vertically into cloud and this fact, coupled with the explosions and red glow seen immediately after this through cloud is taken as the basis for the claim of one Me 110 destroyed.

Cremer fired just forty rounds of 20-mm ammunition to down the enemy aircraft.

Squadron Leader E. W. Kinchin and Flying Officer D. Sellars of 239 Squadron, who had downed a Bf 110 near Frankfurt a month earlier, were shot down and killed by *Oberleutnant* Fritz Krause of *I/NJGr.10* flying a *Neptun*-equipped Fw 190A-5 over Berlin.

Two nights later, on 22/23 April, Flight Lieutenant Tim Woodman and Flying Officer Patrick Kemmis of 169 Squadron were aloft again as the bombers went to Düsseldorf. Tim Woodman recalls:

The Y-Service had informed us that when the bombers were approaching targets in northern Germany and the Ruhr, night-fighter squadrons in the Munich area were being directed to the suspected target area. On this night, therefore, I flew from the Ruhr towards Munich as the bombers approached the Ruhr. We picked up a *Serrate* contact coming towards us and when it was within AI range turned port and came up underneath him. He had not spotted us on his radar. It was a 110 with a small white light on his tail. And there were four other aircraft flying in formation with him, two to port and two to starboard. I switched on the gunsight but it did not light up. I changed the bulb and it still did not work, so I banged the sight with my gloved fist and the socket and bulb fell out on its lead, blinding me with its brilliant white light as it lit up. I switched off and fired a short burst at the 110 tail light but with no strikes.

We were fast approaching the Ruhr searchlight zone so I fired a longer burst, stirring the stick as I did so to spread the shells. There were a number of strikes and the 110 seemed to have blown up. Black sooty oil covered my windscreen and when we got back we found the nose and starboard wing damaged. Pat, on radar, said he could see large pieces going down to the ground. But the Ruhr searchlights were after me and I did not want them to recognize me as a Mosquito. The Y-Service came to my aid. I reached back and pressed the trigger of a fixed Very pistol. Red and green Very lights spread across the night sky. The searchlight crews counted them and doused their searchlights. I had fired off the German 'colours of the day', the Y-Service supplying us with this information. It was the only time I did so. Immediately after the war I was sent to Germany and Denmark to test fly

their aircraft and to cheek up on their radar and other electronic devices. This particular Me 110 I was told was probably a *Nachtjägd* night-fighter escorting Me 109 *Wilde Sau* fighters to the bombers' target area. Seeing their escort aircraft shot down they would all have dived down to ground level, not knowing what was behind them. Maybe this is what my observer saw on radar.

Thirty-seven bombers were lost this night.

Flight Lieutenant R. G. 'Tim' Woodman. On 30 March 1944 he and his observer, Pat Kemmis DFC, had a very eventful night in their Mosquito while the fatal raid on Nuremberg by Bomber Command was in progress. A devastating loss of ninety-five bombers was recorded; Woodman saw forty-four of them go down. (Tim Woodman)

On 23/24 April during a *Serrate* patrol to the Baltic, Flight Lieutenant Graham J. Rice and Pilot Officer Ron Mallett of 141 Squadron shot down an Fw 190 employing *Zahme Sau* tactics against RAF bombers carrying out mine-laying in the Baltic. It was Rice's second victory on the squadron. A few nights later, on 26/27 April, when Bomber Command attacked Essen, Flying Officers William Ranson Breithaupt RCAF and J. A. Kennedy DFM of 239 Squadron shot down a Bf 110 in the Essen area. It was the first of their five victories. Breithaupt had joined the RCAF in August 1941 and was finally off the mark after having no victories flying with 488 and 409 Squadrons. One of 141 Squadron's ace night-fighting crews was lost when Squadron Leader John Forshaw, A Flight Commanding Officer, and his navigator, Pilot Officer Frank Folley, failed to return. Both men are buried in Rheinberg War Cemetery, only about 30 miles (45 km) from Essen. The following night, 27/28 April, 239 Squadron Mosquitoes landed back at West Raynham and submitted claims for three enemy aircraft destroyed. John Forshaw's chosen replacement, Squadron Leader Victor Lovell DFC, and his navigator, Warrant Officer Robert Lilley DFC, failed to return from a patrol to Stuttgart/Friedrichshafen.

In May steps could be taken to increase the strength of the ECM and Mosquito special duties squadrons in 100 Group, which now became known as Bomber Support. A lack of enemy air activity in the Western Approaches had permitted the transfer of Mosquito XIIs and XVIIs of 85 Squadron and Mosquito XIXs of 157 Squadron to Addison's command. These flew in to the recently completed base at Swannington (and in June 23 Squadron arrived from the Mediterranean to operate from Little Snoring, 169 Squadron and 1692 Flight moving to Great Massingham). Wing Commander John Cunningham had commanded 85 Squadron and 157 had been the first unit to be equipped with the Mosquito. All three squadrons were expert in the Intruder role. Corporal B. W. Salmon was a radar mechanic in 157 Squadron, one of many whose work kept the aircraft flying and capable of efficient and effective operations. He recalls:

> At the time, the aircraft were fitted with radio altimeters; either LORAN or *Gee* position-fixing radar; and, most important for the night-fighters, AI, which enabled the crew to find and attack enemy aircraft in the dark, or cloud conditions. Few members of the public were aware of the advanced nature of this equipment, and its contribution to the success of the campaign. The other important item was IFF, Indicate Friend or Foe, which enabled ground defences such as the anti-aircraft radars to identify our own aircraft. Unfortunately, when this was damaged in action, as it sometimes was, the result could be disastrous. We did discover that the radar equipment was an effective tool for spotting rain clouds and thunderstorms and we also used the wave-guides when testing the AI equipment to 'cook' sausages, which we placed on the end of sticks and held in front of the transmitter. This must have been the first microwave cooker!

While the 'new' Mosquito squadrons wrestled with the teething troubles of joining a new group and adapting to their new roles, there was no lack of trade for the existing Mosquito squadrons. On 8/9 May Tim Woodman and Pat Kemmis of 169 Squadron were aloft as the bombers hit targets in northern France and Belgium. Woodman recalls: 'We could clearly see the bombers, as many as ten at a time, but no sign of German night-fighters. We sniffed around for l09s and 190s over the target area but saw none. I saw three Halifaxes weaving like dingbats, up at 6,000 ft (1,800 metres). Below the leading bomber was a twin-engined aircraft climbing up to it.'

The Bf 110, flown by *Leutnant* Wolfgang Martstaller, and his radar-operator/air gunner, of *I/NJG4,* had taken off from Florennes at 0300 hours. In a letter to his parents on 12 May, Martstaller wrote: 'The sky was fully lit, so we could easily see the Tommy. Our crew saw at least ten bombers. However, we could only concentrate on one aircraft. When I was near him and fired (and my burst of fire bloody well blinded me!) the *Schweinhund* fired off a flare with a signal pistol, so that an enemy night-fighter could post us.'

Woodman fired a two-second burst and Martstaller dived into the darkness, Kemmis following him on *Serrate.* Marstaller soared up in a steep climb and Woodman fired from 800 yd. Woodman continues: 'This time he opted out and took us on a chase across the French countryside at treetop height, not seeing him as he flew away from the moon but following him on *Serrate.*'

Martstaller wrote: 'I went into a steep dive to almost zero metres (at night!), but still we could not escape from the Mosquito's attention.'

Woodman continues:

> He made the mistake of flying towards the moon and I saw the moonlight glint off his wings. I fired and got some strikes on his fuselage and wings as he flew across a wide-open space, which looked like an aerodrome. He went into a steep turn and firing 50 yd ahead of him to allow for deflection I hit him again. White smoke poured from his port engine and closing to 150 yd I gave him another two-seconds burst and hit him again.

Marstaller concluded: 'I was fortunate to spot a field in which to belly-land. We were slightly injured from shrapnel. When we found that we were OK we then saw a large explosion 3 km (2 miles) away from us. Next day this turned out to be a *Viermot* [four engine bomber] with seven crew members [Flight Lieutenant Chase and crew of Lancaster ND587 of 405 Squadron] burned to death. We were so happy!' Martstaller was killed in a crash on St Trond aerodrome in August 1944.

At 0010 on 10/11 May Flying Officer Vivian Bridges DFC and Flight Sergeant Donald G. 'Spider' Webb DFM of 239 Squadron attacked Bf 110 3G+El Wrk Nr 740179 of *I/NJG4* near Courtrai, setting one engine on fire. It crashed at Ellezelles, Belgium. *Oberleutnant* Heinrich Schulenberg, pilot, and *Oberfeldwebel*, Hermann Meyer, *bordfunker*, bailed out near Flobeq. Meyer recalled: 'We were shot down with one engine on fire. We could save ourselves by bailing out, and came down near Flobeg. I was wounded on the skull and was badly concussed. I spent three weeks in hospital at Brussels and then had four weeks' leave at home.'

On 11/12 May 429 bombers of the main force made attacks on Bourg-Leopold, Hasselt and Louvain in Belgium. Harry White and Mike Allen reached double figures by bringing down a Ju 88 a few miles north of Amiens, while Lucien LeBoutte and Flying Officer Ron Mallett destroyed a Ju 88 30 miles (50 km) south-west of Brussels. This was LeBoutte's first and only kill during his time on 141 Squadron. His victim was a Ju 88 of *VI/NJG2* flown by Wilhelm Simonsohn who had taken off from Köln-Wahn, a satellite field to the main base at Köln-Butzweilerhof. Simonsohn recalls:

We started around 2200 in Raum Brussels and flew at a height of 6,500 metres [21,000 ft] towards the Channel coast. At times, we saw flak shells exploding. However, compared to the large attacks on the German cities and the huge fires there, this was a quiet area. We were about 1½ hours in the air and now patrolled at a height of around 6,000 metres [19,700 ft]. There were some clouds above us when suddenly a chain of tracer bullets struck our port engine, coming in from the left side. I immediately did a steep dive, hoping that the enemy would break off his attack. The flames from the engine blinded our eyes, which were used to the darkness. I yelled through the microphone at my throat, 'Bail out!'

Franz [*Unteroffizier* Franz Holzer, flight engineer] kneeled at the escape hatch, pulled the red handle and flew out of the plane, together with the hatch. Günther [*Unteroffizier* Günther Gottwick, wireless operator-air gunner], who was sitting with his back towards me, dived towards the hatch and also disappeared. Meanwhile, I loosened my straps, but our aircraft was in a high-speed dive by now. I tried to pull the stick towards me in an effort to reduce the speed. I think that during this manoeuvre the left wing broke off, probably as a result of the attack. The aircraft, or what was left of it, was out of control.

I broke through the cockpit canopy and catapulted myself into the night air. I waited for about five seconds before I pulled the ripcord, then I pulled (I did that so hard that I had the ripcord in my hand!) and there followed a huge jolt. I will never forget that feeling, while I was hanging under that chute and listening to the air flowing through the silk. Far away from me, I saw burning pieces of my aircraft falling towards the earth.

Below me in the light of a white signal flare, I saw another parachute. I pulled my own signal pistol to respond, but it fell out of my hand, which had become stiff in the descent. The landing was without any problem. I landed in the yard of a farm near Mechlen, north-east of Brussels. My chute fell down – there was no wind – and I heard the raid sirens wailing. Next morning I met up with my crew. We were together again, slightly shocked, but happy and we were then transported to Brussels.

Viv Bridges and Spider Webb added another victory on 12/13 May when 239 Squadron dispatched *Serrate* patrols to Belgium in support of the bombers raiding Hasselt and Louvain again. They destroyed Ju 88G-6 Wrk Nr 750922 of *V/NJG3*, which crashed at Hoogcruts near Maastricht. *Unteroffizier* Josef Polzer, pilot, and *Obergefreiter* Hans Klünder, radar operator, were killed and *Gefreiter* Hans Becker, *bordschütze*, was wounded. Flying Officers Bill Breithaupt and J. A. Kennedy DFM also downed a Bf 110 in the Hasselt-Louvain area.

On 15/16 May Pilot Officers Wilfred Handel, 'Andy' Miller and F. C. 'Freddie' Bone of 169 Squadron destroyed two Ju 88s and a Bf 110 near Kiel when Mosquitoes of 8 Group mined the canal. This brought the Welsh pilot and the 38-year-old Birkenhead policeman's score to five enemy aircraft destroyed while in 100 Group (they had got a Bf 110 on 5/6 February and another on 22/23 April) and eight all told. Warrant Officer Les Turner and Flight Sergeant Frank Francis, who had just joined 169 Squadron, had been scheduled for their Freshman trip that same night, but as Turner recalls:

It was thought that the penetration was too deep for an inexperienced crew. The crew that replaced us (Miller and Bone) had a field day that night – two Ju 88s and a Bf 110 – an unbroken squadron record).

For the whole of 1943 I had instructed on Blenheims at Grantham. At the end of 1943 I returned to No. 51 OTU (having gained my first experience of radar-controlled night interception flying on Blenheims and Havocs there in the summer of 1942), this time on Beauforts and Beaufighters, which brought me to April 1944 and to 169 Squadron and Mosquitoes. I found it to be a Rolls-Royce of an aeroplane, easy to fly, forgiving on mistakes and, at that time, a joy because of its high power-to-weight ratio. I had never enjoyed flying more although, until then, I thought the best was a Beaufighter. Seated centrally between those two great radial engines gave a sense of power, which was to be experienced to be believed! At OTU I had crewed up with a radar-navigator Frank Francis and it was with him that I did my first tour of thirty-five trips on bomber support duties. Although perhaps we had little in common on the ground, he was an excellent radar screen 'reader' and our successes were in no small part due to his expertise. No. 169 Squadron was equipped with rather ageing Mosquito IIs with forward- and rearward-looking radar (AI Mk IV) and armed with four 20-mm Hispano-Suiza cannon. Serviceability was a continuing problem until, at the end of June 1944 we got Mosquito VIs. As well as radar we also had *Serrate*. This was a homing device, which was supposed to lock on to German night-fighter radar transmissions. It could not give range or altitude, merely direction, and while it worked after a fashion in practice (we did a two-week course on Beaufighters before going to the squadron) on the one instance where we got *Serrate* indication, it proved abortive.

After about a fortnight's practice both day and night we set out on our Freshman op on 19 May 1944. The Freshman was to Dieppe and Amiens and was totally uneventful over enemy territory but I frightened the life out of myself as we were climbing over southern England to our patrol. There were a number of 'cu-nimbs' – storm clouds – around us and as we reached 12,000 ft [3,650 metres], there was an enormous flash of lightning away to starboard. At that moment, the auto-gear change of the supercharger operated with its usual 'thump'. Such was the state of my nerves, I was sure that we had been struck by lightning until rational reason returned a few seconds later!

On 22/23 May Flight Lieutenant D. L. Hughes and Flying Officer R. H. 'Dickie' Perks of 239 Squadron destroyed a Bf 110. Bf 110G-4 Wrk Nr 720050 05+2 of *III/NJG3,* was shot down by Wing Commander N. B. R. Bromley OBE and Flight Lieutenant Philip V. Truscott of 169 Squadron. *Feldwebel* Franz Müllebner, pilot, *Unteroffizier* Alfons Josten, radar operator, and *Gefreiter* Karl Rademacher, air gunner, were all wounded in action and baled out successfully. The Bf 110 crashed at Hoogeveen, south of Groningen. Two nights later, Bill Breithaupt and J. A. Kennedy added a Ju 88 to their score and damaged a Bf 109 15 miles (24 km) east-south-east of Bonn and north-west of Aachen. While in the Aachen area, Hughes and Perks, and Flight Lieutenant Denis J.

Raby DFC and Flight Sergeant S. J. 'Jimmy' Flint DFM each destroyed a Bf 110G-4 of *VII/NJG6*. Wrk Nr 730106 2Z+AR crashed at 0230 hours in forest between Zweifall and Mulartshuette, south-east of Aachen and *Oberleutnant* Helmut Schulte, pilot, and *Unteroffizier* Hans Fischer, air gunner, both baled out. *Unteroffizier* Georg Sandvoss, radar operator, was killed. The other Bf 110G-4, Wrk Nr 720387 2Z+HR, flown by *Unteroffizier* Oskar Völkel, crashed five minutes later at the Wesertalsperre near Eupen, south of Aachen. Völkel and *Unteroffiziers* Karl Hautzenberger, radar operator and Günther Boehxne, air gunner, baled out safely.

On 27/28 May 239 Squadron sent up eight Mosquitoes on bomber support. The A Flight Commander, Squadron Leader Neil Reeves DSO DFC and Pilot Officer A. A. O'Leary DFC** DFM destroyed Bf 110F Wrk Nr 140032 G9+CR of *VII/NJG1*. It crashed at Spannum in Friesland province in Holland at 0115 hours. *Unteroffizier* Joachim Tank, the 26-year-old pilot, was slightly wounded. *Unteroffiziers* Günther Schröder, the 19-year-old radar operator, and Heinz Elwers, the 24-year-old air gunner, were killed. Meanwhile, Flight Lieutenants Harry White DFC*, now OC Station Flight, and Mike Allen DFC* were one of seven Mosquito crews in 141 Squadron which supported the main force raids on Aachen and Bourg-Leopold. At 0235 hours a little to the west of Aachen, Allen obtained two AI contacts at 14,000 ft (4,300 metres) and 12,000 ft (3,650 metres), crossing right to left. At a range of 8,000 ft (2,400 metres) the two blips merged into one and Allen remarked to White: 'A bomber's about to be shot down in front of us at any minute.' White wrote:

> Still crossing, we turned to port in behind this contact and at 1,200 ft [365 metres], obtained a visual on two white exhausts. We had not increased speed as range was closing quite rapidly but as we assumed the line astern position, the exhausts faded from sight and range was increased to 8,000 ft [2,400 metres] before, at full throttle, we were once more able to decrease the range slowly to 1,200 ft [365 metres] again, obtaining a visual on two white exhausts. We closed to 600 ft (180 metres) where I was able to identify this target as an Me 109. I closed further to 300 ft [90 metres] and opened fire with a two-second burst from 15° below. It exploded with a colossal flash, which completely blinded me for about a minute and a half. I asked Mike to read my instruments for me but his attention was at that moment elsewhere. The flash had attracted his attention from his box and he looked out in time to see a second Me 109 slip slowly by under the starboard wing. With his head now well in the box, Mike commenced reading off the range as this 109 emerged from minimum range behind. But even the best navigator cannot carry out an interception with the help of a blind pilot and the range had increased to 6,000 ft [1,800 metres] astern before I could even see my instruments. We turned hard port but contact went out of range at 14,000 ft [4,300 metres].

Although the second Messerschmitt Bf 109 had escaped, the eleventh victory of Harry White and Mike Allen was duly recorded in 141 Squadron's record book.

A 515 Squadron Mosquito flown by Flying Officers David Kay Foster and 20-year-old Robert Stanley Ling, which took off from Little Snoring at 0155 hours, and was detailed to patrol Leeuwarden, failed to return. They were shot down by airfield defence flak and crashed into a hangar on the airfield. Both are buried in Leeuwarden Northern General Cemetery.

Squadron Leader R. K. Bailey and his navigator also failed to return, as Bailey recounts:

> Intelligence had declared Leeuwarden to be the main reaction base of the German night-fighter force for operations that night. We were detailed to arrive at Leeuwarden when the German fighters would be reacting to the radar indication of the approach of the main force of bombers (we crossed the North Sea at sea level to avoid detection). The plan of operations worked for no sooner had we reached the Leeuwarden area than the navigator called 'Serrate contact'. We followed this target in a climbing orbit to 11,000 ft [3,350 metres] where in conditions of high haze and resultant poor visibility I sighted an Me 110 directly ahead and at very close range. Two bursts from the four 20 mm cannon resulted in an explosion and showers of debris into which we flew. The navigator called out another Serrate contact, which I had to ignore being engaged in feathering the propeller of the starboard engine, which had overheated and stopped. Assessing the situation the navigator said he would give a course for our base in Norfolk. I asked him instead for a course to Calais and thence to Manston, Kent, to avoid a North Sea crossing in a damaged aircraft, the extent of which was unknown. Ten minutes later the port engine failed and I ordered bail out. Within seconds the navigator was gone and I made to follow diving head first across the cockpit to the escape hatch. I had trimmed the rudder for asymmetric flying when the starboard engine failed but I omitted to neutralize trim when the port engine failed. The result was a steep spiral dive. Meanwhile I was trapped, having caught the top section of the hatch. I was head and shoulders out in the slipstream with my legs and torso in the aircraft. I was almost reconciled to this situation when a stupid thought crossed my mind that when the aircraft struck the ground I would be sheared in two! This possibility brought about a frenzied new effort. Suddenly I was free from the whistling slipstream and falling in space. I pulled the ripcord and the parachute opened; I said a prayer of thanks. Some seconds later I made contact heavily with the ground.

Bailey was taken in by the Dutch Underground but his immediate concern was for his wife Jean, who was eight months pregnant on 29 May, and how she would react to the news that he was 'missing'. He spent three months with the Dutch Underground – even taking part in a raid on a post office to augment supplies of ration cards and money – before being sent down the escape lines to Belgium in August 1944. Unfortunately, however, the line had been infiltrated. Bailey, an American Fortress pilot by the name of Bill Lalley from Lowell, Michigan, and Viv Connell, an RAAF Lancaster navigator from Broken Hill, New South Wales, were taken prisoner by the Germans.

In all, 239 Squadron destroyed ten aircraft during May and now led the three Serrate Mosquito squadrons with nineteen victories; 141 Squadron had thirteen and 169 Squadron at Little Snoring had twelve.

On 14 June Harry White and Mike Allen, and Howard Kelsey and Smithy Smith, were posted to the Bomber Support Development Unit (BSDU) at Foulsham. (On 28/29 July 1944 Harry White and Mike Allen returned briefly to West Raynham to fly *Serrate* patrols with nine other Mosquitoes of 141 Squadron. During the sortie they shot down two Ju 88s to bring their tally to thirteen, the highest score in the squadron's history.) In June also, Lucien LeBoutte, who on 24 May had been awarded the DFC (as was his navigator, Mallett) was officially 'tour expired'. Mallet himself was on his third tour. LeBoutte, who had flown over fifty *Instep*, *Ranger*, night-fighter and *Serrate* patrols and damaged three trains in strafing attacks, was given a staff position in London, reaching the rank of Wing Commander DFC CdeG. After the war Group Captain Leboutte served in Brussels at SHAEF and he was one of the founder members of the Belgian Air Force. He served with distinction until retirement in 1956. Replacements arrived at West Raynham during May and June. Two of them, Warrant Officer A. L. Potter and his navigator, Flight Sergeant R. E. Gray, had only just joined 141 Squadron when they were killed on a training flight on 24 May when their Mosquito crashed at North Farm, Clenchwarton, near King's Lynn.

Serrate Mosquito victories were still coming thick and fast in May 1944. On 30/31 May 239 Squadron at West Raynham dispatched ten Mosquitoes on *Serrate* sorties. Bridges and Webb, and Flight Lieutenants Denis Welfare and David B. 'Taffy' Bellis shot down a Bf 110 apiece. Bellis recalls:

> It was in January 1944 that I first heard of 100 Group. I was stationed at TRU Defford, near Worcester, at the time and was on 'rest' after completing a tour of ops at Malta with Denis Welfare. Defford was basically a research station at which new airborne electronic equipment was being tested and life was pleasant, but rather boring. I flew about ten hours a month and there was plenty of time for bridge and sampling the beer and food at the local pubs, especially the White Lion at Upton-on-Severn. By the end of 1943 I longed for an operational squadron again, for the camaraderie that went with it and for the addictive excitement of flying over enemy territory. Thus it was with relief that I was told in January that my posting had arrived. The signal from the Air Ministry read something like, 'You are posted to 100 Group and you will report to O/C 239 Squadron at West Raynham as soon as possible. I had never heard of 100 Group before ; nor had other aircrew at Defford. We all thought there was a mistake; there could not be 100 groups in the RAF! 'Jumbo' Harkness, one of the flight commanders at Defford, said that 239 was a special duties squadron and I had visions of flying VIPs or even dropping agents over occupied Europe.
>
> Denis Welfare had received the same posting and we arrived at West Raynham, where we soon found what 100 Group was about. By the autumn of 1943, a large part of the *Luftwaffe* had been concentrated over western Europe and its night-fighters had developed tactics and electronic equipment that were causing serious losses to RAF bombers on their night operations over Germany. Consequently, 100 Group was formed as a matter of urgency to counteract the *Luftwaffe* night-fighters by jamming their

ground control, organizing spoof raids and by attacking the night-fighters at their bases and in the air.

When we arrived at West Raynham, 239 Squadron, which was previously on low-level reconnaissance, was being reformed and re-equipped with Mosquito IVs for offensive night fighting. Like other crews joining 239 at the time, Denis and I had no experience of offensive night fighting. Our first squadron in 1942 was 141 at Tangmere and Acklington, flying Beaufighters on defensive night-flying duties. This was followed by a tour with 272 Squadron in Malta, also flying Beaufighters, but this time on daylight operations against German and Italian supply lines between Italy and North Africa. Consequently, Denis and I spent the first few weeks at West Raynham on familiarization courses on Mosquitoes and the specialized electronic equipment that they were fitted with, i.e. AI (Airborne Interceptor), *Serrate*, and *Gee* navigational aid.

We had some experience of the Mk IV AI since our days on 141 Squadron. This airborne radar enabled us to pick up an 'echo' from another aircraft and to home accurately on to it. The range of this radar was equal to our altitude – the echoes from the ground below 'drowned' out everything else further away. Thus, successful defensive night fighting depended on ground control guiding us to within, say, 10,000 ft [3,000 metres] of an intruder. There was, of course, no such ground control to assist a Mosquito night-fighter over Germany and the chances of a crew picking up a German fighter on AI was negligible. This is where *Serrate* came in. A radio receiver in the Mossie picked up *Lichtenstein* radar transmissions from a German night-fighter and enabled the Mossie to home in on it – usually an Me 110 or a Ju 88 – until it came into AI range. The *Serrate* receiver had two screens – one giving the vertical and the other giving the horizontal direction of the source of the radar transmission. The Mosquito would home onto the transmitting aircraft until it came within AI range, when the *Serrate* was switched off. *Gee* was also new to me. It made navigation easy; in fact, the old-fashioned skills that I used over the sea and deserts of North Africa on my previous operational tour were now sadly obsolete.

Ground and air exercises followed thick and fast during February and we were operational by the middle of March. Operations were of two categories. The first was to patrol known German night-fighter beacons. These were locations where German night-fighters were held in readiness until their ground control decided where the main bomber stream was going. Here we used AI alone and success obviously depended on our navigation being correct, on the *Luftwaffe* using a particular beacon on a given night, and on our luck – the sky is a big place and 10,000 ft [3,000 metres] range for our AI was not much. The second category of operation was to patrol in the vicinity of the bomber stream, using both AI and *Serrate*. Success was a matter of luck – a German fighter using his own radar at the right time and place. Our first op was on 19 March, when we patrolled Holland and France with no contacts. Similarly no luck with further patrols during the following weeks. Success came at last on the night of 31 May when we picked up a *Serrate* transmission north of Paris. Our first priority was to make certain that the transmission did not come from a fighter homing on us from behind! We then manoeuvred our Mossie to get behind the transmitting aircraft. To our dismay, it switched off its radar before we were in AI range. However, we kept on the same course and picked up an AI contact a minute or so later and converted this to a visual and the shooting down of an Me 110.

Welfare and Bellis, and 239 Squadron, enjoyed more success on 5/6 June, the eve of D-Day, when twenty-one *Serrate* Mosquitoes were dispatched to northern France. Five Mosquitoes were dispatched by 239 Squadron, two returning with problems. Denis Welfare and Taffy Bellis claimed a Bf 110 north of Aachen. Their victim was possibly Wrk Nr 440272 G9+NS of *VIII/NJG1*, which crashed at 0054 hours on the northern beach of Schiermonnikoog. *Unteroffiziers* Adolf Stuermer, the 22-year-old pilot, *Unteroffizier* Ludwig Serwein, the 21-year-old radar operator, and *Gefreiter* Otto Morath, the 23-year-old air gunner, were killed. Flying Officers Bill Breithaupt DFC and J. A. Kennedy DFC of 239 Squadron claimed a Ju 88G-1 off the Friesians. Their victim was Wrk Nr 710454 of *V/NJG3*, which crashed 12 miles (20 km) north of Spiekeroog. *Unteroffiziers* Willi Hammerschmitt, pilot, and Friedrich Becker, *bordfunker*, and *Feldwebel* Johannes Kuhrt, *bordschütze* were killed.

One of the dozen Mosquitoes dispatched by 141 Squadron (of which two returned early) was crewed by Wing Commander Winnie Winn, the new Commanding Officer, and R. A. W. Scott. Ten 515 Squadron Mosquitoes on *Ranger* patrols patrolled and bombed enemy airfields in France and strafed road, rail and canal traffic. Two of 515 Squadron's Mosquito VIs were shot down. Squadron Leader Shaw and his navigator crashed near Dusen and Squadron Leader Butterfield and his navigator were lost off Dieppe. The *Luftwaffe* had managed to put up just fifty-nine fighters to intercept the invasion forces, but only one claim was submitted by a *Nachtjäger* pilot. *Hauptmann* Strüning of *II/NJG1*, flying He 219 *Owl* claimed it. Three more victories were claimed over Normandy by *Hauptmann* Eberspächer, a fighter-bomber pilot flying an Fw 190G-3, of *III/KG51*.

The Mk X-radar-equipped Mosquito Mk XVIIs of 85 Squadron and 157 Squadron's Mk XIXs at Swannington officially began operations on D-Day, 5/6 June, when sixteen sorties were flown. Twelve Mosquitoes in 85 Squadron operated over the Normandy beachhead, while four in 157 Squadron patrolled night-fighter airfields at Deelen, Soesterberg, Eindhoven and Gilze Rijen in Holland. No. 85 Squadron dispatched twelve Mosquitoes over the Normandy invasion beaches and four Mosquitoes of 157 (and ten of 515 Squadron) made *Intruder* raids on Belgian and Dutch airfields. Flying Officer Bob Symon of 85 Squadron recalls:

On 5 June, Wing Commander Michael Miller and myself were transferred to Colerne, arriving at one p.m. There was quite an uproar when nobody was allowed to leave the airfield, no phone calls to wives to say they would not be home for dinner. We flew patrols 75 miles [120 km] inland over the beachhead. We had four Mossies making a line covering the territory on the British and Canadian landings. Michael and I were the first on patrol,

Pavilly-Bernay. This was the beginning of an invasion and there was nothing in our part of the sky. One searchlight groped around for less than a minute and then went out. The real sight was on our way back to Colerne after our relief had taken over. On the return to base looking north over the water we could see for miles the tugs and gliders making their way over the Channel: a fabulous sight.

Radar failure was occurring regularly on operations. In Tim Woodman's opinion it was due to a number of causes, chief of which were inexperienced ground servicing technicians, old equipment, lack of new parts to replace those which became unserviceable, and radar valves which were not designed for operating at the high altitudes which were reached. 'Newly installed aerial systems continually gave wrong altitude readings so that one did not know whether the target was up or down. And, of course, they would not release centimetre AI for our use, and when they did it was to bring in two night-fighter squadrons from Fighter Command, most of the crews having little experience of operating over enemy territory.'

The campaign to acquire the British-designed, American-made AI Mk X culminated in the arrival in 100 Group of 85 and 157 Squadrons at Swannington. At the beginning of May, 85 Squadron, equipped with AI Mk X and already well trained in its use, had been engaged in defensive night fighting, while 157, equipped with AI Mk XV, had supported Coastal Command's daylight anti-U-Boat patrols in the Bay of Biscay. AI Mk X, unlike Mk IV had no backward coverage at all. From the point of view of the Mosquito's own safety, some kind of backward warning equipment had to be fitted before it could be used on high-level operations. To provide a quick interim answer BSDU began a modification of Monica I. Until the tail warner was fitted, 85 and 157 Squadrons would be trained for low-level airfield intrusions. This would mean that the AI Mk X squadrons would eventually be in a position to play a dual role – either high-level or low-level work – which would help considerably in the planning of bomber operations. Mosquitoes of 100 Group continued their support of the invasion forces on 6/7 June.

On 8/9 June West Raynham was the scene of mixed emotions. Flying Officer A. C. Gallacher DFC and Warrant Officer G. McLean DFC in 141 Squadron told of the destruction of an unidentified enemy aircraft over northern France after they had chased it into a flak barrage at Rennes, where it was brought down by a single burst. A popular Free French crew, Flight Lieutenant D'Hautecourt and his navigator Pilot Officer C. E. Kocher, returned from their seventh operation, patrolling over their homeland, on one engine and died shortly after swinging off the runway and crashing into two fighter aircraft. Both Frenchmen had only been with the squadron since February.

That same night Warrant Officer Les Turner and Flight Sergeant Frank Francis flew their fourth trip, which Turner said, made up for the lack of incident on their previous two outings.

While somewhat south of Cherbourg – this was again a beachhead area operation – I noticed that the glycol coolant temperature was rising 'off the clock'. I assumed the worst – a pump failure, possible seizure and maybe fire – and feathered the engine. We set a rough course for UK – 'steer north and you are bound to hit something' – and when we were within radio range of Tangmere got them to give us a course. We then settled down to what turned out to be one hour fifty minutes of single-engined flying at the recommended 170 mph [270 kph] (IAS) at 12,000 ft [3,650 metres]. We had picked what turned out to be one of the worst nights of the year, from the point of view of weather. In fact one of the crews of a neighbouring squadron bailed out when they were unable to get in and were nearly out of fuel. Tangmere kept hold of us all the way. We transmitted for radio fixes every few minutes and eventually I was instructed to commence a controlled descent of say 300 ft [90 metres] a minute until instructed further. I had a marked reluctance to lose height with only one engine and in cloud, and when we reached, I believe, 1,400 ft [425 metres], I asked urgently if further descent was safe. I was assured that it was and we broke cloud at 600 ft [180 metres] over Dante's Inferno – actually the paraffin flares of FIDO at Hartford Bridge. We were given permission to land immediately and executed a very tight circuit to hold the (literally) flarepath in view. We had to lower the undercarriage by pump and this took so long that we didn't have time to get the flaps down! We touched down reasonably well but at 150 mph [240 kph]. Another pilot in the tower said later that it looked like a take-off! When, after about two-thirds of the runway had gone past, the tail-wheel touched down. I locked the brakes but the runway ended and we careered on what seemed like ploughed land for another 100 yd or so when we hit a drainage ditch, slewed to port a bit and stopped. The tremendous silence after the noise of the landing was broken only by the 'chufferty-chuff' of the one Merlin, which was still ticking over. The crash crew arrived almost at once and we clambered down, relieved, somewhat breathless but unhurt. The Mossie suffered a damaged undercarriage and in view of its years was I believe, subsequently written off.

Also on 8/9 June Wing Commander Neil Bromley OBE and Flight Lieutenant P. V. Truscott of 169 Squadron, which had recently moved from Little Snoring to Great Massingham, shot down a Dornier in the Paris area, possibly Do 217K-3 Wrk Nr 4742 6N+OR of *Stab III/KG100*. *Oberleutnant* Oskar Schmidtke, pilot, and *Unteroffiziers* Karl Schneider, observer, Helmuth Klinski, *bordfunker,* and Werner Konzett, flight engineer, were killed. Flight Lieutenant Clements and Pilot Officer Pierce of 141 Squadron safely abandoned their Mosquito in the Wisbech area after losing their port engine over Reading while returning from a sortie to northern France. A 239 Squadron crew overshot the West Raynham runway with the starboard throttle jammed and crashed in a field but both crew scrambled out unhurt. Next day Flight Sergeant Humpreys and his navigator set off from Massingham on a cross-country flight. Near Gayton Mill, Humpreys lost control and the 169 Squadron Mosquito crashed. Humpreys was killed but his navigator managed to bail out successfully.

On the afternoon of 11 June, during another training flight, a Mosquito crewed by Flight Lieutenant P. A. Riddoch and his navigator, 33-year-old Flying Officer C. S. Ronayne, a new crew who had just joined 141 Squadron, disintegrated in mid-air 2 miles (3 km) south of Chippenham village between Mildenhall and Newmarket. Riddoch was blown out of the aircraft and his parachute opened in the action. He suffered a dislocated right shoulder, fractured jaw and lacerations to his face and eyelids but recovered in the White Lodge EMS Hospital at Newmarket. Ronayne was found dead from multiple injuries. A subsequent inquiry found that the cause of the accident was structural failure. That night Irishman Wing Commander Charles M. Miller DFC**, Commanding Officer of 85 Squadron, and Flying Officer Robert Symon, in a Mosquito XIX fitted with AI X, shot down a Bf 110 over Melun airfield. Miller wrote in his report:

> We took off from Swannington at 2215 hours on an *Intruder* patrol to Bretigny and Melun. While orbiting the town of Melun at 3,000 ft [900 metres] we passed over the airfield and were momentarily lit up by searchlights. Shortly afterwards, another aircraft was engaged and it fired a recognition signal – a number of white stars. We turned towards this and a contact was obtained 30° starboard, same level and 2 miles [3 km] range.

Symon recalls:

> I saw the blip on my tube and I had us in position in two and a half minutes behind. We made a very simple interception. Michael insisted that I keep my eyes on the tube even when he had a visual, well that is quite proper, but when I protested that we had closed inside minimum range and there was nothing to look at he relented and said I could look out. So I looked out and saw a completely empty sky. He pointed upwards with one finger and there it was – a Bf 110: I felt that I could have stood up and autographed its underside.

Miller continues.

> We gave chase, the enemy aircraft firing further recognition signals and from 600 ft [180 metres] got a visual of the enemy aircraft silhouette. Closing in to about 50 ft [5 metres] and immediately below, we recognized an Me 110; small fins and rudders, long nose, square wing tips, and drop-tanks. No exhausts were visible from below but a stream of small sparks was seen. We dropped back to about 150 yd, height now about 2,000 ft [610 metres] and pulled up behind, but the silhouette having become rather indistinct, I fired in anticipation of its position. No strikes were seen at first, but by raising the firing point strikes became visible and the aim was steadied. A fire started in the port engine, which spread over the fuselage. Large pieces of flaming wreckage flew back, and enemy aircraft dived vertically downwards, exploding on impact with the ground, about 10 miles [16 km] NE of Melun airfield at 0035 hours. No return fire was experienced.

Miller fired ninety-two 20 mm SAPI and ninety 20 mm HEI rounds to down the Bf 110, although his port outer gun stopped after two rounds because of a loose bullet of the round striking the body of the gun by the chamber entrance. Symon says, 'When we got back to Swannington we found that we had opened the scoring, which I thought was a right and proper thing for the CO of 85 to do! (I regret that 108 days from this event my pilot was compelled to retire due to illness.)'

Denis Welfare and Taffy Bellis of 239 Squadron were also on patrol, between Paris and Luxembourg, on radar watch for night-fighters. Bellis recalls:

> We picked up a German airborne radar transmission about 10 miles [16 km] away on our *Serrate* apparatus and homed on to it. We made a contact 10,000 ft [3,000 metres] away with our own AI and in a few minutes converted it to a visual, showing clearly the twin fins and faint exhausts of an Me 110. We attacked from about 50 yd and the Me immediately blew up. Our Mossie flew into debris and was enveloped in burning petrol. Fortunately, the fire did not get hold, but our Mossie was clearly damaged. We jettisoned the escape hatch ready to bale out quickly and called UK on the mayday channel. The emergency control at Coltishall was most helpful with radio bearings, etc. However, Denis was able to control the aircraft and our *Gee* navigation equipment seemed to be working OK. Thus we decided to dispense with Coltishall's help and return to base, where eggs and bacon never tasted so good! I shall never forget Denis' skill, the ability of the Mossie to take punishment, the spectacular film from the camera gun of the engagement, and last but not least, the discomfort of flying some 300 miles [480 km] home in a plane without an escape hatch.

Meanwhile, the first airfield intrusion results with AI Mk X were very promising and it was found that at a height of 1,500–2,000 ft (460–610 metres) AI contacts at ranges of 3 miles (5 km) or so could be obtained and held. During June, from 176 sorties dispatched, of which 131 were completed, thirty-eight AI contacts were reported leading to the destruction of ten enemy aircraft and the damaging of three others. All these combats, save one of those leading to damage claims, resulted from sixty-two sorties flown between the nights of 11/12 June and 16/17 June.

On 12/13 June Flight Lieutenants James Ghilles 'Ben' Benson DFC and Lewis 'Brandy' Brandon DFC of 157 Squadron in MM630 'E' chased a contact during a low-level patrol of three airfields near Rheims (Laon-Athies, Laon-Couvron and Juvincourt). Finally, Brandon could see the blip on his Mk X AI coming in to 800 ft (245 metres). Then came the words he was waiting for: 'Okay, have a look now. It's a Jerry all right. Looks like a Junkers 188.'

> I looked up, my night vision needing a few seconds to adjust itself. I saw a dark shape, which gradually resolved itself into a Junkers 188. We were almost directly underneath it, just about 400 ft [120 metres] below. Ben eased back the throttles gently; lifted Eager Beaver's nose slightly and at 150 yd range fired a three-second burst at the Junkers.
>
> There were strikes on the starboard wing roots and the starboard engine caught fire. A further two-second burst blew pieces off the port wing tip. A short third burst produced strikes on the burning starboard engine. Then the whole of the port wing outboard of the engine broke off and passed under

us. A second later the Junkers hurtled straight down in flames and exploded on the ground.

I had been entering up my log and then took a *Gee* fix, which showed us to be over the Forest of Compiègne. It had taken just under four minutes from obtaining contact on this second aircraft to seeing it hit the ground. From the light of the burning starboard engine we had seen a swastika on the tail and dark green camouflage on the upper surface of the wing.

The time for the finish of our patrol had been up some minutes so we set course for base, which was reached without further incident. We landed just after 3 a.m. and everyone was highly delighted that the score at Swannington had been opened for 157 Squadron. For our part, it was certainly satisfying to have had an early success with Mk X on this new job. As for our ground crew, they had painted a swastika on Eager Beaver almost before we were out of the cockpit.

It brought Benson's personal tally to five. On 22 December 1940 he had claimed the first confirmed night victory for the Defiant and the next three victories were on Beaufighter IIs and Mosquito IIs with Brandon and his radar operator. Benson had been one of the replacements posted to 141 Squadron in July 1940 after the débâcle of 19 June when six Defiants were destroyed and one damaged by Bf 109s. He suffered a suspected fractured skull following a crash in his Defiant during a night landing in January 1941 but fully recovered and had crewed up with Brandy Brandon to form another highly successful Mosquito night-fighter team. Flight Lieutenants Mickey Phillips and Derek Smith of 85 Squadron destroyed a Bf 110 near Paris.

On 13/14 June, their fifth trip, Warrant Officer Les Turner and Flight Sergeant Frank Francis of 169 Squadron in a Mosquito VI took off from Great Massingham at 2320 hours, still looking for their first victory. They set course at 5,000 ft (1,500 metres) over base at 2331. Turner reported:

In good visibility obtained visual of English coast and subsequently of enemy coast, which we crossed at 0005 at 15,000 ft [4,600 metres]. Tuned on to southerly course and during this log we observed no sign of activity. We then turned West and lost height down to 5,000 ft [1,500 metres] in the hope of finding some joy. The lights of Paris were observed 3 miles [5 km] port of track so we climbed to 9,000 ft [2,750 metres] and orbited lights on the off chance of arousing some reaction. This was however unavailing so we climbed on a Westerly course to 12,000 ft [3,650 metres] where an AI contact was obtained 8,000 ft [2,400 metres] in front showing 20° starboard at 0112 hours. We turned towards aircraft, which was travelling in a Northerly direction at approximately 250 mph [400 kph]. A contact was showing considerably below, we lost height down to 8,000 ft [2,400 metres] from which point aircraft began to weave violently turning alternately port and starboard through 180° at speed approximately 350 mph (550 kph) and losing height to 5,000 ft [1,500 metres] at 12 lb [5.5 kg] boost and 2800 rpm. We closed to 2,000 ft [610 metres] after approximately six minutes. Then enemy aircraft flew into a patch of cloud and as range closed rapidly, I throttled back obtaining visual at 1,300 ft [400 metres] of enemy aircraft above and to port, positively identifying plan view as a Ju 88. We overshot slightly so I let enemy aircraft come ahead and followed partly visually and partly through wispy cloud. When this was cleared I closed to 300–400 yd and opened fire on port engine, which immediately burst into flames. Enemy aircraft turned port and in avoiding enemy aircraft, which was now burning fiercely, I turned port and on to my back, thus upsetting gyro instruments. I regained control on natural horizon and saw enemy aircraft hit the ground and explode at 0122 hours. We then set course towards northerly sky and when instruments had settled down, set course of 350° for coast, which we crossed 3 miles [5 km] West of Dunkirk at 0200 hours. No *Serrate* indications were observed throughout the trip.

They were satisfied with their night's work but on reaching the shores of England they were warned that there were German intruders about. With a pessimism that is probably part of his character, Turner was convinced that they would not make it back to report the combat! They did, however. Turner had fired sixty rounds of cannon with no stoppages to down the Ju 88.

The next victories of 157 and 85 Squadrons occurred on 14/15 June. A Ju 88 trying to land at Juvincourt was shot down by Flight Lieutenant J. Tweedale and Flying Officer L. I. Cunningham of 157 Squadron, and Flight Lieutenant H. B. Thomas and Pilot Officer C. B. Hamilton of 85 Squadron also brought down another Ju 88 near Juvincourt. The third victory of the night went to Flying Officer Branse A. Burbridge DFC and Flight Lieutenant F. S. Skelton DFC of 85 Squadron, who destroyed a Ju 188.

Another inspired 85 Squadron pairing was Squadron Leader F. S. 'Gon' Gonsalves and Flight Lieutenant Basil Duckett. On 15/16 June they were on patrol over Belgium. Gonsalves reported:

> I arrived some nine minutes late on my patrol line owing to some difficulty in finding my last pinpoint just north of St Trond. Eventually decided to do an east to west patrol between two white beacons as St Trond airfield was not lighted. At 0140 hours Flight Lieutenant Duckett reported he had a contact over to port and 10° above (2 miles [3 km] range) and almost immediately afterwards the Visual Lorenz and flarepath were put on at St Trond just a mile or so to port. I followed the contact in a wide orbit of the airfield and closed to 800 ft [245 metres], 15° below where I could see a silhouette but could not identify. I closed to 200 ft [60 metres] and right below and recognized an Me 110 with long-range tanks. Then dropped back to 600 ft [180 metres] and fired a one-second burst which produced a strike on the back of the fuselage – closed in to 400 ft [120 metres] and gave a further burst which blew up the starboard engine. I broke to starboard to avoid the debris flying back and watched the enemy aircraft going down in a starboard turn until finally it hit the ground and blew up in the dispersal area east of the airfield. My height was 3,500 ft [1,100 metres]. Time 0147 hours.
>
> I then resumed patrol and at 0154 hours Flight Lieutenant Duckett again reported contact. This time head-on at 1 mile [1.5 km] range, 15° above.

Closed in to recognize another Me 110 also with long-range tanks. Height 4,000 ft [1,200 metres]. Fired short burst with no results; closed in too fast and found myself flying in formation with him 100 yd away on my port side. Turned back port and gave a good long burst and pulled my nose right through his line of flight. Concentration of strikes seen on upper part of wing outboard of the port engine but no fire. As I was aiming at the top of the fuselage, this struck me as quite odd so I pulled up my nose to have another look at the enemy aircraft but unfortunately he must have been going down because visual was lost and contact could not be regained. No fires were seen on the ground after this combat. One Me 110 destroyed. One Me 110 damaged.

Gonsalves and Duckett's victim was Bf 110 Wrk Nr 5664 G9+IZ of *XII/NJG1*. It crashed 5$^{1}/_{2}$ miles (9 km) west of Tongres, between St Trond and Maastricht. *Unteroffizier* Heinz Bärwolf, pilot, who was injured, and *Unteroffizier* Fischer, radar operator, baled out. *Obergefreiter* Edmund Kirsch, the 23-year-old *bordschütze*, was killed. Not to be outdone, Flight Lieutenant Jimmy Mathews and Warrant Officer Penrose of 157 Squadron destroyed a Ju 188 the same night.

The following night, 16/17 June, Ju 88 Wrk Nr 710590 of *I/NJG2* crashed in the Pas de Cancale, possibly shot down by Flying Officers Andy Miller DFC and Freddie Bone of 169 Squadron. *Hauptmann* Herbert Lorenz, pilot, *Feldwebel* Rudolf Scheuermann, *bordfunker*, and *Flieger* Harry Huth, *bordschütze* were killed. On 17/18 June, at 0230 hours Flying Officer Philip Stanley Kendall DFC and Flight Lieutenant C. R. Hill DFC of 85 Squadron reached their patrol area, the airfield at Soesterberg, at 0100 hours. Their combat report states:

The airfield was not lit, so we proceeded to Deelen, where similar conditions prevailed. At 0126 hours Soesterberg lights were seen to be lit and an aircraft with navigation lights was seen landing. While flying towards the airfield, a red Very light was seen, shot from the ground, and almost immediately another aircraft was seen to put on navigation lights and start to fly round again. We gave chase, putting down wheels and flaps to reduce speed and, with an IAS of 140 [225 kph], intercepted the aircraft at 700 ft [215 metres], just as it was turning onto the flarepath to attempt to land again. Two bursts were given, one second and two seconds, with half-ring deflection, range 150 yd closing to 100 yd, strikes being seen on the wing and in the fuselage. The aircraft caught fire and climbed to 1,500 ft [460 metres], still burning navigation lights, and then dived vertically and exploded on the ground 200 yd short of the end of the runway at 0130 hours. We broke away, retracted the undercarriage and flaps and climbed to 3,000 ft [900 metres] and took cine shots from approximately 3 miles [5 km] range of the aircraft burning on the ground. Patrol was continued near Soesterberg till 0150 hours when course was set for base. Landed 0243 hours.

Kendall and Hill's victim was a Bf 110 of *NJG1*. Müller, the pilot, and two others were killed.

Also at night Flight Lieutenant Geoffrey E. Poulton and Flying Officer Arthur John Neville of 239 Squadron came across some Ju 88s orbiting a beacon and fired at two of

Flight Lieutenant (later Squadron Leader DFC and 'A' Flight Commander) Geoffrey E. Poulton and Flying Officer (later Flight Lieutenant DFC) Arthur J. Neville of 239 Squadron, who destroyed a Ju 88 and damaged another near Eindhoven on 17/18 June 1944. (via Tom Cushing)

them. Neville recalls: 'We claimed one "destroyed" after it plunged earthwards thoroughly on fire, and the second likewise plunged down with one engine on fire which fairly soon went out. This we claimed as "damaged" and both were credited to us.' The first was Ju 88 G-1 Wrk Nr 710866 R4+NS of *VIII/NJG2*. It crashed at Volkel airfield. *Leutnant* Harald Machleidt, pilot, and *Gefreiter* Max Rinnerthaler, *bordschütze,* were killed and *Unteroffizier* Kurt Marth, *bordfunker,* was wounded.

Bransome Arthur Burbridge and Frank Seymour 'Bill' Skelton bagged another Ju 88 on 23/24 June. The 23-year-old Burbridge and Skelton were deeply religious. Burbridge had been a conscientious objector on religious grounds for the first six months of the war before joining up. Both were commissioned from the ranks and served individually on Havocs in 85 Squadron in October 1941 and January 1942 respectively. They only crewed up on their second tour on the squadron in July 1943. Their first victory was an Me 410 *Hornisse* (Hornet) on 22/23 February 1944. A first-class team in every sense of the word, the two men were totally dedicated to their task. Many more victories were to follow but these were put in abeyance when both Mk X Squadrons packed their bags on 25–27 June and left Swannington to return to West Malling for anti-Diver patrols, since the V-1 offensive was now threatening London and southern Britain. Mk X radar was accurate enough to track flying bombs but the Mosquitoes had to be modified to cope with the rigours of anti-Diver patrols. They received strengthened noses to match the Doodlebugs' extra turn of speed and stub exhausts were fitted in place of the exhaust shrouds. Engine boost pressure was adjusted to plus 24 lb (10.9 kg) and the Merlin 25s were also modified to permit the use of 150-octane petrol so that the aircraft could reach around 360 mph (580 kph) at sea level. Just over 130 successful *Intruder* patrols, out of 176 dispatched, had been carried out by the two squadrons before they were transferred (they did not return to Swannington until 29 August).

Meanwhile, 141 Squadron dispatched seven Mosquitoes to France on 14/15 June. Pilot Warrant Officer Harry 'Butch' Welham and his navigator/radio operator, Warrant Officer E. J. 'Gus' Hollis, scored their first victory since joining 141 from 29 Squadron when an Me 410 fell to Welham's guns north of Lille. Although he had volunteered in

Warrant Officer Harry 'Butch' Welham (left) and Warrant Officer E. J. 'Gus' Hollis (right) of 141 Squadron, who destroyed an Me 410 on 14/15 June 1944 and a Ju 88 on 27/28 June. (Harry Welham)

1939, the 28-year-old pilot had been classed 'reserved occupation' because he worked on camouflage paints at ICI at Stowmarket, and had not joined the RAF until 1940. Further success for the Suffolk-born pilot and his Welsh navigator was to follow two weeks later.

However, the *Serrate* squadrons did not always have it all their own way. On 16/17 June, the night Bomber Command began its campaign against the V-1 sites in the Pas de Calais, Flying Officers M. J. G. LaGouge and L. A. Vandenberghe of 141 Squadron lost an engine to enemy fighter action over Belgium and flew home on the other one. Approaching West Malling, they were mistaken for an enemy intruder and the runway lights were extinguished. LaGouge retracted his undercarriage and opened up his one remaining Merlin in an attempt to go round again but he crashed and the aircraft soon burned out. Miraculously, both men survived and were detained in hospital for only one night.

The next night, 17/18 June, more attacks were made on V-1 sites in northern France. The twenty-third kill for 239 Squadron was chalked up by Flight Lieutenant Geoffrey F. Poulton and Flying Officer A. J. Neville when they destroyed a Ju 88 near Eindhoven and damaged another.

Much to the chagrin of 141 Squadron, which had put up with the troubles associated with the Mosquito II, its Merlin engines and its fickle radar equipment longer than anyone else, 169 Squadron had begun receiving brand new Mk VI Mosquitoes for some weeks now. Even so, two or three NFTs were often needed before an aircraft was fit for operations. Considerable trouble was experienced with the Mk IV aerial system fitted to the Mosquitoes and was only solved with the fitting of Beaufighter aerials. No. 169 had still managed to destroy ten enemy aircraft in April and May and in June it shot down four more aircraft.

On 21/22 June Bomber Command attacked synthetic oil plants in Germany. Losses were high, with forty-four out of 139 aircraft dispatched to Wesseling near Cologne being lost. Another eight were lost on the strike on Scholven/Buer by 132 bombers. Four Mosquitoes of 141 Squadron and seven of 239 Squadron took off from West Raynham and Flying Officers R. Depper and R. G. C. Follis from the latter destroyed an He 177. The 141 Squadron Mosquito flown by Pilot Officers Peter Coles and Jim Carter was hit by flak after veering into the Düsseldorf area and they limped home with a broken petrol feed. Approaching West Raynham their undercarriage failed. In the control tower, Wing Commander Winn was in radio contact with the crew for forty-five minutes but his instructions failed to do the trick. Finally, when one wheel was locked in the down position and the other swinging in the wind, Winn ordered them to bail out. They landed 10 miles (16 km) south-west of the station and were returned in an army car. Their Mosquito crashed at Hill House Farm near Swaffham.

On 24 June, Bob Braham and his navigator, Flight Lieutenant Walsh DFC, flew in to West Raynham for a Day *Ranger* from the station on 25 June to Denmark (one of several such 'arrangements' Braham had made since leaving the squadron). Braham scored his twenty-ninth victory. He would get no more. He had just completed an attack on a German staff car on a road on Fyn Island when two Fw 190s attacked him. In one of them was *Leutnant* Robert Spreckels. The Mosquito's port wing and engine were set on fire. Braham tried to crash land on the shore of a fjord when he was attacked again. He managed to set it down and fortunately the aircraft did not explode. Walsh and Braham made a run for it and got behind some sand dunes. Troops from a nearby radar station advanced towards them and opened fire with automatic weapons. Unhurt, Braham and Walsh were marched away into captivity. At 1000 hours next day an ASR search was initiated, and 141 Squadron crews took part, including Paddy Engelbach and Ron Mallett, but their search was in vain. That night Dennis Welfare and Taffy Bellis of 239 Squadron also destroyed a Ju 88 near Paris.

On 27/28 June the Mosquito *Serrate* squadrons helped support 1,049 bombers making attacks on V-l sites and other targets in northern France. At West Raynham, eleven Mosquitoes of 141 Squadron and eight Mosquitoes of 239 Squadron took off between 2200 and 2305 hours and set out across the sea towards France to provide bomber support. At 2235 hours Wing Commander Charles V. Winn and his navigator/radio operator, Flight Lieutenant R. A. W. Scott, led 141 Squadron off, followed at ten and five minute intervals by the remaining ten Mosquitoes.

Flying Officer W. P. Rimer and Warrant Officer H. J. Alexander had to return soon after take-off when their AI set failed. Pilot Officers Coles and J. A. Carter patrolled Beacon Mücke hoping to pick up signals from German night-fighters (otherwise known as 'bashing the beacons'), but also had to abort after both *Serrate* and AI became unserviceable. Problems with engine vibration and instruments and R/T failure made a return to base equally expedient. Francois Vandenplassche and Pilot Officer M. K. Webster, patrolled and chased, but returned empty-handed. It was Vandenplassche's first operation since his return to the squadron after his escape from occupied France after bailing out on 25/26 March 1943.

Meanwhile, Squadron Leader Graham J. Rice and Flying Officer Jimmie G. Rogerson had had better luck. Rogerson recalls:

> It was now approaching halfway house, with unlucky number thirteen of the thirty operations making up the full tour behind us. Action was just around the corner. On 27 June we were given another of the one-hour beacon patrols, taking in two of them in northern France code-named *Emil* and

Goldhammer. We took off just after the last of midsummer's long daylight had faded and a bright full moon was rising into a cloudless sky. Made our way across the North Sea to Flushing, and began our stipulated patrol soon after midnight. The skies were crystal clear, brilliant from the harsh illumination of an unobscured moon, but otherwise apparently empty. After some twenty minutes of stooging calmly up and down, quite unexpectedly a sudden burst of four red stars, exactly like one of Standard Fireworks better rockets, exploded in the air away to our right, followed almost immediately by four more of the same, now slightly closer. Not our own chosen colour combination for the night. My driver promptly turned towards this pretty display of pyrotechnics to investigate, myself with eyes glued to the radar screens searching for non-existent *Serrate* indications. Half a minute later, I had it. A good clean blip, racing out of the ground response and down the time base so rapidly that we were obviously meeting whatever it was head on.

Waiting until the range had closed to 4,000 ft [1,200 metres], I gave instructions to haul round to starboard through 180°, so that if all went according to plan we would finish up directly behind our customer and in a position to chase and intercept. Which is exactly what happened. The Mosquito completed its turn to show me my contact directly ahead at a distance of 2 miles [3 km] but well below our own altitude of 15,000 ft [4,600 metres]. On this occasion I was really going to have to apply myself. The target ahead was weaving steadily about to right and left, added to which it was a question of reducing our height whilst trying to follow spasmodic twists and turns and close the distance respectfully between us. After ten minutes, during which time we found that we had descended some 4,000 ft [1,200 metres], Graham obtained a visual thanks to the clean brilliance of the white moon on an aircraft flying at least 1,500 ft [460 metres] ahead of us.

At that precise moment, our target took a gentle turn to port and finally steadied to fly directly into the full blinding glare of the moon. There was no doubt whatsoever about its identity. The marked dihedral of the longer than average wingspan and the engines close-set to the fuselage shouted Ju 88. But any hopes of closing to a position where my driver could see properly to open fire would have to be deferred. It was back to the radar screens and follow the blip for very nearly quarter of an hour, and that I can tell you was an irritatingly long time.

Finally, it turned once more, this time out of the glare altogether, and we were able to close without more ado right into firing range. Seizing the opportunity whilst we had it, we opened fire at once in two short bursts. Large pieces flew off and passed uncomfortably close above our heads just as they had with the 110 up at Hamburg and this time both engines burst into flames simultaneously. The sequence of events, which followed, is yet another that is burnished into my memory like a roll of cine film. So well alight was the Ju 88 that the black crosses on its wings were clearly visible as it went down beneath us in a steep dive to port, where it disappeared into

Leavesden-built Mosquito II HJ911, which Squadron Leader Graham J. Rice and Flying Officer Jimmie G. Rogerson of 141 Squadron flew when they destroyed a Ju 88 at Cambrai on the night of 27/28 June 1944 and a Bf 110G-4 which crashed 3 miles (5 km) west of Chievres, Belgium, thought to be Wrk Nr 730006 D5+ of II/NJG3. The pilot and Gefreiter *Richard Reiff, who was wounded, both baled out safely.* Obergefreiter *Edmund Hejduck was killed.*

the only bank of cloud anywhere in sight, almost as though it were seeking refuge.

Just as we thought we would not see it again and so be unable to vouch positively for its destruction, it suddenly reappeared out of the cloud in a zooming vertical climb, ablaze from end to end, described a perfect loop directly above, and then came down straight at us, as though by some will of its own it was bent upon revenge by taking us with it in a mid-air collision. Its fiery downward path surged desperately close behind our port wing, and for one awful moment I was absolutely convinced that it would hit us! The whole astonishing performance seemed to last for ever as we sat there watching its progress in open-mouthed amazement. Yet in the event I suppose it cannot have taken more than a couple of minutes before it all ended with a huge explosion as it hit the deck in the Cambrai area of northern France.

It was their third victory.

Warrant Officers Harry 'Butch' Welham and E. 'Gus' Hollis used their well-established rapport to track and hunt an AI contact 5 miles (8 km) north of Eindhoven. Their Mosquito, DZ240, was the same aircraft they had used to shoot down their first enemy aircraft on 14/15 June when an Me 410 had fallen to the Mk II's guns. Clearly painted in large white letters on the pilot's side of the Mosquito's nose was the *double entendre* 'SHYTOT'. Welham reduced height to 14,000 ft (4,300 metres) and closed in on the contact. He recalls:

> The target, a Ju 88, appeared dead ahead, slightly above but we looked as if we were going to overshoot. Gus came on the intercom and in his lilting Welsh accent said, 'Throttle back, pull the nose up, Butch.' His nose was in his set, keeping track of the fir-tree-shaped blip on the *Serrate* scope. 'Left, left, right, right,' he ordered. 'Thirty degrees above. Dead ahead, 2,000 ft [610 metres].' I steered to the ideal spot, 400 yd behind (the four 20-mm Hispanos were synchronized for 400 yd). I lined him up through the circular gunsight, my right thumb ready to press the firing button on top of the stick and aimed between the cockpit and engine. Gus said clearly, 'Go on, shoot!' I said, 'OK,' and let fly a two-second burst. As the cannons fired beneath our feet the seats vibrated and dust flew up from the floor all around the cockpit. A fire started in the engine and the wing and the kite went down in a spiral burning all the while, exploding on the ground about 6 miles [10 km] south of Tilburg.
>
> We continued to patrol and at about 0143 hours about 10 miles [16 km] west of Ghent, we chased another AI contact at maximum range. It developed into a series of tight orbits and contact turned out to be 2,000 ft [610 metres] behind. We did an exceedingly tight turn and it brought 141 Squadron's total victories to seventeen.

Welham and Hollis' victim was possibly Ju 88G-1 Wrk Nr 710455 of *IV/NJG3*, which crashed at Arendonk, Belgium. *Unteroffizier* Eugen Wilfert (pilot), *Obergefreiter* Karl Martin, radar operator and *Gefreiter* Rudolf Scherbaum, *bordschütze,* were killed. Three aircraft were destroyed by 239 Squadron without loss or early return to bring its total to twenty-nine. Flight Lieutenant Denis Welfare DFC* and Flying Officer Taffy Bellis DFC* shot down an Me 410 east of Paris and an Fw 190 was destroyed by their CO, Wing Commander Paul M. J. Evans and navigator Flying Officer R. H. 'Dickie' Perks DFC.

Evans recalls:

> I was returning from accompanying the bomber force to Stuttgart. Near the Channel on the French side we picked up an IFF contact which turned out to be an Fw 190. I shot it down from behind but unfortunately it exploded, covering my aircraft with burning petrol. This burnt off a great deal of the doped control surfaces, which were not wood, and made the aircraft difficult to control. I made a very fast landing at Manston after numerous trials at height to determine at what speed I lost control.

Flight Lieutenant Donald Ridgewell 'Podge' Howard and Flying Officer Frank A. W. 'Sticky' Clay destroyed a Ju 88 near Brussels. Howard reported to Flight Lieutenant C. H. F. Reynolds the Intelligence Officer:

> Mosquito took off West Raynham 2311 hours on a *Serrate* patrol in support of the bombers on Vitry le Francois, crossing in at St Valery and contacting

the bombers at 0106 hours. After intercepting and obtaining a visual on a Lancaster at 0120 hours well away from the bomber stream and at 14,500 ft [4,400 metres] (6,000 ft [1,800 metres] above the other bombers), Mosquito went on to Vitry le Francois. After patrolling there for eight minutes while the bombing was in progress, it was decided to set course for the French coast as the port engine was running very badly. At 0210 hours when north of Laon at 16,000 ft [4,900 metres], 0215 hours, an AI contact at 6,000 ft [1,800 metres] ahead and to the east was picked up but it faded almost at once. When about 5 miles (8 km) north of Cambrai, still at 16,000 ft [4,900 metres], 0215 hours, an AI contact was observed nearly head-on, 12,000 ft [3,650 metres] range, crossing gently port to starboard below on an estimated course of 130°. Mosquito, which was on 320° allowed contact to pass below and then turned round starboard, gradually losing height to 8,000 ft [2,400 metres] and then climbed to 12,000 ft [3,650 metres]. During this climb Mosquito found it was impossible to gain on contact which was doing 260 ASI but fortunately it turned port on to 050°, reduced height and eventually settled down straight and level at 9,500 ft [2,900 metres]. This enabled Mosquito to close in to 1,500 ft [460 metres] where a fleeting visual was obtained on the silhouette of an aircraft 20° above. At 1,000 ft [300 metres] range a clear visual was obtained on what the pilot believed to be a Ju 88 but in order to be quite certain, Mosquito was brought in to within 50 ft [15 metres] and any doubt of the target's identity was removed. Dropping back to 75 yd dead astern and slightly below, a one-second burst of cannon caused strikes on the fuselage and E/A's port engine blew up. As E/A dropped away to port, Mosquito put its nose right down and with another one sec burst set E/A's starboard engine on fire. E/A then turned slowly to starboard, well on fire, and dived vertically into the ground where it exploded. No lights had been visible on E/A and no return fire was experienced. Claimed as a Ju 88 destroyed (Cat. A (1)). E/A was shot down from 9,500 to 9,000 ft [2,900–2,750 metres] at 0230 hours a few miles NE of Brussels.

The AI became u/s after the cannon had been fired and three minutes later the starboard coolant temperature was seen to be 160°, flames started spurting along the starboard engine and fumes filled the cockpit. Pilot feathered the starboard propeller and turned on to 290° climbing into cloud at 10,000 ft [3,000 metres] recrossing the enemy coast at Knocke at 0255 hours. The port vacuum pump was u/s and gyro instruments would not perform. The starboard engine having been put out of action, all electric services had to be switched off to conserve the supply of electricity. Later the navigator tried to get a *Gee* fix, but could not get a normal picture and a fix was unobtainable. R/T was switched on and a mayday call to Kinglsey was given on Channel D with IFF on Stud 3, but after two transmissions and when Kingsley had given a vector to Manston, R/T became completely u/s. Mosquito was holding hard at 10,500 ft [3,200 metres] so an approximate course of 260° was maintained until Sanders lights were seen and the Manston pundit was identified. Mosquito fired the colours of the day several times and then made a perfect landing at Manston at 0330 hours. A number of pieces of '88' and a handful of *Window* (broad) have been recovered from Mosquito's starboard engine.

Two crews failed to return to West Raynham: Flight Lieutenant Herbert R. Hampshire and Warrant Officer Alan W. Melrose, who were on their last operation, and Paddy Engelbach and Ronald Mallett DFC, all of 141 Squadron. Engelbach and Mallett patrolled north Holland for an hour and the navigator could tell they were being picked up by a German night-fighter. The pilot turned south then Mallett suddenly ordered, 'Hard on to the reciprocal.' Engelbach wrote:

> As I threw the aircraft over I asked if there was anything behind. The answer was a series of judders as my tail was shot off and I went into a spin. I pulled the aircraft out but was immediately hit again. At about 2,500 ft [760 metres] the aircraft disintegrated and I was thrown out through the canopy. I opened my parachute after a long search for it, and my fall was broken at about 20 ft (6 metres) and I landed unhurt. Mallett was killed. The Germans said that the aircraft that shot me down was a Heinkel 219.

Paddy Engelbach ended up a prisoner of war and came upon old acquaintances from 141 Squadron behind the wire. One of them was Wing Commander Bob Braham, for whom he had searched on 26 June after Braham had been shot down during a Day Ranger to Denmark. He returned to 141 Squadron at the end of the war and in his flying logbook when recording his search for Braham, he inserted, 'Found him in *Dulag Luft*!' He was killed taking off in a Venom from West Raynham in February 1955. At that time he was commanding officer of 23 Squadron.

Flight Lieutenant Denis Welfare DFC* and Flying Officer Taffy Bellis DFC*, who had shot down a Ju 88 on 24/25 June, added to their score on 8/9 August when they destroyed an Fw 190 near St Quentin (their seventh victory) and damaged two Bf 109s. On 11 October they were credited with the destruction of a seaplane on the water at Tristed. Taffy Bellis concludes:

> By October Denis and I had completed fifty sorties from West Raynham and we were posted to non-operational duties. We were lucky to have been in 239 Squadron at the right time – with fine aircraft and equipment and, most of all, to be part of the happiest squadron imaginable. Firstly, the aircrews, most of them experienced, joined a new squadron more or less together. The type of operations was new and we were 'all in the same boat' and the 'squadron spirit' built up quickly. I shall never forget those heady days of May, June and July. During those gloriously successful months all the squadron personnel – the off-duty crews, the CO, the Adjutant and ground crews – congregated at the watch tower in the early hours, to greet the returning Mosquitoes and to cheer each time a plane signalled a success by 'beating up' the watch tower with its landing lights flashing. Looking back, I realize that the successes belonged to the squadron as a whole and not to the individuals concerned. In this connection, it is too easy to forget that the

dedication and expertise of the personnel who maintained the Mossies and the electronic equipment played a major role.

Another factor was West Raynham itself – it was a pre-1939 station with all the comforts that implied. Important too was the fact that most of the aircrews were flying Mosquitoes for the first time. Many, like us, had been flying Beaufighters before. Everyone respected a Beaufighter – it was sturdy, solid and tough. A Mosquito, on the other hand, was all this and much more. It had the grace, sleek lines, responsiveness and behaviour of a thoroughbred – it was an aeroplane that crews had a lifetime love affair with. In fact, our wives and sweethearts complained that they had to share our affections with the Mosquitoes! Lastly, there were the personnel themselves. Types such as the tolerant CO Paul Evans, the flight commanders, the irrepressible 'Jackson' Booth and 'Golden' Neville Reeves and his navigator 'Mad' Mike O'Leary. Adj. Hawley always had a ready smile and nothing was too much trouble for him. Then there was 'Buster' Reynolds – Buster was the Chief Intelligence Officer. He was a solicitor in civvy life and not only was he a thorough and relentless debriefer of crew returning from ops, but also he was the drinking and singing leader during the never-to-be-forgotten mess parties.

West Raynham holds one very special memory for me – it was during my tour of ops there that Gwyneth and I were married. She came to live in digs in King's Lynn. Living out during ops was frowned upon, but not forbidden. Because it was unofficial, I was not allowed petrol to travel back and fore, nor food coupons. The petrol problem was overcome because I was able to borrow a motorcycle, but how Gwyneth managed to stretch her rations to feed me, I will never know. Fortunately, King's Lynn was within cycling distance of the Crown at Gayton – the pub known to aircrews for miles around because of the quality of its beer and, more importantly, because bacon and eggs seemed to be always available. Those days must, of course, have been worrying for Gwyneth. When I left her in the morning, I could never say 'See you tonight.' If I appeared late afternoon, I would be stood down; if not, I was on ops. Then Gwyneth at dusk would listen to the drone of the heavy bombers heading to Germany and, a little later, the hum of the Mosquitoes flying out after them. She would know I was in one of them. But when she heard them returning some hours later, she would not know if I was coming back until I appeared in the early hours. I shall not forget the night of 25 September, when we landed at Bradwell Bay because West Raynham was closed for fog, and I turned up some twelve hours 'late'. I was one of those who believed that 'it will never happen to me', but I know how worried Gwyneth was. Nevertheless, neither of us would have wanted our lives otherwise – at that time one always lived for today.

CHAPTER V

Moskitopanik

We were hungry tired and dirty,
From our shoulders rifles hung
Our clothes were torn, our faces bronzed
By long hours in the sun.
Here was to be our station,
For the war was not yet won,
When we came to Little Snoring
That fateful June had just begun.

S. F. Ruffle

The mere presence in the circuits of Micawber-like Mosquitoes, 'waiting for something to turn up' as they lurked one by one to cover the whole night period, was enough to cause morale-sapping Moskitopanik throughout Germany in the summer of 1944. On 5/6 July 1944 Mosquito Mk VIs of 23 Squadron flew their first *Intruder* operation from Little Snoring since returning from the Mediterranean, with sorties against enemy airfields. No. 23 Squadron had joined 515 Squadron at the secluded Norfolk base in June after flying *Intruder* operations from Sicily and Sardinia. The main role of 515 and 23 Squadrons was flying low-level Day and Night *Intruders,* mostly concentrating on active German night-fighter bases. Although 515 Squadron had been based at the remote Norfolk outpost since 15 December 1943, it had only been introduced to this role early in March 1944. Before then, it had operated from Northolt, Heston and then Hunsdon, during which time it had conducted *Moonshine* operations using Defiant aircraft. *Moonshine* was the code-name given to an operation which was calculated to alert the enemy defences by causing the approach of a large force of aircraft to be registered on their early-warning radar equipment. The large force was, in fact, one Defiant carrying special radar devices. These tests were highly successful and a flight called the Defiant Flight was formed in June 1942 attached to RAF Northolt, under the direction of 11 Group, Fighter Command. From September to December 1942, as 515 Squadron and equipped with Defiant Mk IIs, it conducted operations with *Moonshine* equipment which succeeded in confusing the enemy. On occasions, over 300 enemy fighters were drawn up by the spoof entirely in the wrong position to ward off bombing attacks by other British aircraft. In December 1942, the role of the Squadron was changed to manipulating a *Mandrel* screen by night, in support of the bomber offensive. *Mandrel* was an American jamming device and was used ahead of RAF night raids and US 8th Air Force daylight raids. Eight predetermined positions were patrolled nightly by 515 Squadron, which operated from forward bases at West Malling, Tangmere and

Wing Commander Bertie Rex O'Bryen 'Sammy' Hoare DSO DFC* one of the leading Intruder *pilots of his generation.*

Coltishall. This work continued until July 1943 when it was decided to re-equip the squadron with Beaufighters.

On 27 January 1944, Squadron Leader Freddie 'Cordite' Lambert was promoted Wing Commander and posted to take command of 515 Squadron. A few days later, information was received from 100 Group HQ that the squadron's work on *Mandrel* was finished and that it would be re-equipped with Mosquito Mk VI aircraft for low-level *Intruder* sorties over enemy airfields. The air gunners were posted away and new crews were brought in to train for *Intruder* work. Beginning on 29 February 1944 515 Squadron's Beaufighters and Blenheims were replaced by Mosquito IIs for training. Some of 605 Squadron's Mk VI Mosquitoes were operated by 515 on detachment at Bradwell Bay and it was in one of these aircraft that Wing Commander Lambert and Flight Lieutenant E. W. Morgan shot down an He 177 in the first squadron sortie on 5 March.

In April Wing Commander B. R. 'Sammy' O'Bryen Hoare DSO DFC*, Commanding Officer of 605 Squadron, assumed the post of Station Commander at Snoring. Despite losing an eye before the war when a duck shattered the windscreen of his aircraft, Sammy Hoare became one of the foremost *Intruder* pilots in the RAF. He had commanded 23 Squadron from March to September 1942 and on 6 July had flown the squadron's first Mosquito *Intruder* sortie. In September 1943 he had assumed command of 605 Squadron, destroying a Do 217 on his first operation, and in January 1944 had notched the Squadron's hundreth victory when he downed a Ju 188. At Snoring, 23 and 515 Squadron crews took bets on which one of Sammy's eyes, one blue, one brown, was real. No. 23 Squadron was commanded by the audacious and admired Wing Commander A. M. Murphy DSO* DFC, Croix de Guerre with Palm. In the Mediterranean, 'Murphy's Marauders' had been like a private air force. Alan Michael Murphy, affectionately known as 'Sticky', had taken over 23 Squadron in December 1943.

Sticky was born on 26 September 1917 at Cockermouth in Cumberland. After spending his early life in South Africa, his father's health forced the family to return to England where Alan went to Seafield Preparatory School at Lytham on the north-west coast until about 1931. Whilst there he played cricket and soccer, and was an outstanding athlete. He jumped high and long, as well as being a top hurdler and 440-yard man. He represented the RAF at athletics, and in a triangular match between Cranwell, Woolwich and Sandhurst, he created a long-standing record for the long jump of 23 ft 1¼ ins (7 metres 4.2 cm) in 1938. Commissioned as a pilot officer in July 1938, Sticky continued his training on 185 Squadron with the Fairey Battle, then trained others in the north of Scotland at an OTU as Station Navigation Officer. In March 1941, Sticky joined 1419 Special Duty Flight at Stradishall, with the primary duty then of dropping secret agents throughout occupied Europe for intelligence and resistance activities. He became one of the pioneer pilots in 138 Squadron, one of the 'Moon Squadrons' which flew the short take-off and landing Lysander to infiltrate and exfiltrate 'Joes' in Europe.

On 1 June 1942, he was rested and attached to the Air Ministry but flew various types of aircraft and enjoyed his married life in the London area. On 20 June 1943 after almost a year, he arrived at High Ercall for conversion to Mosquitoes, and for a rapid course on intruding. Passing this course, he was given an 'exceptional' grading by Wing Commander 'Mouse' Fielden, who had been his commanding officer on 161 Squadron. In late September 1943, he landed in Malta to join the veteran 23 Squadron which had been the scourge of the Axis powers in the area throughout that year, harassing the retreating enemy armies and air forces in North Africa, and in Sicily and Italy throughout 1943. He quickly became the Commander of B Flight. He followed the squadron motto *Semper aggressus* (roughly translated as 'Always have a Go'), which he was more inclined to translate in terms of the ANZACs at Gallipoli, with their war cry, 'Right lads. After the bastards!'

Soon, he became Commanding Officer of 23 Squadron, which quickly loved him for his humanity, his daring leadership and his natural charm, bombing, strafing and intruding from Bordeaux on the Atlantic coast to Udine on the borders of Austria and Yugoslavia. At Little Snoring, the ebullient coryphaeus and his daring crews took the friendly Norfolk hamlet by storm and the locals to their hearts. Always one for a drink and a party, Sticky's discordant rendering of 'Rip My Knickers Away' heralded the real singing sessions. What he lacked in melody, which was to the tune of 'Yip Aye Addy Aye Ay…' he made up for with his usual attack. 'We're a Shower of Bastards', the traditional squadron song, usually followed. One of the navigators, Bucky Cunningham, was a professional cabaret musician and songwriter, and he added original material to the repertoire, such as 'My Gal Sal is the Queen of the Acrobats' and 'She's Got Two of Everything'. No. 23 Squadron left its mark in social as well as operational circles, and Sticky's exploits remain legendary in the memories of the local people of that time. Flight Lieutenant Tommy Smith, one of the new pilots at this time, recalls:

> The atmosphere that came over, was one of lots of fun and games; booze and bawdy songs, prangs and shows and strafing, and not much care for others or the agonies of war. This was all far from the truth. The average aircrews were dedicated, hardworking players in a dangerous game, fully aware of the risks, conscious of the death and destruction they handed out, apprehensive of the agonies of grief and despair their own families would feel on learning they were missing or dead; and also dreading the possible manner of their own death, torn to shreds by bullets or shrapnel, or roasted alive in a flamer.

Tommy, formerly a Glaswegian accountant, had earlier completed a tour of ops with 96 Squadron on Defiants and Merlin-engined Beaufighters, which ended with a trip to the

RAF head injuries hospital in Oxford and a non-operational medical categorization. He spent his 'rest' as a Permanent President of Courts of Inquiry (PPCI), or 'prang basher', in 81 and 9 Groups, which administered the OTUs of Fighter Command. This was a congenial if grisly occupation; congenial because the instructors in OTUs were all operational pilots 'on rest' who were always ready for a party or a session, and included an ever-changing rota of old friends or people who knew old friends; grisly because only fatal accidents required a PPCI, and detailed investigation of prang after prang gave a jaundiced view of flying operational aircraft.

Everyone had the same burning ambition to get back on ops and Tommy was no different. 'I drank my way up the medical profession until I got to an air vice marshal neurologist, who signed me A1 again on the grounds that I was much more likely to be written off by the Hun than by any neurological shortcomings!' From the vantage point of Group HQ, he had decided that the best business to be in was Mosquito *Intruders,* so after a brush-up at Cranfield OTU, he got a posting to the Bomber Support Training Unit at Great Massingham, then on to 23 Squadron at Little Snoring.

> Compared to the Merlin Beaufighter, the Mosquito fighter-bomber was a dream. Although very functional, with a cockpit ranged around you like the console of the 'Mighty Wurlitzer', the Beaufighter felt like a flying dump-truck. By comparison, the Mosquito with its compact, well-appointed accommodation, felt like a luxurious two-seater sports car, and although I felt it was underpowered, it had such clean lines that once it got up speed it went like a bomb and really felt like a fighter. Like all high-efficiency twins, it had a few bad points: It didn't swing on take-off like the Beau, but could drop a wing when near the stall, and I had investigated more than one Mossie prang where this had occurred, spreading a trail of firewood for $1/2$ mile [800 metres]. When a Mosquito crashed, it really crashed.

Tommy Smith had crewed up with Flying Officer Arthur Cockayne, a schoolmaster from Walsall, whose wife was a schoolmistress. 'Cocky', who was in his mid-thirties, pretty old for aircrew, had been called up late in the war and had trained on Catalinas at Pensacola in Florida before becoming a 'radar detective' on bombers in 100 Squadron in a lively way. On their freshman sortie, to Hoorne on the Zuider Zee, they were caught in searchlights which were not supposed to be there, and the following night they went on one of the Squadron's 'transport bashing' operations. Tommy Smith recalls:

> Each crew was allocated bits of railways and canals. I got a stretch of the Weser-Elbe Canal from Hanover to Magdeburg and a railway line from Shoningen to Hildesheim, and it proved to be a hectic bloody caper for me! We set off doing all the things the 'old hands' had briefed us to do. Across the sea high enough for comfort, pull up to dive flat-out over the enemy coast, then weave across the map at 1,000 ft [300 metres] above the scenery. Of course, since the scenery could undulate more than 1,000 ft [300 metres] it was all very dicey!
>
> There was a pearl grey sky with the moon thankfully behind cloud. (Bright moonlight was no good for low-level map reading.) The canal

showed up as a pallid streak. In moonlight it would have been black. The Hun blackout was very good; there were no lights anywhere but people soon woke up. Mosquitoes are the noisiest of aeroplanes, and every boy scout along the canal began firing tracer. They seemed to be hose-piping us from all sides, but they did not put on enough deflection and they missed us. I must have shot at a dozen barges but they were all either carrying scrap iron or cement. All of a sudden there was a colossal 'crump'. I said, 'What the hell's going on Cocky?'

Laconically, he replied in his old man's voice, 'There's a balloon on our tail and its firing at us!

I honked the Mosquito around in a split-arse turn and looked up. On our tail there appeared to be a great big black balloon, with two lines of tracer coming out of it! The enemy gunners had depressed their 88 mm flak guns to rooftop level, and the 'balloon' was actually a flak-burst cloud, and the two lines of tracer fire were coming from the ground below. I learned to fly a little higher after this.

Although they carried out all the normal tasks of *Intruders*, 23 and 515 Squadrons also performed any odd task dreamed up by 100 Group HQ, the Station Commander, squadron commanders, or even, on occasion, the crews themselves. All were likely to form a part of the curriculum. The *Intruder* crews of 23 and 515 Squadrons were excellent pupils. On 12/13 May 515 Squadron carried out anti-flak patrols on the Kiel Canal in support of twenty-two mine-laying Mosquito aircraft of 8 Group by drawing fire from the gun emplacements to themselves and away from the mine-layers. The support given by the squadron has been classified as one of the most important mine-laying operations of the war. Ten Mosquito crews in 515 patrolled the heavily defended canal area. By drawing the fire away from the mine-layers or strafing the gun positions from very close range, they silenced the opposition and enabled the mining of one of Germany's most important waterways to be achieved with the loss of just one 8 Group Mosquito.

Several enemy aircraft were claimed destroyed by 515 Squadron during June, including two He 111s, a Ju 34, a Bf 110G and a Ju 88. The Bf 110, Wrk Nr 440076 G9+NS of *VIII/NJG1*, was destroyed at 1519 hours on 21 June by Squadron Leader Paul Wattling Rabone DFC and Flying Officer F. C. H. Johns during a *Day Ranger* to northern Holland and the Friesians. The Bf 110, flown by 21-year-old *Unteroffizier* Herbert Beyer, had just taken off from Eelde airfield. Rabone and Johns came in from astern and promptly attacked with a three-and-a-half-second burst of cannon. No strikes were observed, so Rabone fired again. This time the two-second burst hit the starboard engine and pieces flew off before it crashed on the northern side of Eelde airfield. Later, Rabone wrote graphically:

Before the Hun got his breath back a delightful third burst of cannon was presented at 50 yds range at a height of about 100 ft [30 metres]. This created havoc – the Bf 110's starboard wing and starboard engine burst into flames, the port engine belched forth black smoke, and the enemy aircraft dived into the ground enveloped in a mass of flames, smoke and destruction.

Mosquito landed at Little Snoring at 1630 hours after a most enjoyable afternoon's sport.

Beyer, *Unteroffizier* Hans Petersmann, the 21-year-old radar operator and *Obergefreiter* Franz Riedel, the 20-year-old *bordschütze*, were killed. It was Rabone's seventh victory of the war. Born in England and raised in New Zealand, he had been a pilot in 88 Squadron on Fairey Battles and in May 1940 his aircraft was hit by flak during an attack on a bridge at Maastricht. He baled out behind enemy lines before escaping in civilian clothes with a refugee column. Returning to England he was shot down again on 12 June by a Bf 109 during a raid on a Seine bridge and he bailed out once more. In August 1940 he transferred to RAF Fighter Command and, flying Hurricane Is in 145 Squadron, shot down a Bf 109E off Dungeness. He added two more victories in late 1940. In October he had joined 422 Flight, which became 96 Squadron in December as a night-fighter unit, flying Hurricanes and Defiants. On 13 April 1941 he and his gunner had to bale out over the Derbyshire Peak District after an engine failure. After a spell on Havocs in 85 Squadron, by the summer of 1943 he was flying Mosquito IIs in 23 Squadron in the Mediterranean and on 15 August, while flying a Spitfire Vc carrying spare parts to Palermo, Sicily, he shot down a Ju 88. Flying a Mosquito II on 8 September he destroyed another Ju 88 and an He 111 and damaged another Heinkel. On 30 June/1 July he destroyed an He 111 and a Ju W34 at Jagel and Schleswig to take his score to nine confirmed victories. In mid-July he rejoined 23 Squadron and his run of luck finally ran out when he and Johns failed to return from a *Day Ranger* on 24 July. His body was washed ashore on Heligoland Island three months later.

On 27/28 June 100 Group Mosquitoes claimed six enemy aircraft shot down. Pilot Officer C. W. Chown and Sergeant D. G. N. Veitch of 515 Squadron set off from Little Snoring to patrol Gilze–Volkel–Venlo-Eindhoven. After three-quarters of an hour, during which they bombed Venlo airfield and created a substantial fire emitting flashes for the odd fifteen minutes, they returned to Eindhoven for a second look. There was no cloud and visibility was good. At 0213 hours they were over the airfield, which had its north-south flarepath well lit. On their approach, four red cartridges were fired from the air and the runway lights changed pattern. Four airfield identification bars were lit at the southern end and then almost immediately three of the bars were switched off and a single red cartridge was fired from the ground followed by a white light flashing. Just then, a green light flashing dashes appeared in the air to the west of the airfield.

Chown and Veitch, their Mosquito at 1,500 ft (460 metres), gave chase and spotted the outline of an aircraft with a green bow light and red downward identification light under the tail. They closed to 200 yd and recognized it as a Ju 88 (actually Wrk Nr 300651 B3+LT of *IX/KG54* flown by *Unteroffizier* Gotthard Seehaber, which was returning after a mine laying operation in the invasion area). Chown delivered a stern attack, with a two-second burst of cannon fire, which recorded one strike on the Junker's fuselage. He closed to 150 yd and delivered a second stern attack, with a burst of about three seconds. The Ju 88 immediately exploded and scattered debris through the sky as it disintegrated before crashing into a house, killing three children. Chown and Veitch orbited the scene and took photos of the burning enemy night-fighter before breaking away and returning home. Seehaber, *Gefreiter* Kurt Völker and *Obergefreiters* Walter Oldenbruch and Hermann Patzel were killed.

On 30 June/1 July Flight Lieutenant Denis. J. Raby DFC and Flight Sergeant S. J. Flint DFM of 239 Squadron destroyed Ju 88 Wrk Nr 711114 of *V/NJG2* over France. They stalked the Junkers and were fired at by the enemy air gunner but his tracer passed harmlessly over the top of the Mosquito, Raby fired a two-second burst from 450 ft (140 metres) and saw strikes all along the port fuselage and wing and the port engine burst into flames. He pumped another two-second burst into the doomed Junkers, which exploded, scattering debris into the path of the charging Mosquito. As it fell vertically to earth Raby continued to pepper the machine, finally breaking away just before another explosion tore the wings off the night-fighter. It crashed south east of Dieppe in a massive explosion. *Unteroffizier* Erich Pollmer was wounded, but other crew details are unknown.

On 4/5 July Warrant Officer R. E. Preston and Sergeant F. Verity of 515 Squadron took off on a *Night Ranger* to Coulommiers airfield via Southwold and Noord Beveland. They reached the enemy night-fighter base at 0205 hours but it was inactive so they stooged around for three-quarters of an hour before returning to the base. This time their approach signalled the double flarepath to be lit. Obviously, the base anticipated that one of its fighters was returning. Preston reduced height to 1,000 ft (300 metres). Verity obtained a visual sighting of the enemy aircraft at 300–400 yd range. It was a Ju 88, and it was on a southerly course at about their height. Preston gave chase but the Junkers started weaving before turning starboard and diving. Undeterred, Preston followed. As the Ju 88 pulled out of its dive at treetop height, it appeared right in his sights and Preston gave it a three-second burst of cannon at 200 yd. It set the Ju 88's starboard engine on fire and the aircraft instantly disintegrated, scattering burning debris into the air like an exploding firework. Preston circled the scene before bombing the airfield with two 500 lb GP bombs, which exploded on the south side. There was no opposition and only four inefficient searchlights vainly probed the cloudy sky. Not satisfied with their night's work, Preston and Verity attacked two small freighters moored side by side in the Zuid Beveland Canal at the Westerschelde lock gates with a three-second burst of cannon fire. Strikes were seen on the bow of one of the ships.

On 5/6 July Sticky Murphy and three other Mosquito VIs of 23 Squadron flew the first squadron *Intruder* operation from Little Snoring since embarkation leave, with sorties against enemy airfields. Ju 88 Wrk Nr 751065 R4+? of *V/NJG2* was shot down by Flying Offcers P. G. Bailey and J. O. Murphy of 169 Squadron and it crashed near Chartres. *OberFeldwebel* Fritz Farrherr, pilot, and *Obergefreiter* Heinz Boehme, *bordschütze*, were killed. *Gefreiter* Josef Schmid, radar operator, was wounded and bailed out. Bf 110G-4 Wrk Nr 110028 C9+HK of *II/NJG5* crashed near Compiègne. It is believed that this was one of the two aircraft shot down at night by Squadron Leader J. S. Booth DFC* and Flying Officer Ken Dear DFC of 239 Squadron. *Leutnant* Joachim Hanss, pilot, and *Feldwebel* Kurt Stein, *bordschütze*, were killed. *Unteroffizier* Wolfgang Wehrhan, radar operator, was wounded.

Five crews in 23 Squadron took part in an uneventful *Night Ranger* on 6/7 July. On 7 July Sticky Murphy and Jock Reid flew a *Day Ranger* to France and attacked a convoy of nine vehicles, claiming one destroyed and a damaged railway engine near Ath. Eight other crews flew patrols that night over France, Holland and Belgium and carried bombs for the first time. An enemy train was destroyed by Flight Lieutenant D. J. Griffiths. Eindhoven was bombed by Pilot Officer K. M. Cotter RNZAF but no results were observed because of flak from the airfield. Le Culot was bombed by Warrant Officer T. Griffiths and a large red glow was seen. A railway junction near Barnefeld was bombed by Flying Officer D. Buddy Badley RNZAF. No flashes were reported but great volumes of smoke appeared. Only the weather stopped 23 Squadron flying between 9 and 11 July and adding to the impressive score of enemy vehicles it had run up in the Mediterranean.

On 7/8 July Squadron Leader Graham J. Rice and Flying Officer Jimmy G. Rogerson of 141 Squadron, meanwhile, had taken off from West Raynham at 2317 hours on a *Serrate* patrol in support of Bomber Command attacks on St Lou D'Esserent and Vaires. Rice reported:

> Enemy coast was crossed on track between Calais and Dunkirk at 0005 hours and patrol was uneventful until approximately 20 miles [30 km] south of Abbeville at 0030 hours and 15,000 ft [4,600 metres] when an AI contact was obtained dead ahead and slightly below. Aircraft turned hard port and contact passed overhead, when a visual was obtained on very bright exhausts. At 1,000 ft [300 metres] range contact was seen to be a twin-engined aircraft travelling at high speed on a NNE vector and looked similar to a Mosquito. Aircraft switched on *Canary* but contact made no response. Contact was followed at full throttle but after two or three minutes it went right away and disappeared in interference and could not be recognized. As contact took no evasive action at any time and made no response to Canary, it is thought contact was probably an Me 410.
>
> Mosquito turned back on track and five minutes later when vectoring 147° a head-on AI contact was obtained dead ahead and below. Contact was allowed to come in to 4,000 ft [1,200 metres] range and Mosquito went into a hard turn through 180° and obtained contact dead ahead and still below at 8,000 ft [2,400 metres] range. Contact was weaving gently and made two hard turns of 90° to starboard with aircraft following hard and losing height to come in from below. No response was made by contact when Mosquito switched on *Canary*, after about ten minutes' chase a visual was obtained at 2,000 ft [610 metres] range at 10,000 ft [3,000 metres] height. Closing in quickly to 600 ft [180 metres] contact was seen to be an aircraft with twin fins and exhausts peculiar to an Bf 110. At this moment enemy aircraft apparently became aware of the presence of Mosquito and took hard turn to starboard. Mosquito gave 1½ ring deflection and opened fire with a four-second burst at 600 ft [180 metres] range. Strikes were seen all along the top of the mainplane leading to a large explosion in the fuselage which was quickly well on fire. The E/A was now definitely established to be an Bf 110. E/A turned over on its back and passed underneath Mosquito and was followed down to 3,000 ft [900 metres] range on AI then blip disappeared. Mosquito straightened up and orbited to look for E/A and immediately a terrific explosion was seen directly below. Scattered pieces of E/A were seen floating down in flames and one large remnant hit the ground with a further explosion. Combat took place at approximately 8 miles [13 km] NW of Amiens at 0050 hours at 10,000 ft [3,000 metres]. After combat AI was no longer wholly serviceable but improved after half an hour and aircraft

made for the target area. Numerous green star cartridges were soon fired in the air on many occasions and aircraft attempted to investigate several times without success. Stoppages on port guns caused by foreign matter in breech. Claim one Bf 110 destroyed Cat A (1).

Their victim was most likely Bf 110G-4 Wrk Nr 730006 D5+? of *II/NJG3*, which crashed 3 miles (5 km) west of Chievres, Belgium. The pilot and *Gefreiter* Richard Reiff, who was wounded, both baled out safely. *Obergefreiter* Edmund Hejduck was killed.

During a *Day Ranger* on 10 July 515 had more success. At 1503 hours Flight Lieutenant R. A. Adams and Pilot Officer F. H. Ruffle and Flying Officers D. W. O. Wood and Ken Bruton, took off and crossed Happisburgh before heading across the North Sea at zero feet for their patrol area in northern Holland and north-west Germany. Both Mosquitoes roared in over the Dutch coast and 'beat up' a German army encampment at Herslake, 15 miles (24 km) west of Quakenbrück soon after crossing into Germany. Strikes were recorded on huts and the Mosquito crews reported general confusion among the German troops. After this exhilarating interlude both crews flew in the direction of Schwishenahner airfield. At 1637 hours and at zero feet, a Ju 88 night-fighter, clearly on an NFT, was spotted 3 miles (5 km) in the distance at 800 ft (240 metres) altitude making its approach to land. The Junkers, quite unconcerned, turned left and lowered its undercarriage. Wood and Bruton approached to within about 250 yd, and from below and astern pumped a two-second burst of cannon into the enemy machine. Its starboard engine immediately burst into flames. The airfield defences opened up on the Mosquitoes with some light flak. Adams and Ruffle went in and finished it off with a further burst of two to three seconds of cannon fire. The Junkers hit a tree near the airfield and exploded. Both crews landed safely back at Snoring at 1814 hours.

In July 515 flew over forty *Day* and *Night Rangers*. The third victory that month occurred on a *Day Ranger* on 14 July when Wood and Bruton again figured in a shared kill, this time with Flight Lieutenant Arthur S. Callard and Flight Sergeant F. Dixon Townsley. Their victim was a Ju-W34 single-engined four-passenger transport, which was unfortunate enough to be in the wrong place at the wrong time as the pair of Mosquitoes approached, 12 miles (19 km) east of Stralsund. Callard and Townsley went in first and gave it a one-second burst from about 150 yd. At this range the Mosquito was hit by flying pieces of debris but no lasting damage was done. The Ju 34, on the other hand, never stood a chance. It went into an almost vertical climb and stall-turned before 'fluttering' to the ground. There was no telling what high-ranking officers were on board, if any, but just in case, Wood and Bruton made absolutely certain by giving the smouldering embers a one-second burst until it exploded. None of the occupants would be keeping their appointment at a top-level meeting, or climbing into their night-fighters later that evening, that was for sure. On 1 September Wood was killed in action and Bruton became a PoW when their Mosquito was shot down whilst attacking a train.

No. 23 Squadron was getting its eye in too. On the morning of 14 July, Sticky Murphy with Squadron Leader H. F. Smith carried out a *Ranger* patrol and took the opportunity to shoot up some German troops on the beach at Stadil. Another famous pilot at Little Snoring at this time was Squadron Leader Harold B. M. 'Mick' Martin DSO DFC who had joined 515 Squadron in April and was supposed to be 'resting' after flying Hampdens and Lancasters (including P-Popsie on the famous dams raid of 18 May 1943). Group Captain

Squadron Leader Harold 'Mick' Martin DSO, DFC (right) of 'Dambusters' fame with Wing Commander Freddie Lambert, CO 515 Squadron at Little Snoring in spring 1944. Martin was supposed to be 'resting' after a Lancaster tour in Bomber Command, but instead he flew many Mosquito Intruders and destroyed an unidentified enemy aircraft on 26 April 1944 and an Me 410 over Knocke in Belgium on 25/26 July. Flying Officer J. W. Smith was his navigator on both occasions. (Tom Cushing Collection)

Leonard Cheshire has written: 'I learned everything I knew of the low flying game from Mick. He was the ideal wartime operational pilot. He had superb temperament, was quite fearless and innovative in his thinking. He was meticulous in his flying discipline and never did make a mistake.' On an operation over the Ruhr, Cheshire broke silence to enquire about the weather. From a Mosquito came Martin's voice. 'What the hell are you doing?' Cheshire asked. 'Sticking my neck out for you types,' replied Martin who was strafing a night-fighter airfield!

That night, 14/15 July Warrant Officer Turner and Flight Sergeant Francis of 169 Squadron took off in their Mosquito VI from Great Massingham at 2310 hours and set course at 2315 hours over base. They crossed the English and enemy coasts and arrived at their orbit point and patrolled for eighty minutes with no activity except for two fleeting AI contacts at maximum range, which disappeared into ground returns before any pursuit action could be taken. Turner reported:

At 0113 hours whilst on vector towards prang at Auderbelck obtained AI contact at maximum range ahead, well to port and slightly below, at patrol height. Turned port immediately and dived and after a few minutes' chase closed range to 3,000 ft [900 metres] where target was held in dead-ahead position. It was then ascertained that target was on port orbit and on closing to 2,000 ft [610 metres] visual was obtained on white light at first believed to be a tail light. Closed visually and when necessary on AI and on nearly overshooting saw that light was exhaust flames. Since target speed was approximately 160 mph [250 kph] throttled hard back and closed slowly in with my navigator calling out airspeeds. We closed to a position about 20 ft [6 metres] below enemy aircraft which was recognized as a Bf 109. I then dropped back to 150 ft [46 metres] and opened fire, seeing strikes on starboard wing, and then fuselage caught fire. Enemy aircraft turned on its back and black crosses, blue camouflage and twin radiators could be seen as it passed underneath. A bright flash was seen as aircraft hit the ground, We took a *Gee* fix and plotted his position. The combat took place at 0128 hours at 13,000 ft [4,000 metres], confirmed by Warrant Officer Scboolbread in Mosquito 169/G. Our patrol time being up we set course for Le Touquet at 0131 hours and returned to base uneventfully. 'Eighty rounds of cannon fired. No stoppages. Camera exposed. One Bf 109 destroyed Cat 1 (A). Slight damage to Mosquito from fragments of enemy aircraft.

On 25/26 July Mick Martin and Flying Officer J. W. Smith flew a *Night Ranger* to Stuttgart and Boblingen. They arrived over the area shortly after midnight and stooged around 'for as long as possible' but the patrol was uneventful and they headed home. Just after crossing the Belgian coast at Knocke at 0350 hours in very hazy conditions, an aircraft was seen about 1 mile (1.5 km) to port flying very fast. Martin swung the Mosquito around to dead astern and below the illuminated aircraft at a height of about 3,000 ft (900 metres). He closed to 50 yd and identified it as an Me 410. He gave the *Hornisse a* burst of cannon fire from astern and slightly below at 70 yd. He was so close the tail light of the Me 410 literally blotted out the spot on his ring sight. Martin recorded:

> This inconvenience was adjusted with no trouble at all, and, with the ring-sight moved to the Hun's starboard engine, a short second burst of cannon set the engine well alight. This obviously shook the Hun, and he speedily dived to port, but an almost simultaneous short second burst of cannon, directed on the port wing, blew the wing off, and the enemy aircraft, burning well, went down in a screaming dive. The 410 was seen to crash on the sea, and continued burning.

Also on 25/26 July Flight Lieutenant D. J. Griffiths and Flight Sergeant S. F. Smith of 23 Squadron recorded the Squadron's first air-to-air victory since returning from the Mediterranean, an unidentified enemy aircraft at Laon Pouvron. The following night, 26/27 July, Sticky Murphy and Jock Reid, one of six Mosquito crews of 23 Squadron aloft from Snoring, damaged a Ju 88 during their patrol to Chateaudun/Orleans airfield. Flying Officer K. Eastwood and Flight Lieutenant G. T. Rogers bombed Clastres airfield and shot up railway trucks and a factory building. On 4 August, thirteen Mosquitoes of 23 Squadron led by Sticky Murphy and ten of 515 Squadron led by Station Commander Sammy Hoare flew to Winkleigh in Devon to escort Lancasters attacking Bordeaux in daylight. When the Mosquitoes arrived over the target, smoke from bombs dropped by the Lancasters was at 11,000 ft (3,350 metres). They flew back over Vannes and Paimpol covering the bombers and landed at Winkleigh for the night. Next day at lunchtime, all the Mosquito crews returned to Snoring in great spirits.

The previous day's operation was to be run again. Twelve crews in 23 Squadron, including Sammy Hoare flying with Flight Lieutenant W. Gregory as his navigator, and seventeen in 515 Squadron flew out and met the Lancasters returning from Bordeaux. Unluckily, Hoare had to abort with a jammed elevator after two hours and landed at Colerne, where all crews returned safely by 2130 hours. Everyone returned to Snoring on 6 August at lunchtime and were rewarded with a 'stand down'. On 12 August, eight

Mosquitoes of 515 Squadron flew to Winkleigh to provide escort for Lancasters of 5 Group raiding Bordeaux again. Flying their first op, in X-X-Ray, were Flying Officer G. M. 'Frank' Bocock and Flight Sergeant Alf 'Snogger' Rogers (a member of a temperance society who did not smoke, drink or swear, but who had a reputation for the ladies). Alf Rogers recalls:

> On low-level Night Intruding Mosquitoes went out singly to *Luftwaffe* night-fighter bases and patrolled around them for an hour at low level while the heavy bombers passed by above. An active aerodrome would be attacked by the Intruder and any aircraft taking off risked an encounter with a Mosquito. So invariably when a Mosquito arrived the aerodrome switched off all lights and closed down. As a result the number of enemy aircraft destroyed was very low. The value of Intruding was not so much that enemy night-fighters were destroyed but rather that they were persuaded to stay on the ground.

Frank Bocock says:

> I was one of those stupid people who liked flying at night and here we were, on our first op, at 18,000–23,000 ft [5,500–7,000 metres] in broad daylight on a Saturday afternoon! We rendezvoused with the Lancasters over the Channel. It was a long boring flight (four hours twenty minutes). We flew out over the Bay of Biscay. The previous flight had flown over Brittany and was shot at by American troops. This time, all our Mosquitoes had invasion stripes painted under the wings.

In two fingers of four, the Mosquitoes patrolled up and down the sides of the bomber force. Frank Bocock's gunsight became unserviceable and he was forced to use extra engine boost to keep up after his gill shutters would not close. He landed back at Winkleigh very low on fuel and rejoined the other seven Mosquitoes at Snoring later.

Frank Bocock and Snogger Rogers flew their first *Intruder* on 18/19 August to the Fw 190 airfield at Leeuwarden. Frank Bocock recalls:

> Wing Commander Lambert told us to keep weaving. That's what I did. We stooged around over Holland at 1,500 ft [460 metres]. Suddenly, four searchlights coned us right in the middle. Gorgeous red, green and orange tracers arced towards us. It looked beautiful but it was even nicer when it missed us! I stuck the nose down. Our tail was damaged and our W/T went dead. We ripped off our helmets and shouted at each other. I told Alf to add a minute to the next leg but as we came back over the airfield, bang, the flak opened up again. The Germans' prediction was terrific, their radar exceptional. Fortunately, I had chopped my height. If I had been flying straight and level, we'd have got the chop.

On 26/27 August 1944 Warrant Officer Turner and Flight Sergeant Francis of 169 Squadron took off from Great Massingham in their Mosquito VI, setting course immediately over base, crossing the English and enemy coasts on schedule. Turner reported:

Nothing of note occurred until at 2345 at 20,000 ft [6,100 metres] where considerable searchlight activity was observed to port. It was apparent there were aircraft of some sort concerned so we decided to investigate and forthwith 'mucked-in' with a Hun searchlight co-op exercise. Occasional fleeting AI contacts were obtained, all showing hard above and from this, the position of the cone, and the firing of apparent colours of the day, it was assumed that there were some aircraft, possibly single-engined, at about 25,000 ft [7,600 metres], which made chances of interception very slim with a Mosquito VI. Having ourselves been coned on two occasions, and discretion obviously being the better part of valour, we proceeded to leave that area and attempt to reach our scheduled patrol area.

At 0030, nothing further having been seen, we turned on a reciprocal westerly course and after about twenty minutes' flying, obtained at 0050, 20,000 ft [6,100 metres], a forward AI contact at maximum range. Target appeared to be crossing port to starboard on estimated course of 030°. We chased for approx. five minutes reducing height to 14,000 ft [4,300 metres] where target was held in dead ahead position at 1,000 ft [300 metres] range. A visual was obtained and range reduced to 500 ft [150 metres] where aircraft was positively identified as a Ju 88. We allowed target to pull away to 1,000 ft [300 metres] range when we opened fire, the port engine immediately bursting into flames. Target turned gently starboard into a diving turn, leaving a long spiral of grey smoke. We followed, firing intermittently, observing strikes all over the fuselage. A tremendous flash was seen as aircraft hit the ground at 0057 hours.

A westerly course was set for base, which was reached at 0225 hours without further incident. 480 rounds of cannon fired – camera exposed. Claimed: one Ju 88 destroyed Cat 1. (A) Weather: starlit and clear – low cloud over most of route.

On 27 August, Flight Lieutenant M. W. 'Joe' Huggins and his navigator, Flight Sergeant Joe Cooper, took off from Snoring at 2210 hours for a *Night Ranger* over the continent. They were returning over the Dutch coast when at 0027 hours one of their propellers ran away. Pilot Officer Chris Harrison, a pilot on the squadron writes:

This problem apparently occurred on several aircraft and we were told to put the pitch lever to full fine should it happen, as this would stop the oil bleeding away – we were told! The engine packed up and caught fire and Huggins told his navigator to bail out, expecting to follow him. However, as he found he could control the slowly descending aircraft, he carried on, calling mayday, and finally bailed out within sight of the English coast, from which his approaching fire was under observation. He was picked up from a calm sea in a relatively short time, and taken to sick bay for check up. [Pilot Officer G. H. Spencer of 23 Squadron came back behind them and put up a good show in staying with them. He made six runs at less than 100 ft [30 metres] and saw Cooper in his dinghy].

The next morning Flight Lieutenant S. 'Josh' Hoskins and Flying Officer 'Jonah' Jones and myself and Flight Sergeant Mike Adams took one of the early stints and proceeded to just off the Dutch coast, where by now the weather was heavily overcast, and an approximately 8 ft [2.5 metres] confused sea was running. We searched for quite some time when suddenly Jonah sighted Cooper's dinghy and Josh called on the R/T and got into a left-hand orbit centred on Cooper. I fell into the circle but because of the sea state it was some minutes before we sighted Joe. We orbited for some time, then decided we would return to base with the good news, but how to know where to find the dinghy when we came back? I noticed a tall chimney on the Dutch coast, so I went inland and made a run back over the centre of Josh's orbit and took a course and time from the chimney, so by flying the same vector would have a reasonable pinpoint on where Joe had been when we left, so off back to Snoring.

We arranged for an ASR Walrus and also a back-up launch to go and pick up Cooper (the sea was considered probably too heavy for the Walrus to land and take off) and to keep Joe company while this was being organized, Josh and I went out again, this time accompanied by Squadron Leader Henry Morley. I duly went inland at the Dutch coast, then flew out my time and direction, and we started to look for Joe but just could not find him. We had more or less decided he had been snatched by the Germans, who would earlier have been able to observe us orbiting and guess what was on, when once again Jonah spotted him, and again the follow-the-leader orbiting. After fifteen minutes or so, eyes fixed on the dinghy; this became very unpleasant, with feelings of dizziness. Just closing your eyes for a few seconds made sighting Joe a great task due to the state of the sea, and we took it in turns to break out of the circle and relax for ten minutes, then back in, and several minutes' search to sight the dinghy. It is my recollection that Henry Morley and his navigator reported they never did sight the dinghy. After a long period of this, under about a 1,000 ft [300 metres] cloud base what we at first thought was a 109 dropped out of the clouds just north of us, and hooray, its half a dozen Church Fenton Polish Mustangs, with the funny old but wonderful-looking Walrus. A couple of passes, and he dropped a smoke float. With this reference, you could scratch yourself and then quickly pick up Joe again, so in went the Walrus, and landed in a great cloud of spray.

While the Walrus was making his circuit, I went in and took camera-gun of Joe in his dinghy, and during the several efforts the Walrus made to take off when the wing floats kept digging into the seas, and spinning it around, I also literally between the silent prayers, flashed over and recorded this on my camera-gun. Eventually, the Walrus got off and we decided to head for home and a celebration and halfway across the North Sea, broken cloud and calm water we met the back-up launch heading for the Dutch coast. This was obviously futile, so what to do? Several passes overhead frantically pointing back to England had no effect, and our VHF was useless, so we decided that whoever was with me would climb up to achieve VHF range to

England to get the launch called on its own frequency. But meanwhile the distance to the Dutch coast was reducing all the time, so in the best nautical tradition I fired a burst of war load 20 mm ammunition into the sea a few feet ahead of the launch, which promptly hove to. However, being a very keen type, after a few more of our futile gesticulating passes overhead, he decided this was just childish over-enthusiasm on our part, and headed for Holland again. Another burst, all recorded on my camera-gun, and he again hove to, and after some minutes the Mosquito up top came back on to Channel C and advised he had passed the message, and after some minutes the launch turned back for England and we headed for Snoring. Joe Cooper, we gather, duly arrived and was promptly put into hospital to recover from the effects of thirty-six or so hours wet through in shocking weather in his dinghy, and I never sighted him again.

On 6/7 September Flight Lieutenant Arthur S. Callard and Flight Sergeant F. Dixon Townsley flew an *Intruder* to Grove and Schleswig/Jägel, returning with claims of one Arado 196 floatplane destroyed and another damaged after sighting five moored in line just offshore at Aalborg. Shore batteries opened up with intense light flak but Callard and Townsley made it safely back to Snoring with a holed starboard outer fuel tank. Meanwhile, Wing Commander Freddie Lambert DFC and Flying Officer 'Whiskers' Lake AFC returned with a claim for a Bf 109 believed destroyed in the Grove-Copenhagen area.

Mick Martin and Flying Officer Smith had a very adventurous operation to Munich and Vienna a few weeks later, on 9/10 September. They made four circuits of Tulin airfield to make sure the coast was clear, before strafing aircraft on the ground. One aircraft was left burning. A second strafing run was made and another 'vivid' fire was seen among the parked aircraft. In the Salzburg area on the way home they attacked and destroyed a train which 'blew up in a terrific explosion followed by vivid blue sparks'. Martin and Smith flew on, pausing to rake installations at Cheim airfield with cannon fire before moving on to the south-east end of Lake Constance, where a seaplane base was also strafed. At Mulhouse, Mick Martin strafed the marshalling yards and had a pop at railway stations, buildings and lights. The former Dambuster reported that strikes were recorded in most cases.

On 12/13 September Pilot Officer Chris Harrison and Flight Sergeant Mike Adams flew an *Intruder* patrol to Hanau/Langendiebach and damaged an enemy night-fighter coming in to land at the airfield. Searchlights and light flak became very active and patrol time was up so the pair decided to set course for home and comfort!

On 26/27 September Squadron Leader Henry Morley and Flight Sergeant Reg Fidler took off on an *Intruder* to Zellhausen airfield, where they destroyed a twin-engined aircraft (possibly an He 111) on its approach. Three days later, they flew to the forward airfield at St Dizier with Arthur Callard and E. Dixon Townsley in T-Tommy for a *Day Ranger* to the Munich–Linz–Vienna area. The two Mosquitoes took off at noon and headed for Holzkirchen airfield 20 miles (30 km) south-south-east of Munich. Morley and Fidler attacked, firing a four-second burst, damaging and probably destroying on the ground two Siebel SI 204 radio, radar and navigation trainers. Their drop tanks gone, they parted company with Callard and Townsley. On the way back they strafed a number

On 30 September Squadron Leader Henry Morley and Flight Sergeant Reg Fidler of 515 Squadron were returning from a Day Ranger *to the Munich-Linz-Vienna area in FBVI PZ440 when their aircraft was hit by a Swiss 20-mm flak battery whilst flying between Konstanz and Zurich at a height of just 200 ft (60 metres). With its port engine knocked out, the Mosquito was intercepted by four Swiss Morane MS.406 fighters and escorted to Dubendorf airfield, over which PZ440's starboard engine also quit, forcing Morley to crash-land near Volketswil. Both men suffered only minor injuries.* (via Tom Cushing)

of Ju 86s parked on the perimeter of Munich/Neubiburg airfield. Between Konstanz and Zurich, when at 200 ft (60 metres), their Mosquito was hit by 20 mm flak from a Swiss battery. Morley feathered the port propeller. Four Swiss Morane 406 fighters appeared and formated on the damaged Mosquito, which was losing height. The firing of Very cartridges and their general behaviour indicated that they wanted the Mosquito to land at Dubendorf. However, when it was over the airfield the Mosquito's starboard engine also quit and Morley crash-landed near Volketswil. Both men suffered only minor injuries.

The crew of T-Tommy meanwhile, had continued their *Day Ranger* with an attack on a seaplane base at Prien. Callard and Townsley attacked at 500 ft [150 metres] and destroyed two Do 24 floatplanes moored near the shore. Satisfied with their work, they carried on to the Salzburg area and investigated a small grass airfield at Friedburg about 20 miles [30 km] north-east of Salzburg. They spotted a Bf 109G parked near a hangar and attacked it. The Messerschmitt exploded and pieces hit the low flying Mosquito. They were returning to base when, passing Prien again, wreckage of their earlier handiwork was seen floating in the water. Callard and Townsley immediately went in to attack the remaining Do 24, which was sunk by a burst of cannon from 200 ft [60 metres]. At about 1435 hours, when south of Munich at zero feet. T-Tommy's starboard radiator began running hot. South-east of Lake Constance as the temperature rose and the needle went off the clock, Callard shut down the right engine and feathered the propeller. He found it difficult to gain height on the one good engine, which was worrying because of the hilly terrain.

Almost an hour later, when north of Zurich, four Swiss Bf 109 fighters slowly overtook and formated on T-Tommy. Two flew off the right wing and the other pair took the left wing. The Swiss made no attempt to attack and the Mosquito crew pretended to ignore their presence but the Swiss fighters closed in and indicated that they had to land. This they did safely on one engine at Dubendorf near Zurich at about 1600 hours. Morley and Fidler were removed to hospital in Zurich and then interned along with Callard and Townsley. All four men later escaped from their captivity and got back to England.

CHAPTER VI

Let Tyrants Tremble

As I was walking up the stair
I met a man who wasn't there.
He wasn't there again today.
I wish, I wish he'd stay away.

Hugh Mearns

Fighter-bomber operations made the headlines almost daily but support units, involved in radio countermeasures (RCM) and electronic intelligence (ELINT), received no mention because of the secret nature of the work. Yet, from the time

Flying Officer N. 'Ali' Barber (left) and Flight Lieutenant Peter W. R. Rowland (right) of 192 Squadron in front of their Mosquito IV. On his first tour in the expert low-level raiders of 105 Squadron Rowland had flown, amongst other raids, the low-level operation to the Gestapo *HQ in Oslo, Norway on 25 September 1942.* (CONAM)

Result of the collision at RAF Foulsham on 27 April 1944 when Halifax III MZ564 of 192 Squadron landed on top of Mosquito BIV DZ377 from the same squadron. (via Alan Hague)

of full-scale operations by 100 Group, main force losses were cut by 80 per cent, with one or two aircraft missing from a total main force strength of between 300 and 500 heavy bombers sent to a major German target becoming typical of the protection which was being given to the bomber stream. Who were these 'mystical' units, few in number but massive in their contribution? On 1 February 1944, 1473 Flight, which up to this time had been under the control of OC 80 Wing, Radlett, and whose activities in the main, consisted of signals investigation over friendly territory, were merged with 192 Squadron at Foulsham. It will be remembered that 192 had transferred to 100 Group from 3 Group on 7 December 1943. The brief was to carry out investigation of German signals from the Bay of Biscay to the Baltic, and along all bomber routes. The amalgamation brought 192's strength up to seven Wellington Mk Xs, ten Halifaxes, seven Mosquito Mk IVs and one Anson. On 20 February, the Halifax Mk II was changed to Mk X and later Mk IIIs were used. The Intelligence Officer at the station, Squadron Leader A. N. Banks, recalls: 'Mosquitoes in 192 Squadron were used to monitor the frequencies being used by ground control of German night-fighters and also to record the verbal instructions used in night-fighter control.'

On 27 April at 0325 hours at Foulsham, Mosquito IV DZ377 of 192 Squadron touched down in bad visibility. Behind it was a 192 Halifax III, flown by Flight Sergeant H. P. Gibson, whose R/T had failed, and on landing he collided with the Mosquito. The RAF Form 1180 (accident record card) recorded that the 'steady green' which was flashed to the Mosquito should not have been given and the pilot should not have been at 500 ft (150 metres) in the funnel or have accepted the steady green as permission to land. The

Squadron Leader Bill Jeffries, (Wing Commander Desmond McGlinn (CO) 214 Squadron's R/O on 5/6 June), Flight Lieutenant Bill Doy and George Wright of 214 Squadron at Oulton 1944. Jeffries and Doy flew the ABC operation in support of D-Day in 5/6 June 1944. (Tom Cushing Collection)

Committee of Investigation concluded that the accident was due to 'juxtaposition of aircraft in the funnel, no navigation lights owing to air raid warning and Halifax's R/T being unserviceable. SFCO [Senior Flying Control Officer] posted and reduced – not considered competent.' Banks adds, 'They both came into land at the same time. They made a good landing and no one was injured. As a matter of fact, the crew of the Halifax were entirely unaware that their aircraft had landed on top of the Mosquito until they got out of the plane.' A second Mosquito in 192 Squadron, attacked by enemy aircraft over France and badly damaged, managed to crash-land at Friston on returning.

On 1 May 1944, 199 Squadron (motto: 'Let tyrants tremble') joined 100 Group at North Creake from 3 Group. Some months before, on 22 November 1943, it had taken part in the last Stirling raid on a major German target – Berlin. From this time an extensive programme of precision sea mining was carried out and attacks were also made on French rail and other military targets. Other useful work was carried out in ASR and, from February to April 1944 199's Stirling IIIs delivered vital food and supplies to the occupied territories. In April, the squadron was stood down to await *Mandrel* jamming equipment to be installed in its Stirling IIIs. They would supplement 214 Squadron's Fortresses over Germany. In January 1944 214 Squadron, then at Downham Market and equipped with Stirlings, had transferred from 3 Group to 100 Group at Sculthorpe. Although he was twenty-eight-years-old, command weighed heavily on Wing Commander Desmond J. McGlinn DFC, who had commanded the squadron since January, and he looked much older. McGlinn and his men were assisted by a small American RCM detachment under the command of Captain George E. Paris, which arrived at Sculthorpe on 19 January to train the RAF crews in jamming using *Jostle* equipment (which began arriving in May). *Jostle* and *Window* patrols would form the bulk of 214 Squadron's work and for the ten months preceding the end of the war, over 1,000 sorties were completed on 116 nights.

Meanwhile, on 10 February, five B-l7Fs and one B-I7G, all formerly belonging to the 96th Bomb Group of the 8th Air Force, and all equipped with *Mandrel* (the B-17G also had ELINT fitted) arrived at Sculthorpe from Snetterton Heath. These were joined at Sculthorpe on 15 May by two more surplus B-17s from the 95th Bomb Group. They received exhaust-flame dampers for night flying and *Gee* navigation equipment

No. 214 Squadron moved to Oulton on 16 May. This was a popular move, nearer to 'civilization' and in the heart of one of the most pleasant districts of East Anglia. Some of the officers were accommodated in Blickling Hall, a fine seventeenth-century mansion reputed to have associations with Anne Boleyn. The park and bathing in the lake were much enjoyed by members of the squadron. Word must have spread about the attractions because, early in May, the American 803rd Squadron, (now redesignated the 36th Bomb Squadron), and equipped with six RCM Fortresses fitted with *Minaret* and

Flight Lieutenant Murray Peden RCAF (front) and Flying Officer Steve Nessner RCAF, special wireless operator, enjoying themselves on a motorcycle in front of 'Canada House' at RAF Oulton. Nessner, born in Yugoslavia of German parents, Canadian by naturalization, flew seventeen trips in 100 Group in American aircraft, bombing his ancestral origins! While recovering from an ear, nose and throat operation his first crew was shot down in the circuit at Oulton on 3/4 March 1945. On 15/16 April Nessner was injured when the Fortress he was in crash-landed in Belgium after being shot up over Schwandorf. (Steve Nessner)

In January 1944 214 Squadron were assisted by a small American RCM detachment (803rd Bomb Squadron) commanded by Captain George E. Paris (seen here in the cockpit of a B-17 at Oulton), which arrived at Sculthorpe on 19 January to train the RAF crews in jamming using Jostle *equipment.* Jostle *(which began arriving in May) and* Window *patrols would form the bulk of 214 Squadron's work and for the ten months preceding the end of the war, over 1,000 sorties were completed on 116 nights.* (CONAM via Stephen Hutton and G. E. Paris)

Early in 1944 eleven war-weary B-17Fs of the 95th, 96th and 384th Bomb Groups, 8th Air Force (B-17F-60-DL 42-3438/F, formerly Dottie J III *in the 337th Bomb Squadron, 96th Bomb Group pictured) arrived to join the 803rd Bomb Squadron. They were immediately fitted with* Mandrel, Carpet *and ELINT jamming equipment, exhaust-flame dampers for night flying and* Gee *navigation equipment. Seven of these, including 42-3438, became drone aircraft packed with explosives and were used in* Project Aphrodite. *On 30 October 1944 42-3438 was used to destroy a German ground installation.* (CONAM via Stephen Hutton)

Wing Commander Desmond John McGlinn CO 214 Squadron RAF; Captain George E. Paris, CO 803rd Bomb Squadron USAAF; Squadron Leader William S. Day RCAF. (CONAM via Stephen Hutton and G. E. Paris)

Air Vice Marshal E. B. Addison with Lieutenant Colonel Hambaugh, CO, 36th Bomb Squadron, November 1944. On 23 November Air Commodore Addison established 100 Group HQ at Radlett, Herts. Its primary duty was to reduce the escalating losses being suffered by the heavy bomber force over Germany. Addison had previously commanded 80 Wing RAF, which, as a wing commander, he had established at Garston in June 1940. (CONAM via Stephen Hutton)

Carpet, moved to Oulton too! By the end of the month, a total of twenty-two crews were fully converted to Fortresses.

On 23/24 May when Bomber Command's main target was Aachen with 264 Lancasters, 162 Halifaxes and sixteen Mosquitoes dispatched, six RCM aircraft and a few dozen *Serrate* and *Intruder* Mosquitoes provided bomber support. One of the three RCM Fortresses despatched by 214 Squadron was SR384/A, flown by Pilot Officer Allan J. N. Hockley RAAF, which was intercepted by *Oberleutenant* Hermann Leube, *Staffel Kaptain* of *IV/INJG3* flying Ju 88G-I D5+KM, which took off from Plantlünne, a satellite airfield between Rheine and Lingen/Emsland at 2303 hrs on 24 May. *Feldwebel* Eberhard Scheve served as *bordfunker* in the crew and *Stabsfeldwebel.* Druschke was the air gunner. Leube went off in pursuit of the bomber stream, as Scheve recalls:

> Until this day our night fighting radar SN-2 was jammed only by *Düppel* (*Window*). On this night, however, a flying transmitter, which caused a flickering of the waves over the full width of the picture tube and which completely prevented the blips from appearing normally jammed our equipment. I tried a few tricks, switched off the transmitter of my SN-2 set, then dimmed the amplifier on the receiver and then had two different flickering bands to the left and to the right of the middle line. I told my pilot to alter his course and established that the flickering bands changed accordingly. I therefore decided that I could use this jamming transmitter as a flying beacon to home on to. As the jamming transmitter probably flew inside a bomber stream to give protection to the formation, we decided to investigate this.
>
> It took us a long time before we spotted the bomber, and we attacked it no less than six times before we were able to shoot it down. At once when the bomber exploded the jamming of the SN-2 ended. Our *Staffel* comrades, who had also flown around aimlessly for several hours, confirmed the vanishing of the jamming at this instant. At debriefing we told of our observations, but we were then told that no such thing existed as a jamming transmitter for the SN-2 and that we had experienced jamming by the overlapping of other SN-2 sets.

Leube's victims were the first Fortress crew lost by 214 Squadron on operations. He first set the fuselage of SR384 on fire, then the wings, and finally the Fortress exploded over the Oosterschelde near Antwerp at 0057 hours. Hockley and his mid-upper gunner Sergeant Raymond G. M. Simpson were killed; the seven other men in the crew escaped alive. The victorious Ju 88G-1 crew returned safely to base at 0220 hrs. Leube met his end on 27/28 December 1944. At the time of his death he had scored twenty-two victories.

On 1 June Capt. Paris, now relieved of his temporary command with the arrival of Captain Clayton A. Scott, took part in the first daylight operation from Oulton. During June, 100 Group began its work of deceiving the enemy, using the airborne *Mandrel* screen and *Window* feint forces. The *Serrate* Mosquitoes and the low-level *Intruders* were also given a part to play in the deception. *Serrate* aircraft accompanied the diversionary forces in order to give the feint more realism and also to be in a position to intercept enemy fighters airborne in reaction to the feint. *Serrate* aircraft and low-level *Intruders* were also on occasions sent to patrol areas well away from the main attack in an attempt to deceive the enemy as to the area in which the attack could be expected.

On 5/6 June, a *Mandrel* screen was formed to cover the approach of the Normandy invasion fleet, and from subsequent information received, it appeared that considerable confusion was caused to the German early warning system. Sixteen Stirlings of 199 Squadron and four Fortresses of the American 803rd established a *Mandrel* screen in a line from Littlehampton to Portland Bill. Five Fortresses of 214 Squadron flown by Wing Commander McGlinn, Squadron Leaders Bill Day and Jefferies, the 'A' and 'B' Flight Commanders respectively, Flight Lieutenant Murray Peden RCAF and Flying Officer Cam Lye RNZAF, also operated in support of the D-Day operation in their ABC (*Airborne Cigar*) role (ABC was a device consisting of six scanning receivers and three transmitters designed to cover the VHF band of the standard German R/T sets and to jam 30–33 MHz (*OHokar)* and later 38–42 MHz (*Benito*) R/T and Beams). A protective patrol lasting over five hours was flown at 27,000 ft (8,200 metres) starting just north and east of Dieppe and running almost at right angles to the coastline carrying out jamming and *Window* dropping in conjunction with twenty-four Lancasters of 101 Squadron of 1 Group. One Lancaster was shot down. Overall, though, the patrol was outstandingly successful and earned a personal congratulation to all concerned by Arthur Harris, to whom he pointed out that 'the work carried out was of paramount importance in connection with the Invasion Forces'.

An Me 410 had the misfortune to choose McGlinn's aircraft, which had Eric 'Phil' Phillips, the Squadron Gunnery Leader, manning the tail turret. Phillips had started his operational tour in 15 Squadron based at Mildenhall, his first trip being on 26 April 1943, and he carried on through the Battle of the Ruhr onto the Battle of Hamburg. Then after fifteen operational trips with that crew he was hit with cannon from a Ju 88 and spent a few weeks in hospital, during which time that crew finished its tour with the Battle of Berlin. Phillips returned to the squadron and completed three more operations with various crews before being sent on a gunnery leader's course prior to his posting to 214 Squadron, where he completed thirty-three operational trips. None was more memorable than the one on D-Day as he recalls:

> We took off at 2250 hours and were cruising on course at 30,000 ft [9,100 metres]. It was a brilliant moonlight night with 10/10ths cloud. Some 5,000 ft [1,500 metres] below the vapour trails from each wing tip stood out for all to see. Inside the Fortress aircraft 'N' with its crew of ten fully trained airmen, all was silent – just the steady hum of the four engines could be heard. There was a click as the wireless operator, Flight Lieutenant Bill Doy, switched on his intercom and spoke. 'Rear-gunner, there is a U/I aircraft approaching very fast from the rear.'
>
> I confirmed that I had it in sight some 2,000 ft [610 metres] astern and approx. 800 ft [240 metres] below. I brought it in by commentary – 1,200 ft [365 metres] – 1,000 ft [300 metres] – and at 800 ft [24 metres] it started to disappear under the Fortress. I handed the commentary back to the W/O who gave the Skipper the order, 'Corkscrew – starboard go!' On the word

'go' I fired one short burst blindly with both .5s fully depressed. The next second with the Fortress in a deep dive to starboard the attacking aircraft I now recognized as an Me 410 was on my port quarter. For a second it appeared to just hang there with the glow of two cannons being fired. I fired two short bursts and also observed an accurate burst from the mid-upper turret. There was no doubt that the Me 410 was hit as I saw smoke. He then disappeared from my view and I did not see the aircraft again. I gave the Skipper instructions to resume course as the attack had ended. The navigator gave him an intermediate course to fly. The Skipper then asked me if we had been hit. I replied in the negative (although we did find when we landed that a cannon shell had passed through the tailplane). The engineer, when asked, confirmed that all was well with the engines. The Skipper then asked for a course for home. Owing to our loss of height and possible damage to our aircraft from stress caused by the evasive actions he decided this was the correct thing to do. Once again silence reigned until we arrived back at base. If you were to ask me how long it was from when I first sighted the Me to the breakaway of the attack I would possibly say thirty seconds.

At the debriefing the Skipper, mid-upper gunner, and the port waist gunner all stated that they last saw the Me 410 on a downward path with smoke pouring from one of the engines. It then disappeared into the cloud and the port waist gunner was sure that he saw a red glow through the cloud shortly afterwards.

Phillips was awarded the DFC in 1943 and recommended for a bar to the DFC in 1944 (not awarded) and Mentioned in Dispatches in 1945.

D-Day saw 192 Squadron in a new operational role. A constant patrol was maintained between Cap Gris Nez and the Cherbourg area to see if the enemy was using the centimetric band for radar, all the known enemy radars being effectively jammed. No positive results were obtained but centimetric investigations continued right up until the end of the war. At a later date, it was confirmed by the Y-Service that the enemy was indeed using centimetric radar and it was believed that it was in fact captured 'friendly' equipment. No. 192 Squadron used sound recorders, both on film and on wire on investigations into the enemy's radar secrets. It had always played an important part in the interception of enemy VHF R/T and W/T traffic, both air-to-air, and air-to-ground. Its value was doubly increased from D-Day onwards due to the old question of optical range and such transmissions being outside the normal interception of a Y-Service ground-listening station.

A sound recorder also played a very important part in establishing the use by the enemy of the *Bernardine Gerdte*, a complicated system, ground-to-air, involving the transmission of *Hellschreiber* traffic, operative only for about ten seconds a minute. Without a sound recorder this particular type of transmission could not have been broken down. Sound recordings were also of considerable assistance in assessing the efficiency of friendly RCM. Sound recordings made of RAF countermeasures, with the actual signal as it was being jammed in the background, meant that the efficiency of the jammers could be assessed accordingly. Cameras such as Leica, Contax, Kodak Cine and Bell and Howell were also used. Because the duration of certain enemy transmissions was so short, it was not always possible for a detailed analysis of a signal to be made by the special operator, but in many instances it did permit a photographic record to be made, enabling further information to be obtained. Cine cameras played a very important part in establishing the polar diagrams of enemy radar transmitters. Some very good results were obtained on the *Jagdschloss* type of transmitter.

During June Pilot Officer Don Earl, a Londoner, and his crew, all fresh from 12 OTU at Chipping Warden, where they had trained on Wellingtons, arrived at Foulsham for operations with 192 Squadron on the Wimpy. Earl and the rest of the crew, all flight sergeants – Jimmy Jones, navigator, Frank 'Doc' Elliott, signaller, bomb-aimer Walter 'Buck' Rogers, a Canadian, and Jack 'Shorty' Short, tail gunner – had expected to be posted to a HCU and Lancasters. They had never heard of Foulsham or 100 Group. Before the war Short had been a child prodigy of impresario Carroll Levis. He recalls:

Ground and flight crews of Wellington X HE472 B-Bambi of 192 Squadron, RAF Foulsham. Aircrew back row L–R: Flight Sergeant Jim Jones; Pilot Officer Jack Short, tail gunner; Pilot Officer Don Earl, pilot; Frank 'Doc' Elliott; Flight Sergeant Bob Webster; special wireless operator; Flight Sergeant Walter 'Buck' Rogers RCAF. B-Bambi survived the war and was reallocated to 11 Air Gunners' School at RAF Andreas, Isle of Man. (Group Captain Jack Short)

On arrival crews were thoroughly briefed about the importance of total secrecy. We did not expect to fly ops in a 'Welly', stooging around for five hours or more. Our allotted Wellington X was christened *B-Bambi* by kind permission of the Walt Disney office in London, who supplied suitable stencils. Our first op was flown on 23 June, to Brest–Cherbourg. Most aircraft were fitted with two banks of oscilloscopes with a special operator (ours was Flight Sergeant Robert Webster), using a 35 mm German Leica camera (which amused us no end), to record the incoming German signals data for subsequent interpretation. Externally the aircraft carried an array of different aerials which were the subject of much attention when landing away from base, particularly as it called for a guard to be mounted.

Pilot Officer Jack Short, tail gunner of B-Bambi. (Group Captain Jack Short)

On one occasion, a 192 Squadron Halifax diverted to Manston after a raid accompanying 3 Group Stirlings. The captain of the aircraft was so pressed by the Stirling aircrew to disclose the function of his aircraft that he made up a code-name to fend off the interest. He whispered – 'in the strictest confidence' – that his was a 100 Group 'clothes line' aircraft and that in consequence the 3 Group loss rate would be minimal, and truly, that night it had been! Through the post-raid intelligence debriefing, information emerged about 'clothes line'. This resulted in a request from 3 Group HQ to 100 Group HQ for the attendance of another aircraft similarly equipped for the next operation. Tracing quickly identified the pilot as Hayter-Preston, a pre-war Fleet Street journalist, who was using his acquired skill with words. He was appropriately admonished by the Wing Commander Flying. He had previously used his skill at off-the-cuff remarks when landing at an OTU by stating that the squadron dropped bags of flour across the Continent to leave a dotted white line to the target for the Pathfinder force to follow!

Throughout June, *Mandrel* screens were flown on a number of nights, sometimes as cover for main force bombers, and on a few occasions as a diversion to alert the enemy defences unnecessarily. At this early stage, it was necessary to experiment in order that the best uses of the *Mandrel* screen might be determined. It was found that to a considerable extent, more was achieved in practice than the theoreticians had dared hope for. A consideration which also arose immediately was that, owing to lack of aircraft, only a small screen could be put up. It was, of course, necessary to fly RAF aircraft in pairs to give full coverage. The American aircraft flew singly, but did not cover as wide a frequency band. A very high standard of flying by the pilot, and of dead reckoning on the part of the navigator, was essential, for the Stirlings always flew at their maximum operational height, often in cloud conditions. Some *Gee* chains were jammed by the

Mandrel itself, and thus there was no means of wind-finding once the racecourse pattern had started. As the aircraft were not fitted with AFIs, even a good direction finding (DR) position could not be established from the last found wind velocity once jamming commenced. (Many of these problems were overcome with the changeover to Halifaxes, but this was not completed until March 1945.)

June 1944 was not without loss. On 16/17 June Bomber Command lost thirty-one bombers from 321 Squadron dispatched to the synthetic oil plant at Sterkrade Holten in Germany. Six B-17s of the 36th Bomb Squadron joined sixteen Stirling IIIs of 199 Squadron in routine *Mandrel* sorties to cover the attack. Stirling EX-N LJ531 of 199 Squadron failed to return to North Creake. Pilot Officer T. Dale RNZAF, his six crew, and Warrant Officer F. Lofthouse, the special wireless operator, all perished. On 21/22 June 214 Squadron was detailed to cover an attack on the Nordstern oil plant at Gelsenkirchen. Flight Lieutenant Murray Peden and his crew took off in F-Fox. Peden, a Canadian, saw in the darkening sky the spire of Norwich cathedral looming in the distance as he swung on to an easterly heading and made for the coast and the unfriendly stretches beyond.

> I never saw it without thinking of that wonderful, brave woman, Edith Cavell, sleeping in its shadow. We had read about her as kids when we were at school, and I always had the greatest admiration for her courage. I read more about her as I grew up, and used to remember, too, that she had spent many summer holidays at the coast at Cromer. And many times Cromer was our point of departure from England on operations.

At a point approximately fifteen minutes from the target area, F-Fox was attacked by an Me 410. In the ensuing combat, the Fortress was seriously damaged, the starboard inner engine was set on fire, and the intercom system was put out of action. Both Flight Sergeant Alfred 'Stan' Stanley, the wireless operator, and the special operator were wounded in the attack, and Flying Officer J. B. Waters, the air bomber, gave them some timely first aid. Waters also helped to restore the intercom. A few minutes later the Fortress was attacked by a Ju 88 but coolness and good shooting on the part of Flight Sergeant Johnny Walker, the air gunner, drove off the night-fighter. Strikes were obtained on both enemy machines.

With one engine still on fire, Murray Peden set course for home and, displaying great ability, successfully reached the long emergency airfield at Woodbridge. He made a spectacular arrival on two good and one partially serviceable engines, and came straight in. He was unable to acknowledge instructions because of the damaged equipment, which rendered the instructions almost unintelligible. The Fortress put down but burst a tyre, causing it to swing violently off the runway towards a Lancaster of 61 Squadron, which had just landed without hydraulics after an encounter with night-fighters. Fortunately, the Lancaster crew and the maintenance personnel milling around were able to get clear before the Fortress cut the bomber in two. Murray Peden recollects:

> Years later, when I tracked down Dennis Copson, the only survivor of Butch Passant's crew, he gave me a laugh. You have to understand that he had been wounded that night near Gelsenkirchen, and had to be more or less chopped

out of the turret when Passant landed. He had just been assisted out of the turret by a groundcrew man named Corporal Francis, who had been wielding the emergency axe from the aircraft to help free him. They somehow managed to leave the scene at a handsome pace a few seconds before we arrived on the scene at a rate of knots and cut the Lancaster in half.

Four crashes occurred in all, in the space of thirteen minutes. There were no injuries from any of them. Later, Peden was told that the Lancaster had a 12,000 lb (5,400 kg) bomb on board! Murray Peden, Waters and Walker were commended for their actions and Stanley was awarded the DFM for continuing to carry out his duties after being wounded. Murray Peden concludes:

> Stan still remembers, as his clearest recollection of the crash landing at Woodbridge, his skipper coming over for a look at him on the grass, in a rather breathless state, and offering the Mayo Clinic medical opinion: 'Oh … the poor bastard … he's had it.' He was still conscious when this encouraging prognosis was announced and now we have a good laugh about it every time we get together and I point out that I didn't actually put a time limit on the occurrence!

This story is one of many related in full in Murray Peden's autobiographical classic, *A Thousand Shall Fall.*

Another Fortress, flown by Flying Officer Johnny Cassan, failed to return from the Gelsenkirchen operation. The bomb-aimer, Warrant Officer Doug Jennings, was the only survivor. He eventually returned to Oulton during August after first being signalled as killed, reclassified as a POW and again reclassified as 'now in the UK'.

July 1944 saw the operational birth of two new and important countermeasures, *Jostle* and the special *Window* force. The former made its first appearance on 4/5 July and the latter on 14/15 July when all available spare aircraft from 100 Group's heavy squadrons were used. The *Mandrel* screen was used on sixteen nights in August, on several occasions over south-east England, giving coverage to bomber attacks on V-l sites in the Pas de Calais.

On 14 August the 36th Bomb Squadrons in B-24H/J Liberators moved to Cheddington and continued to operate in 100 Group, principally on daylight missions, until January 1945. (In August, 199 Squadron was increased to three flights to give added cover at night.) The greatest success achieved by a Spoof force to date occurred following the main force attacks on Kiel and Stettin on 16/17 August. On 17/18 August, no major bomber attack took place, but a *Window* force, strengthened in numbers by a *Bullseye,* and covered by a *Mandrel* screen, headed towards northern Germany. The *Windowers* kept on almost to the Schleswig coast, and created in the enemy mind a complete impression that the previous night's attack was to be repeated. No less than twelve *Staffeln* were sent up against the bomber stream. An even more important after-effect of this Spoof took place on 18/19 August when a main force actually did go to Bremen, on a route similar to that of the spoof force. The German defenders, thoroughly confused, took this attack to be another Spoof, and left it entirely unopposed by fighters.

B-24J-FO-1 42-50665/K Lady in the Dark *was the first Liberator assigned to the 803rd Bomb Squadron when it arrived at Oulton in June 1944 and received Mandrel and Jackal AN/ART-3 tank communication jamming equipment.* (Dr. Robert F. Hambaugh Jr. via Stephen Hutton/CONAM)

On 23 August, 223 Squadron took the Americans' place at Oulton, formed initially with a handful of B-24H/J Liberator aircraft from the 8th Air Force for operations using *Jostle* jamming equipment. The B-24 was capable of carrying as many as thirty jamming sets. This and its long-range capability made it a much more ideal aircraft for the task than the Fortress, which equipped 214 Squadron. Unfortunately, 223 Squadron's B-24s, some of which had accumulated as many as 350 flying hours in 8th Air Force service, had seen far better days.

During August, Wing Commander McGlinn left 214 Squadron after fourteen months' tenure, to be replaced by Wing Commander D. D. Rogers, and for a short period commanded 223 Squadron. Although 223 Squadron was originally formed as the second *Jostle* unit, its role was set to change when in mid-July 1944 the wreckage of a German rocket, thought to be a V-2, was flown to England for scrutiny at RAE Farnborough. The missile had landed in Sweden after a test firing from the German research station at Peenemünde. Immediately, urgent steps were taken to develop a countermeasure and *Jostle* equipment was subsequently modified to the *Big Ben* configuration. However, the wreckage in the hands of the RAF Farnborough belonged not to the *V-2* but the *Wasserfall* anti-aircraft missile, although this was not realized until after the war.

B-24H-DT-30 Liberator 42-51188/O Lady Jane *was assigned to the 803rd Bomb Squadron in July 1944.* (Charles M. Todaro via Stephen Hutton/CONAM)

B-24H-CF-25 42-50385/H Beast of Bourbon *was also assigned to the 803rd Bomb Squadron in July 1944. This aircraft crash-landed on 19 February 1945 and was salvaged.* (Donald Burch via Stephen Hutton/CONAM)

A Jostle *R/T jamming transmitter on a special transporter at Oulton ready for insertion into the ball turret opening of a B-24 Liberator of 223 Squadron.* (IWM)

With the advent of the V-1 and V-2 192 Squadron was prepared in as much as Mosquito, Halifax and Wellington aircraft were suitably equipped and kept on standby for immediate take-off in order to investigate the possibility of some form of radio control being used, with weapons. In the initial stages of the V-2 the squadron maintained a twenty-four-hour patrol. Shorty Short, tail gunner of B-Bambi recalls:

> While on a North Sea patrol, Robert Webster, the special signals operator, had picked up on one of his oscilloscopes some unusual returns emanating from the area of The Hague. Having photographed these signals and logged the relevant data an immediate return to base was initiated. Unfortunately, the weather made a recovery to Foulsham impossible and the aircraft diverted to Methwold. The usual guard was placed on the aircraft and the 'spec-sigs' crewman with his secret information was rushed off by staff car to 100 Group HQ for urgent analysis. Not long after this occurrence, a major 'gas explosion' which had demolished a row of houses in London, was reported on the front pages of national newspapers. This was generally accepted by the populace, as there had been no air raid in progress. A few days later there was a similar explosion, again without warning. Hitler's

random terror weapon was directed against the civilian population. It was a good day's work by Bob Webster, special operator!

At midday on 16 August B-Bambi was taken aloft for an air test but failed it after just fifteen minutes. For the night's operation to the Friesian Islands, Don Earl was given D-Dog. 'No one was ever happy about a change of aircraft,' recalls Shorty Short, the tail gunner. 'It meant a change of luck.'

> We took off at full throttle. At 100 ft [30 metres] the starboard engine backfired and began to run rough. Don did a full circuit at 200 ft (60 metres] and came in for an emergency landing. Downwind the signaller fired off a red flare and the pilot shouted his intentions over the R/T. He made the bomb-aimer flash 'SOS' on the nose light. So we were shouting, flashing and firing! I was dead worried. To me it seemed we were still at nominal flying speed. The controller's caravan went 'pumpff' as we passed it at 140 mph [225 kph] instead of drifting gently past. We only had a 2,000 yd runway. I knew either we were going to go off the end or shed rubber. We did the latter. I'd turned the turret 90° and unlocked the doors as we

On 16 August 1944, Wellington XLP345 D-Dog, piloted by Pilot Officer Don Earl of 192 Squadron, crashed at Foulsham shortly after take-off. The explosion was caught on film by the station photographer. All the crew had a narrow escape. (Group Captain Jack Short)

The skeletal remains of Wellington XLP345 D-Dog. (Group Captain Jack Short)

clobbered the runway hard – the oleos penetrated the wings. The tyres burst and sparks from metal on concrete set the ruptured bomb-bay overload fuel tanks alight. Flames came back along the fuselage. I had my bum out of the turret and my fingers on the rim. If the wing dug in I'd be flung out like a tennis ball. The undercarriage crumpled and we want off the runway. Flames immediately roared up through the fuselage. I literally fell out backwards on to the grass. I tried to run but after two paces I found I was still plugged into the aircraft intercom! I went back and unplugged and sprinted. Everybody scrambled clear in eleven seconds (practice paid off!), although Jim Jones grabbed hold of the already hot astrodome rim to get out and burned his hands to the sinews. We all scattered. Ammo soon began exploding.

CHAPTER VII

Dare to Discover

We are the heavy bombers, we try to do our bit,
We fly through concentrations of flak with sky all lit ...

'When asked to design a crest and motto for 100 Group,' recalls Jack Short, 'one wag produced a drawing of an aircrew officer peering through the keyhole of a bathroom [ostensibly at a young lady in a tub] with the motto, "We snoop to conquer"! As things turned out not too far removed from the *Chester Herald* approved version of "Dare to Discover" and a bright-eyed owl over a signals motif.'

In the investigation for signals in connection with the V-2, assistance was given by the 8th Air Force which had already detached a flight of four P-38J Lightnings to Foulsham, arriving on 24 August under the command of Captain Kasch. (In July 1944, an ELINT P-38 of the 7th Photographic Group (Reconnaissance) arrived at Foulsham to operate alongside 192 Squadron.) A total of four P-38s was eventually based at Foulsham for daytime *Ferret* sorties. (One P-38, crewed by Captain Fred B. Brink Jr and Second/Lieutenant Francis Kunze, was lost on 26 October 1944 and in March 1945, when the 36th Bomb Squadron assumed all RCM tasks for the 8th Air Force, the three surviving Lightnings were relocated to Alconbury.) Although V-2 jamming proved impossible, during August, 192 Squadron had some success when it found and established the identity of an enemy radar transmission on 36.2 MHz. By means of a Fuge 16 homing loop, which was fitted to one of the Wellingtons, homing runs were made and its site on the coast of north-west Holland established.

By the end of August, 214 Squadron, which shared the twenty-four-hour watch on the V-2 rocket launchings with 192 and 223 Squadrons, had completed 305 successful operational sorties as a countermeasure squadron with the loss of only three crews. It had achieved a record of no flying accidents for six months. Oulton took on a flurry of activity. By early September, 223 Squadron was up to nearly full strength. Training was begun and two American Liberator pilots helped to check out the captains. Five Liberators were allotted for this and other training. On 19 September, Flight Lieutenant A. J. Carrington DFC carried out the first *Big Ben* patrol for 223 Squadron. The patrols were of four hours' duration and at 20,000 ft (6,100 metres) – a new experience for many Coastal Command crews. On 23 September, Wing Commander H. H. Burnell AFC arrived to take command of 223 Squadron. The new commander continued with the training programme and operated those crews judged fit for patrol duty. Later, the squadron was left solely on this task and all crews were placed on the work. It served as a useful start for squadron crews, for these four-hour patrols entailed full briefing, debriefing and careful maintenance of flight plan.

Very few of the groundcrew at Oulton had any experience of American aircraft, no perfect tool kits, and because of the urgency of provisioning, the Liberator aircraft were far from new. Yet they never lost heart and although the coast of England turned out some of its most bitter winter weather they kept on trying and did exceptional things. Ernie Frohloff, a Canadian radar mechanic in 214 Squadron at Oulton, recalls:

> Life for the groundcrews was a daily routine of getting a maximum number of aircraft serviceable for the next op. Leisure time was spent at the large, modern NAAFI in Norwich; lunches of fresh crab on the cliffside at Sheringham and Cromer, where we played golf but were warned never to try and retrieve a ball from the beach, as they were mined! After the day's work we went to our favourite pubs; the Bird in Hand opposite the main gate at Oulton; the White Hart at Marsham and the Buckinghamshire Arms adjacent to Blickling Hall, for a few quiet pints, a few games of darts, or shove-halfpenny, or just to talk. At Christmas 1944 we augmented our food parcels from home with a large goose, purchased from a local farmer and cooked by the landlady of our favourite pub in North Creake. No one instructed us in how to pluck a goose, with the result that the Radar Hut, and surrounding countryside, was white with goose feathers for weeks after!

Fellow Canadian Murray Peden recalls:

> Blickling was our home in effect. Our officers' mess was only about 100–150 yd clear of the box hedges of Blickling Hall, and our Nissen hut billets only another 200 yd further on. When we went into Aylsham, or into Norwich, or went away on leave the place to which we were always returning to lay our heads on the pillow was the billets hard by Blickling Hall. When we wanted to have a bath, we walked over to Blickling Hall and up to the top floor of the old mansion where we got a cold (make that frigid) bath. Oulton, on the other hand, was the place we returned to when we'd been airborne for a while. To go to work every morning, we left our 'homes' at Blickling and rode by bus up to the flights at Oulton. Sometimes during the morning or afternoon, if things were slack, we'd walk off the station, out past the guardroom and just across to the opposite side of the road to the Post Office there, where we would buy a cup of tea and a muffin or scone.'

Such had been the urgency to get 223 Squadron operational that crews, drawn from Coastal Command Liberator OTUs, became operational after only fifteen hours' flying training. Sergeant Don Prutton, a flight engineer, was among the first to join the special duties squadron at Oulton. 'In the early hours of 3 September 1944 myself and a party of sergeant flight engineers fresh from technical school at St Athan, arrived slightly puzzled at Norwich railway station. We gathered that 100 Group, to which the newly formed 223 Squadron belonged, was a special group; we would be on "special duties" and would be joined by "special operators".

They were not the only ones on a Norwich railway station in August 1944 who were slightly puzzled. The 32-year-old Squadron Leader John Crotch and his crew, who had

Halifax BIII V-Victory, which was flown by Squadron Leader John Crotch DFC and his crew in 192 Squadron at RAF Foulsham. (John Crotch)

flown twenty operations in Halifax BIII MZ706, V-Victor, in 76 Squadron at Holme-on-Spalding-Moor, had had enough of 'life' at the bleak Yorkshire air station. It had not taken too much urging on the part of their skipper to consider a posting to 100 Group, which he assured them, 'would be good because it was near Norwich' (Crotch had been a practising solicitor in the city since 1935). They were duly given a posting to 192 Squadron at Foulsham, which was equipped with the Halifax. When their train steamed into Norwich, Crotch went home for the night and told his crew to stay at the Bell Hotel, with instructions to meet him at the station at 1000 hours the next morning. They did. So far so good, but the Midland & Great Northern line (otherwise known as the 'Muddle and Go Nowhere' line) involved many stops and they did not get to Guestwick station near Foulsham, until 1500! John Crotch never lived it down.

My crew said, 'Hey Skip, we thought we were going to a base near Norwich!'

There were lots of boffins at Foulsham. Our job was to fly Halifax IIIs over enemy territory in the bomber stream and monitor German fighter frequencies with a bank of a dozen radar sets in the back of the aircraft. An operator would establish the frequencies and then photograph the radar displays, which were lit by anglepoise lamps. The photographs would be developed and next night the frequencies would be jammed with engine noise. It would take the Germans a week to change their frequencies. My

B Flight, 192 Squadron in front of Halifax III B-Babe *at RAF Foulsham.* (via CONAM)

boys felt it a waste of time not to carry bombs so I got six American 500-pounders, had them put in the wings, and we dropped them on occasion. On nights when there were no main force operations we flew what were called 'Foulsham Follies'. Two Halifaxes would be sent on shallow penetration over the continent, dropping *Window* (long strips of metal foil) all the way to simulate raids by 50+ aircraft. Each Halifax then dropped flares over its target to raise 150 fighters. It was reckoned that at least ten would crash on take-off or landing so it was more effective than *Intruder* operations.

On 28/29 August we flew an eight-hour four-minute round trip to Stettin in Poland. We flew over Sweden, received a few warning shots of ack-ack, and carried out ELINT support for the main force. The next day we flew five Halifaxes to Lossiemouth to take part in an ELINT operation against the *Tirpitz,* at anchor in Altenfjord in Norway. This meant a 1,500 mile [2,400], nine-hour 45-minute round trip, all of it over water. Two Halifaxes were sent

Flying Officer Clarkson and his crew in front of Halifax III B-Babe *of 192 Squadron at RAF Foulsham.* (via CONAM)

back to Foulsham with faulty radar and the three of us set out at 1900 hours that evening. One returned early with engine trouble. We flew in at 200 ft [60 metres] to avoid enemy radar. Near the Arctic Circle it is difficult to judge your height above sea level because there are no whitecaps and the water gives an 'oily' appearance because it is half frozen. We monitored the *Tirpitz* radar frequencies and found blank spots for the Lancasters to come in on.

On 15 September, Lancasters of 9 and 617 Squadrons, operating from Yagodnik airfield, Russia, attacked the *Tirpitz,* scoring one hit. The warship was finally sunk in Tromsö

Wellington X D-Donald *of 192 Squadron at RAF Foulsham.* (via CONAM)

fjord by 12,000 lb (5,400 kg) Tallboy bombs dropped by 617 Dambusters Squadron Lancasters, on 12 November 1944.

On 13 September Squadron Leader John Crotch and his crew flew one of twenty-four aircraft which stooged around Holland, escorted by Spitfires, waiting for the V-2s which were normally fired at around 1700 hours, to get the supposed frequency. Starting on 9 September, 214 Squadron Fortresses, equipped with a special modification to the *Jostle* apparatus, had also started *Big Ben* patrols. Extensive modifications were made in the Liberators belonging to 223 Squadron and the crew was reduced by one, as the front gunner was unnecessary. A large floor space in the rear bomb cell was provided for *Window* storage and the whole of the navigator's position was enlarged and improved. Additional jammers were installed and the squadron was ready to begin *Window* patrols.

Fitters cleaning Wellington X D-Donald *of 192 Squadron at RAF Foulsham.* (via CONAM)

Sergeant Don Prutton did his first operational flight in a Liberator on 2 October 1944 in B-Baker. 'We patrolled in daylight off the Dutch coast at about 20,000 ft (6,100 metres), hoping to spot a V-2 on its way up from its launching pad. We carried two special operators who were doing mysterious things with radar-jamming devices but security was so good that even the rest of the crew did not have the slightest idea of what they were up to.'

All this was in vain – the V-2 could not be jammed. In November 1944, *Big Ben* was deleted and replaced with *Carpet* and *Dina* jamming devices.

Meanwhile, with operations against the enemy reaching a climax, the Air Ministry decided to supplement the already powerful Bomber Support force by forming 171 Squadron on 7 September 1944 at North Creake within 100 Group. Initially, the squadron, commanded by Wing Commander M. W. Renaun DFC, was formed with Stirling Mk III aircraft and crews, pending the allocation of twenty Halifax IIIs. In order to get the new unit operational, one flight of 199 Squadron was posted in. No. 171 Squadron's first operation took place on 15 September, when two Stirlings took off on a

Flight Lieutenant 'Hank' Cooper DSO DFC, navigator-radar operator and Flying Officer Kelt RNZAF of 192 Squadron in front of BIV 'H' at Foulsham, Norfolk during the winter of 1944–5. This dedicated ELINT squadron within 100 Group also operated Halifaxes and, for radar and radio investigation, Mosquito NFII DZ292. All their aircraft were fitted with various receivers for the detection of German nightfighter AI frequencies over the continent, which they recorded on Bagful *and* Blonde *recording equipment.* ('Hank' Cooper Collection)

special mission, which was completed successfully. Shortly after, fourteen Halifax crews were posted in from squadrons under the operational control of 4 Group HQ but they were unable to operate as 171's Halifaxes were at St Athan undergoing installation of *Mandrel* and *Window* chute equipment (Stirlings would continue to be used until 21 November). Finally, on 21 October 171 Squadron Halifaxes took off on a *Window*ing operation. While *en route* the operation was cancelled and the aircraft recalled, but one aircraft failed to receive the signal and pressed on to the target, where it was plotted as 'a force of some thirty heavy bombers', a successful, if unintentional start for the squadron!

Meanwhile, on 5 October, Mosquito Mk IVs of 192 Squadron flew over enemy territory in an attempt to pick up FuG 200 transmissions and, the following night, checked on the density and characteristics of German AI on 90 MHz while another Mosquito crew carried out *Jostle* jamming of enemy VHF signals. On 19 October a Mosquito of 192 Squadron flew to Stuttgart to try and discover low-frequency *Würzburg* signals and on 30 October another Mosquito was dispatched to Berlin to determine if FuG 216 or FuG 217 *Neptun* could be intercepted. On 2/3 November five Mosquitoes of 192 Squadron listened in on German radio communications. On 4 December, a Mosquito flew to Karlsrühe to determine whether coastal observation units were being used on inland flak control.

During October 1944 meanwhile, daily 'intention of 100 Group operations' were sent to all groups in the main force in order to keep everyone in closer touch with each other's activities and also show just how much protection and assistance they were getting. On 7/8 October, in riposte to the enemy R/T communications used in its *Zahme Sau* operations, Lancasters of 101 Squadron, fitted with *Airborne Cigar* carried out jamming of the enemy R/T frequencies. These special Lancasters also carried a specially trained German-speaking operator. That night the order 'All butterflies go home' was broadcast on the German night-fighter frequency, resulting in many enemy night-fighter pilots returning to their airfields!

The most outstanding *Window* success of the month was perhaps on 14/15 October when 1,013 heavies went to Duisburg and 200 to Brunswick. It was anticipated that the Duisburg raid, by low approach, radar silence and shallow penetration, would get through with little trouble, but that the Brunswick force might be strongly opposed. A *Window* force was therefore routed to break off from the Brunswick route and strike at Mannheim. This succeeded beyond all expectations, for the Brunswick attack was almost ignored because the Mannheim area was anticipated as the main target. Just fourteen bombers were lost this night. Pilot Officer Morris and his crew from 223 Squadron, which completed its first *Window* patrol this night, was hit by flak and the navigator was badly wounded.

October also saw the introduction of *Dina*, the jammer used against FuG 220 Lichtenstein SN-2. *Dina* was installed in the *Jostle*-fitted Fortresses of 214 Squadron. This was frequently used in the *Window* force, as were *Jostle*, H2S and *Carpet*, thereby more effectively giving the simulation of a bombing force. A further realistic effect, also born in October, was created through the co-operation of PFF, which, on several occasions *Oboe*-marked and bombed the *Spoof* target. (The *Window* force itself had not yet arrived at the bomb-carrying stage.) The noise of *Oboe*, which had until that time always preceded real attacks only, was thought to confuse the enemy controller still

Fortress III HB774 of 214 Squadron. Note the prominent Jostle *transmission mast behind the radio room, H2S scanner nose radome and rear-mounted Airborne* Grocer *and* Dina *aerials.* (via Martin Staunton)

more, who, as the 100 Group diarist put it 'was already thinking furiously about many other forms of deceit'. It was also found in October that *Window* forces could only be increased by deductions from the *Mandrel* screen and jamming forces. It was a point to be considered very seriously, for there was every indication that the enemy was trying to see through the screen, thus making it very likely that more aircraft might shortly be needed to increase the screen effort. So, after the daylight patrols by 223 Squadron came to an end on 25 October, crews began their 'real work', which involved night operations with the rest of Bomber Command. Don Prutton recalls:

> These operations were of two distinct types. In the first, two or three of our aircraft would accompany the main bomber stream and then circle above the target; the special operators used their transmitters in particular, *Jostle* to jam the German radar defences while the Lancasters and Halifaxes unloaded their bombs. Then everyone headed for home. Our friends in 214 Squadron seemed to do more of these target operations than 223 Squadron. My own crew did a small number of these but the majority of our operations

Fortress III W-William *of 214 Squadron from RAF Oulton over the Norfolk countryside.* (via Martin Staunton)

were of the second type, the *Window Spoofs.* The object of these *Window* raids was to confuse the enemy as to the intended target. There was a radar screen created by other aircraft patrolling in a line roughly north to south over the North Sea and France. A group of us, perhaps eight aircraft, would emerge through this screen scattering *Window* to give the impression to the German radar operators that a large bomber force was heading for, say, Hamburg. Then, when the Germans were concentrating their night-fighters in that area, the real bomber force would appear through the screen and bomb a totally different target, perhaps Düsseldorf. After several nights, when the Germans had become used to regarding the first group of aircraft as a dummy raid, the drill was reversed. The genuine bombers would appear first and with luck be ignored by the German defences, who would instead concentrate on the second bunch, which was of course our *Window Spoof.* So we rang the changes, sometimes going in first, sometimes last, in an attempt to cause maximum confusion to the enemy, dissipation of his resources and reduction in our own bomber losses.

The *Window* was carried in the rear half of the bomb bay which was floored and separated from the rest of the aircraft so it was impossible to have a low light on. The rear bomb doors were fixed shut, unlike the front ones, which were still operational and were the means of getting into and out of the aircraft. The *Window* was wrapped in brown paper bundles about a foot [30 cm] long and perhaps 2 or 3 ins [5–8 cm] across. Each bundle had a string loop and the idea was that as you pushed the bundle down the specially installed chute near the floor of the compartment you held on to the string loop. This ripped the brown paper wrapper and as the slipstream drew out the bundle the contents were scattered on the night air.

It was normally a two-man job, usually the flight engineer and one of the beam gunners, and was quite hard work bearing in mind we were in bulky flying suits, helmets and oxygen masks. At the pre-flight briefing the rate of discharge was stipulated; it was to start at, say, forty bundles a minute and then as we approached our 'target' it must increase to perhaps sixty a minute! In practice we knelt or sat on the floor surrounded by the mountain of bundles and when the navigator gave the word the plane started weaving gently and we started pushing the stuff out fast. When the time came to increase the rate

Flight Sergeant Ron 'Jimmy' James helps fellow air gunner 'Taffy' Williams into the ball turret of a Fortress at Oulton. Although these turrets, which were equipped with the Sperry computing sight, were excellent for daylight sorties they were found to be unsuitable for night raids and were removed from 214 Squadron's Fortresses towards the end of 1944. (Ron James via CONAM)

we just went even faster, but whether it was correct or not we never knew.

We normally used Type 'A'. We also carried a few bundles of Type 'C' and always made sure we knew where these were because Type 'C' was for our own protection. If the anti-aircraft fire started getting too close for comfort we would sling out some Type 'C' and miraculously the flak would drop behind us. I believe our *Window* operations were reasonably successful; certainly our bomber losses were greatly reduced in the last months of the war. I think we also helped the Germans use up their aviation fuel.

Flight Lieutenant C. J. Merryfull AFRAeS (back row, centre) and other ranks of 199 Squadron at North Creake. Merryfull established the BSDU at Foulsham and during the latter months of 1944, he designed a machine to eliminate entirely manual launching of Window. *During February 1945 it was decided to form a* Window *Research Section under Merryfull's command at Swanton Morley. Squadron Leader Merryfull MBE was killed while performing aerobatics in a Mosquito, which broke up in flight over Docking on 8 July 1945.* (RAF Swanton Morley)

During the latter months of 1944, a machine to eliminate entirely the manual launching of *Window* was designed by Flight Lieutenant C. J. Merryfull AFRAeS of 199 Squadron at North Creake. During February 1945 it was decided to form a *Window* Research Section under Merryfull's command at Swanton Morley. Squadron Leader Merryfull MBE was killed while performing aerobatics in a Mosquito, which broke up in flight over Docking on 8 July 1945.

100 Group's deceptive powers were never better illustrated than when Flying Officer Jackson's crew in 214 Squadron took off from Oulton to join a *Window* force from Manston, which failed to materialize owing to a last minute recall. They continued on to the Ruhr, blissfully unaware of their isolation. They returned safely and were greeted with the news that the German defences had plotted them as a force of fifty aircraft! Jackson was lost on 6 November.

On 9 November Flying Officer Briscoe and his crew completed a *Window* and VHF *Jostle* patrol in the face of the worst weather, including snow; and a personal message of commendation on RAF Station Oulton's effort was sent from the AOC, Air Vice Marshal Addy Addison.

November 1944 produced a new and rather different use of the *Window* force. With the frequent repetition of heavy attacks on the Ruhr, the enemy adopted a policy of keeping fighters there, regardless of attempts to draw them away by Spoofs. The *Window* force was therefore used on several occasions to infest the whole Ruhr area with vast quantities of *Window* immediately prior to the arrival of the main force from behind the covering influence of the *Mandrel* screen. It was assumed that the enemy fully expected attacks on the Ruhr area, and could not be persuaded otherwise. Therefore, the *Window* force's aim, which seemed highly successful, was to confuse the enemy so that they could not distinguish the bomber track in the maze of *Window* echoes. Still the confusion was increased when once or twice this tactic was employed and there was no bomber force. Always, however, the *Mandrel* screen was present if the weather allowed, to keep the *Nachtjägdgesehwader* crews in their cockpits and the controllers at their desks, just in case the bombers were *en route*. Don Prutton cites an example of this:

> On 10/11 February 1945 there were twelve of us against the *Luftwaffe*. We had a briefing in the afternoon but weather was clamping down all over Britain and the bombing plans were later 'scrubbed'. However, two crews each from 214 and 223 Squadrons were put on standby. At 9 p.m. we had another briefing and learned that as East Anglia seemed likely to remain clear it had been decided that 100 Group should deny the German forces a night off. So just after midnight a dozen assorted aircraft from the group took off on a *Window* raid to Krefeld in the Ruhr. It was bright moonlight above the clouds; the occasional searchlight filtered through and at one stage a fighter tailed us for a few minutes but other than this we saw no enemy activity and all returned safely. In all we felt the trip was probably a waste of time, but when we landed at about 5 a.m. we were greeted by our commanding officer, Wing Commander Burnell, with the news that 'half the German air force' had been up looking for us. We later had a message from the AOC confirming that the operation had been 'an unqualified success and in every manner achieved its object'.

Meanwhile, on 14 January 1945 223 Squadron lost its first aircraft when B-24 'R' piloted by Flight Lieutenant Noseworthy RCAF was hit by an enemy fighter and crashed near Antwerp. Noseworthy and one gunner had miraculous escapes but the rest of the crew were killed. On 20 February, Flying Officer J. Thompson RCAF was shot down by a night-fighter. The third Liberator to be lost was 'T' flown by Flying Officer N. S. Ayres. The only survivor was one of the special operators, who escaped after the aircraft was hit and plunged into a pine forest. When he recovered consciousness, which as he said, 'was a shock that nearly killed him', he found the *Jostle* weighing over 600 lb (270 kg) lying on him. He later recovered from multiple injuries in an English hospital. Don Prutton recalls:

Our own losses were comparatively light. Of the six flight engineers I arrived with, four survived, but in the squadron as a whole the survival rate was probably slighter higher than this. It used to be said sometimes that we were in more danger from the unserviceability of the aircraft than from enemy action. By the late stages of the war we had become somewhat blasé. Because of the shortage of fuel, German fighter activity was severely restricted; we no longer did a detour via Gravesend, but flew straight back to base across the North Sea and our gunners unloaded their guns as soon as we crossed the Dutch coast.

During March 1945, 223 Squadron learned that it would be converting to the Flying Fortress. The changeover went on apace and on 15 April Don Prutton's pilot, Flight Lieutenant Gordon Bremness, completed the first successful operation in a Fortress.

Like 223 Squadron, 214 Squadron had its bad times as well as good at Oulton. On 16 November one of its B-17s crashed near Foulsham while landing and all the crew were killed. If a crew came down on the continent they could not always expect to reach safety. On 21/22 November a Halifax III of 192 Squadron, flown by Warrant Officer B. H. Harrison, was shot down by fighter attack during an operation to the marshalling yards at Aschaffenburg, Germany. The navigator, Sergeant Stan Wharton, recalls:

> We flew at 14,000 ft [4,300 metres] and we lost *Gee* as we crossed the Dutch coast due to German radar jamming. But I had calculated an accurate wind speed and direction at that height which took us within pinpoint precision to the target. I was twenty-five seconds early. As we did not carry bombs, we were told at the briefing to 'skirt' the target. I instructed the pilot to turn to port, did a 180° turn south-east of the target and came on to my 'return to base' course. On both sides of the track were German air flares, lighting up the return course like a main road. I instructed the pilot to increase to maximum speed, nose down, and after a few minutes in this attitude I heard the rear gunner shout: 'Fighter attacking. Corkscrew starboard skipper!' Tracer bullets passed between my feet and the two starboard engines were on fire. As there was no response from the pilot I gave the order to bale out, jettisoning the escape hatch in the forward part of the aircraft. I pressed the 'destroy' buttons for all the secret equipment and went through the hatch. In my haste, I had forgotten to unfasten my oxygen supply and found myself dangling under the crashing aircraft. I felt a boot on the top of my head which I think belonged to Sergeant Bloomfield, the bomb aimer, which snapped the oxygen connection, and I lost consciousness.

Stan Wharton and Jack C. Smith RAAF, the wireless operator, were taken prisoner. Harrison was killed in the crash. Sergeant R. B. Hales, the flight engineer, and Bloomfield, after first being apprehended by villagers, were handed over to the police. Later, the two fliers were taken under guard by a party of *Volkssturm* (Home Guard) who, *en route* to Erbach, murdered them in cold blood. Two of the perpetrators died in a car crash three weeks later, one committed suicide and four more were later given sentences of fifteen, twelve, seven and five years.

The worst case of 'retribution' when a crew fell into enemy hands occurred on the night of 14/15 March 1945 when 244 Lancasters and eleven Mosquitoes of 5 Group attacked the Wintershall synthetic oil refinery at Lützkendorf near Leipzig. Sixteen Lancasters were lost. 100 Group lost two Mosquitoes and a Fortress of 214 Squadron piloted by Flight Lieutenant Norman Rix DFC, which performed *Jostle* radio countermeasure duties in support of the main force. HB802 was shot down by a Ju 88 G-6 flown by *Hauptmann* 'Tino' Becker of *Stab IV./NJG6* and his *Funker* (Radio/Radar operator). In all Becker and Johanssen claimed nine bombers, the highest score by a German night-fighter crew in any single night. Becker shot down six Lancasters of the Lützkendorf force. After expending his last ammunition on the sixth Lancaster he positioned his Ju 88 to the side of two more Lancasters and finally HB802, which were all shot down by *Unteroffizier* Karl-Ludwig Johanssen manning the twin rear-facing machine guns. Johanssen's burst of gunfire hit the Fort's No. 2 engine and the bomber went down 5 kms SE of Baiersbronn, West of Eutingen at 2337 hrs. Johanssen's three victims counted towards the grand total of his pilot so the B-17 was Becker's 57th official victory. Johanssen was awarded the *Ritterkreuz* two days later. (Becker's score at the end of the war was 58 confirmed night victories).

Next morning crews coming down to breakfast in the mess at Oulton heard that Flight Lieutenant Johnny Wynne, the pilot of Fortress III HB799/K, had flown his aircraft home alone. Murray Peden recalls:

> It was the talk of the mess. It turned out that, like us, Johnny had a fire in an engine. It got so bad that he'd ordered the crew to bale out, and intended doing the same himself. His chute accidentally opened inside the aircraft, and left him with no choice but to try to bring his Fortress home. He had a hell of a time but Johnny made it to Bassingbourn. The tragic side of the story is what happened to his crew ....

The two Fortresses flew at around 24,000 ft (7,300 metres) while the Lancs flew towards the target at 20,000 ft (6,100 metres). For the homeward trip both were to fly at 3,000 ft (400 metres) above sea level to make it difficult for the German night-fighters to locate and attack them. However, this of course made the heavies more susceptible to flak and small-arms fire. Wynne comments, 'I had to obey orders ... I had

Flight Lieutenant Johnny Wynne DFC, who brought Fortress III HB799/K back alone from Lützkendorf near Leipzig on the night of 14/15 March 1945, in the cockpit of Take It Easy. (CONAM)

trusted that the planners had routed the force away from towns, airfields and other places which would be defended by guns. We now know that this was not the case. Of the sixteen bombers shot down on this attack on the Lützkendorf oil installations almost all were brought down by light flak between Nuremberg and the Rhine.'

Wynne's Fortress was within half an hour's flying time of the Rhine when it was hit in the No.2 engine, though he did not see a flash from the gun. 'That is why I thought that we were being attacked by a night-fighter from below. The fact that I did not see the flash means the gun was more or less vertically below us or slightly behind us. It would not have made much difference if I had seen the flash. We would still have been hit, perhaps in a fuel tank instead of the front wheel bay, which would have been bad news for us.'

He soon found that the oil pressure on the No.2 engine was falling rapidly. The propeller refused to feather and about six minutes later the engine burst into flames. Wynne and his co-pilot, Flying Officer James Vinall DFM, knew that they had only twenty minutes to fight the fire before it reached the firewall behind the engine. The fuel tank, which by now was half full, could explode at any time. Wynne flew on as the Fortress gradually lost height. By now they had flown 80 miles (130 km) with the No.2 engine on fire and they were 60 miles (95 km) from the Rhine, where the land south west of the river was occupied by the Allied armies. Unfortunately, strong winds had caused the main force to fly south and east of the planned track and the Fortress had been hit 25 miles (40 km) east of the position recorded in the navigator's log. The No.2 engine gradually disintegrated but Wynne was sure that they had by now reached the safety of French territory, though Flight Lieutenant 'Tubby' Pow, his navigator was unable to confirm their position. Wynne gave the order for his nine crew to bale out. They did so, but later, when he tried to do so the D-ring release handle on his parachute pack snagged on something and the canopy spilled out. Wynne released the harness and threw it onto the flight deck, and still clutching his maps and papers, followed as quickly as he could. He found the log and began to sing. Thirty minutes later the engine started to burn once more but after another 10 miles (16 km) the fire again died down and finally went out. He knew he had to find an airfield and make an emergency landing. He crossed the Channel at 0240 hours and amazingly reached England and sighted an airfield beacon just after reaching Beachy Head. Despite circling and firing off the colours of the day no light came on and he was forced to fly on. After a nervous fifteen minutes he saw a searchlight and he fired a red flare before circling and flashing his landing light. The searchlight gave him a heading straight over London to Bassingbourn in Cambridgeshire, an 8th Air Force B-17 base. Wynne made two circuits and received a green from the control tower to land. The landing was going to be hazardous because the No. 2 propeller had separated from the engine and was only held on by the pressure of the slipstream. Wynne skillfully went along the runway for 1,000 yd and then went down on the rim. The No.2 propeller flew off and made a hole in the nose of the aircraft. The B-17 ground to a halt, Johnny Wynne was home safe!

Wynne was sent on leave to await the return of his crew from France. He wrote to all the relatives to assure them that their sons or husbands were uninjured when they left the aircraft and that they would soon be returned. However when the logs were examined it looked as if the crew had baled out while the Fortress was over the east side of the Rhine. The strong winds at low level had completely altered the situation. Most likely they had all become PoWs so Wynne wrote again to all the relatives telling them that it was most likely that they had been captured. (This is what happened to Rix and five of his crew, who baled out after their Fortress was hit by ground fire south of Stuttgart, some 30 miles (50 km) south of the planned track, and exploded. The four other crew landed safely in a suburb of Stuttgart and drove westwards in a fire engine they found. Whenever they were confronted they simply rang the fire bell and were waved on!)

Norman Rix was lucky to survive. His parachute opened a few seconds before he crashed into the top branches of a pine tree. It is an ill wind that blows nobody to good. Rix, as PoW, saved the Bavarian village of Ettringen from destruction by the advancing US 7th Army in 1945. Having arrived at Ettringen he persuaded his guards to lay down their arms. He then took control of the village. Next day he went forward to meet an American tank patrol and informed the astonished commander that Ettringen was already in British hands. A formal handover was arranged for the following day. No shots were fired and no civilians were injured. Sadly, Rix's achievement was never recognised by the authorities but the villagers of Ettringen have not forgotten.

Sadly, there was no such happy outcome for five of the nine men who baled out of HB799. Flying Officer Tom Tate, the special operator, and Flight Sergeant Norman Bradley DFM, one of the waist gunners, landed close together and were soon captured. 'Tubby' Pow, the 2nd navigator, who was severely burned on the face and neck, landed in telegraph wires. He had also broken his ankle and he was hospitalized. The first navigator, Flying Officer Dudley Heal DFM, landed on the roof of a tall building in the centre of Buhl and was brought down by soldiers who cut a hole through the roof to get him and was made a PoW. (Heal was one of the most accomplished low-level navigators in Bomber Command. As a Sergeant navigator on 617 Squadron, he flew on the famous dam buster raid on 16/17 May 1943, for which he was awarded an immediate Distinguished Flying Medal by King George VI). Tate was put into a cell, where he was reunited with six of the crew. Vinall and Bradley were there, as were Flying Officers Harold Frost DFM, the top turret gunner, and Gordon Hall, the radio operator, Flight Lieutenant Sidney Matthews DFC the gunnery leader, and Flight Sergeant Edward Percival DFM, the other waist gunner, whose wife Maud was expecting a baby on that very day.

On 17 March the seven crewmen were taken by armed guard in a lorry to Pforzheim about 20 miles (30 km) further south, near the Black Forest. The city had been bombed three weeks before on the night of 23/24 February by over 360 Lancasters and thirteen Mosquitoes of 1, 6, and 8 Groups in the first and only area-bombing raid on the city from only 8,000 ft (2,400 metres). Some 1,825 tons of bombs dropped in just over twenty minutes killed more than 17,000 people, and 83 per cent of the town's built-up area was destroyed in 'a hurricane of fire and explosions'. Ten Lancasters were lost.

At the village of Huchenfeld the crew were put in a school basement before being hauled into the street and confronted by a lynch mob. Tate, in bare feet, managed to get away and was later apprehended by the *Wehrmacht and* taken into custody by two *Luftwaffe* soldiers who escorted him to PoW camp in Ludwigsburg. Bradley and Vinall managed to get away from their captors but Matthews, Frost, Percival and Hall were murdered in cold blood. Vinall was free for a day and then he gave himself up to some *Wehrmacht* soldiers. He was handed over to the police, who had to give him up, and he was later murdered by a civilian mob and Hitler Youth. Bradley evaded recapture and reached the village of Grunbach southwest of Pforzheim. The five men of HB799 are buried in the Dürnbach RAF Cemetery.

Hans Christian Knab, the Nazi *Kreisleiter* (District Leader) of Pforzheim was hanged in 1946 following war crimes proceedings. He had instructed the commander of the local Hitler Youth, *Sturmabteilung* or SA and the *Volkssturm* to assemble with their men in Huchenfeld in civilian clothes and had incited the crowd to murder the RAF airmen.

Wynne concludes:

> The losses on the Wintershall raid were unusually high for the period of the war. It appears that most of the losses occurred in the low-level withdrawal from Nuremberg to the Rhine. The bombers were routed at approximately 1,000–1,500 ft [300–460 metres] above the ground, without navigational aids, using a pre-briefed met wind and without route markers to keep them on track. This sort of activity is fine for a single aircraft because it arrives and disappears before ground fire is alerted. But to pass 224 bombers over a thirty-minute period, i.e. seven per minute along the same general corridor was by any standard stupid.

Between 8 February and 22 March 1945 six other 214 Squadron crews failed to return to Oulton. The captains of these crews were Pilot Officer Robertson, Flying Officers Shortle and Stewart, (all of whose crews were reported to be PoWs) and Anderson (all except two of his crew were reported safe), Flight Sergeant R. V. Kingdon and Flight Lieutenant Allies. Air gunners destroyed two Ju 88s, one in July 1944 and another in February 1945, plus two probables. Nine enemy aircraft were claimed as damaged. Towards the end of February, when the heavies in 100 Group had started carrying bombs as well as *Window,* it was obvious to the squadrons from events on the continent that a still greater air effort was going to be needed. This was made quite clear by the Air Staff branch at Bylaugh Hall, when information was received that the only stand-downs would be through adverse weather conditions that rendered operational flying impossible.

As well as the heavies in 100 Group for the last few months of the war controllers in *Fliegerkorps XII* and their plotters at their Seeburg tables also had to contend with increasing numbers of *Intruder* aircraft in the circuit over the night-fighter bases. (On 2 May 1945, a *Window* Spoof over Kiel by four Fortresses and five Liberators was the last operation of 223 Squadron as a heavy Bomber Support squadron operating with the main force of Bomber Command in Europe.) Over the German airwaves the triumphant German battle-cries of a few months previously had now given way to '*Achtung Moskito*': the 'bed of heavenly bliss' had become a bed of nails.

CHAPTER VIII

'Dutch'

Press on regardless – never mind the weather
Press on regardless – it's a piece of cake
Press on regardless – we'll all press on together
Cos you're bound to see the Dummer or the Steinhuder Lake

(To the tune of 'Poor Joey')

Pilot Officer Leslie 'Dutch' Holland had flown five hours short of a thousand when he first joined 515 Squadron on offensive operations. This late baptism of fire came nearly two years after having done about six months on home-defence night-fighters. In the period between, a year spent instructing pilots destined for night-fighters and on a refresher course at an Operational Training Unit, had nurtured a gradual build-up of confidence, capability and a certain amount of fatalism.

At Cranfield one evening in August 1944, the OTU Beaufighters were lined up on the spare runway with engines running in readiness for the night's training exercises, when a V-1 came blathering along over our aircraft. All of us fully armed and unable to do a thing about it. Unfortunately, a Czech pilot with an Australian navigator broke the rules and went down to London looking for it, only to run into balloon cables instead.

On arriving at an operational station one is naturally eager and perhaps a little anxious about the task soon to be undertaken and above all keen to makes a decent showing. But the welcome from the Commanding Officer, Wing Commander 'Cordite' Lambert made two things clear. In his own words, 'Your names on the squadron status board are in chalk and it is easy to erase. This will be done for one of two reasons. First, if you have an accident and put an aircraft out of service, in which case you will be immediately posted: second, if you allow yourself to succumb to enemy action. Either event is referred to as "wastage". See to it that neither of these occurs.'

Air operations have always been a matter of teamwork. The aircraft; the groundcrew; the flight crew. In each of these aspects I was extremely fortunate. Groundcrew – fitter and rigger – worked all hours to keep aircraft on the top line. Always cheerful, never complaining, although like so many of their unsung brethren, constantly working in the open, often in atrocious weather, at hours of the day or night intended for comfortable repose, and waiting faithfully and patiently for our return.

In 1944 515's Mosquito FB Mk VI aircraft carried no air interception radar (still referred to by us as AI) but did have *Gee* as a navigational aid, helpful for course checking on approach to the enemy coast but little use beyond that. For armament they carried the full complement of four .303 in Brownings and four 20 mm Hispano cannon. A 63 gal [286 litre] fuselage fuel tank could be removed and two 250 lb [113.4 kg] bombs or incendiaries or flares fitted instead. Wing 'stores' carriers would take a 250 lb [113.4 kg] bomb each or a 50 gal [227 litre] tank. These bare facts tell nothing of the Mossie and the Mk VI in particular in which a crew could have complete confidence under all circumstances and equally, in the Merlin engine and the DH propellers.

And the long-suffering bloke in the right hand seat, the navigator on whom one depends for more than finding the way in the dark. I was particularly lucky to have teamed up with a very down-to-earth Geordie – one Flight Sargeant Robert Young, ex of the 43rd and 52nd of Foot, the Oxfordshire and Buckinghamshire Light Infantry, transferred to the RAF for which I remain always humbly grateful. It does help to have someone as phlegmatic as Bob in the other seat when things are getting hot. 'What colour's blood?' was his only comment if he thought we might be exceeding our duty.

[The] 28th October 1944 being Bob's birthday was a very appropriate occasion for our 'Freshman operation'. This consisted of a very easy trip as far as the Zuider Zee without any hanging about. We were only airborne two hours and it was uneventful except for some useful exercise in dodging searchlights. Blacked-out Holland looked very much the same as blacked-out Norfolk. Somewhat to our surprise, next morning 'Charlie', our Flight Sergeant in charge of groundcrew, informed us that there was a bullet hole in one wing.

After this trip the squadron received a Mosquito XIX fitted with Mk X AI (SCR 720) and which Bob and I flew twice only before taking it back to Swannington, where it probably lived with 85 Squadron. We never had another Mk XIX at Little Snoring.

Up to late 1944 *Day Rangers* had been flown occasionally but usually by more than one aircraft. Wing Commander Lambert was particularly keen on these and Squadron Leader Walter Gibb, the Bristol Aircraft Company test pilot who was on 515 until shortly after I joined them, described to me a somewhat hairy run down to Brest or Bordeaux, a region in which one was bound to run into a great deal of trouble. I believe it was in the course of this effort that, legend has it, Lambert shot the wheels off a Storch because it didn't seem right to blast such a small aircraft out of the sky.

A *Day Ranger* was flown by 515 on 29 October 1944 by two aircraft when they were still without radar: Flight Lieutenant F. T. L'Amie and Flying Officer J. W. Smith, and Pilot Officer Terry A. Groves DFC and Flight Sergeant R. B. 'Doc' Dockeray DFM. Between them, they left a trail of destruction across Bavaria and on to Prague. Both crews took off at 1420 hours from St Dizier and crossed liberated territory south of Nancy at 8,000 ft

Flight Sergeant R. B. 'Doc' Dockeray DFM and Pilot Officer Terry A Groves DFC of 515 Squadron destroyed a Bf 110 in the air and damaged several Bf 109s on the ground, during a legendary Day Ranger *with Flight Lieutenant F. T. L'Amie and Flying Officer J. W. Smith on 29 October 1944 that resulted in nine aircraft shot down and five damaged.* (Tom Cushing Collection)

(2,400 metres). Allied ack-ack fired at them as they sped overhead but no lasting damage was sustained. At zero feet at Heehingen, 30 miles (50 km) south-south-west of Stuttgart, a Fw 190 was spotted to port on a reciprocal course. L'Amie and Smith did a climbing turn and came behind it. They attacked below and astern, with L'Amie giving the enemy machine a one-second burst of cannon fire from about 100 yd. The Fw 190 immediately burst into flames and disintegrated. At Ingolstadt just minutes later, a Bf 110 was seen at about 500 ft (150 metres). This time it was the turn of Terry Groves and Doc Dockeray. They got astern and fired three bursts of cannon fire from 100 yd. Pieces fell off and the Messerschmitt crashed to the ground and continued burning.

The two Mosquitoes continued on their patrol. At Straubing at 1632 hours a Ju 34 crossed from starboard to port at a height of about 1,000 ft (300 metres). The pilot spotted the Mosquitoes and took evasive action but L'Amie and Smith got into position and made a starboard quarter attack from 50 yd range. L'Amie gave the Junkers a one-second burst of cannon and it exploded in flames. Then the starboard wing blew off and the rest of the transport aircraft disintegrated. L'Amie and Smith flew through the burning oil and petrol, which severely scorched the fuselage and rudder surfaces of the Mosquito. Flying debris from the Ju 34 punched a small hole in the tail plane but it remained airworthy and L'Amie and Smith were ready for more. Just over a quarter of an hour later, they attacked a Bf 109 taking off from a grass airfield in the Beroun area. It stopped and swerved to port and although a number of strikes were seen all around the enemy aircraft they could not confirm its destruction.

About a dozen Bf109s were seen parked on the grass airfield and both Mosquito crews went in to attack. Altogether, four strafing runs were made on the field and they left nine aircraft burning fiercely with three damaged. A hangar was set alight by the fires and burst into flames. L'Amie and Smith claimed three Bf 109s destroyed and two damaged. Terry Groves and Doc Dockeray also claimed three Bf 109s destroyed and two damaged. There was no opposition, save for a lone machine-gunner who put a hole in Groves's starboard engine cowling. Groves and Dockeray landed at Juvincourt at 1905 hours and L'Amie and Smith put down at Amiens/Glisy thirty minutes later, both crews well satisfied with their work. L'Amie and Smith were killed on 21 November 1944.

Dutch Holland and Bob Young's first 'op in earnest' was to Kitzingen which, says Holland,

> ... lies about 25 miles [40 km] south of Schweinfurt, and between Würzburg and Nuremberg. That makes it nearly 500 miles (800 km) from base. *Intruder* sorties were flown at low altitude, generally around 2,000 ft [610 metres] above ground, and a straight course was not usually held for more than about half a minute at a time as no area could be regarded as entirely 'safe'. A more-or-less continuous weave about the required course was adopted so as not to let the opposition have it all their own way. I never was especially good at flying straight courses.
>
> All navigation after crossing the coast was by contact flying, or if the ground was obscured, by dead reckoning. Contact flying means simply map reading and endeavouring to anticipate prominent ground features. It is an art, which improves with experience, but I had been fortunate in having been on a two-week course in 1942 at No. 2 School of Air Navigation at Cranage, which specialized in low-level pilot navigation. It taught how to look ahead for the next line features; how to assess, reasonably correctly, the size of area features like woods and lakes and built-up areas and how to work out course corrections in one's head. That was in daylight. At low level at night it's a different story but that course provided an invaluable grounding.
>
> On the run to Kitzingen, a half moon gave us good sightings of rivers, canals, lakes and railway lines. As a result, we arrived on target within two minutes of scheduled time. An hour's patrol was normal, calculated to cover either the approach of the main force to their target or return. Sometimes a follow-up patrol was laid on, but it was not usual. The object was to cause as much disruption as possible to German night-fighter operations. As this was a fairly deep penetration requiring the fuselage fuel tank, no bombs were carried but the 20 mm guns could be used whenever there were signs of activity on the airfield. Intelligence sources led us to believe that Me 163 rocket-propelled fighters were based at this airfield but we saw no sign of them. A mild strafe of the airfield produced only a half-hearted reaction from ground defences and there was no evidence of any air activity.
>
> It was also a part of the briefing for all *Intruders* to attack transport of all kinds. However, this was not entirely a one-sided activity. Many trains carried light flak batteries, which made it foolhardy to make the simpler

Armourers, 20 mm belts around their necks at the request of the cameraman, attend to a Mosquito Intruder *at Little Snoring. Both 23 and 515 Squadrons flew day and night* intruder *operations in 1944–5 from the airfield, where, over 500 years earlier, longbowmen practised their archery skills in firing butts nearby.* (Tom Cushing Collection)

lengthways attack. It is very much easier to aim the length of a train and much more difficult to get elevation and range in a crossing attack, even in daylight. In addition, night trains were more likely to be carrying some very explosive loads. All fuel for V-2 rockets was taken to launch sites by rail. Activity of this type occurred on most sorties and only occasionally got a mention in our logbooks if really positive results were observed.

While on patrol at an airfield, light flak was usually encountered, and at some airfields various devices were kept in readiness for the protection of aircraft landing or taking off. These included flak screens on the final approach path which probably accounted for several *Intruders* who went missing. We were repeatedly reminded at briefing to be wary of following an aircraft into the runway threshold and to refrain from continuing an attack below 200 ft [60 metres]. But at such times the eyes are not on the altimeter but at the gunsight and it is easy to misjudge height, especially on a dark night with ground details not too clear. Discretion gets elbowed aside.

A five-hour flight without much activity on the patrol and two hours each way out and back tends to get a bit tedious strapped to the seat the whole time. But the need to stay alert and keep a look out does not cease until the wheels are firmly on the ground. Some months later the aircraft were fitted with *Monica,* a rearward looking radar which was intended to indicate the presence of an aircraft behind, but it gave so many false alarms that it became a normal practice to try a couple of turns to see if the pursuer followed exactly. If it did, it was pretty safe to assume that it was a spurious 'ghost'. There will always be the one occasion when the cry 'wolf' is not to be ignored. There were also rumours of balloons on lengths of wire and I am bound to say that some of the 'ghosts' behaved very much as if they were just that.

There followed several sorties of a similar nature to patrol night-fighter airfields; Marx and Varel, near Wilhelmshaven; Vechta and Quakenbrück, north of Osnabrück and near the Dummer Lake; Hanau; Lippstadt: Erfurt and one to Schwabisch Hall. This last was a departure from the norm in that we had a partner, our great buddies Bunny Adams and Frank Widdicombe. As this was after the aircraft had been equipped with radar of very limited capability, we spent most of the patrol time intercepting and identifying each other – a dreadful waste of time. I do not remember that this rather frustrating pairing was repeated.

The Dummer Lake was one of a pair in north-west Germany which were easily identified landmarks. In impromptu sessions round the piano in the mess 'Press on Regardless – Never Mind the Weather' a little ditty commemorating the fact was a regular favourite. Among other things we saw in our comings and goings there were of course several sightings of flying bombs. Although the jet flame could be seen from a long way off in clear conditions it was extremely difficult to assess the actual distance. On more than one occasion we witnessed the launch of a V-1 in the middle of the North Sea but a bit of simple trig will show that apart from failing to make our own target on time, it would be an impossibility to make an interception of an object travelling on its own vector at around 400 mph [650 kph].

I did go down to Lowestoft one evening and while I was waiting for my date who was on duty at the Fire Brigade HQ, went up to the clifftop at Sparrow's Nest to see if there was any 'trade'. There was a layer of cloud at about 2,000 ft [610 metres] but otherwise clear and dark. Sure enough a small gaggle of them could be heard throbbing their way westwards and two flickering orange flames increased in brightness. [The] 40 mm guns opened up but only when they were less than ½ mile [800 metres] out. Suddenly, a great orange ball bathed the sea in glare and two seconds after, an almighty 'BLAM' and blast wave was shortly followed by a repeat performance. But there was still the same fluttering drone above the clouds. An unseen battery of 'heavies' suddenly blasted off and a further explosion lit the clouds from above. When my ears had recovered they could detect one solitary 'bug' droning it's way inland.

One sortie brought us back on a course to pass north-westwards, well clear to the east of Antwerp. This was at the time when it was the principal supply port for the Allied armies. We picked up a V-1 and set off after it but it was too low for us to range it in the ground returns on the ASH. However, it ought to be possible to tell if one was within about 400 yd, or so one would think. A handy patch of moonlight suddenly revealed that we were going along a heavily wooded valley at treetop height. This was not the spot to generate a cataclysmic explosion even if one could be sure of doing so and it was deemed prudent to delay the attack until circumstances were more propitious. Further progress in our stalk was made inadvisable by the rise of a wall of tracer ahead. We had crossed it clear into the Antwerp Diver defences and our only option was a very steep turn out of it. All Diver defences were ordered to shoot at everything but everything – flying below a certain height unless specifically ordered (for which on a later occasion I had reason to be thankful).

At Little Snoring at this time, morale wasn't good – it was excellent. And one of the chief reasons was that the Station Commander was none other than the redoubtable 'Sammy' B. R. O'Bryen Hoare, with multiple DSOs and DFCs. A legend in his own time, he had done heaven knows how many *Intruder* sorties both day and night from as early as 1941, during which he had left a trail of wrecked German aircraft on airfields in Germany and occupied territories. Most if not all of this was achieved with only one eye and without radar. After we had a small anti-surface-vessel radar (AN/APS4) fitted to our aircraft, my own being out of service for an inspection, he did me the great honour of letting me have his personal aircraft with the comment, 'You will find that my aircraft does not have radar: I don't need it!' Needless to say, I was also requested not to bend it.

By late 1944 many of the veterans of earlier years were less directly in contact with operations. Sammy Hoare was still flying occasional sorties and showed no signs of losing any enthusiasm. Briefings were sometimes a bit daunting when particularly 'dicey' jobs were on but Sammy's attitude of courtly chivalry never waned. Stroking his immensely long moustache (you could see both ends at once from behind), he would conclude with, 'Let us sally forth and do battle with the Hun', or, on one memorable occasion, a quote which should be engraved in stone: 'Gentlemen, there will be flak; almost certainly quite heavy flak. If you cannot go over, you will go under. If you cannot go under, you will go through!'

Sadly, this reference to a very gallant character has to end with the recollection that after surviving the war he went missing on a flight in a Mosquito.

Squadron Leader Ginger Farrell, whom I had previously known for a brief spell on 85 Squadron, was our Flight Commander. On a unit like 515 naturally one could not be nursed along by the flight commander during the actual operation as one was on day fighters but he could and did in his own very pleasant fashion give us all the tips we needed and the feeling that he was 'with us'. Life at the squadron dispersal was somewhat informal. A good-natured camaraderie served in place of subservience to rank without prejudice to respect for commanders or obedience to orders. After our somewhat late arrival in the mornings, the first thing to interest us was the schedule of crews for the night's operations. If you were 'You're ON' the day would then be occupied with going over the aircraft with the groundcrew, perusing intelligence reports and aerial photographs of enemy airfields, and conscientious air testing of the aircraft which was done before every sortie.

Air tests, always referred to as night-flying tests or NFT, consisted of a full cheek of systems and engine performance as far as could be done in about thirty minutes and without going much above 2,000 ft [610 metres], our normal operating height. Being near the sea gave us the chance to test the guns and a ship stranded on Brancaster sands provided an excellent target for practice. Naturally it was too large an object for precise aiming, so we concentrated on trying to be the one to fell the funnel. It was like a cheese-grater before it finally went. Other units used the same target and there was no control as on target ranges so that a very sharp lookout was required and this added to the value of this exercise. Other aircraft firing at the ship were not too hard to spot but on one occasion a Swordfish appeared to be trying to convey a message by frantically waggling its wings. The intent of this gesture became clear when a fountain of smoke and sand erupted alongside the hull. Clearly, RAF and RN were not on the same frequency.

It will be appreciated that night-fighter crews put in a lot of effort to keep up to scratch in aircraft recognition. Many hours were spent in a very specialized approach to this art. In a totally dark room, a special projector threw a silhouette on to a screen. It showed accurately the shapes of all types of aircraft which we were likely to encounter, friend or foe, from all angles, but mostly different aspects from astern, including the exhaust glow. The silhouettes were only just visible against a dark background but with progressive reduction of the exposure, it proved to be possible to get correct identification in as little as a fifth of a second.

Before November was out we took part in a couple of Spoof raids on Bonn and Wiesbaden. The object was to come out through the front of a screen of *Window,* representing a major raid and to drop a couple of 250 lb [113 kg] bombs to give the impression that an actual raid was developing. The defences took it very seriously and made good but not perfect practice on the one blip showing clearly on their radar. Heavy (large bore) flak was not something we frequently encountered but on these occasions saw plenty and actually encountered it too. The Mosquito VI of course, had no bombsight, and bomb aiming entailed no more than letting go once the target had disappeared under the nose regardless of altitude or attitude, but we did attempt to aim at pinpoints such as junctions in a railway siding or airfield buildings. Both Bob and I had experienced too much on the receiving end of haphazard bombing from the *Luftwaffe* to be particularly worried where our bombs went but also believed that they could be more usefully employed on targets of some tactical or strategic significance rather than on the populace at large. Probably because we did our usual best not to present too easy a target, our aircraft suffered no damage despite almost continuous illumination by radar-controlled searchlights. These would suddenly and very accurately swat the aircraft with a blinding blue light, whereupon several lesser minions would latch on and follow any frantic effort to evade until out of range. Fortunately, I had heeded the injunction never to look at the lights but keep eyes glued to the instruments.

At this stage in the proceedings, the aircraft of 515 Squadron began to be equipped with the AN/APS4 radar (ASH). This was a small torpedo-shaped installation more often seen on Fleet Air Arm Fireflies. Originally intended for searching for surface vessels and reading coastlines, it had the tiniest plan position indicator (PPI) of all airborne radars, measuring about 3 ins by $1^{1}/_{2}$ ins [7.5 by 3.8 cm], and was proportionally efficient for air interception. During the re-equipping some practice in its use was carried out on Ansons with the 'bomb' slung under the nose. After a week or two of this, and almost before we had digested our Christmas dinner a very different sort of task awaited us for which the newly fitted ASH was of very little consequence.

At the end of December German troops were being moved from Norway, presumably to reinforce the Ardennes front. Consequently, it was required that mines be laid in the intervening waters, especially in Oslo Fjord. This task was to be performed by Lancasters and 515 was to do its best to divert the attention of local anti-aircraft defences. The briefing was extremely exact. First, the timing had to be spot on otherwise the defences would either be alerted too early – this meant not more than one minute before the arrival of the mine-layers – and secondly, attention must be directed to those batteries whose exact position, calibre and number was described in considerable detail. The underground intelligence service must have been very active.

So we set out on the two-and-a-half-hour flog across the North Sea, taking a final fix and wind check with *Gee* about 100 miles (160 km) out. After that it was necessary to start losing height, flying the last 100 miles [160 km] at about 50 feet [15 metres] in fair visibility but only a little starlight. Using the new wind and corrected course from the Gee fix, it was dead reckoning the rest of the way, aiming to avoid the radar on the Danish coast. How much it was luck would be hard to say but, all credit to Bob, we arrived within our time slot and, helped by the enticing lights of a Swedish coastal town (should be able to make that on one engine), were able to identify Moss, about 20 miles [30 km] south of Oslo opposite Jelo [Jeloy] Island. Our ASH would have been no use for coast reading at that height and would only have betrayed our presence. The channel between the mainland and this island was one of those to be mined.

A few dimly discerned features were enough to tell us roughly where the supposed batteries were situated and we had only just taken up a position about half a mile inland when a stream of tracer curved seaward nicely pinpointing for us the exact location. From about 500 ft [150 metres], a shallow dive brought the sights nicely to bear on its source and a burst of 20 mm must have caused some consternation. A tight turn brought us round for another attack across their line of fire. Part of the battery had picked us up and returned fire. By this time flak and air-to-ground fire was lacing the fjord in all directions, particularly on the opposite side of the fjord, and the operation was evidently in full swing.

The brief had been to draw fire away from the minelayers so the next attack was made from the landward side. The annoyance of the gunners became apparent when all their guns opened up in our direction. It was like driving into snow with headlights on. There appeared to be several 20 mm and possibly 40 mm, judging from the different colours and rounds per burst. By this time the party seemed to be over so we were happy to break off and not continue the confrontation. As it was we used all our 400 rounds. The fireworks over the water transpired later to have been largely due to the late arrival of a cruiser, which fact caused Flight Lieutenant Lawrence, who was dealing with that particular patch, to remark when he was informed in debriefing afterwards that there did seem to be a bit more reaction than he had been led to expect. Then it was straight down on to the water and set a course for home. Fortunately, no searchlights followed us but reaction from fighters remained a distinct possibility at the start of the long sea crossing. Setting the radio altimeter to 20 ft [6 metres] made the indicator lights flash continually red, amber, green, amber, red, due to the wave height, and it proved easier to judge height visually by what could be seen of the wave tops.

After about half an hour we came up a bit to ease the strain. The constant drone of the engines and the visible swish, swish, swish of the sea below become hypnotic after a while and the mind drifts off into hallucinations which turn the instruments into jazz pianists with big white teeth and suchlike. Worse, one starts to nod. Bob stirs uneasily in his harness when bank begins to exceed 30° and I do my best to pretend I am doing a little turn as a normal precaution. Neither of us refers to the lost fifty ft [15 metres]. It is with a warm feeling of relief that we touch down and taxi in with our minds firmly fixed on the prospect of one fried egg, one rather small rasher of streaky bacon and a few greasy chips. Then to flop out on a three-biscuit mattress with damp sheets and blankets which smell like they have been on a horse all day.

CHAPTER IX

Fluctuating Fortunes

Tighter and tighter turned the fighter
Till he blacked out Pilot Officer Paine,
Then he gave max boost and revs
And turned just half as tight again

During November 1944 there was not one single *Serrate* contact during the month's operations on any one of the three *Serrate* Mosquito squadrons – 141, 169 and 239. The situation had been getting worse since the summer of 1944. Although 141 Squadron had successfully destroyed three enemy aircraft in air-to-air combat on *Serrate* operations in October, these were all through AI contacts and not *Serrate.* It was a poor month for all three squadrons, with only five enemy aircraft being destroyed, three by 141 and two by 239 Squadron. The former had only one *Serrate* contact all month and 169 and 239 had only four between them.

For the reasons, one must go back to May 1944. In the early months of 1944 the *Nachtjägd* had begun to bring into service the new FuG 220 Lichtenstein SN-2 AI radar which was not affected by *Window* and the *Serrate* homer fitted to the Mosquitoes was calibrated to the frequencies of the old Lichtenstein AI sets. For some time, *Serrate* crews had noticed on operations that the enemy night-fighters quickly took evasive action when picked up on AI radar. By May, the majority of German night-fighters had been fitted with SN-2 sets, which rendered the *Serrate* sets practically useless and the *Nachtjägd* had also introduced backward-looking warning devices. During June and July 1944, the number of *Serrate* contacts obtained during operations had noticeably started to tail off. All *Serrate* Mosquito crews could do was rely on their old Mk IV AI radar for interceptions. These were few and far between. The few *Serrate* contacts that were made were almost all found to radiate from ground stations. In July, only one in ten sorties on average reported a contact – in May it had been one per sortie, and in the early part of the year each sortie was reporting a large number of contacts.

When the frequency band of the SN-2 was discovered in June, work was at once started to develop a homer, later called *Serrate* Mk IV. An aural presentation was decided upon with dots and dashes, similar to the *Lorenz* beam system. Considerable trouble was experienced due to the interference caused by *Freyas* on the same frequency band, but eventually a satisfactory filter was devised. (*Serrate* Mk IV was not used operationally until January 1945.) The development of another homing device, *Perfectos,* was started in June 1944. It was known that the *Egon* system was one of the main methods the enemy used for controlling his fighters. In this system, the *Freyas* interrogated an IFF (Fuge 25A) in the fighter, and so were able to direction find and range on them. There was no reason why the bomber support fighters should not do the same as the ground stations, and *Perfectos* was to interrogate the enemy IFF and then direction finding and ranging on the return signal. *Perfectos* would clearly have one advantage over the *Serrate* type of homing since ranging would be given. However, it was not found possible to provide the *Perfectos* equipment with the elevation planning. (The first *Perfectos* operations would not be carried out until November.) One further homing device, *Benito,* was under development for a considerable time but was never used operationally. It was intended that this equipment should allow homing on to the 38–42 MHz transmissions from the enemy fighters when they were being controlled from the ground under the *Benito* system. However, it was never found possible to devise an aerial system which could be carried satisfactorily on a Mosquito and eventually, the project was dropped.

Meanwhile, another German prize fell into the RAF's lap when *Obergefreiter* John Maeckle landed his Ju 88G-1 night-fighter 4R+UR of *III/NJG2* at RAF Woodbridge on 13 July. The crew had taken off from their base at Twenthe at 2305 and had become lost in thick cloud, which had a ceiling of about 14,000 ft (4,500 metres). For forty-five minutes, the *Bordfunker* tried to establish radio contact but without success. After four hours in the air and very low on fuel, Maeckle told his crew they might have to bail out. However, the flight engineer informed him that he had not packed his parachute. Maeckle decided to get the Ju 88 down. He wrote:

> Fuel gauges showing empty and descending at 6 ft [1.8 metres] per second, we broke through the clouds at 600 ft [180 metres] and miraculously discovered we were coming down right on top of an airfield. I did not waste any time landing the aircraft. When I saw the big white flashing light on the control tower and all the four-engined airplanes, I had no doubts where we were. After we touched down, the plane rolled to a complete stop in the middle of the runway with both engines dead. While bright spotlights aimed at our plane, we sat there for twenty minutes or longer before we were finally approached by an armoured vehicle and thus had plenty of time to burn classified material and demolish valuable instruments. We were happy to be alive and well, especially the flight engineer.

Gerhard Heilig, a special operator with 214 Squadron from March to July 1944, heard a different story. He recalls:

> The Ju 88 did not get lost but was misled by our own people. On one of my leaves I had lunch with my father at a Czech émigré's club in Bayswater. Amongst the group of his friends there was a WAAF sergeant and I made polite conversation with her. To my opening questions she replied that her work was so secret that she could not even tell me where she was stationed. However, before many minutes had passed, I knew that her job was my own counterpart on the ground with 100 Group. When I started to grin, she told me indignantly that it was nothing to laugh about, it was all terribly important but she was mollified when I told her that I was in the same racket. She then told me the following story.
>
> Receiver operators passed *Luftwaffe* radio traffic to a controller who then issued co-ordinated false instructions to transmitter operators designed to

cause confusion to the enemy. One night there was nothing happening whatsoever. Then the controller was roused from his torpor by repeated calls for a homing, which evidently remained unanswered. Mainly in order to relieve the utter boredom of a routine watch he decided to give the lost sheep a course to steer – to Manston airfield in Kent. The German pilot had been faced with the prospect of having to abandon his aircraft and was going to buy everyone concerned a beer on his return to base. He came down safely – to find himself a prisoner and could hardly be expected to keep his promise to stand drinks all round. The aircraft was a Ju 88 stuffed with the latest German equipment, quite a catch for Intelligence. The capture of this aircraft was made public at the time, but not how it had all come about.

Scientists from TRE investigated the Ju 88's FuG 220 Lichtenstein SN-2, FuG 227/1 and FuG 350 Z Naxos radars, the last two types being previously unknown to the RAF. They confirmed *Serrate's* ineffectiveness and discovered that the Nachtjägd was using the FuG 227/1 equipment to home on to the *Monica* tail-mounted warning device, and the FuG 350 Z Naxos to home on to H2S radar bombsight transmissions. RAF bombers were ordered immediately to restrict the use of H2S while *Monica* sets were removed from the Lancasters and Halifaxes. *Window* was modified to jam the new Lichtenstein radar.

In June almost all the contacts obtained over enemy territory had been by the Mosquitoes' AI radar with its limited range. This was due to the success of beacon patrols. It became clear in June that the enemy was making more and more use of his assembly beacons in France. The area of these beacons proved to be the most profitable type of patrolling for the *Serrate* squadrons. Many of the Mosquitoes' successes at the beacons were obtained before the enemy fighters had attempted to intercept the bombers.

On 28/29 June Pilot Officer Harry 'Shorty' Reed and Flying Officer Stuart Watts of 169 Squadron picked up an AI contact two minutes after their arrival at Beacon Mücke. Reed turned hard to starboard in an attempt to get behind the enemy aircraft. After losing the contact twice through fading and interference, it was eventually picked up again at a range of 15,000 ft (4,600 metres) dead ahead and just below, after two hard orbits and some weaving. Harry Reed closed to about 5,000 ft (1,500 metres) after some difficulty due to unreliable elevation signals. The Mosquito's height was now 12,000 ft (3,650 metres). A visual was obtained at 3,000 ft (900 metres) and the enemy aircraft continued weaving. Harry Reed called 'Bogey bogey wiggle wings' but there was no reply. It had to be an enemy aircraft. Then it fired off four star red cartridges. Range was reduced to about 150 ft (45 metres) when the enemy aircraft was recognized as a Bf 110 with external wing tanks. Harry Reed fired two two-second bursts and the Bf 110 exploded. The Mosquito's AI and *Serrate* failed immediately after the guns were fired. The Bf 110 was seen to go down in flames until it entered cloud at 4,000 ft (1,200 metres). A bright flash followed on the ground. With their radar now unserviceable. Harry Reed and Stuart Watts turned for home.

June seemed to offer much for the *Serrate* squadrons. For instance, 239 Squadron reported 89.7 per cent of sorties completed (compared with only 62.5 per cent in January) and registered eleven victories. But 141 and 169 had shared only eight evenly between them. July was the same. Both 141 and 169 notched six victories, while 239 Squadron racked up seven, without any operational losses.

On 4/5 July Squadron Leader N. A. Reeves DSO DFC and Pilot Officer A. A. O'Leary of 239 Squadron destroyed a Bf 110 north-west of Paris, and Flight Lieutenant J. D.

Flight Sergeant C. G. A. Drew (left) and Flight Lieutenant A. B. A. Smith being debriefed by Flight Lieutenant C. H. F. 'Buster' Reynolds, the Intelligence Officer, at West Raynham following a Night Intruder sortie. (Tom Cushing Collection)

Peterkin and Flying Officer R. Murphy of 141 Squadron bagged an Me 410 near Orleans. Flight Lieutenant J. S. Fifield and Flying Officer F. Staziker of 169 Squadron added a Bf 110 at Villeneuve. Near Paris on 5/6 July, Reeves and O'Leary destroyed a Bf 110, and Flying Officer P. G. Bailey and Pilot Officer J. O. Murphy of 169 Squadron destroyed a Ju 88. Four of 239 Squadron's seven victories in July came on the night of 7/8 July. An Fw 190 was destroyed by Wing Commander P. M. J. Evans and Flight Lieutenant Tommy Carpenter in the Pas de Calais and Flight Lieutenant Viv Bridges DFC and Flight Sergeant D. G. 'Spider' Webb DFM shot down a Bf 110 near Charleroi. Their Mosquito went into a violent spin, which tore the rear hatch off and damaged the wing tip and elevator. Bridges feathered the starboard propeller and the door was jettisoned. They landed at Woodbridge safely. Two Bf 110s were destroyed at Paris by Squadron Leader Jackson Booth DFC* and Flying Officer K. Dear DFC. Booth celebrated his double victory by performing a slow roll over West Raynham's No. 4 hangar at 0100 hours. He explained later that he did not think his action was at all dangerous as he had practised several times on the way back. His moustache grew at least an inch longer overnight and he blushed modestly as he introduced himself to newcomers by saying, 'Just call me ace!'

Comparison of *Serrate* with AI contacts May-September 1944

	May	June	July	Aug	Sept
Average No. of *Serrate* contacts per sortie completed	1.1	0.2	0.1	0.02	0.005
Average No. of AI contacts (without initial *Serrate*) per sortie completed		0.3	0.5	0.8	0.5	0.3
AI contacts per successful combat		9	9	10	16	60

No. 141 Squadron salvaged some pride on 7/8 July when Squadron Leader Graham J. Rice and Flying Officer Jimmie G. Rogerson destroyed a Bf 110 north-west of Amiens.

A famous night for 169 Squadron, now established at Great Massingham, occurred on 20/21 July with the destruction of '100 Group's 100th Hun'. Harry Reed and Stuart Watts got a Ju 88 in the Hamburg area while Wing Commander Neil B. R. Bromley OBE DFC the Commanding Officer and Philip Truscott destroyed Bf 110G-4 Wrk Nr 730218 G9+EZ of *XII/NJG1,* which crashed near Moll in Belgium. *OberFeldwebel* Karl-Heinz Scherfling, the 25-year-old pilot, who was a *Ritterkreuzträger* since 8 April 1922 and who had thirty-three night victories, was killed. So too was *Feldwebel* Herbert Winkler, the thirty-one year old air gunner. *Feldwebel* Herbert Scholz, the twenty-five year old radar operator, baled out seriously injured. The squadron was presented with a coveted silver tankard inscribed 'To the hungry Hun hunters of 169 Squadron', a reference to the squadron's motto 'Hunt and Destroy' on its proud crest, which was designed by Squadron Leader Joe Cooper. The former 4th Hussars' trooper cleverly featured a hunting horn, signifying the intruder role, against a midnight-blue hurt, representing the night.

On the night of 23/24 July Bf 110G-4 Wrk Nr 730036 G9+ER of *VII/NJG1,* was shot down by Flight Lieutenant R. J. Dix and Flying Officer A. J. Salmon of 169 Squadron at very low level around midnight. It crashed near Balk in Friesland Province in Holland. *Feldwebel* Heinrich Karl Lahmann, the 25-year-old pilot, and *Unteroffizier* Günther Bouda, the 21-year old *bordschütze,* both baled out. *Unteroffizier* Willi Huxsohl, the 21-year-old radar operator, was killed. This same night two other *NJG1* night-fighters were lost. At 0125 hours Bf 110G-4 Wrk Nr 730117 G9+GR of *VII/NJG1* was shot down north of Deelen airfield. *Leutnant* Josef Hettlich, pilot, *Feldwebel* Johann Treiber, radar operator and the *bordschütze* all baled out safely. (Flying Officers N. Veale and R. O. Comyn of 239 Squadron claimed a Bf 110 that night.) The third Bf 110 lost was Wrk Nr 441083 G9+GR of *III/NJG1* or *VII/NJG1,* which was shot down at 0147 hours during landing at Leeuwarden airfield

Flying Officer Viv Bridges DFC and Flight Sergeant Don 'Spider' Webb DFM of 239 Squadron who on 10/11 May 1944 destroyed Bf 110 Wk. Nr 740179 3C+F1 of I/NJG4 piloted by Oberleutnant *Heinrich Schulenberg near Ellezelles, Belgium. Two nights later they shot down Ju 88C-6 Wk Nr 750922 of V/NJG3, flown by* Unteroffizier *Josef Polzer at Hoogcruts near Maastricht. On 31 May/1 June Bridges and Webb scored their third kill (a Bf 110) followed on 7/8 July by another Bf 110 near Charleroi for their fourth, and last, victory of the war.* (Don Webb Collection)

and which crashed at Rijperkerk, just to the north of the base. *Hauptmann* Siegfried Jandrey, the 30-year-old pilot, and *Unteroffizier* Johann Stahl, twenty-five, the radar operator, were killed. *Unteroffizier* Anton Herger, twenty-four, *bordschütze,* was injured.

Pilot Officers Doug Gregory and D. H. Stephens of 141 Squadron returned from their patrol triumphant. The intelligence officer at West Raynham compiled their report during debriefing.

> Mosquito took off from West Raynham 2310 hours and set course for patrol area crossing enemy coast at 2350 hours. Proceeded to Chameleon and then to Willi, arriving at 0025 hours. Shortly after leaving Willi on the way to Biene, at 15,000 ft [4,600 metres], AI contact obtained on aircraft crossing starboard to port way below at maximum range. We turned in behind it and lost height. E/A was doing mild evasive action and half orbits. Chase continued for ten minutes with A/C closing range giving fleeting visuals at 600 ft [180 metres]. Closed further to 300 ft [90 metres] and E/A was identified as a Ju 88. We were now at 9–10,000 ft [2,750–3,000 metres]. On identification panic set in and we desperately tried to get the sights on. Meanwhile, greater panic took hold of the 88 type who promptly peeled off and visual and contact was lost, although we also peeled off.
>
> Taking a psychological view of the situation we orbited for ten minutes, hoping he would return; sure enough he did and came in head-on well below. We opened up everything and got on to his tail. He was going very fast still weaving and it took us ten minutes to close range and get another visual when we again identified contact as a Ju 88. Due to slightly faulty elevation he appeared much more above than was expected.
>
> Pilot said, 'He's miles above.'
>
> Navigator said, 'Gee, have a go,' whereupon we stood on our tail and at a range of approximately 60 yd, let fly with a one-second burst which exploded E/A's port engine. We continued upwards in a starboard climbing turn and watched the 88 spiral down in flames and, after going through cloud blew up on the ground with great gusto and much flame. He was still burning on the ground when we left ten minutes later. Patrol completed we returned to base through the usual channels. Claim one Ju 88 destroyed.

Gregory fired forty-eight rounds to down the Ju 88, which crashed south-west of Beauvais.

On 28/29 July parity with 239 Squadron was almost restored when 141 destroyed three aircraft in one night. None other than Flight Lieutenants Harry E. White DFC* and Michael S. Allen DFC* emulated Booth's and Dear's feat, getting two Ju 88s in the Metz-Neufchateau area. In the same area, Pilot Officers Doug Gregory and D. H. Stephens destroyed their second Ju 88 of the month, as Gregory recalled.

> We took off from West Raynham at 2315 hours, set course for enemy coast, crossing in at Overflakee at 16,000 ft [4,900 metres] at 2357 hours. Route uneventful until leaving Ida on way to Christa. At 0031 hours at 16,000 ft [4,900 metres] we got an AI contact slightly port and below crossing port to

starboard. We turned in behind him and went down. A/C then led us on a vector of 210°M. we closed and after an eight-minute chase obtained visual. Closing still further we got into various positions and finally when about 200 ft [60 metres] directly below, identified A/C as a Ju 88. He was flying quite straight at 14,000 ft [4,300 metres] without a clue.

We pulled up to his level and at approximately 100 yd and let fly with a one-and-a-half-second burst. Our shells apparently found their mark for his port engine immediately gave up the ghost and burst into flames, and smoking pieces came back at us. We broke off to port and watched him burning satisfactorily and going down. He entered cloud at 8,000 ft [2,400 metres] and after a few seconds he lit up the cloud as he exploded on the ground. Time was now 0045 hours and his grave may be found 16 miles [25 km] NW of Metz. We then set course for base via Overflakee, crossing out at 0140 hours. Here endeth the second lesson.

Ju 88G-1 Wrk Nr 713649 R4+KT of *IX/NJG2* was shot down over France. It was flown by *Hauptmann* August Speckmann, pilot, with *OberFeldwebel* Wilhelm Berg, flight engineer and *Unteroffizier* Otto Brüggenkamp, *bordschütze* who were all killed and *OberFeldwebel* Arthur Boos, radar operator who was wounded. It was probably one of the Ju 88s destroyed by Gregory and Stephens and Harry White DFC* and Mike Allen DFC* of 141 Squadron.

When 239 Squadron was told, at the end of July, that it was to be called upon for greater efforts in order to offset a shortage of trained crews and a lack of serviceable aircraft in the two sister squadrons, the general opinion was that nothing better could happen. At the beginning of August, however, German-originated radar, which had begun to bother crews in June, became rapidly more troublesome, and in the next four months the maximum detection range of 10,000 ft (3,000 metres) became a rarity. Even the most experienced and successful crews returned from sortie after sortie with reports of jamming so intense that, as one navigator remarked, it was flooding the tubes and spilling over the cockpit.

100 Group Mosquito victories were on the wane, largely owing to successful German counter-measures to the *Serrate* homing device used in the Bomber Support units. In August, 331 *Serrate*/AI Mk IV sorties yielded just eight successful combats. No. 141 Squadron claimed just one, while 239 Squadron, which completed 93 per cent of all sorties it dispatched, destroyed three but lost two crews, one killed in landing, the other disappearing without trace on a non-operational night flight. No. 169 Squadron destroyed four. Tim Woodman and Patrick Kemmis destroyed an Fw 190 near Abbeville on 9/10 August when the heavies attacked V-l sites in the Pas de Calais.

On 26/27 August Warrant Officer Les Turner and Flight Sergeant Frank Francis destroyed a Ju 88 near Bremen to add to the Bf 109 they had shot down on 14/15 July. Turner reported:

Took off from Great Massingham at 2235 hours in Mosquito T, setting course immediately over base, crossing English and enemy coasts on ETA. Nothing of note occurred until we reached a position at 2345 hours at 20,000 ft [6,100 metres] where considerable searchlight activity was observed to port. It was apparent there were obviously aircraft of some sort concerned as we decided to investigate and forthwith 'mucked-in' with a Hun searchlight co-op exercise. Occasional fleeting AI contacts were obtained, all showing hard above and from this, the position of the cone and the firing of apparent colours of the day, it was assumed that there were some aircraft, possibly single-engined, at about 25,000 ft [7,600 metres], which made chances of interception very slim with a Mosquito VI. Having ourselves been coned on two occasions, and discretion being obviously the better part of valour, we proceeded to leave that area and attempt to reach our scheduled patrol area.

At 0030, nothing further having been seen, we turned on a reciprocal westerly course, and after about twenty minutes' flying obtained at 20,000 ft [6,100 metres] a forward AI contact at maximum range. Target appeared to be crossing port to starboard on estimated course of 030°. We chased for approximately five minutes, reducing height to 14,000 ft [4,300 metres] where target was held in dead ahead position at 1,000 ft [300 metres] range. A visual was obtained and range reduced to 500 ft [150 metres] where aircraft was positively identified as a Ju 88. We allowed target to pull away to 1,000 ft [300 metres] range when we opened fire, the port engine immediately bursting into flames. Target turned gently starboard into a diving turn, leaving a long spiral of grey smoke. We followed, firing intermittently, observing strikes all over the fuselage. A tremendous flash was seen as aircraft hit the ground. A westerly course was set for base, which was reached at 0225 hours without further incident.

Turner and Francis's victim, which was brought down by 480 rounds of cannon fire, was Ju 88G-1 Wrk Nr 710542 D5+BR of *VII/NJG3*, flown by *Leutnant* Achim Woeste. He and *Unteroffizier* Anton Albrecht were killed. *Unteroffizier* Heinz Thippe and *Gefreiter* Karl Walkenberger, who were both wounded in the action, baled out. The aircraft crashed near Mulsum, 26 miles (42 km) east of Bremen. Turner adds, 'The large number of cannon rounds used was, in the main, due I fear to a feeling of extreme anger at the time. Just before take-off I had read the press reports of the discovery of the extermination ovens at Lübeck and I was so incensed that I was determined that any *Nazi* within range was not going to aid that war effort.'

The two other 169 Squadron victories in August went to Flying Officers Andy Miller DFC and Freddie Bone DFC. Their Bf 109 over Dijon on 10/11 August was their tenth victory of the war. Their eleventh, scored the following night, was not confirmed until after the war, for Andy Miller and Freddie Bone failed to return from a patrol near Heligoland. Miller recalls:

> Freddie picked up a contact crossing slightly at quite a lick. We eventually caught up with it. Vertically above it I identified it as an He 219. I dropped back to about 150 yd and gave it four two-second bursts. We were hit by debris and lost coolant in both our engines. I glided in over the coast of Holland and Freddie bailed out at 1,200 ft [365 metres] and I followed, at 800–900 ft [240–275 metres].

Freddie Bone was captured early next morning and later sent to *Stalag Luft III*. Andy Miller evaded capture. For four weeks he was sent along the Dutch Underground, then the network was betrayed. He was among evaders captured at Antwerp and handed over to the *Gestapo*. At *Dulag Luft* the pilot of the He 219 he had shot down in August confronted him! He was not too pleased and his arm was in a sling. Andy Miller was sent to *Stalag Luft I*. Freddie Bone DFC* returned to the police force after the war and was promptly put back on the beat!

In September three Mosquitoes were lost. On 6/7 September Neil Bromley and Philip Truscott were killed by flak near Oldenburg during a night bomber support operation for Mosquitoes bombing Hamburg. (Wing Commander I. A. Heath assumed command of the squadron on Bromley's death.) No. 239 Squadron lost Bill Breithaupt DFC and Flying Officer J. A. Kennedy DFM DFC on 12/13 September. Their grave was found on 15 January 1947, when it was determined from witnesses that they had been shot down by a Bf 110, but had in turn brought this down before their Mosquito crashed. It was their fifth victory. The German crew had baled out safely and they had confirmed the story. Flying Officer W. Osborne and Flight Sergeant Acheson were also lost. Despite 93 per cent of all sorties being completed, 239 Squadron had nothing to show. In fact, the 240 sorties flown during the month by the *Serrate* squadrons bore little fruit – on the 7th, Flight Lieutenants Paul Mellows and S. L. 'Dickie' Drew of 169 Squadron had damaged a Ju 88 15 miles (24 km) south of Wilhelmshaven – and produced only one successful combat. On 11/12 September Flight Lieutenant Peter Bates and Pilot Officer William Cadman of 141 Squadron destroyed a Bf 110 south of Mannheim. Despite these successes there were obvious signs that the German defences were countering the Mosquitoes' *Serrate* homer. On 26 September, Squadron Leader Tim Woodman, who had taken over 'B' Flight in 169 Squadron from Joe Cooper, found that there were 'plenty of Huns airborne' during a sortie near Frankfurt but found that his radar was completely jammed.

Group obviously took notice of the changing fortunes, for that month the *Serrate* squadrons began more practice (more hours of practice flying were actually recorded than on operations in August) and low flying in anticipation of a new role that was to be found for them. In September, the three *Serrate* squadrons joined 85 and 157 Squadrons which had returned to the fold at the end of August following their anti-Diver patrols at West Malling, on low-level strafing and *Intruder* attacks over enemy territory. No. 85 Squadron, which had destroyed thirty-three V-1s, and 157 Squadron's Mosquitoes retained the modifications they had received for anti-Diver operations except the stub exhausts, which were replaced with shroud exhausts. Both Mk X Squadrons were also used on high-level patrols and the results for both kinds of operation were very encouraging. From 167 Mk X high-level patrols, forty-seven suspicious AI contacts were reported, leading to twelve successful combats. Ben Benson and Brandy Brandon, who had destroyed six V-1s, opened the scoring for 157 Squadron since returning to Swannington by destroying two Ju 188s at Zeeland on 11/12 September. A Bf 110 was knocked down on 12/13 September by Squadron Leader Robert Daniel 'Dolly' Doleman and Flight Lieutenant D. C. 'Bunny' Bunch, and Flight Lieutenant Vincent and Flying Officer Money destroyed an Me 410 *Hornisse* on 29/30 September. In 85 Squadron Branse Burbridge and Bill Skelton destroyed a Ju 188 on 11/12 September, the first squadron victory since returning to Swannington.

Another six enemy aircraft were destroyed by 85 Squadron by the time the month was out. These included two Bf 110s, which fell to the guns of Flying Officers Alan J. 'Ginger' Owen (whose brother Don was killed early in 1944 while flying as a navigator on the squadron) and S. Victor McAllister DFM on 17/18 September. Their victims – both of which crashed east of Arnhem, Holland – were Bf 110 G-4 Wrk Nr. 740358 G9+MY of *XI/NJG1* (*Unteroffiziers* Walter Sjuts, Herbert Schmidt and Ernst Fischer were killed) and Bf 110G-4 Wrk Nr. 740757 G9+GZ of *XII/NJG1* (*Unteroffiziers* Heinz Gesse and Josef Kaschub and *Obergefreiter* Josef Limberg were killed). A Ju 188 was destroyed by Flight Lieutenant Micky Phillips and Flight Lieutenant Derek Smith on 28/29 September. (Phillips and Smith failed to return on 6/7 November after a British bomber fired on them, setting one engine ablaze, and were then shot down by an He 219. Phillips and Smith baled out. Captured, they spent the remainder of the war in *Stalag Luft I.*

Besides patrols in the target areas after bombing and around the assembly beacon, escorting the stream was tried with the Mk X-equipped Mosquitoes of 85 and 157 Squadrons flying at 10–15 miles (16–24 km) from the mean track. A number of contacts were also obtained on the rearward-looking *Monica* equipment carried by the AI Mk X high-level *Intruders*. It was found that these contacts could generally be evaded fairly easily but that it was often difficult to convert them to forward AI Mk X contacts – only about a quarter of the *Monica* contacts reported were converted. Thus it appeared that the main value of *Monica* was the prevention of surprise attack from the rear rather than as an additional interception aid. The Mosquitoes of 85 and 157 Squadrons did not, in general find much activity at the airfields to which they were sent. They did, however, achieve three successful combats from thirteen AI contacts.

A few weeks earlier, 141 Squadron had at last begun receiving Mosquito Mk VIs. No. 169 Squadron had had them since June, and 239 had received just one on 31 December 1943. The Mk VI was standard *Intruder* equipment in 100 Group and 2nd TAF. Meanwhile, a modified *Serrate* Mk IV was being tested and flown operationally by the BSDU. There was also increased German jamming and interference of the old Mk IV AI sets and although frequencies were changed from 193 MHz to 188 MHz, it was not a success and introduced complications in interrogating IFF and beacons.

On 2 September Wing Commander Winnie Winn had held an aircrew conference at West Raynham, giving a lecture on the operational aspect of low flying. Another was given two days later, although the first victory of the month for 141 Squadron was the result of an AI contact on a *Serrate* patrol on 11/12 September when Bomber Command visited Darmstadt. A head-on AI contact was obtained by Flight Lieutenant Peter A. Bates and Pilot Officer William G. Cadman 10 miles (16 km) north-west of Frankfurt at 2350 hours at 18,000 ft (5,500 metres). Both aircraft went into a dogfight lasting some twenty minutes with neither aircraft getting anywhere. *Canary* was tried without result but eventually the contact made off to the north-west. A chase lasting five minutes ensued but the contact eluded them.

Bates and Cadman returned to the target area, and as the bombing had ended, decided to fly slowly westward in the hope of deceiving enemy fighters that it was a straggling bomber. Twenty miles (30 km) west of Darmstadt, a backward AI contact was picked up 12,000 ft (3,650 metres) behind crossing starboard to port. Bates turned and followed. For almost twenty minutes the Mosquito tailed the enemy machine through twists and turns towards Darmstadt. Eventually, Bates closed to 900 ft (275 metres) range and a visual was obtained on two exhausts. Bates and Cadman dropped back but the visual was lost. Closing again a pale bluish-white light was seen underneath the dim silhouette of an aircraft. At that moment, the enemy aircraft opened up from the upper gun position and tracer hit the Mosquito's starboard drop tank. Bates pulled up, visual was regained on the exhausts and he gave the enemy aircraft a burst of two-to-three seconds of cannon fire from 600 ft (180 metres) range. The enemy's starboard engine exploded and Bates had to pull up to avoid a collision as it passed underneath. It was then that they could see in the light of the explosion that it was a Bf 110. Cadman watched the contact going down on his AI set before the Bf 110 hit the ground and exploded. Five other victories that month can be attributed to Mosquitoes of 85 Squadron. During the month, *Intruder* and escort operations for the four-engined bombers in 100 Group were the order of the day, or rather the night.

Bob Symon of 85 Squadron recalls:

> The 12th of September 1944 was a frustrating night's work. I found two sitting duck targets, a Ju 88 and an Me 110. For the first one the gun-sight suddenly flared up and wrecked Michael's (Miller) night vision. We fired some rounds waving our nose around hopefully but saw no strikes. The second sitting duck was equally fortunate – gunsight dead. The 15th of September the trip to Kiel was short on targets for us but we found that we were an excellent target for them. I have never felt so embarrassingly naked as I did on top of that searchlight cone. Like taking over from Eros in Piccadilly Circus on boat-race night with all the car headlights trained on me. I was thankful that Michael had done two tours in Wellingtons and was quite at home taking evasive action. This was my first experience of this treatment: at one moment one is being pushed through the bottom of the aircraft and the next one is picking up pencils, bits of paper, a bar of chocolate and whatever is floating around in the cockpit. To give the Germans their due I confess that they were pretty good with their heavy metal. When one can hear the shell explode over the engine noise it must be pretty close.

On 13/14 September Flight Lieutenant Bill House and Flight Sergeant Robert Denison MacKinnon of No. 85 Squadron patrolled Germany looking for a ninth victim to add to the tally. No. 85 Squadron had been short of navigators when MacKinnon had been posted to the squadron straight from training and he had never been to night flying training school. In fact he had never been in an aircraft that had occasion to fire any guns. MacKinnon recalls: 'I guided Bill onto an Me 110 near Koblenz and managed to get behind it without the crew being aware of us. Bill opened fire and I thought it was us who were being attacked. The noise, to me, was terrifying but to the enemy it must have been terrible. The whole plane just blew up in front of our eyes.'

Their victim was Bf 110G-4 Wrk Nr 440384 G9+EN of *V/NJG1* piloted by *Oberleutnant* Gottfried Hanneck. Hanneck was a very experienced pilot who served with various *Luftwaffe* units flying forty different aircraft types for five years before he joined *V/NJG1* at Deelen in April 1944. On his fourth operational sortie, on the night of 11 May 1944 he shot down his first RAF night bomber and went on to claim another five *4-Mots* (four-engined bombers). He recalls:

After the successful invasion by the Allied armies in the summer of 1944, the second *Gruppe* of *NJG1* was posted from Deelen to Düsseldorf airfield at the end of August 1944. The big problem of our night-fighter controllers at this time was the loss of the radar stations in France and along the coast of the canal. Thus, the preparations by the RAF for incursions over the *Reich* could not be established in time and effective countermeasures could not be prepared anymore. Instead, our leadership, suspecting an RAF raid, had to scramble a number of night-fighter crews and keep them in the air in case a raid developed.

Thus on 13 September 1944 me and my crew of *Unteroffiziers* Erich Sacher, radar/radio op and Willi Wurschitz, who on this mission served as air gunner but normally was a radar operator, were ordered to take off and fly to a radio beacon in the Frankfurt area and await further developments. We took off at 2234 in our Me 110 G9+EN. Once we had arrived at the radio beacon, we flew around in wide circles and listened to the messages from our controllers on the radio frequency relating the developments in the air.

Then my radar operator reported a blip on his SN-2 radar set – he could not quite determine it but gave me courses to steer to the target. The target flew in a westerly direction at a distance of about 6,000 metres [19,500 ft]. It could be a homebound enemy aircraft. I followed it and tried to reduce the distance by increasing my airspeed. The blip on the radar screen, however, did not become clearer, and since we had been chasing it for about twenty minutes and by now had probably arrived over the front line, we had to turn around and return to the radio beacon.

At this very instant we were fired upon and I saw many hits striking the wings of my aircraft. The control column was shaking, a clear indication that the controls were heavily damaged, and I ordered my crew to 'prepare to bale out'. At this time, the intercom was still functioning and my crew was not injured. After I told my crew to prepare to bale out, we received another burst of gunfire and the 110 immediately caught fire in both wings and the pressure on my control column was completely gone. The aircraft was plunging down out of control! There was only one option left to save our lives: the parachute. I counted for four or five seconds to give my crew the opportunity to 'hit the silk', and then I opened the roof of my cockpit and jumped out through the ball of fire. Again, I counted for several seconds before I pulled the chord of my parachute, for fear of colliding with my crashing plane. The canopy unfolded and I floated down towards the dark earth. In order to be able to estimate my height, I fired off a Very light towards the ground. It fell into a meadow, and I swung to and fro three or four more times before I hit the ground. I glanced at my watch and saw it was 2335 hours. I had come down east of Pruem in the Eifel. I had suffered second- and third-degree burns to my head and hands, and stayed in cover at the edge of a small wood for the remaining hours of darkness, as I did not want to walk into the arms of enemy soldiers. At the break of dawn I sneaked to the east and soon I ran into German soldiers.

My crew had been killed in the crash. In this way, an RAF long-range night-fighter 'avenged' my six night-kills of four-engined bombers.

The 110 crashed at Birresborn in the Eifel at 2335 hours.

On 16/17 September, Bomber Command's operations were in support of the Allied airborne landings at Arnhem and Nijmegen in Holland. Six Mosquitoes of 239 Squadron supported attacks on German airfields in Holland and Germany during the night and 141 took part at dawn on the 17th. Winnie Winn and five other Mosquito crews carried out a low-level attack on Steenwijk, one of three airfields bombed during the night. Four Mosquitoes were damaged by flak. Winn damaged a twin-engined Junkers on the ground, and buildings and personnel were strafed. Trains were attacked on the way home. *XI/NJG1* lost Bf 110 G-4 Wrk Nr 740358 G9+MY when it was shot down east of Arnhem by Ginger Owen and Flying Officer McAllister DFM of 85 Squadron. Walter Sjuts and *Unteroffiziers* Herbert Schmidt and Ernst Fischer were killed. The same RAF crew also shot down Bf 110G-4 Wrk Nr 740757 G9+GZ of *XII/NJG1* in the same area. *Unteroffiziers* Heinz Gesse and Josef Kaschub and *Obergefreiter* Josef Limberg were killed.

Six more Mosquitoes from 239 Squadron kept up the momentum, with support raids on the airfields again the following night. At last light on 18 September, two Mosquitoes of 141 Squadron flew protective patrols for nine Fortresses of 214 and 223 Squadrons supplying a *Mandrel* screen off the Dutch coast, and the action was repeated again at first light on the 19th. The Fortresses were covered by two 141 Squadron Mosquitoes again at last light on the 22nd. By the end of September, the score for the two *Serrate* squadrons at West Raynham stood at thirty-eight destroyed by 239 Squadron and twenty-five by 141 Squadron. Despite the problems with *Serrate,* these sorties still predominated, 141 Squadron, for instance, flying sixty-two *Serrate* sorties on eleven nights and fourteen *Intruder* sorties.

Bob Symon of 85 Squadron recalls:

> On 27 September 1944 we did an *Intruder* patrol to Ober-Olm. Nothing seen. Very thundery. This was my last flight with Michael and his last too. He has done two tours in Wellingtons, and I think that this was his third tour with night-fighters. He was sent to see the MO after we came back from this flight and was sent to hospital for examination. They found he had diabetes. When one considers the work he has done since the beginning of the war it is a wonder he lasted that long. Captain Svein Heglund of the Norwegian air force came to the squadron at the beginning of October. He had no nav/rad waiting for him and I was asked to show him around until his nav/rad turned up. After a couple of flights we got on so well that I went to the CO and asked him to let me have him permanently.
>
> We flew our first op on 14 October, a bomber support run to Brunswick. We had one chase but it was one of ours. We did four more ops in October, all of them different. The first was hunting for Heinkels, which launched flying bombs from over the North Sea. This involved flying at less than 500 ft [150 metres] on a bumpy windy night. We never found anything, but I was mightily impressed by the way Svein handled the Mossie. The next one was supporting our minelayers in the Kattegat. We had one chase but it was, again, one of our own. The next was a low-level ranger patrol to Vechta/Diepholz, which we didn't reach as the radar set gave up and died. It was a bright night so we stayed low and kept our eyes open for a likely target on the ground. At one point we were shot at by light flak, which

seemed to cover the ground for miles around. Tracer was coming from all sides and I wondered how we were going to get out of this mess. My unflappable Norwegian put our nose down and all was peace. I said, 'Thank God we are clear of that horrible place.'

'Not yet,' said Svein, 'but at this height if they shoot at us they will shoot each other.' At this point my breathing got back to normal and the adrenalin took over. Hedge-hopping by moonlight! We had a pot shot at a train and missed, I think we had more luck with a car, we hoped it was full of Gestapo agents. As we turned away a pair of cooling towers faced us: no room to climb over, so go between. Svein had to bank a bit to get through. This brought us to a small town. I looked up at the church clock as we passed – it was just after 10 p.m. I did some research with the map and decided that we had passed over Meppen. I don't think I want to do that ever again. The final op on the 31st was a bomber support run to Frankfurt.

October saw a great decrease in the effectiveness of the enemy opposition to the night bombers. This was a combined result of the Allied advance and the technical and tactical countermeasures employed. The enemy warning and inland plotting systems were thrown into confusion and the low-level and high-level *Intruder* played no small part by causing the enemy to plot hostile aircraft over very wide areas as well as forcing them to broadcast frequent warnings of the presence of hostile aircraft to their own fighters. In fact, 100 Group fighters made a very important contribution to Bomber Support. The fighters also took part in the *Window* feints flying with them to add to the effect of deception and then fanning out to take advantage of enemy reaction.

In October the *Serrate* squadrons led the rest of the field, with six enemy aircraft destroyed to the Mk X Mosquito squadrons' five. No. 141 Squadron shot down three enemy aircraft, although it was accomplished using AI and not *Serrate.* No. 239 also scored three. No. 169 Squadron, which damaged three enemy aircraft that month, was already having nine of its *Serrate* homers replaced by *Perfectos,* a homer which gave a bearing on the enemy night-fighter's IFF set and had a range of 40 miles (65 km). Stopgap arrangements were made to fit some of 141 Squadron's Mosquitoes with ASH, a centimetric radar originally developed in the USA as an ASV (air-to-surface-vessel) radar for US Navy aircraft and the Fleet Air Arm. ASH was a wing-mounted radar but as it could not be fitted to the Mosquito wing it was installed in a 'thimble' radome in the nose.

The first of the victories by 141 Squadron occurred on 6/7 October when Flight Lieutenant A. C. Gallacher DFC and Pilot Officer G. McLean DFC destroyed a Ju 88 during a *Serrate* patrol to Dortmund and Bremen. Their victim was Ju 88G-1 Wrk Nr 710639 D5+EV of *X/NJG3,* which crashed near Groningen. *Oberleutnant* Walter Briegleb, pilot, *Unteroffizier*s Brandt, flight engineer and Bräunlich, air gunner were wounded. *Feldwebel* Paul Kowalewski, radar operator, was killed.

The following night, 7/8 October, Flight Lieutenant Jimmy Mathews and Warrant Officer Alan 'Penny' Penrose of 157 Squadron picked up a contact at 6 miles range west of Neumünster while on a high-level support sortie. Mathews narrowed the range and as they got a visual at 1,000 yd the target straightened out. It was recognized as an Me 410 with long-range tanks. Mathews opened fire with a short burst from 100 yd dead behind.

Strikes were seen and a small explosion occurred in the starboard engine. Another burst and the starboard engine caught fire. It dived to the ground burning and exploded.

Flight Lieutenants Paul Mellows and S. L. 'Dickie' Drew of 169 Squadron on a support patrol to Egmond returned with a claim for a Ju 88 damaged. Mellows wrote:

> Mosquito arrived in patrol area at 2005 hours, flying at 15,000 ft [4,600 metres]. Two beacons flashing 'QC' and 'CT' respectively were observed near two airfields 15 miles [24 km] to the North so Mosquito proceeded to the area to investigate. At 2022 hours an AI contact was obtained hard port at maximum range, our height being 14,000 ft [4,300 metres]. Mosquito closed to 7,000 ft [2,100 metres] when target commenced hard turns to port through a number of orbits. Enemy aircraft then straightened out and climbed at low IAS and Mosquito closed to 100 ft [30 metres] to identify enemy aircraft as Ju 88 vertically above height 18,500 ft [5,600 metres]. In climbing at 140 IAS to attack, Mosquito dropped back and opened fire at 500 ft [150 metres]. Time 2037 hours. Strikes being observed between the starboard engine and fuselage. Enemy aircraft immediately peeled off to port and visual was lost, but contact was held at 10,000 ft [3,000 metres] range and Mosquito closed again losing height to 14,000 ft [4,300 metres] and obtained another visual while in hard starboard turn, at 500 ft [150 metres] on enemy aircraft which was losing height and turning starboard. However visual could not be held and no further AI contact was obtained on enemy aircraft, which was inside minimum range. Mosquito continued to patrol the area, where three aerodromes were now lit, until 2120 hours at heights ranging between 7,000 and 15,000 ft [2,100–4,600 metres], numerous sisters were seen to be fired mostly well below but no further contacts were obtained. Course was then set for base. Rounds fired: 140. No Stoppages. Claim, one Ju 88 damaged Cat.III (B).

AI contacts made by 100 Group Mosquitoes September 1944–April 1945								
	Sept	**Oct**	**Nov**	**Dec**	**Jan**	**Feb**	**Mar**	**Apr**
Average No. of AI contacts per sortie	0.28	0.24	0.38	0.34	0.25	0.18	0.18	0.11
Average No. of AI contacts per successful combat	3.9	5.6	3.5	2.4	3.1	4.6	5.2	5.3

On 19/20 October, when 853 bombers raided Stuttgart and Nuremberg, 141 and 239 Squadrons dispatched a total of twenty-six Mosquitoes. Warrant Officer Falconer and Flight Sergeant Armour of 239 Squadron shot down an enemy aircraft and two Ju 88s fell to the guns of 141 Squadron. A Ju 88 claimed by Pilot Officer J. C. Barton and Flight Sergeant R. A. Kinnear as 'damaged', which they attacked on three separate occasions 10–15 miles (16–24 km) north of Nuremberg, was confirmed as a victory upon their return to West Raynham by Squadron Leader Goodrich, whose inspection revealed the

Squadron Leader 'Dolly' Doleman and his dog 'Towser' with Jimmy Mathews' dog 'Shadow'. (via Richard Doleman)

leading edge of the Mosquito's starboard spinner and starboard mainplane were extensively covered in oil from their victim, while several indentations in the aircraft were found to be caused by flying debris.

The second Ju 88 was destroyed by Flight Lieutenant G. D. 'Charlie' Bates and Flying Officer D. W. Field approximately 10 miles (16 km) south-east of Karlsruhe after a ten-minute chase. Charlie Bates gave the Ju 88 a two-second burst of cannon fire from 300 ft (95 metres) dead astern. After what seemed like hours, the enemy aircraft's starboard engine burst into flames and the Ju 88 pulled up in a hard starboard turn. Bates turned hard port and came in to deliver a second attack. However, the Junkers was by now well alight and after firing red and white Very lights, went into a steep dive into cloud. Two seconds later, two explosions of great force were seen below, the second one lighting up the whole cloud. The Ju 88 split into three pieces, which were picked up on AI, scattering themselves into the night. their victim was possibly Ju 88G-1 Wrk Nr. 712312 2Z+EB of *I/NJG6*, which crashed at Vaihirgen/Marksdorf east-north-east of Pforzheim, Germany. *Oberleutnant* Wilhelm Engel, the pilot was wounded; the radar operator safe.

Four aircraft were destroyed by 85 Squadron and 157 Squadron scored one victory, a Bf 110, which fell to the guns of Flight Lieutenant Jimmy Mathews on 7/8 October. On 14/15 October and 19/20 October, Branse Burbridge and Bill Skelton destroyed a Ju 88 on each night and on the latter Squadron Leader Dolly Doleman and Bunny Bunch DFC shot down a Ju 88 and claimed a Ju 88 'damaged'. Doleman wrote in his report:

> We were airborne Swannington at 1924 hours on high-level support patrol to Nuremberg. Patrol was uneventful from 2056 hours to 2102 hours when a contact was obtained head-on, same height, at 4 miles [6 km] range at Beacon Fritz. Turned round on to a target at approximately the same height. Closing in with visuals at 2,000 ft [610 metres] when we went through searchlight cone. Target pooped off some colours, about six stars, mixed green and white,

Flight Lieutenant 'Bunny' Bunch (right) Squadron Leader Doleman's navigator. (Theo Boiten via Richard Doleman)

illuminating us. Searchlights doused. Target on course of 310, which seemed very 'phoney', so closed to 400 ft [120 metres] and identified as a Ju 88. Dropped back to about 800 ft [240 metres] and in spite of having a screened sight, when I put spot on him he disappeared. Had a squirt and missed. Target continued straight and level. Repeated process with strikes all along fuselage from dead astern. Target just seemed to drop straight down and went into 10/10ths cloud at 8,000 ft [2,400 metres], contact disappearing from C scope on –15 with extreme speed. Fanned around, then did a reciprocal at about 11,000–12,000 ft [3,350–3,650 metres]. Contact obtained port, turning port at 4 miles [6 km]. Closed at full boost and revs and identified another Ju 88 with night glasses at 14,000 ft [4,300 metres], about 600 ft [180 metres] range. Had a squirt with no results, and target peeled off port down to 10,000 ft [3,000 metres]. Followed on AI and closed into 800 ft [240 metres] on target, climbing port. It levelled off again at 14,000 ft [4,300 metres], so had another squirt. Target again peeled off to port to 10,000 ft [3,000 metres], and again contact held. Climbed and closed to about 800 ft [240 metres] at 12,000 ft [3,650 metres], squirted once more with mass of strikes on port wing root, and thereabouts. Target slowed down very quickly and in spite of throttling right back overshot to starboard, as he dived to port. Inaccurate *trace* came from dorsal position. Much profanity as we thought he had got away, but when he was below at about 7,000 ft [2,100 metres] range on *Monica*, he caught fire, and went down burning though not fully alight, in a 45° dive, the flames spreading quite nicely until he hit the deck, somewhere near a steady searchlight. No more joy, so set course for base at 2200 hours.

Flight Lieutenant Bunch was 'wizard' on the infernal machine, never making a mistake. I should like to add that the night glasses are really invaluable, being an incurable optimist I had them slung round my neck before starting the patrol – in any case that is about the only place vacant in the flying power-house.

Doleman and Bunch's possible victim was Ju 88G-1 Wrk Nr 714510 2Z+CM of *IV/NJG6* which crashed at Murrhard SE of Heilbronn, Germany. *Unteroffiziers* Georg Haberer (pilot) and Ernst Dressel (radar op) were killed.

The other victory was on 15/16 October when Flight Lieutenant C. K. Nowell and Warrant Officer Randall of 85 Squadron bagged a Bf 110. A number of Day and Night *Intruder* operations were carried out by the *Serrate* Mosquitoes during the month. On 17 October, Tim Woodman flew a daylight *Intruder* sortie to north-east Germany. He recalls:

> Squadron Leader Mike O'Brien DFC, a pilot from 23 Squadron, came as my observer and Pilot Officer Pierre Dils DFC (Belgian) as my No. 2. Fifty miles [80 km] off the Danish coast Dils saw two men in a dinghy. They did not wave and looked like 'krauts'. I sent him back to call up and radio their position. The Germans were informed as they were too far out for our rescue services. We pressed on alone, crossing into the Baltic without any trouble. Flew past German airfield at Eggebec, which looked deserted. Low-level flak with tracer had me doing ducks and drakes at 50 ft (15 metres) to avoid it. Crossed into the main coast at Barth. What I thought was a forest fire lookout platform in the conifers proved to be a sentry post at Barth *Stalag Luft*. [Flight Lieutenant Patrick 'Paddy' Barthropp was shot down over France on 17 May 1942.] Barthropp was a prisoner there and a test pilot with me at Boscombe Down after the war. He said I had flown right over the camp at midday.
>
> Some 50 miles [80 km] inland I shot up a long train of tanker wagons (empty) plus the loco. On the way out I shot up the Heinkel factory at Barth. No aircraft on the airfield or in the air. Was able to put some cannon shells into a converted M/Y, which had shot at me on the way in. Crossing Schleswig-Holstein there was a small passenger train entering a small station. I shot up the engine. Passengers got out and started to run across a field. I dived down on them as they stared terror-struck at me. 'Don't shoot,' Paddy O'Brien said. 'They're nice people up here.' I had no intention of doing so, only giving them something to tell their grandchildren about. Machine-gun bullets in our starboard engine when we got back. Probably from a sentry on one of those platforms at Barth.

Warrant Officer Turner and Flight Sergeant Francis of 169 Squadron meanwhile, had been piling up their ops and on 22/23 October they flew their thirty-second trip, a *Serrate* patrol to Denmark. It was to prove a rather frustrating patrol, as Les Turner confirmed in his combat report:

> We took off from Great Massingham at 1744 hours in Mosquito Y, reaching patrol area at 1915 hours, without event. At 1920 hours whilst on course west of Nissun Fjord height 15,000 ft [4,600 metres], contact was obtained at maximum range showing hard starboard and below. Pursuit action was immediately taken and for the next five minutes we indulged in tight turns eventually reducing range to 2,000 ft [610 metres] where a visual was obtained of an aircraft believed to be a Ju 88 standing on its port wing, also tight turning. The enemy aircraft must have seen Mosquito and peeled off, whereat we lost some range. Contact was held and after a further three minutes of hectic dog-fighting range was once again closed to 2,000 ft [610 metres], where aircraft was identified as a Ju 88 travelling at about 150 mph

[240 kph]. We throttled back and put down full flap opening fire at about 400 yd observing large strike on port wing-root. Enemy aircraft peeled off starboard and an ineffective burst was fired leaving Mosquito in an awkward position at about 145 mph [230 kph] – full flap and being curiously knocked about by slipstream from the Ju 88. We followed down on AI to about 4,000 ft [1,250 metres] height, where contact was lost in ground returns.

We patrolled off the coast for another thirty minutes with no further joy. Course was set for home at 2005 hours and reached without further event at 2120 hours. Rounds fired: 160 of cannon, including one one-second burst by accident during chase. Camera exposed. Weather: moonlight, clear, some scattered low cloud. Claimed one Ju.88 damaged (Cat.B.)

He thought they could only claim a 'damaged' although Turner was convinced this aircraft crashed subsequently as there was a fire on the ground some ten minutes after the attack. He adds:

I am fairly certain that the R/T listening group known as the 'Y-Service' monitored the German R/T and confirmed this combat. For security, there was no mention of this on the paper. I am also fairly certain that this aircraft crashed subsequently. There was fire on the ground some ten minutes after the attack. On a personal level, I was commissioned. Frank was promoted to warrant officer and we were awarded the DFC and DFM respectively. These awards were effective before my commission and Frank's promotion, hence the DFM rather than DFC.

On the 23rd Squadron Leader Tim Woodman flew another daylight *Intruder* to north-east Germany.

Squadron Leader Mike O'Brien was again my observer, another volunteer crew – a black West Indian flying officer pilot – as my No.2. I let them lead the way across the North Sea, doing the *Gee* navigation. They brought me right up the main street of Westerland, the *Nachtjägd* fighter base on Sylt, 40 miles [65 km] from where I had intended to cross in! I flew down the coast with white Very lights being fired by shore stations. Surprise factor was essential and we had lost that. Suddenly all hell broke loose as a number of Oerlikon cannons fired at us from Eggebec, no longer deserted. Total blue skies too, no cloud cover. I decided to abandon. Told the West Indian to break to starboard, hit the deck and pour on the coal to the North Sea. Took me twenty minutes to catch him up. He looked like he intended to make it all the way to Barbados. Some hits on my Mosquito from machine gun bullets.

Squadron Leader O'Brien and his navigator Flight Lieutenant P. A. Disney, who had flown with Woodman on 6 October, were killed on their 23 Squadron *Intruder* operation on 22 March 1945.

On 28/29 October Flight Lieutenant Donald R. 'Podge' Howard and Flying Officer Frank 'Sticky' Clay, who had shot down an Fw 190 over Holland a few days earlier on

14/15 October after a considerable dog fight, destroyed a very slow-flying Heinkel 111 at Stendal-Handorf. The Heinkel exploded with such force that it was probably carrying a V-l flying bomb, which would account for its slow flying speed. On 29/30 October six crews in 239 Squadron made low-level *Intruder* patrols over north-west Germany and left a trail of destruction, including nine trains, a lorry and a marshalling yard. Eight Mosquitoes of 141 Squadron also operated. Gallacher and McLean of 141 Squadron were gratified to see clouds of steam as 'their' train stopped with seven wagons damaged. Six other 141 Squadron crews destroyed or damaged locomotives and trains this night. On 29/30 October fifty-five Mosquitoes operated on *Serrate* and *Intruder* patrols. On the night of 30/31 Ocotober, when 905 aircraft attacked Cologne, fifty-seven Mosquitoes patrolled the night sky. Squadron Leader D. L. Hughes and Flight Lieutenant R. H. Perks of No. 239 Squadron returned with bullet holes through the tail unit and both wings, including one through the port wing tank. Flight Lieutenant F. Wimbush and Pilot Officer Fraser 'tangled' for thirty-five minutes with a German fighter.

November saw the same pattern of operations with bomber support and night and day *Intruder* and *Ranger* patrols. No. 85 Squadron continued its run of success with a superb individual effort during a night Intruder on 4/5 November when Bomber Command's main thrust was against Bochum, with smaller raids on the Dortmund–Ems Canal and on Hanover. Three Bf 110s were claimed shot down, one each by Wing Commander K. H. P. Beauchamp and Flying Officer Mony of 157 Squadron, Flight Lieutenants N. W. Young and R. H. Siddons of 239 Squadron, and Squadron Leader Tim Woodman and Flying Officer Arthur F. Witt of 169 Squadron. Bf 110 of *II/NJG1* was shot down at 1900 hours at a height of 20,000 ft (6,100 metres). *Unteroffizier* Gustav Sario, the pilot, was injured and baled out. *Unteroffizier* Heinrich Conrads, the radar operator and *Obergefreiter* Roman Talarowski, the air gunner, were both killed. Bf 110G-4 Wrk Nr 440648 G9+RS of *VIII/NJG1* crashed at Bersenbrück, 20 miles (30 km) north of Osnabrück. *Feldwebel* Willi Ruge, the pilot was wounded and baled out. *Unteroffizier* Helmut Kreibohm, the radar operator, and Ober*gefreiter* Anton Weiss, the air gunner, were both killed. Also shot down that night by a Mosquito was *Leutnant* Heinz Rolland, the 26-year old pilot of *IV/NJG1*, who had fifteen victories at night. Rolland, *Feldwebel* Heinz Krueger, 25-year-old radar operator, and *Unteroffizier* Karl Berger, the 22-year-old air gunner, were killed when their Bf 110 crashed south-west of Wezel. By far the greatest achievement that night, though, went to Squadron Leader Branse Burbridge DSO* DFC* and Flight Lieutenant Bill Skelton DSO* DFC*. They were airborne from Swannington at 1731 hours on a high-level Intruder patrol south-east of Cologne, crossed the enemy coast and headed into Germany. Burbridge wrote later:

> We were returning to our patrol point from Limburg at 15,000 ft [4,600 metres], on a north-westerly course, when Bill reported contact at 1904 hours, range 4 miles [6 km], crossing starboard to port at about our level. We turned in behind it, flying west, looking vainly for Type F response while closing in. I obtained a visual at 1,500 ft [460 metres] range. At 1,000 ft [300 metres], I believed it to be a Ju 88, and using night binoculars Bill identified it as a Ju 88G. I fired a short burst from 500 ft [150 metres], producing strikes on the port engine. A dull flame appeared. A second short burst gave the same result, and a fire slowly developed in the engine as the

enemy aircraft lost height. Soon it began to dive steeply, exploding on the ground at 1909 hours.

By the time we had climbed up again to our patrol point, the markers were beginning to appear in the target area, so we set course towards it. On returning to a reciprocal brief investigation of further flares south-west of us were fruitless, but at 1953 hours Bill reported contact at 4 miles [6 km] range. We dived after it and found that it was taking regular evasive action by losing height at high speed, weaving up to 45° in either direction. After about five minutes we had lost height to 7,000 ft [2,100 metres], and I obtained a visual at about 1,200 ft [365 metres] range. Again no Type F response or exhausts were seen. We closed in and identified the target with binoculars as a Ju 88. At 500 ft [150 metres] range, having finger trouble, I pressed the camera button by mistake, but the absence of thunder and the mocking buzz of the camera on the R/T put me right. A short burst (cannon) gave strikes and a flash from the port engine and fuselage, but owing to the dive I lost the visual against the darkness of the ground. Bill regained contact, and although the evasion of the enemy aircraft had increased and became irregular, we closed in again to visual range of about 1,200 ft [365 metres] after a further five minutes, our height now being 3,000 ft [900 metres]. Another short burst at 2002 hours at the same engine produced the same results, and once again the visual was lost below the horizon. We searched around, but were unable to pick him up again; our position was roughly 5 miles [8 km] SE of what we took to be the dummy flarepath of Bonn. At 2005 hours, an aircraft exploded on the ground some distance ahead of us. Two minutes later I saw what I believed to be another crash on the ground.

We now proceeded to regain a bit of height, and when at 8,000 ft [2,400 metres], set course from the last-named position to join the bomber homeward route near Duren, which point we reached at 2020 hours. It was our intention to fly on the reciprocal of the route, towards the target, and to intercept contacts coming head-on: these would most likely be hostiles attempting late route interceptions, as the bombers should all have been clear. After two minutes flying on 50° my attention was attracted by a recognition cartridge (red and white) fired about 25 miles [40 km] east of us. We hurried in its direction losing height on the way, and shortly the red perimeter lights of an airfield appeared. Then I saw the landing light of an aircraft touching down east to west at 2028 hours.

A minute later we had a snap contact and fleeting visual of an aircraft above us, but were unable to pursue it. On commencing a right-hand circuit of the airfield, however, Bill obtained a contact (on the north side of the aerodrome) at 2 miles [3 km] range and at our height, which was about 1,000 ft [300 metres] above the ground. Following round the south side, we closed in to identify an Me 110. He must have throttled back rather smartly when east of the airfield for we suddenly found ourselves overtaking rapidly, horn blaring in our ears, and finished up immediately below him about 80 ft (24 metres) away. Very gradually we began to drop back and pulling up to dead astern at 400 ft [120 metres] range, I fired a very short burst. The whole fuselage was a mass of flames, and the Me 110 went down burning furiously, to crash in a river about 5 miles [8 km] north of the airfield, which we presumed to be Bonn/Hangelar. The time was 2032 hours.

We flew away to the north for a few minutes, and then turned to approach the airfield again. As we did so Bill produced yet another contact at 2 miles [3 km] range, 80° starboard. When we got in behind him he appeared to be doing a close left-hand orbit of the airfield. Again we followed round the west and south sides, and as he seemed to be preparing to land, I selected 10° of flap. I obtained a visual at 1,500 ft [460 km] range; no a/c was visible, so I took the flap off again. We identified the target as a Ju 88 and a very short burst from dead astern, 400 ft [120 metres] range, caused the fuselage to burst into flames. The cockpit broke away, and we pulled up sharply to avoid debris. Crosses were clearly visible in the light of the fire, and the Ju 88 dived towards the airfield. He finally turned over to starboard and exploded in a ploughed field just north of the aerodrome at 2040 hours.

We could see intruder warnings being fired from aerodromes in every direction by this time, and although we tried to investigate one further recognition signal some distance from us, we obtained no joy, and presumed that we had outstayed our welcome.

Burbridge and Skelton landed back at Swannington at 2223 hours and submitted claims for one Bf 110, one Ju 88 and one Ju 88G destroyed and one Ju 88 probably destroyed. Their Bf 110 victim was a *II/NJG1* machine which crashed into the River Rhine near Hangelar airfield at 2150 hours. *Oberleutnant* Ernst Runze, the pilot, was killed and *Obergefreiter* Karl-Heinz Bendfeld, the radar operator, and the *bordschütze* baled out safely.

James Lansdale Hodson, a newspaper reporter, visited Swannington and in his subsequent article attributed Burbridge's and Skelton's great success to 'intelligence'.

They know before they set out precisely where they will be at a certain time. They carry a picture in their head of the whole night's operation ... the various bomber streams, times, targets. They try to read the enemy mind ... they visualize at what time he will discover what is happening, how far he will be misled, what he will do, what airfields he will use, what times he will rise, whether he will fly, what his tactics will be. They act accordingly. If one expectation fails, they know which next to try. After they had shot down three on the night they shot down four, Burbridge said, 'Time we were starting for home, Bill.' To which Skelton replied: 'Well if you like, but I've got another Hun for you.' They went round after him and destroyed him too. Then they had a further look round, 'But,' says Burbridge's combat report, 'we found no joy and presumed we had outstayed our welcome.'

The popular press dubbed Branse and Bill the 'Night Hawk Partners'. Such was the need for morale-boosting headlines. Less happy reading was that although 100 Group Mosquitoes claimed six enemy aircraft that night it had been a sorry twenty-four hours for Bomber Command. Despite the actions of the Mosquito crews (239 Squadron and

157 Squadrons also destroyed an enemy aircraft apiece) and a *Window* Spoof by 100 Group, out of a combined 1,081 sorties during the day (to Solingen) and night, thirty-one bombers were lost, the highest for some time.

Two nights later, on 6/7 November, the bombers attacked the Mittelland Canal at Gravenhorst. It was about of the worst night's weather Tim Woodman had ever flown in.

> We left the target area and flew into a cold front of exceptional violence. We were thrown all over the place, ice quickly froze on the windscreen and static electricity began to spark about the cockpit. We would drop like a stone and I feared my wing tips would come off. Down at 800 ft [240 metres] the ice cleared but it was too dangerous so close to the sea so I went back up to 2,000 ft [610 metres]. Flying Officer Witt had his straps loose in order to operate the *Gee* set but after he had hit the top of the cockpit for the third time I told him to lock his straps and I would fly due west until we reached better weather. I listened out on the radio. Other crews were obviously in dire trouble from the nature of their calls. Outside the propellers were whirling discs of violet fire, the aerials on the wings glowed violet like neon tubes. The inside of the windscreen was a lattice of static and, as I leant forward concentrating on the instruments the static struck across like pinpricks on my face. We dropped out of the sky in another violent air disturbance, the instruments went spinning and we waited to hit the sea. Arthur Witt then said, quite calmly, 'Another one like that, why not let the controls go'. Then it will all be over. I am quite easy about dying.' We made it after some more dicey episodes. But poor Arthur was killed a fortnight later flying with another pilot. Eleven aircraft were lost due to the weather, including two 100 Group Mosquitoes.

On the night of 6/7 November 100 Group crews claimed two Ju 188s, a Bf 110 and a Ju 88 and Ju 188 as probables. Two Ju 88G-6 aircraft were lost. 620396 R4+KR of *Stab/IV/NJG3* was shot down by a Mosquito and crashed at Marienburg. *Hauptmann* Ernst Schneider, the pilot, was killed. *Oberfeldwebel* Mittwoch, the radar operator, and *Unteroffizier* Kaase both baled out safely. Wrk Nr 620583 R4+TS of *XI/NJG3* was shot down in air combat and crashed south-west of Paderborn. *Oberleutnant* Josef Foerster, the pilot, survived. *Feldwebels* Werner Moraing, the radar operator, and Heinz Wickardt were both wounded. Squadron Leader Dolly Doleman and Flight Lieutenant Bunny Bunch DFC of 157 Squadron at Swannington received confirmation of a Bf 110 destroyed. Doleman reported:

> We were airborne at 1734 hours and before reaching our patrol point obtained a contact to starboard on 090 just by the Rhine. Chased and obtained a visual on exhausts like a Mosquito, but on closing in to identify definitely, aircraft did steep turn to port. Chased on AI on target, which was taking evasive action, and obtained a second contact head-on, which we chased and got a visual on an Me 110 going west. The position and time are somewhat uncertain after the first chase. Minimum range on weapon was poor, but opened fire on a visually estimated range of 500–600 ft [150–180

metres] with a short burst. Strikes and explosion occurred instantaneously and poor Hans went straight down in flames.

Contacts were obtained on bags more, Mosquitoes and the odd bomber throwing out *Window*, and also on two aircraft (at different times) going north-west at very high speed. Mosquito flat out but contacts drew steadily away. One visual obtained on two pairs of exhausts, one of these at 6,000 ft [1,800 metres] range. Do not know what they were but most certainly they were not Mosquitoes on one engine.

Returned from these chases towards Koblenz, and was followed by some crab in a friendly for about fifteen minutes, in spite of G band, Type F and calling on Command Guard. At 2040 hours set course for base as supplies of chewing gum were running low. Saw one beacon lit up. No contacts obtained and *Monica* was unserviceable by then anyway. Near Brussels was challenged by an American on Channel C and put navigational lights on as second American was advising our chum to 'Shoot the basket down' – only he didn't say 'basket'. Landed base with nasty smell of burning in cockpit at 2155 hours. Claim one Me 110 destroyed.'

When the fitting of AI Mk X into 100 Group Mosquitoes began there were not sufficient equipments available for the whole force. Tim Woodman recalls:

Although 85 and 157 Squadrons had been attached to 100 Group since May 1944 with 10 cm AI we considered they were not shooting down the numbers of Hun night-fighters they should have. Our Mk IV radar was completely jammed over Germany. Only half a dozen crews of 85 and 157 were getting scores; two or three doing quite well. I challenged the SASO, Air Commodore Rory Chisholm, to let two of 169 crews have the use of 85 Squadron's aircraft for five ops each, guaranteeing to shoot down a Hun apiece. We went over to Swannington, myself to fly with Flying Officer Simpkin, an 85 Squadron observer, plus Mellows and Drew from 169. What a delight to have 10 cm radar which could range up to 8 miles [13 km] ahead and no jamming. Mellows proved my challenge by shooting down a Heinkel 219 on the second of his five ops. I failed but nearly got a Ju 88 on my fifth op on 2 January. Chased three Huns but had partial radar failure. Shot at a Ju 88 as it entered cloud. Followed him down through, shooting blind on radar. Clear below cloud. A light on the ground and another pilot said he saw an aircraft crash. Made no claim, however, and climbed back up as unsure of the height of the ground.

This was Tim Woodman's fifty-first op, and his last with 169 (85). He was assessed as a 'Bomber Support pilot: exceptional'. He received a commendation from 100 Group's AOC for meritorious service and was appointed to be operational test pilot at the BSDU at Swanton Morley. There he, Squadron Leader Gledhill, and Flight Lieutenants Arthur Neville and Tommy Carpenter, specialist radar observers, checked out ASH, *Perfectos*, *Piperack*, centimetric homer and other electronic devices, and flew eight more operations.

ASH was not as elaborate an AI as the Mk X, and was expected to be much better than Mk IV for bomber support operations. It was decided to equip 23, 515 and 141

Squadrons with it. On 8 November, Mr Willis of Western Electric and Mr Glen Turner, the US technical representative, visited West Raynham. The reason for their call was to inspect the ASH Mk XV AI installation, which had been fitted to an Anson (and an Oxford) for testing by 141 Squadron. Some weeks later, on 21 November, Flight Lieutenant R. A. W. Scott DFC and Flying Officer W. G. Cadman DFC flew in the Anson on ASH training and obtained excellent results, especially at minimum range. Two days later aircrew at West Raynham were shown a two-hour film on ASH. It required a very high degree of skill for successful operation. With a very highly skilled operator, 100 Group hoped that it might become a really valuable weapon in bomber support.

On 11/12 November Flying Officers Ginger Owen and Victor McAllister DFM of 85 Squadron shot down an Fw 190 30 miles [48 km] south-east of Hamburg and Flying Officer Jimmy Mathews DFC and Warrant Officer Penny Penrose of 157 Squadron claimed a Ju 88 'probable' at Bonn. Ju 88 Wrk Nr. 712268 of *I/NJG4* crashed near Giessen. The pilot and radar operator baled out safely but *Gefreiter* Alfred Gräefer, the *bordschütze,* was killed.

Bob Symon recalls:

> On 16 November 1944, We were airborne 0010 hours a bomber support ops for the Dortmund raid. No reaction, no searchlights no gunfire. The met briefing before we left warned us that Swannington probably would be clamped down on return. When we were over the sea on the way back all our electrics went out, no radio, no blind flying panel. We were above cloud at around 10,000 ft [3,000 metres]. Svein reckoned that our only way out was to fly until we were sure of being over land, pointing our Mossie towards the sea and making a jump for it. I wonder who has tried this one? I suggested to my pilot that our Mark X AI (which has its own generator and was functioning) could give me a good enough clue as to whether we were nose up or nose down or which wing was up or down. A short check on my claim satisfied us that a controlled downward spiral was possible and we proceeded to do so until the ground return suggested that we were at about 3,000 ft [900 metres]. At this point the tube told me that we were in a straight steep dive. I protested but was calmly informed that there was a hole with a light beyond and he was going for it. And so we landed at Coltishall.

On 25 November, two Mosquitoes of 141 Squadron carried out low-level night *Intruder* sorties to enemy airfields in Germany. One crew returned early after failing to find Sachsenheim airfield, but Flying Officer R. D. S. Gregor USAAF and his navigator/radar operator Flight Sergeant F. S. Baker attacked vehicles *en route* to Hailfingen and Eutingen. The latter was all lit up but there was no sign of any aircraft so they blew up some more vehicles before returning to Norfolk. Low-level and high-level *Intruders* continued to be flown during the month and, starting on 25 November, two 500 lb (227 kg) MC bombs were carried by 141 Squadron Mosquitoes for the first time on attacks on German airfields. Alternatively, eight 40 lb (18 kg) bombs could be carried. The small bombs caused little damage but helped disrupt the German night-fighter airfields. High-level bombing sorties were also flown, using *Gee* navigation fixes to pinpoint targets, to help foster the impression that the 100 Group Spoof *Window*-dropping aircraft were, in fact, a bombing force and so divert German night-fighters

Wing Commander 'Sticky' Murphy DSO DFC (left, centre) and Group Captain Bertie Rex O'Bryen 'Sammy' Hoare DSO DFC* (right centre) during a function at Little Snoring with local farmer, Mr. Whitehead (right) where Murphy commanded 23 Squadron and Hoare was Station Commander. (Tom Cushing Collection)

from the main attack by the heavies and by Mosquitoes of 8 Group.

On 30 November Wing Commander Howard Kelsey DFC* and Flight Lieutenant Edward M. Smith DFM of 169 Squadron destroyed an He 177 on the ground at Liegnitz. That night Squadron Leader F. S. Gonsalves and Flight Lieutenant Basil Duckett of 85 Squadron destroyed a Ju 88 and Flying Officers R. J. V. Smythe and Waters of 157 Squadron destroyed a Ju 188. No. 141 Squadron dispatched eight Intruders. Pilot Officers F. A. Lampkin and Bernard J. Wallnutt were shot down during their patrol to Diepholz airfield. Lampkin was last heard transmitting 'Winball 20 pranging in Holland.' Wallnutt was killed and Lampkin was captured. Eight Day-*Intruder* sorties and thirty-five Night *Intruders*/Rangers and night bomber/*Intruder* sorties were flown during November by 141 Squadron. On 2/3 December two Mosquitoes in 141 Squadron carried out the last *Serrate* patrols of the war, having been the first to fly *Serrate* sorties on 14 June 1943 from Wittering. No. 239 would continue with *Serrate* patrols for a little longer during December 1944 and, starting on 7 January, some of their Mk VIs were transferred to 141 Squadron as 239 received new Mk XXXs. Some patrols using Mk IV *Serrate* were carried out by 169 Squadron at Great Massingham right up until the end of the war. Mosquitoes from 141 Squadron started ASH operations in December, thus joining their sister squadrons, 23 and 515, at Little Snoring. Since late 1944, both squadrons had begun training with ASH for low-level raids on German airfields. For many months with and without ASH, these two squadrons had been established in this deadly, incisive form of airborne warfare. No. 23 Squadron was led by Wing Commander Sticky Murphy, whose panache and aggressive leadership had created a fresh élan, which boded ill for the *Nachtjägdgeschwader gruppen*.

CHAPTER X

December Days

Here both men and maidens tended
To the harsh and warlike needs,
Of men who through the dark hours
Flew their man-made steeds.
The sky at night their hunting ground
In which they sought their prey.
Returning only when the night
Gave way to breaking day.

S. F. Ruffle

Jock Reid was uneasy. Sticky Murphy's trusty navigator had flown on almost all of his commanding officer's sorties from Malta, Sardinia and Little Snoring but the period between operations was becoming longer and longer. It was 2 December and their previous operation together had been on 26 November:

> The reason for so long a gap between ops was to lengthen his stay as Commanding Officer of 23 Squadron. Sticky was a swashbuckling character, proud of the fact that his identity card carried the description 'Colour of eyes: bloodshot blue'. Only one other I knew had this mark of identification, 'Mick' Martin, one of the Dambusters, who came to 515 for a rest!

Jock was the perfect foil of practical navigational skill to complement Sticky's audacity and exceptional experience. A rather dour Scot, he saved his unexpected moments of humour for special occasions. Saturday, 2 December was not one of them. He met the Commanding Officer going into the mess for lunch. '"We're flying tonight [an *Intruder* trip to Gütersloh]." he said. I then told him I was grounded for a few days because I had seen the MO that morning. 'That's OK – we'll just scrub it,' Murphy said. Murphy, however, took off from Little Snoring at 2018 hours, his eighty-sixth op. All told sixteen crews (eight from 23 Squadron and eight from 515) flew *Intruder* patrols over airfields in Germany, Denmark, and Norway while 504 bombers attacked Hagan. The 21-year-old Flight Sergeant Douglas Darbon had gone with Murphy. The route to and from Gütersloh had offered an ideal opportunity for the experienced leader to blood young Darbon in the art of *Nacht Zuster* (night nurse) tactics. (Most towns and cities in Holland had their 'night nurse'. The Dutch were glad to hear any aircraft of the RAF and USAAF flying. It gave them a lift.) Darbon most probably noticed that his wing commander had inexplicably shaved off his prized handlebar moustache. (He had once clipped $^1/_4$ inch (60 mm) off each end of his moustache so that it did not 'outrank' Sammy Hoare's, which was 6 inches (15 cm), 'wing tip to wing tip'.)

Earlier in the day Sticky had called to see his friends the Andersons at a farm near the base where he shot pheasant, but they were out. Caretaker Eric Myhill had watched as Murphy rocked up and down on his heels in front of the log fire roaring in the grate. He noticed that the wing commander was wearing his favourite American brown flying boots. 'Tell Mr and Mrs Anderson I'll be back tomorrow' he had told him. 'I'm on ops tonight.' Sticky's wife Jean, whom he had met when she was a WAAF officer while he was instructing at an OTU in Scotland in 1941, has fond memories of him: 'rough shooting through the corn stubble for rabbits and any game – Sticky was an excellent shot with a .22.'

When 23 Squadron had moved to Snoring Jean had moved to Norfolk from Berkshire with their daughter Gail (born three days before Sticky returned from Sardinia) and had lodged at a farm some distance from the airfield. (Crews were not permitted to 'live out'.) Living there was Spartan and cold, and Jean became ill. She moved to a more congenial farmhouse at Tuddenham, where the farmer was also a butcher, so they lived well! Illness persisted, however, and Jean had to spend several weeks in the Norfolk and Norwich hospital, where Sticky visited whenever possible. After her spell in hospital, Jean had moved with Gail to lodgings in a terraced house in Fakenham where they saw much more of Sticky. On 2 December, he visited and told Jean he was flying that night. She argued, 'Surely you've done enough, Sticky?'

'Don't worry,' he said. 'It's a wing commander's moon tonight.'

It was 10 o'clock on Sunday morning before Jock Reid knew that Sticky had gone flying and who had gone with him. 'When I met some of the boys who were at church, they said, "Oh, so you got back." I replied that I hadn't been anywhere. I didn't even know the flight sergeant who was his navigator that night.' This was not the first time that something like this had happened. 'In Pomiglicino d' Ario (Naples) after a rowdy party, he went off with a friend. I was asleep but got up and waited for three and a half hours till he returned. They had attacked boats in a harbour (suicide). It all came as a shock to me on the morning of 3 December.'

Two crews took off early on ASR patrols to search the North Sea but they met with no success. Intermittent rain with much low cloud and gale-force southerly winds made the task even more difficult. 'The only information that came through, quite early in the morning, was that the squadron would be stood down for the night,' Jock Reid recalls, 'There was no mourning, spirits were kept up. In fact that Sunday night there was a party at North Creake, to which 23 Squadron were invited. It went ahead as usual.'

The flight to and from the target had passed without incident but approaching the Zuider Zee on the return, Murphy's aircraft was hit by flak. Murphy had been Squadron Commander for almost a year and a flight commander for some months before. On 4 December; Sergeant Pieter de Jong of the military police at Wezep, Holland, and two labourers, went to the scene of the crashed Mosquito. Close by the two bodies of Sticky Murphy and Douglas Darbon, de Jong found a silver cigarette case, twisted by the inferno, with the words 'A. M. Murphy RAF' engraved on it. (It was later sent to the Air Ministry in London with other effects.) The labourers laid the bodies in two coffins and took them to the cemetery at Oldebroek. Sammy Hoare broke the news to Jean. On

10 December, a postagram was received from Air Chief Marshal Arthur T. Harris, which was forwarded to Jean. Four days earlier Sticky had been awarded a Bar to his DSO.

Squadron Leader Philip Russell was promoted wing commander and assumed Murphy's mantle. He had suffered the after-effects of untreated diphtheria contracted in Sardinia but after treatment at the RAF rehabilitation unit at Loughborough College he had returned to the squadron on 7 October completely recovered. Returning to the squadron was a bit of a wrench, as he admits.

Wing Commander Philip Russell who assumed command of 23 Squadron at Little Snoring on the death in action of Sticky Murphy. (Philip Russell via Tom Cushing)

The rehabilitation unit was run by Dan Maskell of subsequent tennis fame. I had to learn to walk again, helped with lots of massage from attractive nurses and swimming lessons with even more attractive ones. At the end of September I went for an RAF medical examination and (and here I have to admit rather shamefacedly) to my mild disappointment I was passed fit for flying duties. The European picture had changed considerably since we had left the UK and our targets were now principally in Germany and all rather heavily defended. In December we were fitted with radar and I took on a new radar operator, Hugh Boland, who was as mad as a hatter and totally without a trace of fear. As we were crossing the enemy coast amid curtains of flak, he would laugh out loud and say, 'Gosh, isn't that pretty?' and he meant it!

He also carried a flute stuck in his flying jacket and would play happily to himself until I told him to belt up and find out where we were. His hobby on the ground was making up anything explosive such as bombs and rockets. He made a sort of Very pistol, and on the way home from a rather wild night in Norwich, during which we had stormed the castle, he sat on the back step of the aircrew bus firing Very lights along the road at following traffic. Judging by their evasive action, it must have been quite upsetting, seeing these coloured lights bouncing along the road towards them. To be frank, in the aircraft I would sooner have had a navigator who was as frightened as I was but he did enjoy it so much.

Philip Russell proved to be a very inspiring leader in the long tradition of 23 Squadron commanding officers. He used to attend the daily briefings at 100 Group HQ at Bylaugh Hall near Swanton Morley, which was also home to the Mosquito Servicing

Section and, conveniently, to aircraft of 100 Group Communications Flight. Russell recalls:

> It was fascinating to watch the plot being hatched out, and then, on the next day to be able to see what results had been achieved. It all worked out very well and the losses in Bomber Command fell dramatically. The Germans very much resented our efforts to prevent their night-fighters becoming airborne. The airfield flak was increased heavily and we lost rather a lot of crews. We were quite often within sight of the mainstream bomber attack and a big raid was a most dramatic sight.

A big raid was indeed an impressive sight; probably even the Germans thought so on their *Würzburg* radar scopes. Of course, for reasons of secrecy, the vast majority of 100 Group were not privy to the overall picture. Crews, unaware of the important role they were playing, could easily become disillusioned. Many resented being used as 'bait' night after night. Being restricted to dropping nothing more volatile than *Window* did little for their psyches.

Bylaugh Hall was a beautiful mansion in secluded woodland, where Air Vice Marshal Addison and his staff approved the night's complex RCM and *Spoof* operations. Battle summaries for the previous night's work went each day to fifty-two different recipients in twelve groups and nine OTUs, as well as to the Air Ministry, the HQs of Fighter and Bomber Commands, and twenty-five stations and squadrons within 100 Group itself. Even Section 22, its opposite number in the south-west Pacific, was kept appraised of the role 100 Group was playing.

Throughout 1944 the Fortresses of 214 Squadron and the Liberators of 223 Squadron had been jostling for every major bombing raid. By December, all were of still greater assistance, being fully equipped with *Carpet (anti-Würzburg))* and *Piperack* (anti-SN-2) besides *Jostle* (anti-HE and anti-VHF). Mosquitoes began operating this month at jammers. Their role was a dual one. They flew to target areas on routes which took them well clear of the main force and on the way they made 'Y' recordings of enemy R/T traffic. Arriving at the target area, they jammed the enemy AI with *Piperack* and they stayed there until well after the attack was over; thus covering the withdrawal of stragglers. It was intended to increase and prolong the AI jamming in the target areas to which the enemy fighters would ultimately gravitate. During December, the *Mandrel* screen and *Window* forces also kept up the good work of confusion and diversion. The Ruhr was still the favourite target, and *Window* flooding continued to be used with success. Even though 141, 169 and 239 Squadrons did not shoot down any enemy aircraft during the month, their part in the overall scheme of things was of great importance. It started on 1/2 December when a Spoof *Window* attack on the Ruhr by forty-nine aircraft of 100 Group with no losses among the eighty-one heavies that attacked Karlsrühe, Duisburg and Hallendorf, was supported by *Intruder* and high-level patrols by the *Serrate* squadrons. They continued this type of operation throughout the month.

The following night, 2/3 December, was again judged successful, with only two aircraft missing from the 504 dispatched to Hagen and Giessen. The operation was supported by 110 aircraft of 100 Group, with one lost (Murphy), and two aircraft claimed destroyed in the air. Low-level *Intruder* squadrons bombed enemy airfields and strafed rolling stock. On patrol at Fassburg airfield, Flying Officers F. X. A. Huls and Joe Kinet of 515 Squadron saw four twin-engined aircraft on the ground and attacked them. Two He 177s were set on fire and claimed as destroyed. A Ju 88 was destroyed by Flight Lieutenant W. Taylor and Flying Officer J. N. Edwards of 157 Squadron a little to the east of Stagen at 2136 hours. The German night-fighter was possibly Ju 88 Wrk Nr 714819 3C+WL of *III/NJG4*, which crashed at Rheine. *Oberfähnrich* Erhard Pfisterhammer, the pilot, *Unteroffizier* Wolfgang Sode, the radar operator, and the air gunner were all wounded.

Captain Tarald Weisteen, a Norwegian serving in 85 Squadron, obtained a contact at 5 miles (8 km) going west across the target area. Range was closed to 4,000–5,000 ft (1,200–1,500 metres), and at 2,000 ft it was identified as a Bf 110. Weisteen opened fire at 200 yd and portions of the aircraft broke off and the starboard engine caught fire before the Bf 110 spun down. The explosion could be seen through the cloud half a minute later. The victim was Bf 110G-4 Wrk Nr 180382 of *XII/NJG4*, which had taken off from Bonninhardt at 2047 hours. It crashed at 2145 near Lippborg near Hamm. *Leutnant* Heinz-Joachim Schlage, the pilot survived, but Fiebig and *Unteroffizier* Kundmüller were killed. A 223 Squadron Liberator rear gunner obtained a visual on an aircraft carrying an orange light on the starboard quarter, which closed very fast at 2,000 yd. He ordered the pilot to corkscrew starboard and nothing more was seen. It was presumed to be a German jet.

There were no 100 Group operations on 3/4 December. An outstanding piece of spoofery occurred on 4/5 December when 892 heavies set out for Karlsruhe, Heilbron, Hagen and Hamm in the north and south of the Ruhr. The *Window* force (altogether 112 aircraft of 100 Group were aloft, including a Liberator of 223 Squadron, captained by Flight Lieutenant Haslie on the squadron's first target patrol at Karlsruhe) went straight into 'Happy Valley', supported by PFF marking, and held no less than 90–100 fighters in the area until much too late for their deployment against the heavies. Losses to the main force were kept to fifteen aircraft, or 1.5 per cent of the force. On this night 100 Group Mosquitoes shot down five aircraft and probably destroyed another. The Mk IV AI squadrons obtained numerous contacts in the Ruhr area, but AI was mainly unworkable owing to heavy interference from *Window*. Contacts in the south showed great superiority in speed and in all cases drew away from the aircraft. Low-level *Intruder* squadrons, meanwhile, bombed airfields, but results could not be observed because of adverse weather conditions.

Victories were recorded by the Mk X AI squadrons. A contact was obtained by Flight Lieutenant W. Taylor and Flying Officer J. N. Edwards of 157 Squadron in the Frankfurt area at $4^1/_2$ miles (7 km) range. Taylor chased it for ten minutes, the enemy all the time taking violent evasive action. He closed to 1,500 ft (460 metres) and identified it as a Bf 110. At 250 yd he gave it a two-second burst from dead astern. The Bf 110 burst into flames, dived and exploded on the ground near Limburg. Flight Lieutenant Jimmy Mathews DFC and Warrant Officer Penny Penrose DFC, meanwhile, obtained a contact in the Ruhr area at 5 miles (8 km) range and chased it for forty minutes before it was identified as a Ju 88. Mathews dispatched it near Dortmund.

Old Flight Lieutenants Richard 'Dicky' Goucher, twenty-five and C. H. 'Tiny' Bullock, thirty-three, of 85 Squadron completed their patrol and set course for

Swannington. They had crewed up in North Africa in 1943 and remained together until the end of the war, being posted to 151 Squadron at Hunsdon on 18 January 1945. Thoughts of home were abandoned when a *Monica* contact was obtained. Tiny Bullock successfully converted it to a forward contact at 8,000 ft (2,400 metres) range. The enemy aircraft was going in the direction of Karlsruhe at 2,000 ft (610 metres). In the light of flames from Karlsruhe, Dickie Goucher identified it as a Bf 110. He gave it two bursts without apparent result, but a third put out the port engine. The fourth caused the aircraft to explode and it crashed in the vicinity of Germersheim close to a red beacon. Almost immediately another contact was obtained at 4 miles (6.5 km) range. After several orbits around the beacon visual was obtained on a Bf 110 at 2,000 ft (610 metres). Two short bursts caused the enemy aircraft to explode and crash in approximately the same place as the first one. Goucher's and Bullock's Mosquito was struck by flying debris but returned to Swannington safely.

The German night-fighter force was run ragged by 85 Squadron. Captain Svein Heglund DFC and Flying Officer Robert O. Symon, who were airborne in their Mosquito XXX from Swannington at 1730 hours on a high-level support patrol in the Karlsruhe area reached their patrol at 1855 hours. Contacts were obtained on bombers and later two targets, with violent evasion, were chased eastwards. At 2005 Schwabish Hall airfield was seen lit and several fleeting contacts appeared well below. Heglund went down to 2,500 ft (760 metres) to investigate but all lighting was doused. The Norwegian regained height and at 2015 hours, north-east of Heilbronn Symon obtained a contact. Captain Heglund recalls:

> We had just regained height at 10,000 ft [3,000 metres], after investigating Schwabish Hall airfield and were flying on about 260° when, at 2015 hours, my N/R said he had contact and told me to turn 100° port. Our position then was about 10 miles [16 km] north-east of Heilbron. Contact was then obtained 6 miles [10 km] ahead and well below. The aircraft was doing a mild corkscrew on an easterly course and we came in behind at 4,000 ft [1,200 metres] (about 2,500 ft [160 metres] above the ground). The aircraft being chased was travelling very slowly – 190–200 IAS – and we overshot, recognizing it as an Me 110 by its square wingtip and two fins and rudders, as we pulled away to starboard 400 ft [120 metres] away. Contact and visual were momentarily lost but contact regained and maintained to bring a further visual at 400 ft [120 metres] we were still overtaking and I lost the visual in making further S turns to lose speed, and remained behind the enemy aircraft. Contact was maintained, the whole time and finally the visual was obtained at 400 ft [120 metres], and held steady. I fired a one-second burst obtaining strikes immediately on the starboard engine and wing root. The enemy aircraft burst into flames, lighting up the crosses on wings and fuselage and showing up the radar aerial display on the nose. Enemy aircraft side-slipped into the ground near Rothenburg, where it exploded. Time 2025. At 2026 course was set for base via Frankfurt area where several airfields were seen active. Unfortunately petrol was low and we had to land at Brussels at 2200 hours. After refuelling, we took off at 2320 and landed back at base at 0010 hours.

Heglund, who expended just twenty-four rounds of SAPI and sixteen of HEI put in a claim for a Bf 110 destroyed. Robert O. Symon DFC remembers:

> Captain Svein Heglund DFC* who joined 85 Squadron (and his fellow group of Norwegians) in October 1944, was a delightful and modest young man, who, I found later, was Norway's Ace. As a point of interest check the number of rounds it took my friend to bring down three 110s compared with the number of rounds fired to bring down No.1. I can only assume that this was the first for Swannington and he was going to be sure that it would never fly again.

Flying Officers Ginger Owen and Victor McAllister DFM, also of 85 Squadron, got an AI contact in the Ruhr area at 4½ miles (7 km) range and chased it for twenty-six minutes before a visual on a Ju 88 was obtained before shooting it down. It was 85 Squadron's 100th enemy aircraft at night. Their victim was probably Ju 88G-1 Wrk Nr 714152 of *VI/NJG4*, which crashed near Krefeld. *Unteroffizier* Wilhelm Schlutter, the pilot, was wounded and *Unteroffizier* Friedrich Heerwagen, the radar operator and *Gefreiter* Friedrich Herbeck, the air gunner, were killed.

Flight Lieutenant Edward R. Hedgecoe DFC of the Fighter Interception Unit at Ford, who was attached to 85 Squadron at Swannington for a ten-day period, finished an uneventful patrol except for chases and visuals on other Mosquitoes before setting course for home. However a minute later, a contact at 4 miles (6.5 km) head-on was obtained. The 34-year-old former accountant officer had remustered to aircrew and joined 85 Squadron where he crewed up with Flight Lieutenant Norman Bamford. On 24/25 March they had a narrow escape when their Mosquito, O-Orange, had been severely scorched with the rudder fabric being burned away following their shooting down of a Ju 188 at 300 ft (90 metres) range off the south coast. Hedgecoe had nursed O-Orange back to base, where a piece of debris from the Ju 188 was removed from the port wing. He and Bamford both received the DFC after this encounter. This harrowing experience appears to have had an effect on Hedgecoe, who now adopted a more judicious approach on the bogey behind which he turned and gave chase for eight minutes. Over Detmold airfield at range of 1,000 ft (300 metres) at 6,000 ft (1,800 metres) the unmistakable outline of a Ju 88 was made out. Its identity was confirmed at 300 ft (90 metres). Dropping back to 150 yd, Hedgecoe gave it three short bursts and saw strikes all over the aircraft. Burning debris flew in all directions. Hedgecoe overshot and was unable to regain contact before a shortage of petrol forced him to set course for Brussels/ Melsbroek to refuel. He put in a claim for a Ju 88 probably destroyed.

On 5/6 December, 553 aircraft attacked Soest, Duisburg, Nuremberg and Mannheim. Seventy-six aircraft of 100 Group supported the operation, which cost one heavy bomber. Reports indicated: 'There was probably no fighter reaction. Only a few contacts were obtained. This was probably due to adverse weather conditions over enemy airfields.'

A very severe ground frost heralded a bright and clear morning on 6 December, and all anticipation was for a maximum effort. Low-level *Intruders* bombed and strafed enemy airfields but the weather conditions were not good for this type of operation. That night, 1,291 aircraft attacked Bergesburg, Osnabrück, Giessen, Berlin, Schwerte and

157 Squadron gathered on the steps of the Officers' Mess (Haveringland Hall) at Swannington. Front row L–R: Flight Lieutenant R. J. V. Smythe; Stevens; Squadron Leader J. H. M. Chisholm (KIA 15.9.44); Wing Commander H. D. U. Dennison (CO, March–June 1944); Towser; Flight Lieutenant J. O. Mathews DFC; Squadron Leader Giles 'Ben' Benson; Squadron Leader Dolly Doleman. Others identified are F/L E. L. Wilde (KIA 15.9.44) (back row, third from right); to his right is Flight Lieutenant Lewis Brandon; Smythe's navigator, Flying Officer Waters, (second from far right). (Richard Doleman via Dr Theo Boiten)

Hanau. Eighty-nine aircraft of 100 Group supported the operations and one was lost. The heavies lost twenty-one, or 1.7 per cent of the force. Squadron Leader Neil Reeves DSO DFC and Flying Officer M. Phillips, attached to the BSDU, were carrying out a *Perfectos* patrol when they obtained a contact west of Giessen at 12 miles (19 km) range. They followed and eventually got a visual on a Bf 110. After a long chase they shot it down. It was the first victory to *Perfectos*.

Bad weather did not prevent 157 and 85 Squadrons from running up the score. A contact was obtained at range by Flight Lieutenant Jimmy Mathews DFC and Warrant

NFIIs and XIXs of 157 Squadron at Swannington, Norfolk. Far left is NFII HJ9ll. (BAe)

Officer Penny Penrose DFC of 157 Squadron, which they chased for thirteen minutes through several orbits and changes of height. A visual was gained at 1,000 ft (300 metres) range on a Bf 110 with long-range tanks. They closed to just 50 yd and gave it a one-second burst, scoring strikes all over the fuselage. The Bf 110 burst into flames and crashed at Limburg. A second contact at 5 miles (8 km) led to a visual on a Ju 88 at 1,500 ft (460 metres) range. Mathews gave it a short burst from close range and the enemy aircraft broke its back and crashed 15 miles (24 km) south-west of Giessen. Their Ju 88 victim was Wrk Nr 712268 of *I/NJG4*, which crashed near Giessen killing the air gunner, *Gefreiter* Alfred Graefer.

Squadron Leader Dolly Doleman and Bunny Bunch of 157 Squadron were airborne from Swannington at 1835 hours in their 'plywood pantechnicon' and set course for patrol. Doleman describes the flight.

> Got hung up in the bomber stream west of the Rhine, and saw the flares being laid on Biesson. We saw bags of four- or five-star reds being fired from the Frankfurt searchlight belt so bogged off to have a look. No joy so returned to Giessen, which was being inundated with incendiaries (wizard alliteration) and saw lashings of Lancs flying across the target. We stayed overhead to see if we could pick off someone trying to pick off a Lanc, but nothing happened so went NW to clear the bomber stream. We had just arrived, at 2030 hours, when we picked up an almost head-on contact at

15,000 ft [4,600 metres] at 6 miles [10 km], same level. Target dived to 11,000 ft [3,350 metres] on bomber withdrawal route then did a figure of eight and stooged off eastwards. Closed in and identified as an Me 110 and shot it down at 2040 hours in Kitzingen area. Night glasses were used to advantage. We had a persistent *Monica* contact before and after the happy event and as he wouldn't close to less than 8,000 ft [2,400 metres] we had to turn and try to catch him. He must have seen what we were trying to do, for he had no forward contact but saw the Hun colours fired in the direction he should have been, but out of range. Looked in at an aerodrome near Zelhausen and later at Bonn, but no bon, as they say, so returned to base, where we landed at 2320 hours – the landing as usual, being the most exciting thing of the evening for Bunny. Claim one Me 110 destroyed.'

Doleman fired fifty-two SAPI and forty-eight HEI rounds to dispatch the enemy night-fighter.

Flight Lieutenant Hedgecoe took off in O-Orange, an 85 Squadron Mosquito XXX with Flight Sergeant J. R. Whitham as his radar operator. They obtained several contacts at 15,000 ft (4,600 metres). One was selected and chased westwards for ten minutes. A visual was obtained at 800 ft (240 metres) on a Bf 110 (an *VIII/NJG4* machine flown by *Hauptmann* Helmut Bergmann, a *Ritterkreuzträger* with thirty-six victories). Hedgecoe gave it a one-second burst between the exhaust flames. It crashed and exploded on the ground 25 miles (40 km) west of Munster. Several more contacts were obtained in the target area. One at 4 miles (6.5 km) coming towards the Mosquito was selected. After a five-minute chase, a visual was obtained on another Bf 110. A one-second burst produced strikes and a flash on the port engine. Visual was lost. When it was regained, the Bf 110 was going very slowly with its port engine feathered. Hedgecoe closed in again but overshot owing to ice on the windscreen. He tried a second time but the Mosquito stalled and the enemy aircraft was lost. He claimed it as a 'damaged'. Hedgecoe and Whitham's second 'victim' may have been Bf 110G-4 Wrk Nr 740078 G9+HZ of *XII/NJG1*, which crashed 6 miles (10 km) north-west of Handorf. This aircraft was flown by 23-year-old *Hauptmann* Hans-Heinz Augenstein, *Staffelkapitan*, *XII/NJG1*, who was found three days later in a ditch, his parachute unopened. *Feldwebel* Günther Steins, his *bordfunker*, was killed when he was hurled from the aircraft in the crash. Augenstein had forty-six night victories, including forty-five RAF night bombers, and had been awarded the *Ritterkreuz* on 9 June 1944. *Unteroffizier* Kurt Schmidt, *bordschütze*, who was wounded, baled out and survived. A Ju 88 was also claimed as a 'damaged' by a Fortress gunner, Flying Officer Corke of 214 Squadron, while on a *Jostle* patrol.

For two nights following, 100 Group flew no operations. Then on 9/10 December, when seventy-nine aircraft of 8 Group attacked Duisburg, Koblenz and Berlin, 100 Group dispatched sixty-eight aircraft. One, a Halifax of 171 Squadron piloted by Warrant Officer Powe RAAF, failed to return from *Windowing* Koblenz. All Mosquito patrols were 'completely uneventful', probably owing to adverse weather conditions over Germany. No operations were flown the following night for the same reason. The morning of 11 December was much milder and warmer in contrast to the previous day's sleet and rain but that night's operations were also scrubbed. Late that evening, the crews were told that it was to be 'a lovely day tomorrow', but then it broke dull and wet.

That night, 12/13 December, 592 bombers attacked Essen and Osnabrück. Six, or 1 per cent of the force, failed to return. Ninety-one aircraft were dispatched by 100 Group. No. 192 Squadron played its first operational role as an airborne jammer when the first Mosquito fitted with two channels of *Piperack* operated. (In time, all the squadron's Mosquitoes would be fitted with *Piperack.* The aircraft played a dual role: signals investigation continued to and from the target, while *Piperack* itself was used over the target). The group shot down five more German night-fighters.

The Mk IV AI squadrons, meanwhile, obtained only two contacts but no combats resulted and in the main, the low-level *Intruder* squadrons were once again defeated by the weather. Not so 85 and 157 Squadrons. In 85 Squadron Flight Lieutenant Edward R. Hedgecoe DFC and Flight Sergeant J. R. Whitham destroyed two Bf 110s and Squadron Leader Branse Burbridge DSO* DFC* and Bill Skelton DSO* DFC* added a Ju 88 and a Bf 110 to their rising score. Hedgecoe and Whitham in O-Orange obtained a contact at 6 miles (10 km) range, head-on and below them. Violent evasive action followed before Hedgecoe was able to close to 1,000 ft (300 metres) and obtain a visual. He closed right in and positively identified it as a Bf 110. Hedgecoe dropped back to 75 yd and fired a short burst, which caused an explosion in the fuselage. The Bf 110 dived steeply, burning furiously, and disappeared into 10/10ths cloud at 7,000–8,000 ft (2,100–2,400 metrres), 20 miles (30 km) south of Hagen. A second contact was obtained at 4 miles (6.5 km) range, slightly above them and orbiting. It eventually settled down on a course towards Essen. Hedgecoe closed the range to 2,000 ft (610 metres) and saw exhaust flames at 1,000 ft (300 metres). Obtaining a visual, he closed right in and recognized it as a Bf 110. A two-second burst from 100 yd caused the enemy aircraft to disintegrate and fall vertically in approximately the same area as the first one. At the end of the month Hedgecoe and Norman Bamford were posted to 151 Squadron at Hunsdon where the promoted Hedgecoe was a flight commander. On 1 January they both died in a crash-landing on their first flight with the squadron. Hedgecoe had shot down eight enemy aircraft and Bamford had taken part in the destruction of ten. The award of a Bar to Hedgecoe's DFC was gazetted in March.

Squadron Leader Branse Burbridge DSO* DFC** and Bill Skelton DSO* DFC** were on patrol when a contact was obtained at 7,000 ft (2,100 metres) and $2^1/_2$ miles. Burbridge followed it at a low air speed through port and starboard orbits. A visual at 1,000 ft (300 metres) confirmed the contact as a Ju 88. Burbridge gave it a one-and-a-half-second burst from 500 ft (150 metres) and set one of the engines on fire. The Ju 88 G-1, Wrk Nr 714530 of *VI/NJG4*, crashed at Gütersloh airfield. *Unteroffizier* Heinrich Brune, the pilot, *Unteroffizier* Emil Hoffharth, the *bordfunker,* and *Unteroffizier* Wolfgang Rautert, the *bordschütze*, were killed.

Flying towards Essen, another contact was obtained at 4 miles (6.5 km) and 12,000 ft (3,650 metres). Burbridge and Skelton dashed towards the target area at high speed and climbing. Luckily, a burst of flak illuminated a Bf 110, and Burbridge closed to 400 ft (120 metres) for final identification. He gave the Bf 110 a half-second burst from 500 ft (150 metres) and the enemy aircraft exploded before spinning down in flames, the tail unit breaking off. It crashed about 2 miles (3 km) west of Essen. Burbridge and Skelton finished their second tours early in 1945. Both were awarded Bars to their DSOs to go with the Bars they had already been awarded to their DFCs. They finished the war as the top-scoring night-fighter crew in the RAF, with a final total of twenty-one victories. Bob Braham and Wing Commander John Cunningham both destroyed nineteen enemy aircraft at night. After the war, Branse Burbridge became a lay preacher, while Bill Skelton was ordained as a clergyman in the Church of England and became chaplain at Clare College, Cambridge.

Captain Eric Fossum and Flying Officer S. A. Hider, another Norwegian crew on the strength of 85 Squadron, obtained a contact crossing port to starboard. A hard turn brought it dead ahead at a range of 4,500 ft (1,400 metres) and he closed in. At 300 ft (90 metres), the silhouette was made out to be that of a Ju 88. Fossum dropped back to 600 ft (180 metres) and fired a short burst. Strikes on the tail unit were seen and debris flew off. A further burst produced more strikes on the fuselage and the Junkers spun to port. A few seconds later, a faint glow was seen through the clouds.

Wing Commander K. H. P. Beauchamp DSO DFC, Commanding Officer of 157 Squadron and his navigator, Flight Lieutenant Leslie Scholefield, patrolled uneventfully until the main force bombing commenced. At 1925 hours the markers were seen on Essen and Osnabrück. At 2010 hours at 12,000 ft (3,650 metres) Scholefield got a contact at 6 miles (10 km) range, 30° to starboard and going away to starboard. Beauchamp wrote:

> I turned after it, and chased for twenty-five minutes, first on course 120 and then on 150, and descending during chase to 10,000 ft [3,000 metres], just above cloud tops. At 2035 hours the target did a port orbit over a lit airfield, believed to be Aschaffenburg. I closed to 200 ft [60 metres] below and on the quarter, and identified it as an Me 110 with long-range tanks, and burning an orange light inboard of the starboard engine. Identification was checked by Flight Lieutenant Scholefield, using night binoculars. I dropped back to 600 ft [180 metres] astern and fired two short bursts at 2037 hours, 10,000 ft [3,000 metres]. Saw strikes on the starboard wing and there were two large showers of sparks. Immediately after this, visual was lost, and as the AI had been upset by firing the guns, contact was also lost. I patrolled in the area hoping to regain contact. We had had two forward *Monica* contacts during the chase and got another AI contact at 2040 hours, which was followed down to 5,000 ft [1,500 metres] and lost in violent manoeuvres. I claim one Me 110 damaged.

On 13 December the day broke under a very heavy frost and towards mid-morning fog 'thick enough to shame any Manchester could boast about' enveloped stations in Norfolk and operations were scrubbed very early. Therefore, 100 Group did not support Bomber Command operations in northern Denmark and Norway that night, or *Gardening* operations in the Kattegat on 14/15 December. On 15/16 December seventy-three aircraft were used to support main force operations against Ludwigshafen, Osnabrück, Hanover and Duisburg. Seven Mosquitoes of 141 Squadron led a Spoof raid and dropped 500-pounders (227 kg) and 250 lb (113.5 kg) yellow target indicators through solid cloud over the target. Spoofing was adjudged successful; only one heavy bomber was lost, in the main attack on Ludwigshafen. Only two AI contacts leading to chases were made. The following night, 100 Group stood down again.

On 17/18 December ninety-six aircraft in 100 Group, including a Spoof raid by four Mosquitoes of 141 Squadron on Mannheim, supported a massive operation by 1,174 aircraft, which bombed Ulm, Munich, Duisburg, Hanau, Münster and Halendorf. Three Bf 110s were destroyed that night. Dickie Goucher and Tiny Bullock obtained a contact about 40 miles (65 km) from Ulm. Their prey was above them and because of evasive action was at first thought to be a Mosquito. Goucher closed to 2,000 ft (610 metres) and got a glimpse of a green resin light. At 1,000 ft (300 metres), he obtained a visual and closed to 400 ft (120 metres). It was a Bf 110. A short burst set fire to the port engine and the Bf 110 pulled up and dived, hitting the ground about 8 miles (13 km) from Ulm where it continued to burn.

No. 157 Squadron also reaped rich rewards that night. About 5 miles (8 km) west of Duisburg Warrant Officer D. A. Taylor and Flight Sergeant Radford obtained a contact at 8 miles (13 km) range and 13,000 ft (4,000 metres). Taylor chased it for five minutes, closing to 1,500 ft (460 metres) and obtained a visual on a Bf 110. Closing to 300 ft (90 km), he pumped a two-second burst of cannon into the Bf 110's airframe and it exploded, covering the Mosquito with oil and debris. It crashed north-west of Neiss. Thirty miles (48 km) north-north-east of Ulm, another Bf 110 was shot down by Flight Sergeant Leigh. One of the crew bailed out before it crashed in flames. A Ju 88 was damaged by Squadron Leader James Giles Benson and Flight Lieutenant Lewis Brandon during a dogfight lasting an exhausting forty minutes after obtaining the contact near a cone of searchlights. Lewis Brandon recalls:

We had not chased a Hun for over a month and were hoping our luck would change. It was a long way to go, two solid hours each way for only a twenty-minute patrol. We wasted no time and made straight for our patrol point, crossing in over the Belgian-Dutch border and plodding on over land at 15,000 ft [4,600 metres] until we reached our destination. For

Squadron Leaders Giles 'Ben' Benson DSO DFC*, and Lewis Brandon DSO DFC* who shared in eight victories flying in 157 Squadron 1943–5. Benson, whose first victory with Brandon as his radar operator was in a 141 Squadron Beaufighter If on 15/16 February 1940, finished the war with ten victories, four damaged and six V-1s destroyed. (via Theo Boiten)

twenty minutes we scoured the skies between Stuttgart and Ulm without anything appearing on our AI, although we saw lots of activity where the bombing was taking place. We tried flying at 10,000 ft [3,000 metres] and 18,000 ft [5,500 metres], but there was just nothing doing for us.

We had plenty of petrol left so we decided to go out of our way a bit and see what we might find in the Frankfurt-Koblenz area. This proved a happy decision. As we approached Frankfurt at about 12,000 ft [3,650 metres] I got a contact on an aircraft flying south. It was well above us so we whipped around and climbed after it.

Whatever it was, it was certainly flying fast and high. Try as we could, we just could not catch it. Eventually, when we were up to nearly 20,000 ft [6,100 metres], we lost him, still well above us and going like a bat out of hell.

It seemed as if this was just not our night.

Round we turned, heading for Frankfurt again, when we spotted a cone of searchlights shining up into the sky near Wiesbaden. We made for these, and a minute later I had another contact. Our combat report read as follows:

Squadron Leader Benson reports:
Contact obtained near a cone of five steady searchlights. Our height 16,000 ft [4,900 metres]. We followed down to 6,000 ft [1,800 metres] and up again to 12,000 ft [3,650 metres]. Target weaving violently and making steep turns in either direction. Then followed down to 2,500 ft [860 metres] still on AI and we found ourselves on the circuit of a fully lit airfield. Visual obtained on Junkers 88G, indicated air speed 320 mph [512 kph], height 2,500 ft [760 metres]. At this time certainly not more than 50 yd away and below the enemy aircraft. I raised the Mosquito's nose and was about to open fire (despite the fact that I thought we were too close,) when we were illuminated by a searchlight. At this moment the Junkers 88 fired a four-star cartridge – two reds, two whites. These completely blinded me. As I knew we were dead behind him, I opened fire but saw no strikes. Then I saw the enemy aircraft, illuminated by the falling cartridges below and peeling off to port. I jammed the nose down and had a quick shot which produced several strikes outboard the starboard engine. He continued steeply down to port and we followed him round to the other side of the airfield, going very fast.

We were again illuminated, this time by two searchlights. The enemy aircraft fired another cartridge, which illuminated it, and it was seen above us and slightly behind. Our height was then only 800 ft [240 metres]. We could not get into firing position and contact was lost. Several white cartridges were fired from the airfield, which we continued to patrol for some time afterwards without obtaining contact again. Excellent work by Flight Lieutenant Brandon, who kept contact despite violent and continuous evasive action of every sort, especially when below 2,500 ft [760 metres]. The dogfight on AI before the visual lasted for nearly forty minutes. Claim: one Junkers 88G damage.

On 18/19 December 308 bombers attacked Gdynia, Munster, Nuremberg and Danzig. Forty-eight aircraft of 100 Group supported the operation. Four heavies and a Mosquito flown by Flying Officers Desmond T. Tull DFC and Peter J. Cowgill DFC of 85 Squadron failed to return. Tull accidentally rammed Bf 110 G9+CC of *Stab IV/NJG1* flown by *Hauptmann* Adolph Breves (with *Feldwebel* Telsnig, *bordfunker* and *Unteroffizier* Ofers, *bordschütze*) which was coming into land at Düsseldorf airfield at 2230 hours. A large part of one of the wings of the 110 was torn off but Breves (who finished the war with eighteen victories) managed to land the aircraft without further damage. The Bf 110 was repaired and test flown on 31 December. Tull and Cowgill, who were both killed, are buried in Reichswald Forest Cemetery near Kleef.

Low-level *Intruders* reported no combats and the Mk IV AI squadrons did not operate. The one victory that night went to Flight Lieutenant William Taylor and Flying Officer Jeffery N. Edwards of 157 Squadron. At first their patrol was uneventful. Having set course for base, they ran into *Window* but were able to pick up a contact at about 6 miles range. Their target was climbing steeply and orbiting. At 2,000 ft (610 metres) and 800 ft (240 metres) above they obtained a visual. Taylor was nearly overshooting so he dropped back and weaved gently. Another visual was obtained 30° above him. After chasing for another five minutes, the contact was identified as an He 219, He 219A-O Wrk Nr 190229 G9+GH of *I/NJG1*. Taylor opened fire from 250 yd but the Mosquito was caught in the enemy night-fighter's slipstream and his shooting was erratic. Strikes were observed and minor explosions appeared in the fuselage before the Owl turned slowly to port and peeled off. Visual was lost, but the Heinkel was followed on AI until contact was lost at 12,000 ft (3,650 metres). A few seconds later, it exploded on the ground at Suedlohn. *Unteroffizier* Scheürlein, the pilot, bailed out safely. *Unteroffizier* Günther Heinze the radar operator was killed. Taylor and Edwards were killed on 22/23 December when they crashed while attempting to make an approach to land at Swannington after informing Flying Control over the R/T that they had no aileron control.

Bad weather interfered again before operations resumed on 21/22 December. Only 28 aircraft supported 475 heavies attacking Cologne, Bonn. Politz and Schneidemuhl. Three bombers failed to return. Low-level *Intruder* and Mk IV AI Mosquitoes did not operate. The only contact of the night was obtained by Wing Commander K. H. P. Beauchamp DSO DFC and Flight Lieutenant L. Scholefield DFC of 157 Squadron south of Bonn. Beauchamp reported:

> We had completed our patrol uneventfully at 1852 hours and were on the way home at 12,000 ft [3,650 metres], just west of Koblenz when my navigator got a contact 60° to port at 5 miles [8 km] range, going port. This was chased on an initial heading of 150°, turning port slowing on to 060°. We were losing height and eventually overtook him at 4,000 ft [760 metres] having been flying at 300 mph [680 km] for most of the time. A visual was obtained at 2,500 ft [760 metres] and was identified as a Ju 88 in the light of a half-moon from 200 ft [60 metres] on his starboard quarter below. I dropped back to 200 ft [60 metres] dead astern and fired a short burst, causing strikes. Enemy aircraft immediately peeled off port and went down on to the top of some stratus cloud, which appeared to be just above ground level. I thought he had dived right through this as I had lost visual contact,

but as there was no resultant explosion I followed down and regained a visual on him as he was weaving away violently just above cloud. I closed in on his port quarter and slightly above, opening fire at about 600 yd, as I was anxious to inflict further damage before he could make good his escape. Strikes were obtained from this burst and from two more, the last of which set his port engine on fire. I pulled up and did a port orbit over him watching the fire increase until the enemy aircraft flew into the ground in a shallow dive and exploded … in view of the length of time of the combat and the final behaviour of the enemy aircraft it seems likely that the crew had time to escape by parachute.

Beauchamp fired 176 rounds of SAPI and 172 rounds of HEI to down the Ju 88.

More Ju 88 losses occurred on the following night, 22/23 December, when forty-five aircraft were dispatched to cover 274 heavies attacking Koblenz and Bingen. High-level ASH patrols were carried out but no contacts resulted. The mercurial Mk X AI squadrons worked their magic once again with a 'wizard prang' or two. Branse Burbridge and Skelton, and Dolly Doleman and Bunny Bunch DFC of 85 Squadron destroyed a Bf 110 and a Ju 88 respectively. Doleman reported:

Arrived at patrol at 1825 hours and at 1835 hours obtained contact. We were at 15,000 ft [4,600 metres] and chased it up to 20,000 ft [6,100 metres], just north of Bingen. While staggering up the last few thousand feet a *Monica* contact whistled in, and position became so uncomfortable, we had to leave the original contact and try to catch the other type. As we turned to port the *Monica*, which had been frantically jammed, cleared (we think the first contact might have been a Dinah [sic] Mosquito) and we saw the type behind showing IFF. After several conversations on the R/T, starting with 'Please go away', and finishing '——— off, you silly ———' we neared the bomber stream and dived into a cloud of *Window* where we lost him. This had wasted about twenty minutes of valuable time, and as bombing had finished we went along north of Frankfurt to have a look at Limburg. This proved a good bet, as we obtained a contact at 10 miles [16 km] range and well below. We were at 15,000 ft [4,600 metres] and time 1925 hours. We closed range and descended to 8,000 ft [2,400 metres] and obtained visual at 3,000 ft [900 metres]; the target by this time was doing a hardish port turn. Identified at 1,500 ft [460 metres] from below in the turn as a Ju 88 then the silly clot slackened his turn and we were able to close in nicely to 500 ft [150 metres] and prang him with only ½-ring deflection. The fuselage and port engine burst into flames. We hung behind just to make sure, but he dived straight in 5 miles [8 km] west of Limburg at 1935 hours. We wished him a Merry Christmas on the way down – literally cooking his goose for him.

No more joy, so left patrol at 1949 hours. Saw a buzz bomb in Malmedy area on way back. Just getting nicely in position when some brown job opened up with one solitary gun, missed the buzz bomb and frightened us away. I hope it landed on their headquarters. Landed base 2107 hours. Claim one Ju 88 destroyed.

Doleman fired 52 SAPI and 48 HEI rounds to dispatch the enemy night-fighter.

Flying Officers A. J. 'Ginger' Owen and J. S. V. McAllister also went on the rampage, scoring a hat trick of victories, with two Ju 88s and a Bf 110. First they shot down a Bf 110 north of Saarbrücken. Then a *Monica* contact was obtained almost immediately afterwards. It was converted to AI at 14,000 ft (4,300 metres) range. At 1200 ft (3,650 metres), visual was obtained, and confirmed as a Ju 88 on closing dead below it. Owen gave it a 'medium' burst from 150 yd which set the port engine on fire before crashing in the same area as the Bf 110. Twenty minutes later, a third contact was obtained 4 miles (6.5 km) ahead. Closing to 2,000 ft (610 metres), a visual was obtained well above him. It was another Ju 88 and it was taking evasive action. A short deflection burst scored strikes on the port wing and pieces flew off. The Ju 88 dived vertically and contact was lost at 7,000 ft (2,100 metres). Four minutes later, an explosion occurred on the ground. Ju 88 Wrk Nr 621441 27+HK of *II/NJG6* crashed at Landstuhl killing *OberFeldwebel* Max Hausser, the pilot, *OberFeldwebel* Fritz Steube, the radar operator and *Feldwebel* Ernst Beisswenger, the air gunner. Ju 88G-6 Wrk Nr 621436 2Z+DC also of *II/NJG6*, crashed at Lebach, north of Saarbrücken. *Unteroffizier* Werner Karau survived, while the two other crew were killed.

Flight Lieutenant Hannowin obtained a visual on a Ju 88 but contact was lost because of violent evasive action by the enemy aircraft. For twenty-four minutes, Warrant Officer Taylor chased a contact. When a visual was obtained, it was seen to be a Ju 88, and

NFXIX of 157 (SD) Squadron at its dispersal near St Peter's Church, Haveringland on whose land part of RAF Swannington airfield was sited.

throwing out *Düppel (Window)*. The Mosquito overshot and contact was lost. A 199 Squadron Stirling crew obtained a visual on an Fw 190 dead astern at 450 yd. Both the rear and mid-upper gunners opened fire before the enemy fighter could attack.

On 23/24 December sixty-one aircraft of 100 Group supported operations by Bomber Command when 105 heavies attacked cities in Germany. Low-level *Intruders* had no combats but took advantage of the moonlight to bomb and strafe a variety of aerodromes and any other targets. Again the aerial victories went to the Swannington squadrons. A contact was obtained by Flight Lieutenant G. C. Chapman and Flight Lieutenant J. Stockley of 85 Squadron at 8 miles (13 km) range and 11,000 ft (3,350 metres) in the Mannheim area, which turned out to be a Bf 110. After a prolonged dogfight, Chapman finally shot it down just south of Mainz. Flight Lieutenant R. J. V. Smythe and Flying Officer Waters of 157 Squadron destroyed a Ju 88 about 10 miles (16 km) west of Koblenz.

On Christmas Eve 100 Group supported two raids, by 104 Lancasters of 3 Group on Hangelar airfield near Bonn, losing one aircraft, and by 97 Lancasters and five Mosquitoes of 1 and 8 Groups on the marshalling yards at Cologne/Nippes. The Mosquito squadrons in 100 Group celebrated the festive season in style, claiming four Me 110s and one Ju 88 shot down. Low-level *Intruders* covered enemy airfields and carried out *Ranger* operations in the Breslau area. Locomotives, rolling stock and motor transport were bombed and strafed by the Mk IV AI Mosquito squadrons operating as low-level *Intruders*. Meanwhile, Wing Commander Howard C. Kelsey DFC, the new 515 Squadron Commanding Officer, and Flying Officer Edward M. 'Smithy' Smith took off from Little Snoring in the afternoon for a night *Intruder* operation. Edward Smith recalls:

> We had been interested in night-fighter training areas and felt the Breslau area might be fruitful. We landed at Laon/Juvincourt to refuel as this station was supposed to provide facilities for Bomber Command aircraft. On arrival we found some panic on there as the Battle of the Bulge had just started. However, we managed to make arrangements to refuel and have a quick meal before starting off at 1650 hours across southern Germany, passing near Bayreuth at quite a low level; 200–300 ft [60–90 metres].

The commanding officer and his navigator reached Rosenhorn airfield at 1952 hours. It was not lit but several aircraft were seen parked around the perimeter. Kelsey made several low runs over the airfield but, as there was some ground haze with poor visibility, he decided to continue his patrol and return to Rosenborn later. They had the same problems at Ohlau airfield so they returned to Rosenborn. Several Ju 52 transports were seen parked at the south end of the airfield while a single He 111 was parked on the north side near a radio station. Kelsey took the Heinkel first, broadside on, from 1,300 ft (400 metres) down to 150 ft (45 metres), breaking off at 200-ft range. Kelsey's cannon shells ripped into the Heinkel but it did not catch fire. Then the crew turned their attentions to the Ju 52s and a lone Ju 88. Again Kelsey attacked from broadside on, breaking off the attack at 200 ft (60 metres) range at a height of 150 ft (45 metres). Kelsey claimed one Ju 52 and the Ju 88 as 'damaged'. Smith adds, 'On the way back we damaged two trains severely in the Prague area.'

The Mk X AI Mosquitoes, meanwhile, enjoyed almost total air superiority over the *Nachtjägdgeschwader* that night. Squadron Leader James Benson DFC* and Flight

Lieutenant Lewis Brandon DFC* of 157 Squadron in Mosquito XIX were airborne Swannington at 1819 hours on high-level support patrol for Bomber Command attacks on Cologne and Hangelar. Lewis Brandon recalls:

We decided to have our Christmas dinner on Christmas Eve. As a maximum effort had been asked for from the station for the night's operations, we were very pleased that we all had an early time for take-off. It was arranged that dinner would be held back until we returned, giving us something to look forward to. We left Swannington at 1630 hours on our way to Limburg. We had put in quite a lot of flying time in that area during the past few weeks and considered ourselves rather as specialists around Frankfurt – a couple of Frankfurters almost.

We had been on patrol at 14,000 ft [4,300 metres] for about half an hour when we obtained a contact. We were just north of Limburg and the aircraft was well below us. Down we went pretty smartly to 8,000 ft [2,400 metres] after a target that was flying level at that height but weaving quite violently. As we closed in, Ben had fleeting visuals two or three times. Each time, however, he could not hold on to them nor could he identify the aircraft. We continued to follow him on AI, and he turned through two complete orbits before settling down on a north-westerly course. Shortly afterwards we saw some target indicators go down ahead of us. We had closed in on the aircraft and Ben got a visual on a Messerschmitt 110 at a range of 2000 ft [610 metres], silhouetted against the light of the target indicators.

'Okay. I can see him all right now,' said Ben. 'Just look at that. No wonder we've taken such a while to close in.'

As I looked up, I saw the Messerschmitt go across us from starboard to port. It went a fair way out to port, then went right up on one wing and came back in front of us, crossing the other way in this violent weave. Ben followed it through several of these weaves, fairly well throttled back and far more gently than the Messerschmitt. Then, from about 150 yd he gave it two short, sharp bursts, firing at the exhaust flames. The second burst set the port engine and the whole of the port side of the fuselage alight. We dived under some large pieces of debris that came flying back and heard them swoosh above the cockpit. The Messerschmitt was well alight now and going over to our starboard. We saw it hit the ground and explode near a small town by the name of Dottesfeld [about 10 miles (16 km) west of Mainz], where we could see it burning brightly.

'About bloody time we shot one down again,' remarked Ben. 'Look at it burning. I wonder if the camera gun would pick that up?'

'Why not have a go?' I suggested. So we did.

We had a good look around to see that there was no high ground and Ben did two runs right down to within a few hundred feet of the burning aircraft. All in vain, though, nothing appeared on the film when it was developed.

We landed back at Swannington at five minutes to nine. Dinner had been laid on for half past so after a pretty rapid debriefing we set off for the mess. We were fortified with the news that, in addition to our Messerschmitt,

Jimmy Mathews and Penrose had destroyed a Junkers 88. [Flight Lieutenant Jimmy Mathews and Warrant Officer Alan Penrose of 157 Squadron blasted a Ju 88 of *V/NJG2* with a one-and-a-half second burst, which resulted in the starboard engine bursting into flames. As it turned to port, three parachutes came out in quick succession and three bodies sailed to earth. The aircraft then spun down and crashed at Roermond 3 miles (5 km) south-west of Cologne]. As can be imagined, this gave the squadron something to celebrate. Four enemy aircraft destroyed in one night was by no means a record, but this had been accomplished on Christmas Eve, just before a party.

Benson added: 'About time too after two damaged recently.'

Another success went to Captain Svein Heglund DFC and Flying Officer Robert Symon of 85 Squadron, who obtained an AI contact at 1850 hours. Heglund reported:

We were flying on a south-easterly course away from target area and towards a visual beacon in Wiesbaden area when we obtained a contact head on and below at 6 miles [10 km] range. We turned port and dived, levelling out at 14,000 ft [4,300 metres], coming in behind an aircraft doing a mild corkscrew, range 1½ miles [2.5 km]. We chased rapidly to 3,000 ft [900 metres] and aircraft climbed rapidly to 14,000 ft [4,300 metres], weaving all the time. A visual was obtained at 2,000 ft [610 metres], on a faint outline and a dim white light inboard of the starboard engine. Following the white light through several turns range was closed to 150 ft [45 metres], when aircraft was recognized as an Me 110 by twin fins and rudders, general outline and large drop tanks. We dropped back to 600 ft [180 metres] and fired a half-second burst, obtaining strikes on starboard wing root. Aircraft exploded immediately and we dived hard to avoid flaming debris which showered back over us.

We once again turned on original south-easterly course and almost immediately obtained another contact dead ahead at 6 miles [10 km], height being 15,000 ft [4,600 metres], travelling on the same course as ourselves. We increased speed and went into a shallow dive slowly overhauling the aircraft, which was travelling at about 300 mph [480 kph] IAS. Shortly before arriving at the beacon and when we had closed range to 2,500 ft [760 metres], aircraft dived hard to starboard then climbed hard, contact being lost for some seconds. Contact was regained and aircraft dived hard again turning as it did so. Contact was finally lost. During the last part of the chase the port engine was getting very rough, cutting intermittently and vibrating. Claim: one Me.110 destroyed. Aircraft landed base 2041 hours.

It was Heglund's fourteenth victory of the war, having scored twelve and one-third kills flying Spitfires with No.331 Squadron.

Squadron Leader Dolly Doleman and Flight Lieutenant Bunny Bunch of 157 Squadron were airborne from Swannington at 1626 hours at the start of a very auspicious high-level support patrol for Bomber Command attacks on Cologne and Hangelar.

Doleman wrote:

> Just before reaching patrol had a radar dogfight with something. We presumed this to be either friendly or single-engined. We found on landing this was RSD. Reached patrol area and saw an aircraft hit the deck dead below us near Siegen. Things seemed pretty dead, so went towards Cologne and just as we arrived, obtained a contact: range 6 miles [10 km] well below. Overhauled fairly quickly and just managed to slow down into an ideal position, where we identified an Me 110 doing an orbit at 9,000 ft [2,750 metres]. I think the crew must have been full of the festive spirit as we were directly up moon at 600 ft [180 metres] when we opened fire with very long burst. The pride of the *Luftwaffe* caught fire immediately but we gave them another burst just for fun, and he went down and pranged just west of Cologne at 1905. We immediately had another contact at 10 miles [16 km] range, well above. Chased this at full bore and luckily the tyke dived down and we closed in very rapidly, eventually slightly overshooting. About 50 yd to port, having a wizard view of another Me 110. We did a hard port orbit and picked him up at 3 miles [5 km] – by this time we were at 8,000 ft [2,400 metres], going NW slap across the Ruhr – closed in and identified again and opened fire from about 500 ft [150 metres] with long burst. He caught fire and pieces of debris fell off including one quite large piece. He continued flying evenly so we gave him three more bursts, when he went down in the Duisburg area at 1921 hours. We headed west, as we could not fix on *Gee* and found ourselves near Krefeld and flew straight home. Cannot write any more as there is a party on in the mess. Claim two Me 110s destroyed. Aircraft landed at base 2024 hours.

Doleman fired 484 rounds of SAPI and HEI.

One of their victims was Bf 110G-4 Wrk Nr 740162 G9+OT, flown by *Hauptmann* Heinz Strüning, *Ritterkreuz mit Eichenlaub* (Knight's Cross with Oak Leaves), *Staffelkapitän* of *IX/NJG1,* which was shot down at 2200 hours and crashed at Bergisch Gladbach/Rheinland. The *bordfunker* and *bordschütze* baled out safely but the 32-year-old ace, who had fifty-six night victories, was killed when he hit the tail of his 110. His body was found two months later. *Luftwaffe* losses included Bf 110 of *VII/NJG1,* which crashed near Roermond killing the crew and one Ju 88 of *V/NJG2* which also crashed near Roermond, killing one of the crew while three were captured. This may have been the aircraft claimed by Mathews and Penrose of 157 Squadron. One Ju 88 of *V/NG1* crashed south of Afferden; one crew member was killed, two were reported 'missing' and one was captured.

Also over Christmas, 462 (RAAF) Squadron, the last unit to join 100 Group and equipped with Halifax BIIIs, transferred to Foulsham airfield, initially as part of the *Window* force. The reaction of crews commanded by Squadron Leader P. M. Paull DFC to being taken off bombing operations in 4 Group in order to drop strips of silver paper in 100 Group is unknown, but bombs were carried until the installation of Airborne *Cigar* was completed in March and the Aussies could begin jamming operations. (The squadron CO at Driffield had been Wing Commander David Shannon DFC of Dambusters fame, but he had completed his tour and was to return to Australia to join QANTAS.)

Halifax BIII MZ913 Z5-N Jane of 462 (RAAF) Squadron, which began operations in 100 Group on 1/2 January 1945 and by the war's end had lost twenty-three Australian and twenty RAF aircrew on spoof and jamming operations. Note the ABC transmission aerial under the nose. (via Jerry Scutts)

Staying at the Crown in Fakenham over Christmas were six wives and girlfriends of 23 Squadron crews. At lunchtime on 28 December Flying Officer Lewis Heath, a pilot who was on leave, volunteered to go to Snoring to collect the mail. He did not return until the following day. His wife Pauline asked, 'Where have you been?' Lewis smiled and said, 'Oslo Fjord!' Despite their protests he and his navigator, Flight Sergeant Jack Thompson, had been told that they were 'on' for an escort to Norway for Halifax minelayers of 6 Group!

On 31 December/1 January five aircraft were destroyed. The last of thirty-nine *Luftwaffe* aircraft to fall to 100 Group in December were two Ju 88s and an He 219 Uhu on New Year's Eve. On that night Flight Lieutenants A. P. Mellows and S. L. 'Dickie' Drew of 169 Squadron, attached to 'B' Flight 85 Squadron at Swannington to try interceptions with AI Mk X, also had good fortune on their patrol that same night. Mellows recorded:

> We took off at 1654 hours on a high-level support patrol west of the Ruhr. Patrol was reached at 1758 hours and at 1808 hours AI contact was obtained at 6 miles [10 km] range and ceased turning slowly port and climbing from 15,000 ft to 18,000 ft [4,600 to 5,500 metres]. While this contact was still well above another came in at 3 miles [5 km] range from the west nearly head on. This was found to be at our height so we turned starboard as it

passed us and came in 4,000 ft [1,200 metres] behind. A visual was obtained at 2,000 ft [610 metres] on four white exhausts and on closing to 400 ft [120 metres] twin tail fins were seen, and shortly after black crosses on the blue undersurface of the wings were seen in the light of a searchlight. On the strength of this I fired a two-second burst from slightly below causing debris to fly off and a small fire in the fuselage. Another two-second burst caused an explosion, by the light of which Flight Lieutenant Drew clearly saw the dihedral and slanting fins of an He 219, which I confirmed. A further short burst set him well alight and from 1,000 ft [3,000 metres] to starboard we saw him climb for a few seconds before plunging to earth, where he exploded with a bright orange flash at 1824 hours in the Cologne area, Throughout the combat the He 219 was flying straight and level and appeared to have no knowledge of our presence. Mosquito landed Manston 2005 hours and crew returned to base 1.1.45.

Their victim was He 219A-2 Wrk Nr 290194 G9+KL of *III/NJG1* which crashed at Schleiden, 30 miles (50 km) south-west of Cologne. *Oberleutnant* Heinz Oloff, the pilot, and *Feldwebel* Helmut Fischer, the radar operator, who were wounded, both baled out and survived.

Two of the New Year's Eve victories were the first using ASH. The first went to Squadron Leader C. V. Bennett DFC and Flight Lieutenant R. A. Smith of 515 Squadron. In the Lovns Bredning area during an *Intruder* patrol to Grove, Bennett and Smith's Mosquito was fired at with tracer from *Oberleutnant* August Gyory's Ju 88 of *IV/NJG2*. Bennett returned fire at 400 yd with a two-second burst of cannon and strikes were seen on the port wing. A second burst cut the Ju 88 in two. Gyory spun in and dropped into Lim Fjord. No. 515 Squadron received a congratulatory signal from Air Vice Marshal Addison, 'Heartiest congratulations on opening the batting for the Ashes.' During the New Year's party which followed, they were joined by Squadron Leader J. Tweedale and Flight Lieutenant V. Cunningham of 23 Squadron, who scored their squadron's first victory using ASH by destroying a Ju 88 of *NJG5* at Alhorn. It brought the number of victories during the month to thirty-seven. It is no coincidence that 85 Squadron, which claimed eighteen victories, and 157 Squadron, which claimed thirteen, were the only squadrons in 100 Group which were equipped with the excellent Mk X AI radar. *Intruder* incursions over *Luftwaffe* bases were being made with haunting regularity and there was much 'joy' as the predators enjoyed rich pickings from among the returning flocks of unsuspecting, weary, *Nachtjägdgeschwader* crews.

On 13 January Bennett and Smith were lost when they went down in the North Sea on the way home.

CHAPTER XI

No Joy?

At times when hope was fading
They would patient vigil keep,
Rejoicing if their crew returned
But often they would weep.
They wept for those who ere the sun
Had warmed the fresh turned clod,
Had fought in their last battle
And were at peace with God.

S. F. Ruffle

Crews of the *Gruppenstab* and the VIIIth and IXth *Staffeln* of *III/NJG2* at Marx/Varel were given the usual 'meteorological and signal' briefing on 31 December and the commanding officer told the crews that in view of the suitable weather conditions, an RAF raid was to be mounted that night. At 1800 hours his eight Ju 88s were ordered to take off. The first 4R+0S, was sitting at the end of the runway awaiting the signal when a Mosquito *Intruder* dropped a bomb which exploded on the runway about 30 yards away. No damage was apparently suffered by 4R+0S and it took off after a short delay. The crew made for Hanover and soon saw the first cascade flares. On arrival, they saw the incendiary bombs and fires. A four-engined bomber was seen to be held in searchlights and heading south-west. The Naxos and SN-2 of 4R+0S had been unserviceable for some time and the four-engined aircraft was lost. The Ju 88 first turned west-north-west in the hope of finding the bomber stream but after fifteen minutes the starboard engine cut out. It was a coolant leak, caused by the *Intruder's* bomb.

The *Intruder* was crewed by Lewis Heath and Jack Thompson of 23 Squadron, which had taken off from Little Snoring at 1700 hours on 1 January. The Ju 88 pilot turned due east to return to Marx/Varel but soon afterwards the crew, believing themselves to be over German territory and anxious to find their exact whereabouts, fired a recognition signal followed by two 'reds' which they repeated. They were then surprised by a night-fighter attack from aft. The pilot lost control and all the crew baled out. They all landed in Allied territory and were taken prisoner.

This account was extracted from one of the crew on interrogation and subsequently Air Commodore Chisholm hoped that Flying Officer Heath would be credited with a destroyed enemy aircraft as it was considered that 4R+0S was hit by splinters from bombs dropped on the airfield by the Mosquito crew before take-off.

Sixteen aircraft were claimed shot down by 100 Group Mosquitoes in January 1945. On 1/2 January, when eight Halifaxes of 462 Squadron flew their first Spoofing operation in 100 Group, Mosquitoes on bomber support covered heavy operations over Germany. Eight crews in 85 Squadron participated in a maximum effort in the Kiel and Ruhr areas while the main force attacked the Mittelland Canal, rail yards at Vohwinkel and Dortmund. Dickie Goucher and Tiny Bullock chased a contact for eleven minutes before obtaining a visual. It was a Ju 188. Goucher gave it a couple of bursts and it fell in flames, crashing ten miles north of Munster. Almost immediately, Tiny Bullock got a second blip on his Mk X scope, apparently dropping *Düppel.* Goucher got closer and they could see that their enemy was a Ju 88G. Goucher gave it a long burst from dead astern as the Junkers turned to port. Flying flaming debris struck the Mosquito, causing it to vibrate badly and lose height. Goucher jettisoned his drop tanks and the port tank came over the top of the wing, damaging the tail plane and at the same time shearing off the pitot head. They landed safely at Brussels/Melsbroek and were flown home in a C-47 the next day. Their second victim was Ju 88G-6 Wrk Nr 621364 27+CP of *V/NJG6,* which crashed at Dortmund. *Oberleutnant* Hans Steffen, pilot and *Unteroffizier*s Josef Knon, Helmut Uttler and Friedrich Krebber, were killed.

Four Mosquitoes of 239 Squadron carried out low-level *Intruder* patrols. One of these, flown by Flying Officers Walker and J. R. Watkins, crashed on return at Narford Hall just north of RAF Marham and both were killed. One of the six Mosquitoes dispatched by 141 Squadron on a high-level ASH patrol was forced to land in France with oxygen trouble. Another, flown by Flight Lieutenant Ron Brearley and Flying Officer John Sheldon, took off at 1710 hours on a low-level *Intruder* patrol to the airfield at Luneburg. They crossed in at Egmond, Holland, at 1749 hours at 200 ft (60 metres) and flew to Luneburg, arriving at 1846. The airfield was lit on their approach but the lights were doused as they arrived. Brearley orbited for ten minutes and as there was no activity flew off to the south. At 1906 hours he approached the airfield again and again it was lit. The Mosquito orbited about 1 mile (1.5 km) away and the crew saw the exhausts of an aircraft taking off but this was then lost. Four searchlights were exposed around the airfield, two pointing in their direction.

Brearley and Sheldon continued to patrol the airfield until 1940 hours. When crossing it at about 100 ft (30 metres) they saw two very small green lights moving along the flarepath. It was an aircraft which had just landed. They executed a tight turn and came in over the flarepath and over the aircraft. Brearley opened fire. Many strikes were seen all over it but it did not burn. They turned again, giving a longer approach, and once more Brearley opened fire. Again many strikes were seen resulting in pieces being scattered in all directions. This time the German night-fighter burst into flames and burned furiously. Searchlights were exposed all over the area and flak came up all around them. Brearley took evasive action and then stood off and watched the enemy plane burn before setting course for home at 1945 hours.

On the night of 5/6 January Captain Svein Heglund DFC and Flying Officer R. O. Symon of 85 Squadron in their Mosquito XXX flew an eventful high-level support patrol to northern Osnabrück. Heglund and Symon were airborne from Swannington at 1955 hours. Patrol was reached at 2100 hours and after fifty minutes a contact was obtained and chased for twenty minutes, finally being identified by exhausts and behaviour as a Mosquito. At 2225 hours in the patrol area a head-on contact was obtained and chased on 240°. Heglund reported:

After having patrolled beacon in Munster/Osnabrück area without any contact we set course for Hanover and arrived just as the target indicators were sent out. We got contact, which we chased in a westerly direction for twenty minutes with everything pushed forward. We just got a visual of exhaust flames, which looked like a Mosquito and took it for one of the pathfinder force and turned back towards target.

At 2223 hours we got another head-on contact north of Osnabrück and turned in behind it. It was slightly above and we closed in to about 2,000 ft [610 metres], when my operator lost contact owing to scanner trouble. We made one orbit and picked up contact again at 4 miles [6.5 km] range. We closed in again and got visual of Me 110 recognizing square wings and twin fins and rudders. As we were slightly overshooting I weaved underneath enemy aircraft keeping visual contact all the time. At 500 ft [150 metres] range I pulled up behind it and gave it is a short burst, which caused an explosion in fuselage. Lots of smoke and debris was flying off and enemy aircraft continued flying straight and level. I rather think the crew was killed right away. I fired another burst, which missed and noticed small explosions going on all the time. The third burst put enemy aircraft well on fire and it crashed on the ground with a large explosion at 2230 hours. We got two more contacts afterwards, which turned out to be Mosquitoes and then set course for base.

Claim: one Me 110 destroyed. Mosquito landed base 2355 hours.

It was his fifteenth and final victory of the war. Another top scoring team, Flight Lieutenants Ben Benson DSO DFC* and Lewis 'Brandy' Brandon DSO DFC* notched their ninth combined victory that night, shooting down He 219A-0 Wrk Nr 190188 G9+CK of *II/NJG1*. It crashed 3 miles (5 km) south of Wesendorf. *Oberfeldwebel* Josef Stroelein, the pilot, was killed. *Unteroffizier* Kenne, the radar operator, baled out safely. Ju 88 Wrk Nr 620513 R4+CD of *II/NJG2* is possibly the aircraft shot down by Flight Lieutenant A. S. Briggs and Flying Officer Rodwell of 515 Squadron. It crashed at Jägel airfield. *Oberleutnant* Bruno Heilig, the pilot, *Unteroffizier* Günther Kulas, the radar operator, *Gefreiter* Johan Goliasch, the flight engineer, and *Obegefreiter* Horst Jauernig, the air gunner, were killed.

Meanwhile, Flying Officer Frank Bocock and Flight Sergeant Alf 'Snogger' Rogers of 515 Squadron had found little joy in recent weeks. Alf Rogers recalls:

A typical night *intruder* op. began by crossing the North Sea at less than 500 ft [150 metres]. In this way they were too low to be detected by German radar. The Dutch coast was crossed at a point 5 miles [8 km] north of the town of Egmond. From there-on navigation was by map-reading which could be difficult on a dark night. Water features showed up quite well so these were used as pinpoints. After crossing the coast the next turning point was the distinctive mouth of the Ijsell River on the eastern side of the Zuider Zee. Then on to the Dortmund–Ems Canal, next Dummer Lake, then Steinhuder Lake. Depending on which aerodrome was being visited the *Intruder* would turn off at one of these points and head for the target.

If the target was in southern Germany the route would be via Belgium. This involved another problem as the Allied armies moved in. They created several 'artillery zones' where the gunners were free to fire on any aircraft flying lower than 10,000 ft [3,000 metres]'. *Intruders* never flew higher than 2,000 ft [610 metres] so they had to avoid these zones to avoid being shot down by what is now euphemistically called 'friendly fire'. Sometimes the target was Lista in Norway. This involved a 500 mile [800 km] sea crossing where *Gee* was not available. Then it was a matter of trusting that the Met Officer had been accurate in forecasting the wind velocity and that the navigator had worked out his flight plan correctly. Occasionally *Intruders* carried bombs, HE or incendiary, in which case the primary target was the *Luftwaffe* base. Failing that, any other legitimate target that presented itself was attacked. So low-level night *Intruders* contributed to the safe return of many a bomber crew.

One night in December we were assigned an *Intruder* target at Giessen in southern Germany. The previous few days had been very wintry and there was a good deal of snow on the ground. The snow plough had been busy keeping the runways usable. As we walked out to dispersal the sky was heavy with more snow and as we climbed into our Mossie the snow began to fall heavily. We settled ourselves into the cockpit, started the engines and began to move off. After we had moved just a yard or two Frank said 'Can you see anything at your side?' I said 'No – but I have an uneasy feeling that we are not right.' Frank said, 'So have I – we'd better stop.' He put the brakes on and we strained our eyes in an effort to see something through the darkness and the falling snow. We spotted a groundcrew coming round in front of us carrying two marshalling torches. He stood with his back towards us, put both torches together and shone them straight ahead. In the light of the torches we were just able to see directly in front of us a petrol bowser. The groundcrew pointed us in the right direction and we began to creep around the perimeter track.

We had not gone far when over the R/T a voice from Control said, 'Aircraft on runway – return to dispersal.' So it seemed that ops were scrubbed. We were about to turn round and return when another voice on the R/T said 'It's all right, Control, we can cope.' After that silence. We didn't quite know what to make of that so Frank called Control and asked, 'Do we go or don't we?' Back came the reply, 'You can go if you like.' Go if you like! On ops! We decided that having gone so far we might as well continue. So we taxied round and took off along the snow-covered runway.

We always flew over the sea at a maximum of 500 ft [150 metres] so it was no problem to stay below cloud at first. But eventually we had to climb in an effort to get above the weather. Being a low-level squadron our engines had a rated altitude of 2,000 ft [610 metres]. On this occasion we climbed steadily up through the cloud but never quite out of the top. There was a spectacular display of St Elmo's fire and serious icing. Icing on the control surfaces prevented any manoeuvering and we had no alternative but to fly straight and level, hoping to run into clear skies. When we did eventually run out of the cloud we had passed our target area. There was no possibility of carrying out a low-level *Intruder* so once we were free of the ice we just had to turn round and come back. In a way that was worse. On the outward flight we had pressed on in the hope of finding better weather. Now we knew exactly what lay ahead – all the way back to base. We had not encountered enemy action, but that was one occasion when we were glad to get back home.

Bocock and Rogers flew their nineteenth operation on 28/29 December, a flak patrol off Jeloy Island in Norway in support of a raid on Oslo Fjord by sixty-seven Lancasters and one Mosquito of 5 Group. Strong winds blew Bocock and Rogers south to the northern tip of Denmark on the way home. On the 30th they flew all the way to Stavanger where they dropped flares over Lista airfield only to discover there were no aircraft, 'not even a light'. Adding to their frustration was the fact that no RAF bombers were headed that way either. (Much later, Frank Bocock was told that agents were being dropped in Norway that night.) Long missions over water were flown at 150 ft (45 metres) above the surface of the sea using the radio altimeter. In complete contrast, their operation on 7 January, to Hailfingen in J-Jig, was at very high level indeed! Bocock was forced to climb to 23,000 ft (7,000 metres) to get above cloud. The heating failed and the temperature registered –37°C outside, or 70°F of frost. Rogers was so cold that he wrapped his hands around the bulb on the *Gee* box to try to warm them. They landed back at Snoring after four hours. Bocock and Rogers came through but there were periods when the 'chop rate' became very high. Frank Bocock says, 'You learned not to be so damned inquisitive sometimes.'

On 12 January, two Mosquito VIs of 169 Squadron gave high-level and ASR support for a raid by thirty-two Lancasters and one Mosquito of 9 and 617 Squadrons on U-boat pens and shipping in Bergen harbour, Norway. Two Mosquitoes of 169 Squadron flew long-range escort for an ASR operation. Nearing the target, NS998 encountered five Fw 190s. Undaunted, they attacked two of them and damaged one. In NT176, Squadron Leader John Wright was chased by them.

Two days later, the first five Mk XIX Mosquitoes arrived at Great Massingham from Swannington and joined 'A' Flight for high-level patrols and intruding. 'A' Flight had been flying *Serrate* patrols since November, while 'B' Flight, which operated Mk VIs, used *Serrate* and *Perfectos.* No. 169 Squadron flew its first Mk XIX Mosquito operation on 21 January. This same night 239 Squadron operated Mk XXX Mosquitoes for the first time.

Meanwhile, on 14/15 January, the main Bomber Command thrust was aimed at a synthetic oil plant at Leuna, near Merseberg, railway yards at Grevenbroich, and an oil store at Dulmen. Ron Brearley and John Sheldon of 141 Squadron again proved successful. Brearley wrote later:

> We contacted the bomber stream at the front line and overhauled them at a height of 20,000 ft [6,100 metres]. On reaching the target area we proceeded eastward through defended area between the banks of searchlights for seven–eight minutes, then struck north in the hope of intercepting enemy fighters from the Berlin area. An airfield was seen lit,

subsequently identified as either Jüterborg or Pretsch, but which doused on our approach.

We patrolled, sweeping north and south, for some time, noting three horizontal searchlights pointing south near Wittenberg. At 2130 hours, fifteen minutes after the Merseberg bombing had finished, an ASH contact was achieved at 13,000 ft [4,000 metres], 2½ miles [4 km], which we followed down to 6,000 ft [1,800 metres] before losing it in ground returns. Enemy aircraft was losing height rapidly and obviously heading for aforesaid airfield which was plainly visible and which now fired a green Very light. (The flarepath was unusually wide, about 300 yd with aircraft landing close to left-hand line of lights. Hangars and buildings plainly seen in light of flares). Smelling blood and knowing that none of our *Intruders* was operating thus far afield, we rapidly knocked off the remaining height and orbited the airfield at 1,500 ft [460 metres]. Navigation lights of an aircraft were seen on the approach, between the 'artificial horizon' and flarepath, at 2135 hours, so with a twitching thumb we turned hard port and came down in a diving quarter attack opening fire at 500–600 yd with half ring deflection. Strikes were seen in line with the enemy aircraft, but on the ground as he neared the runway. This was easily countered by raising the nose and continuing to squirt. Many strikes were seen on him and he hit the deck just off the flarepath, bursting into flames immediately. By the light of flares which had been put up, enemy aircraft was seen to be a twin-engined job, but these things happen much too quickly for positive identification.

While doing a hard turn over the airfield after this encounter another set of navigation lights was seen at the other side of the circuit, so we kept on the hard turn and hared after him, determined to get as much joy as we could with our seriously diminishing petrol. Deflection and range estimate being somewhat difficult at night we allowed home one and a half rings for luck and fired at 500 yd as we closed in on him from the port side. After a two or three second burst some strikes were seen on him and flame streamed out behind him. Enemy aircraft dived away as we passed behind him and, as we watched, in a somewhat expectant manner, for him to prang. Instead he made a panic circuit and tried to land in spite of reds, which were being popped off from the ground. He failed to make it and opened up again, just as our attention was distracted by some flak, which hurtled up at us, necessitating evasive action, with the result that we did not see him again. However, yet another 'hod' was seen almost instantly, with his navigation lights on, and once again we gave chase. After our first burst at him he was evidently stirred by strong emotions, for he commenced weaving violently, and we followed as best we could, squirting as opportunity offered in the pious hope that something would hit him. Much to our regret no strikes were observed and he eventually pulled his finger out and switched off his lights.

As our petrol supply was really getting low we had to set course for home immediately, feeling somewhat peeved that we could no longer take advantage of such promising opportunities. Height was gained at 8,000 ft [2,400 metres] and while still well in enemy territory another enemy aircraft was seen burning navigation lights crossing to port some distance away. We turned after him but he soon switched them off and we turned back on course as a long ASH chase could not be contemplated even if we could have picked him up, in view of diminishing petrol. What a situation! Several lighted airfields were seen on the way back, and about 0600°E port radiator temperature was seen to be high (110°). Immediately throttled it back to -4 boost and reduced revs in order to nurse it. Temperature remained constant until 0400E when it shot up right round the clock. Feathered the propeller and proceeded to base to find cloud down to 700 ft [210 metres] and bad visibility. In view of this we had no alternative but to belly-land on the grass. *Gee* of course expired with the port engine and we were 'homed' by Coltishall and base. 215 gallons of petrol in tanks after landing.

Brearley and Sheldon, who were uninjured, submitted claims for one twin-engined aircraft destroyed and one damaged.

Flight Lieutenants K. D. Vaughan and Robert Denison MacKinnon of 85 Squadron shot down two enemy aircraft during January 1945, the first of these on the night of 14/15 January. Vaughan wrote:

Whilst on high-level patrol supporting attack on Merseburg at 2125 hours on last leg of patrol navigator reported contact 4½ miles [7 km] eleven o'clock port side crossing starboard to port, above. Our height 15,000 ft [4,600 metres]. Chased target flying straight in south-westerly direction gradually losing height. Closed in on target to identify. At range of 100 ft [30 metres] directly beneath, identified target as Ju 188 by pointed wings, underslung engines, no protruding leading edge between engines and fuselage and no exhausts. I increased range to 600 ft [180 metres] and fired a one-second burst dead astern, which produced a large explosion from starboard engine. I pulled away to starboard, but seeing no further results followed again on AI and closed in to 900 ft [270 metres] firing a two-second burst which produced no strikes. Closed in to 600 ft [180 metres] on target now rather rapidly losing height and decided to make certain this time. I fired a one-second burst, range 500 ft [1500 metres], producing strikes and explosion again in starboard engine with pieces flying off past Mosquito. Target then disappeared straight down to explode on ground right beneath us at 2143 hours lighting up countryside and cockpit of Mosquito with large orange glow. We orbited fire on ground. I claim one Ju 188 destroyed. Mosquito landed base 2315 hours.

Their victim was possibly Ju 88G-1 Wrk Nr 710818 D5+EP of *Stab/NJG3*, which crashed 2 miles (3 km) south-east of Friedberg, north of Frankfurt. *Oberfeldwebel* Johann Fels, the pilot, *Unteroffizier* Richard Zimmer, the radar operator and *Gefreiter* Werner Hecht, *bordschütze*, were killed.

When Bomber Command attacked Magdeburg and oil plants near Leipzig, and Brux in Czechoslovakia, on 16/17 January and 100 Group again flew support, Flight Lieutenant Vaughan and Flight Sergeant MacKinnon of 85 Squadron were airborne from

Swannington at 1902 hours for their high-level support in the Frankfurt area. Vaughan reports:

> We had completed uneventful patrol east of Frankfurt supporting raid on Zeitz and set course for base at 2140 hours. At 2145 hours, on vector 290° navigator reported contact 3½ miles [5.5 km] range crossing starboard to port. We closed in on target, losing height to 10,000 ft [3,000 metres], IAS 260. At 4,000 ft [1,200 metres] range two pairs of brilliant white exhausts could be seen. We closed to 150 ft [45 metres] below and astern and identified target as He 219 by twin fins and rudders, narrow wings with marked taper on trailing edge outboard of engines, long nose and those brilliant exhausts. Confirmation was obtained as to target's identity from my navigator using night glasses.
>
> I dropped back to 600 ft [180 metres] range astern and fired a two-second burst between the pairs of exhausts but no strikes were seen. Closed in to 400 ft [120 metres] range and fired another two-second burst and immediately a large explosion occurred in the port engine and we pulled up to starboard to avoid debris, which was coming back at us, and passed over enemy aircraft which went down to port with port engine on fire. We did a quick starboard orbit and saw burning fragments of aircraft falling and small fires starting on ground suggesting it had disintegrated in the air. Claim: one He 219 destroyed. Mosquito landed base 2345 hours.

Vaughan expended sixty-two SAPI and fifty-six HEI to destroy the Owl, and it was 85 Squadron's fourth and final victory of the month.

That same night five Mosquitoes of 239 Squadron made a Spoof bombing raid on Stuttgart, while eleven Mosquitoes of 141 Squadron patrolled to Zeitz and Magdeburg. Two of the three crews detailed to patrol the Magdeburg area were Flight Lieutenant D. H. Young and Flying Officer J. J. Sanderson, and Flying Officer R. C. Brady and Flight Lieutenant M. K. Webster. Young wrote up his combat report in a laid-back manner thus:

> We patrolled to the north and east of Magdeburg, watching it burn somewhat and we continued patrolling the furnace until 2220 hours when we decided to follow up the bomber stream and set course in that direction. Just as we were leaving Magdeburg at 2225 hours, our height being 20,000 ft [6,100 metres], a contact was got on the starboard side going further starboard, we followed it round the southern side and up the western side of the still furiously burning target, the searchlights very kindly pointing at the aircraft we were chasing. After about half a minute all the searchlights doused simultaneously (no doubt the Boche told them to put those —— lights out). Shortly after this, having followed him round on to a NE heading (weaving slightly) and closed to about 2,000 ft [60 metres], I saw a bluish green light being situated inboard of the starboard engine nacelle. I pulled the nose up and pressed the button and precisely two rounds came out. We both nearly burst into tears. Then for some inexplicable reason, I tried the gun master-switch and found that it had been flicked off

so I put it back on again. By this time I had dropped back to 800 ft [240 metres] but the Bf 110 continued flying straight and level. I was now afraid I should lose it any second so I closed in again as fast as possible – much too fast – and found myself about to ram the brute so I got him in the sight and opened fire again at what must have been 50 ft [15 metres]. He immediately exploded in a blinding flash, so I pulled back the stick and bounced over the top. A little later I saw the explosion on the ground where he crashed, blew up and burned furiously. We orbited the crash and put its position down. The ASH was now unserviceable so we set course for base and landed at 0033 hours.

Brady and Webster, meanwhile, were also heading for Magdeburg. As Webster went over to ASH on the 'downward tilt', the Dummer and Steinhuder lakes were picked up and valuably assisted navigation. They also used the H2S side of ASH to reach their patrol point, which was the Brandenburg Lake. They obtained an ASH contact at a range of 5 miles (8 km), well above them and crossing from port to starboard. Brady recalls:

We chased and after following the aircraft through some mild evasive tactics, obtained a visual, fifteen minutes after the initial contact, at 17,000 ft and 1,000 ft [30 metres] range. It was a Halifax. We followed it for a few minutes and it appeared to be orbiting the target of Magdeburg. We carried on with our patrol.

At 2245 hours whilst patrolling on a westerly vector south of Magdeburg at 14,000 ft [4,300 metres], a contact was obtained at 4–5 miles [6.5–8 km] well above and crossing gently to port from starboard. We gave chase and the aircraft appeared to be flying more or less straight and level. Range was closed to 2,000 ft [610 metres] behind, height 17,000 ft [5,200 metres]. At this point the aircraft appeared to get backward warning of us and began to take violent evasive action, in a wave of tight turns with loss of height. We managed to hang on to him but about 1½-miles [2.5 km] range. This continued for some time until finally the other aircraft seemed to give up and flew straight and level. We positioned ourselves dead behind him and at 1 mile [1.5 km] range and rapidly closed in and obtained a visual at 1,000 ft [30 metres] range. My 'good man' had the night glasses and identified the aircraft as an Me 110. Upon closing in I noticed a dim yellow light showing from outside the starboard engine nacelle of the enemy aircraft. Range was further closed to about 200 yd and below, so that looking up I was able to confirm the aircraft as being an Me 110. I was still tending to overshoot and was a little to port. I gave the enemy aircraft a one-second burst using 20° deflection from 200 ft [60 metres] and strikes were observed on the side of his fuselage. The enemy aircraft immediately fired off colours, which lit up the side of the aircraft. I turned away to port to allow the Bf 110 to get ahead of me, which he did, still flying straight and level – quite clueless. We came in behind him and slightly above and at 200 yd opened up with a five-second burst. Very many strikes were seen on the cockpit and thereabouts. Bits flew off and much black smoke belched out, then the port engine burst into flames. The 110 spiralled down burning furiously and hit the ground with a terrific explosion. It crashed approximately 25 miles [40 km] SW of Magdeburg at 2310 hours. We were very short of fuel by this time and headed straight back for base, landing at 0115 hours.

On 16/17 January Flight Lieutenant Tommy Smith of 23 Squadron, who by now was within two or three operations of completing his second tour, and his navigator, Flying Officer 'Cocky' Cockayne, were on ops. Tommy Smith recalls:

It was a dirty night – thick as a bag up to 16,000 ft [4,900 metres] – and we went on an ASH patrol to Stendal fighter airfield near Berlin. I used a square search system for nearly an hour, but picked up nothing and when the time was up, we set course for home. At the point when we should have been over the area of the Steinhuder Lake, we came across an airfield where aircraft with nav. lights on were taxiing. This was unheard of. I went in to have a bash. There was a chap sitting at the taxi point. He was my target: his nav. lights and the hooded runway lights were on. I opened up and saw a good cluster of cannon strikes on the aircraft, and was about to break away when I saw exhaust flames of another aircraft halfway up the runway. 'God, someone's taking off! I'll have him,' I thought. (I was trained to recognize an aircraft by the number, type and disposition of its exhaust flames and I reckoned it was a Ju 88.) So instead of breaking off, I closed in and opened up. My muzzle flashes lit up the Hun right under my chin! (I was so close I was practically looking at the back of the pilot's head.) It wasn't a Ju 88, it was an Me 109! (What I had taken for exhausts of two engines were the flames from either side of one engine.) Because of the difference in line between my gunsight and the guns beneath my feet, I was shooting low, being so close, and ripped the bottom out of the Me 109. He crashed at the end of the runway.

However, as I was pursuing this chap, I had passed between two flak towers at the downwind end of the runway. Light flak [from eight guns, the Germans said later] had the cannon flashes to aim at, and my Mosquito was hit coming in over the perimeter track at a height of about 200 ft [60 metres] in a dive. Flak set my right engine on fire and I automatically feathered the prop and pressed the extinguisher button. I zoomed up to 1,000 ft [30 metres]. My mind was running on how to get organized to fly home on one engine, when, all of a sudden the other engine stopped! The first engine was blazing merrily and the prop was feathering and unfeathering. I said to Cocky, 'That's it! Bale out!' It's not easy to get out of a Mosquito. Cocky was having trouble jettisoning the hatch door. Time and height were running out. I switched on the landing lights. Treetops showed up below. We were too low. I shouted, 'Knock it off. Do your harness up.' Cocky didn't answer. A burst of flame lit up the open hatch. He had baled out. I found out later that his parachute didn't open fully, and he had broken his neck.

The forest came up and I was skimming over the treetops, and preparing to stuff the nose in while I still had flying speed. I could feel the 'whiffle' which indicated the approach of the stall. Suddenly, there was a field covered in snow. I stuffed it in at about 200 mph [320 kph]. Next thing, I was hurtling along the ground heading for more trees. I thought it was a wood but it was only a line of trees; a windbreak! The trees ripped off the outer wing sections and something, possibly a stump, knocked a hole in the cockpit alongside me. I still had my hand on the throttle control and it was ripped away by the tree stump! Then I was out of the trees and into the snow again before the aircraft came to a stop. A feeling of relief came over me. All I could think was, 'A forced landing in the dark! What fantastic luck to be alive!'

All I had to do now was lift the roof emergency hatch, climb out, and run away. Except that in the crash, the whole of the seat had come adrift and shot me underneath the instrument panel, and the cockpit cabin was full of earth. The left rudder bar had taken my foot back under the seat and locked it. I had some grim moments trapped in the middle of a bonfire trying to extricate my foot. By the time I got out of the hole the port radiator and its contents were burning fiercely right outside the hole. I crawled out badly burned, and stuffed my face and hands into the snow. When I got up, I found I had a broken leg, caused by the rudder pedal. [He had also lost an eye.] By the light of the fire I could see a farmhouse and crawled over to it. Two soldiers hiding in the hedge, expecting the bombs to explode, carried me into the barn and about an hour later a *Luftwaffe* ambulance from Fassburg collected me. I was sadly aware that my wartime flying was over.

He was treated at Fassburg sick quarters. The Germans confirmed his destruction of the two 109s he had shot at and also credited him with another 109 which spun in due to the presence of the intruding Mosquito. It crashed and burnt out, killing the pilot. Tommy stayed at Fassburg for a month before being transferred to *Dulag Luft* at Frankfurt for another month. He was bombed out by the RAF then transferred to Homemark, a convent hospital being used for RAF POWs. On 28 March 1945, he and the other inmates were released by the US 3rd Army and flown home from Paris. At the POW reception centre at RAF Cosford, his assorted burns were treated in hospital. After discharge he was given a posting to Fighter Command HQ at Bentley Priory where the 'Prang Basher' once again took up crash investigation duties. When it came to demob he was invalided out of the RAF and sent to East Grinstead for further plastic surgery. It was there that he met a nursing sister who was to become his wife. Her name was Joy.

After the war, a *feldwebel* who had befriended Tommy when he was blind sent him photos of Cockayne's grave. It showed Tommy's grave, on the left, waiting for him! Tommy adds, 'The Huns were a tidy-minded lot and would have put the two of us alongside each other. Luckily I was "late for my own funeral".'

CHAPTER XII

I Dance With Gisela Tonight

Ganz alleine auf der Reise,
Jängt der kleine Kahn am Firmament,
Joch das stört in keinster Weise
Or ist in seinem Element.

'Das Lied von der "Wilden Sau"' by Peter Holm

On 21/22 January 239 Squadron attempted its first AI Mk X patrol when three Mosquitoes from West Raynham supported an attack on Kassel by seventy-six Mosquitoes, but the Mk XXXs returned early with radar problems. The two 141 Squadron Mosquitoes completed their patrols. The following night, fourteen Mosquitoes from 141 Squadron and three from 239 Squadron supported Bomber Command operations to Duisburg. One crew reported their first sighting of an enemy jet aircraft. German jets could certainly outpace the Mosquito but their introduction had been too little too late (the first ground units of 100 Group were established on the Continent, at Wenduine, Belgium, during January), and while on occasions they caused havoc with the US daylight bombing missions, they were less effective against the Mosquitoes at night.

More of a problem was the bad weather, January being the worst month since 100 Group began operations in December 1943. There were sixteen days of snow. A big freeze from 19 to 31 January prevented many operations. However, 100 Group Mosquitoes destroyed seventeen enemy aircraft and damaged three in January. One of the latter was credited to Flight Lieutenants A. P. Mellows and S. L. 'Dickie' Drew of 169 Squadron, attached to 'B' Flight 85 Squadron at Swannington on 28/29 January. Mellows reported:

> Shortly after completing patrol on Beacon *Fritz* single white flare was observed to north-west, presumably over Darmstadt. We proceeded in that direction and Biblis airfield was seen to be lit and had a canopy of four searchlights 2 miles [3 km] to the west. From 6,000 ft [1,800 metres] three single-engined aircraft in the airfield were outlined against the snow. As there were no signs of airborne activity and time was short it was decided to make an attack. The airfield was approached from the south-west and one single-engined aircraft, believed to be Fw 190, was attacked with two three-second bursts from a height of 1,500–1,000 ft [460–300 metres]. No results were observed from first burst defences opened up when we were over the centre of the airfield but without results. Claim one single-engined UEA damaged on ground.

By the end of the month, re-equipment with ASH was almost complete. All 141 Squadron's Mk XV AI radar and the *Monica* Mk IX backward AI ASH had been fitted and the squadron had only experienced four early returns from eighty sorties – a great tribute to the radar mechanics and their abilities in difficult conditions.

In February Mosquitoes of 100 Group shot down ten enemy aircraft, probably destroyed one other and damaged six. On 1/2 February *Oberleutnant* Gottfried Hanneck of *V/NJG1*, who had been shot down by House and MacKinnon on 13/14 September 1944, returned to Bf 110 operations, with a new crew of *Feldwebel* Pean, radio/radar operator, and *Unteroffizier* Glöckner, air gunner. Hanneck continues:

> After seven practise flights in January we arrived at Düsseldorf airfield on 1 February to fly on operations again. By this time, the night-fighter control organization was experiencing severe problems when trying to assess the plans of the enemy, as we had lost the complete advanced defence line (Holland, Belgium and France were already occupied by the enemy). Therefore, on this day a number of crews were ordered to fly to several night-fighter beacons, and wait there at the height at which the bombers were expected to fly in. I received orders to take off [in Bf 110G-4 Wrk Nr 730262 G9+CN] at 1945 hours, proceed to a beacon in the Frankfurt area and wait for any reports of enemy aircraft movements. Thus, we were flying around in wide circles and figures of eight in the prescribed area and waited for the enemy reports. These however, did not reach us, but something else did – the enemy in the shape of a Mosquito (which we were expecting because who else would have come?), which completely by surprise gave us a short burst of fire. We were hit. The intercom was put out of action, and the landing light in the wing came on. I stood the aircraft on its nose to avoid a second attack and to find shelter in a layer of clouds beneath us. My crew, who couldn't contact me any more, must have assumed I was hit as I was slumped over the control column. They baled out – and landed safely.
>
> I was now alone in the machine. I safely reached the layer of clouds and was now confronted with the question: should I bale out or attempt a crash-landing? There was no question that I should continue with my flight without any radio contact and with the light on. I decided to crash-land. I could only switch off the light by stopping both engines and glide towards the ground in an aircraft which weighed several tons. But where should I land? Fortunately, I could distinguish between the dark forest and the snow-white fields and I steered towards such a field where I let the tail unit touch the ground first (to avoid nosing over) and then with retracted undercarriage, slid over the ground on the motor gondolas. I had come down 2 km [1 mile] west of Kettershausen in the Westerwald. The time was 2110 hours. My face slightly hit the gun sights but I was able to scramble out of my seat and withdraw from the machine through the snow and shouted for help. A farmer 'collected' me on his horse-drawn sleigh and took me to the nearest army post. There I received first aid and large quantities of Cognac as a remedy for the shock and pain. Then I was transported to the nearest hospital, which was at Wissen on the Sieg.

It is believed that Hanneck's adversary was either a 157 or 239 Squadron Mosquito. Squadron Leader Ryall and Pilot Officer Mulroy of 157 Squadron claimed a Bf 110 'probable' at Oberolm, while Wing Commander Walter Gibb DSO DFC the 239 Squadron Commanding Officer and Flying Officer R. C. Kendall DFC destroyed a Bf 110 at Mannheim. Two more enemy aircraft fell to the squadron's guns during the month.

Flight Lieutenants A. P. Mellows and S. L. 'Dickie' Drew of 169 Squadron, attached to 'B' Flight 85 Squadron, were also airborne at night, on a high-level support patrol to Stuttgart. Mellows reported:

> Airborne Swannington 1700 hours. We arrived at our patrol point at 1845 hours and after ten minutes proceeded in a north-westerly direction. A red-star cartridge was seen to be fired some way off to the north so we proceeded to investigate, losing height to 10,000 ft [3,000 metres] a head-on contact was obtained and after being once lost was converted to an intermittent visual on a blue light at 2,000 ft [610 metres] range, height then being 11,000 ft [3,350 metres]. We closed on AI to 1,000 ft [300 metres] where navigator identified it as an Me 110 with the aid of night glasses. Target was climbing and weaving 30° each side of course. We closed to

This graphic photograph shows the damage suffered by Flight Lieutenants Paul Mellows's and 'Dickie' Drew's NFXXX NT252 as a result of their combat with a Bf 110 near Stuttgart on 1/2 February 1945. (Paul Mellows Collection)

200 ft [60 metres] to confirm and opened fire at 300 ft [90 metres] from slightly below with a two-second burst from which a small explosion sent debris flying back. A second burst resulted in a very large explosion and for a few moments the Mosquito was enveloped in flame, the heat of which was felt in the cockpit. We broke to starboard and watched enemy aircraft in the light of which a black cross and all details of the aircraft were plainly visible. A further explosion occurred whilst it was going down and enemy aircraft eventually exploded on the ground at 1910 hours. As combat had affected rudder control, the patrol was terminated.

Mellows fired seventy-two rounds of SAPI and sixty-eight rounds of HEI to down the Me 110. The victim was probably Bf 110 Wrk Nr 730370 2Z+EL of *III/NJG6*, which crashed 16 miles [25 km] south of Stuttgart. *Oberleutnant* Willy Rathmann, the pilot, *Feldwebel* Erich Berndt, radar operator and *Obergefreiter* Alfred Obry, the air gunner were killed.

On 2/3 February Wing Commander Kelsey DFC, Commanding Officer of 515 Squadron, and Flight Lieutenant Edward M. Smith DFC patrolled Gütersloh to no avail before obtaining a visual on a Ju 88 near Vechta. From astern and below Kelsey dispatched it with a short burst of 100 rounds of cannon fire. The starboard engine burst into flames, the port wing outboard of the port engine fell off, and pieces of debris flew back and damaged the Mosquito's air intake and undercarriage doors. Kelsey managed to land safely at Little Snoring.

That same night Pilot Officer Les Turner flew the first operation of his second tour. He says:

> I can recall nothing but a feeling of pleasure that we had reached the end of my first tour unscathed. After Christmas at home I was posted to the BSDU at Great Massingham, flying Ansons loaded with pupil navigators learning ASH radar. My original navigator, now Flight Lieutenant Jimmy Wheldon, was there as an instructor and, somewhere along the line, we agreed to rejoin 169 Squadron, then equipped with Mosquito XIXs with Mk.X radar, for a second tour. Jimmy had served in another 100 Group squadron as the wing commander's navigator and I was quite flattered that he wished to fly with me again! Needless to say, he was an excellent radar operator and I always felt safe in his hands.
>
> We trained throughout the second half of January 1945 and did our first op on 2 February. This was to the Ruhr and the logbook records one chase without results. Trip No.2 was another 'beacon' patrol, where German night-fighters were supposed to assemble, but we had no contacts. Jimmy then took some leave to complete his studies for and sit his LlB finals. He was an intellectual throughout and after the war attained a high position in the Civil Service. To keep me occupied I was attached to Massingham's Gunnery Flight and it was there that I experienced my second incident of engine failure, only this time, rather unnervingly, as passenger. I must confess that I had less than 100 per cent faith in the pilot's ability but, by leaving him to control the flying and with me dealing with undercarriage and flaps and keeping up a running commentary on our approach speed, we

landed without incident. Jimmy and I 'squeezed in' trip No.3 to Mannheim on 13 February and then it was back to the Gunnery Flight. I didn't distinguish myself particularly at practice air-to-air firing, although I once shot the drogue off, having 'led' too much with the sight!

Meanwhile, on 7/8 February 239 Squadron crews were prominent when the main force targets were Cleve and Hussum. Flight Lieutenant D.A.D. Cather DFM and Flight Sergeant L. J. S. Spicer BEM shot down Bf 110G-4 Wrk Nr 730322 G9+HR of *VII/NJG1*, which crashed west of Soest in the Ruhr. *Feldwebel* Heinz Amsberg, the pilot, and *Unteroffizier* Matthias Dengs, the radar operator, were killed, while *Gefreiter* Karl Kopperberg, the air gunner, who was wounded, bailed out.

Flight Lieutenants Anthony J. Holderness and Walter Rowley DFC of 239 Squadron had taken off from West Raynham at 2025 hours and reached their patrol area at Zandvoort at 2117 hours. The pilot's report of the sortie and successful combat is as follows:

We carried out the first part of our patrol quite uneventfully, before and while the targets, Cleve and Hussum were being bombed. Towards the end of the bombing we moved closer in to the targets and were doing a short 'square search' patrol when, at 2200 hours 13,000 ft [4,000 metres], we got a contact at 2240 hours at about 6 miles [10 km] range, and heading towards the targets. It was only slightly above but difficult to close, as it was taking what appeared to be precautionary evasive action, diving and climbing through a series of steep turns. Throughout this part of the chase our altimeter was reading anything from 11,000 to 15,000 ft [3,350–4,600 metres]. Several times I caught sight of the exhausts' glow, but was unable against the starlit sky to hold them for more than a few seconds at a time. After about ten minutes of this, when we had closed to 1,000 ft [300 metres] we suddenly found ourselves overshooting very fast and some way above, and had to turn 60° to port, then back onto our original course to recover the blip. This time the contact was headed away from the target, flying on an easterly course and at a height of about 12,000 ft [3,650 metres]. The pilot must have thought either that there was no longer any need to evade, or that he had shaken us off because he was flying straight and level. We closed in fairly fast and from only about 200 ft [60 metres] below and behind identified as Me 110. I dropped back to about 250 yd and opened fire. Quite a lot of debris flew back past us and the port engine immediately caught fire. Then the nose came up and he went into steep climb, which I tried to follow, still firing. Although I throttled right back we were rapidly overtaking him and had to pull away quickly to starboard. Just then he seemed to stall and flick over to port. I turned as slightly as our low airspeed would allow and saw him diving very steeply with the port engine now a mass of flame. My navigator could still see burning pieces coming off when he went into the cloud. Almost simultaneously there was a terrific white flash which lit up the clouds. We followed through about 3,000 ft [900 metres] of cloud to come out at 4,000 ft [1,200 metres] on the altimeter, and there it was, burning immediately beneath us, and only about a mile [1.5 km] from a white beacon flashing the letters L.F.

The 'A' Flight Commander in 141 Squadron, Squadron Leader Peter Anthony Bates DFC, and his navigator, Flying Officer William Guy Cadman, who had destroyed a Bf 110 on 11/12 September, failed to return from an ASH patrol to Ladbergen on 7/8 February. Bates was twenty-three years old and Cadman, the son of Major William H. Cadman MBE of nearby Redenhall, Norfolk, was just twenty-two. Both men are buried at Hanover War Cemetery. Apart from the air-to-air victory they had destroyed one locomotive, damaged three more, and damaged a ship and a train. On a happier note, on 13 February Harry White and Mike Allen were posted back to 141 Squadron at West Raynham. They had flown twenty-one and twenty operations respectively while with BSDU, testing new radar equipment for 100 Group. In September both men had received a second Bar to their DFCs.

White and Allen continued flying operations into 1945. On the night of 1/2 January they took off on a high-level *Intruder* in MM797, known as the 'dreaded XXX' because of its recurring engine problems. They crossed the Dutch coast near Ymuiden at 15,000 ft (4,600 metre) at 1803 hours and patrolled uneventfully until 1830 hours. When a wide, straggling bomber stream was contacted at 1915 hours at 15,000 ft (4,600 meters) Mike Allen soon obtained two AI contacts, one to port, one to starboard, at 7 miles (11 km) range. They chased the first one, which was weaving violently, until White closed the range to 3,000 ft (900 metres). They obtained a fleeting visual but the enemy aircraft took evasive action and extended the range to 7,000 ft. The two adversaries jockeyed range constantly until, at 200 ft (60 metres), White could identify his quarry as a Ju 88. Allen confirmed it using night glasses. White dropped back to 250 ft (75 metres) and opened fire. Several strikes were seen, followed by an explosion, and small pieces were seen to come away. The flash caused Harry White to lose visual contact and as the Ju 88 broke away in a hard diving turn to starboard, his navigator tried to follow it on AI but without success. White fired a second short burst at the estimated position of the aircraft but was unable to confirm results. It went down in the record books as a 'damaged'. If it had not been for stoppages in both port cannons they might have been more successful.

The next day, 2 January, they wanted to go again and try to find another Ju 88 to make up for the one they had lost. Flight Lieutenant Dennis Welfare and his navigator, 'Sticky' Clay, also wanted to go so he and Harry White had tossed a coin to see who would fly the operation. It was the first time White ever tossed a coin for an operation and he won. There was no time for an NFT before briefing so White and Allen decided to take it without one. They had never done this before in three and a half years of night fighting. At 1715 hours they took off again in MM797 in support of a raid by the main force on the Ruhr. It was their ninety-first operation. When glycol started pouring out of the port engine shortly after take-off, White pressed the feathering button and jettisoned the long-range drop tanks. He was at 600 ft (180 metres), too low to think about turning to get back into Swanton Morley and too low for either of them to bale out. When he found the propeller of the dead engine would not fully feather, he knew he could not maintain height for very long. He realized his only chance was a belly landing into a field, if he could spot one in the gathering darkness. The field would have to be almost in their line of flight because to turn would mean losing precious height and it would have to be soon. White wrote later to Rodney Allen, Michael's brother:

> To my mind, no-one can learn much from what happened before we touched down. The Pilot's Notes will tell you what to do – it is not possible to make a mistake. But there is always something to learn from any accident. And the first thing is never take off at night without having done an NFT during the day. This was the first time we had tried and it stood fair to be the last.
>
> The touchdown, which soon became inevitable in the half light, was very heavy, much heavier than it should have been with the possible excuse that a glide approach with such a load at 140 mph [225 kph] could not be otherwise.

Mike Allen recorded in his logbook, 'Harry put up a terrific show in crash-landing the kite in a field in the half-light and very poor visibility.' Allen had jettisoned the perspex canopy cover over the top of the Mosquito's cockpit just before they touched down. All that should have been necessary was a rapid abandoning of MM797 and an Olympic dash for the nearest ditch in case it exploded in flames. Unfortunately both men were trapped. As they bounced across the field White's seat had shifted on its mountings. They both knew that they did not have long before MM797 blew up. Fortunately, Herbert Farrow, a farmer, James Andrews, one of his labourers, and Walter William Ward, known as 'Old Walter', had seen the Mosquito crash. They hurried to the scene and at the risk of their own lives, tried to pull the men free. At one point Allen remembered hearing one of the men say, 'I think she's going to go up now!' He thought so too. Virtually giving up the struggle, he sat back and started to contemplate what death would be like. He felt a warm sense of anticipation; in fact he was looking forward to it. It was going to be good. He also made a mental note he would probably find out what had happened to his parent, who had been killed on 28 October when a V-2 rocket exploded in Ashford, Middlesex. His younger brother Rodney, who was in the house, had escaped injury, but he was killed after the war flying a Meteor from RAF Stradishall. Allen felt exhilarated by the prospect of dying in the next few seconds. Harry White, who had certainly not given up, rudely woke him. He kept urging him to greater efforts, with forthright language. The Mosquito had now been on the ground for three minutes and time was running out. In a superhuman effort, with the help of the three rescuers, they succeeded in escaping. Then they all sought the safety of a ditch. During the whole time there were explosions of ammunition and the flames grew in intensity. A second or two after all five men had flattened themselves in the ditch, the petrol ignited and the Mosquito exploded. Allen knew they owed their lives to the three men. On 8 May Farrow, Andrews and Old Walter were awarded the BEM. It was bitter for Mike Allen to learn from Herbert that, after the war was over, they had received their medals in the post! However, he did not seem to be too troubled by this. What he really seemed to value was his silver tankard!

Harry White was promoted Squadron Leader and became 'A' Flight Commander. He remained with 141 until it disbanded at Little Snoring in September 1945.

On the night of 13/14 February 1945, when the bombers' targets were Dresden and Leipzig, Flight Lieutenant Donald R. 'Podge' Howard DFC and Flying Officer Sticky Clay DFC of BSDU at Swanton Morley were airborne in their Mosquito XIX. Howard joined 239 Squadron on 2 May 1944 and had completed thirty-two operational sorties by 9 November 1944, during which he destroyed three enemy aircraft and damaged eight trains. During four other sorties he damaged eight trains in Holland and Germany. He was awarded the DFC on 9 November 1944.

Sticky Clay recalls that at BSDU,

> … my time was enjoyable. The nature of our operations was such that we (more or less) planned our own trips after seeing the morning Bomber Command broadcast, which gave details of the targets for the night. It was nice, too, to try out various 'boxes' dreamed up by George Baillie (one of the boffins), and then use them operationally. I remember him sitting on a chair on the perimeter track with earphones on, listening to pulses emanating from a sort of Walls Ice Cream tricycle being ridden around the other side of the airfield by some poor 'erk'.

George Baillie was one of the small group of scientists who pioneered electronic warfare at the Royal Aircraft Establishment, Farnborough, in the late 1930s. Inspired by Group Captain Addy Addison. Baillie's team anticipated that the *Luftwaffe* would use radio beams to guide bombers to targets in Britain. As a result of their dedicated efforts in the run-up to the outbreak of war, the RAF was amply prepared for the Battle of the Beams, and in 1940 radar started to be introduced in night-fighters. At the height of the Battle of Britain Baillie was posted to Radlett, Herts, where Addison had formed Bomber Command's 80 Wing to counter enemy beams. Equipment was scarce, but Baillie employed all the ingenuity for which the cash-starved Farnborough scientists were renowned to turn hospital radiotherapy sets into beam-benders. After America's entry into the war Baillie paid regular visits to the United States to pass on Britain's growing expertise in electronic warfare. His overall contribution to the development of Britain's radar capabilities played a significant part in the eventual success of 100 (Bomber Support) Group.

Howard and Clay's patrol 13/14 February was to prove very rewarding, as Howard reported:

> Aircraft BSDU/H was airborne Swanton Morley at 1906 hours to carry out a patrol of beacons Kolibri, Ida, Elster, Nachtigall and Otto with Mk.X AI and *Serrate* IV with lowered frequency band of 80 m/cs. Beacon Kolibri was reached at 2011 hours (six minutes after start of *Mandrel* Screen) and proceeded to Ida where at 2015 signals were heard on *Serrate* IV (77.5 m/cs). The D/F on this low frequency was very suspect and we were not surprised when we found we could not D/F these signals. It was, however, an indication that Huns were around. We then set course in an easterly direction and the signal strength increased. We obtained a Mark X contact about 5 miles [8 km] 30° to port and down. We turned after it and lost height and eventually discovered it was in a climbing port orbit and the range closed fast. The A/C did not show Type F and by now the George [George Baillie] box was trilling furiously (still in dashes) and A/C apparently levelled out. A visual was obtained on an A/C at 1,000 ft [300 metres] and at 600 ft [180 metres] in a rate 1–1½ turn to port the A/C was recognised as

an Me 110. At a range of about 600 ft [180 metres] with a ¼ ring deflection a short burst was fired but no strikes seen. Increased deflection and fired another burst which caused strikes all over starboard engine, wing root and starboard side of cockpit. A fire started in starboard wing root and the Me 110 turned over to port burning well and dived straight down and entered cloud; shortly after there was a vivid white explosion on the ground at 2033 hours, our height being 12,000 ft [3,650 metres]. Claim – one Me 110 destroyed.

Two minutes after this type had bought it, another Mark X contact appeared crossing starboard to port and above range 12,000 ft [3,650 metres]. Turned after it and range closed fast and after turning about rate one for about two complete circles and got visual on an A/C at 1,000 ft [300 metres] with George box still pushing out its very loud Hun note. At 600 ft [180 metres] this A/C was identified as another Me 110 in a port turn. Opened fire at 600 ft [180 metres] and missed and the Hun promptly rolled into a starboard bank during which he presented no deflection and he received a one-second burst which caused strikes on the cockpit fuselage and port wing-root. The type then dived away to starboard and we gave him another burst, which set his port engine on fire and caused bits to fly off. He then dived vertically into cloud, burning very well. We had to pull up and out of our dive and we didn't see it hit the deck but as the cloud was only about 5,000 ft [1,500 metres] and he was well on fire this is claimed as an Me 110 destroyed. Cat A (1).

At 2040 hours, 5,000 ft [1,500 metres] we obtained yet another Mark X contact almost at once but although we chased him in an easterly direction for about twenty minutes at full bore we could not overtake him so we decided he was very fortunate and returned to our patrol area and came back to base via Kolibri and West Kappelle.

Podge Howard fired eighty rounds of HEI and eighty rounds of SAPI on the sortie. One of the downed aircraft, Bf 110 Wrk Nr 480164 C9+ of *V/NJG5*, crashed near Bodenbach in the Frankfurt area. *Feldwebel* Heinrich Schmidt, the pilot, *Unteroffiziers* Erich Wohlan, the radar operator, and Adam Zunker, the air gunner, were killed.

On 14/15 February Bomber Command attacked Chemnitz and an oil refinery at Rositz near Leipzig. Leslie 'Dutch' Holland of 515 Squadron recalls:

Our designated patrol airfield was Hailfingen, in the area east of Stuttgart, where nearly every town ends with 'ingen'. After we had mooched around the vicinity of the airfield for the best part of an hour Bob announced that he thought there was something on the *Monica*. A port turn caused an increase in range whereupon I immediately opened the taps and made the turn as steep as possible. The blip disappeared so we started a starboard turn to make a sweep. A head-on contact came up on the ASH at about 2 miles [3 km] closing fast. As he appeared to be on a parallel course slightly right we went straight into a hard right turn. The bogey must have done exactly the same because he failed to appear on our screen after the turn. Reverse

Pilot Officer Leslie George 'Dutch' Holland of 515 Squadron at Little Snoring, 1944, in front of his FBVI, D-Dog, which was equipped with AI.Mk XV ASH radar. ASH was a wing-mounted radar but could not be fitted to the Mosquito wing so it was installed in a 'thimble' radome in the nose. FBVI PZ459 was assigned to 'A' Flight, 515 Squadron, at Little Snoring, where it was coded 3P-D 'D-Dog' and flown almost exclusively by Holland and Flight Sergeant Robert 'Bob' Young. Following service with 515 Squadron, 141 Squadron briefly used PZ459 before it was placed in storage and was eventually sold as scrap in July 1947. (Leslie Holland)

course again and have another go. Sure enough, another head-on. Port turn this time and lose him again. Suddenly, Bob yells into the intercom, 'He's coming in from …

WHOOSH, and a Heinkel 219 flashes by under our nose about 20 ft [6 metres] away – the radar operator clearly visible in the after part of the canopy. No time to depress the nose and have a squirt, not even to get the ginger on the button. And he's in a 600 bank to his right going to my left, so he's probably got a Lichtenstein radar with all-round performance superior to our miserable little ASH, so the only course is to try and outguess him, and at the same time bear in mind that we have now been making inroads at full throttle into our get-home fuel. We make a sweep and try to make a bit of westing. But a break in the clouds reveals that the North Star is to port. I've been steering by the directional gyro compass and it has spun in the tight turns. A quick look at the compass which has just about settled down confirms the 'astro' observation and we are actually working our way deeper into enemy territory.

Obviously, our adversary had been expecting us to do exactly as we had intended so we must have ended up going in opposite directions at a separating speed of something over 500 mph [800 kph]. We never saw each other again, which may be just as well considering the performance of his mount and the great superiority of his radar.

Another anti-flak covering mine-laying in Oslo fjord at Rygge was made. It was very near the scene of our previous sortie. The cloud cover was low and on this occasion we made our approach over the mountains of southern Norway There was a good moon but letting down into the fjord through a gap in the clouds was a trifle nail biting. Near the south-east coast we intercepted a Halifax while still below cloud and passed fairly close to him without being seen. The minelayers were supposed to be Lancs so I expect he was from 38 Group on some clandestine activity.

While 141 did not score during February they destroyed two enemy aircraft on the ground, damaged two more and destroyed a train and damaged nine more. On 13 February two of 141 Squadron's favourite sons, Squadron Leader Harry White DFC** and Flight Lieutenant Mike Allen DFC**, had arrived back at West Raynham after their stint with the BSDU. On 21/22 February they flew their first operation since rejoining the squadron but drew a blank. On 23/24 February a 239 Squadron Mosquito flown by Flight Sergeant Twigg and his navigator Flight Sergeant Turner, overshot as it was landing on the FIDO strip at Foulsham and hit a parked Halifax. Twigg was killed and Turner was injured. The following night, Warrant Officer E. W. 'Bunny' Adams and Flight Sergeant Frank A. Widdicombe of 515 Squadron damaged a Ju 88 in the circuit at Bonn. Adams throttled hard back and lowered his flaps to avoid overshooting and gave the Junkers a two-second burst before he was forced to pull away hard to starboard to avoid hitting the ground.

That same night, ten Halifaxes of 462 (RAAF) Squadron, each carrying three 750 lb (340 kg) incendiary clusters and a 500 lb (227 kg) GP bomb, were despatched on a special duty Spoof and bombing raid in the Neuss area of the Ruhr. Four failed to return.

One was MZ447 A-Able flown by Flight Lieutenant Allan J. Rate RAAF and his six crew on their twenty-ninth operation. It carried a 'spare bod', Flying Officer D. N. Kehoe RAAF, the new squadron bombing leader. Flight Sergeant Reg Gould, air bomber and the only crewmember to survive, recalls:

> We were in the area of Krefeld in the Ruhr when we were hit in the port wing by flak, which set the wing on fire. I was sitting in the nose of the aircraft on my tubular metal folding seat, which covered the escape hatch, and I could see flames through the navigator's window, which wasn't quite blacked out. I had been asked by Alan to take a *Gee* fix for Flight Sergeant J. Maslin, the navigator. Finding the set placed rather high I had taken my parachute from where it was stored to put on the seat. So by a quirk of fate I had my parachute immediately to hand when we were hit. We were in a very steep dive, doing about 340 mph [540 kph] in an attempt to get from 18,000 ft [5,500 metres] to below 14,000 ft [4,300 metres] before crossing the Allied front line which was about 40 miles [65 km] away. The Allies had started a push and their artillery had orders to open fire on any aircraft flying above 14,000 ft [4,300 metres]. I faced the rear of the aircraft and baled out backwards but the slipstream was so strong it jammed me on to the back of the escape hatch and my parachute caught on a metal strip. I did not have enough strength to push myself off although I was kicking the underside of the aircraft in a desperate attempt to get clear. I heard Malcolm Husband, the rear gunner, yell 'Dive to starboard.' This was the order used by gunners when an enemy aircraft was attacking. Alan responded immediately and as he did so I was rolled out of the side of the hatch, dislocating my right shoulder as I went. That was the last time I saw the aircraft.

Reg Gould was soon taken prisoner and placed in a vehicle with three downed aircrew from Flight Lieutenant F. H. Ridgewell's Halifax.

> Sergeant R. C. Hodgson, the flight engineer, who was about nineteen years old, was injured. Flying Officer J. R. Boyce RAAF, the wireless operator, was badly burned. His parachute had been on fire. It was obvious that he was in very severe pain as the smell of his burnt flesh was terrible. Later I learned that the third person was Pilot Officer W. J. Mann, who navigated for Ridgewell's crew. Some time after the war I read a letter from the mayor of Krefeld in which he spoke of the remainder of my crew and the aircraft being scattered over an area of 100 square metres [120 sq. yd]. They had crashed in Boishiem and had been buried in a cemetery at Bieyelle. Later, the Allies interred them in the Reichwald Forest War Cemetery.

Dutch Holland's last trip in February was another unusual one in that it was a close escort for a raid on Wilhelmshaven by Liberators of the 492nd Bomb Group, 8th US Air Force. He recalls:

It was a sort of trial run to see how they made out on a night sortie and involved about three dozen B-24s. We were to rendezvous with them at a DR position halfway out at 20,000 ft [6,100 metres] and run close escort rather like riding herd. We picked them up easily on our little sets then shut them down after getting visual contact. There was no difficulty in running up one side of their stream, turning and coming back for another run. There was no room to speak of but enough starlight to see them clearly from about 100 yd on the beam. As we neared the target, we widened our sweep to about ½–1 mile [800 metres–1.5 km] in order to intercept any interceptors. (Our radar was now switched on again or in the official code of the period, we were 'flashing our weapon.') Our separation from the stream incidentally kept us nicely clear of the large-calibre flak, which was now coming up by the bucketful.

They turned for home without any spectacular disasters and we resumed our role of guard dogs back to our rendezvous, feeling we had done a fairly good job even if we hadn't run into any fighters, but, after our return, a message came through from the American group, 'Where the hell were you guys?' Ah well, I suppose night vision isn't learned in a day (or night). This addendum is of course slightly apocryphal and they were grateful for our support.

He also recalls that on 2/3 March:

… there was a full moon, which was a deterrent to a main force effort but on such occasions experienced *Intruder* crews were allowed to go on a night *Ranger*. Generally a distant target would be chosen at which worthwhile aircraft could be found on the ground or even with luck in the air. All such ventures had to be approved by Group HQ and they were usually given the OK if not either too footling or too foolhardy – like an attack on the *Tirpitz*. Several hours would be spent poring over intelligence reports and air photographs. Our little efforts were very tame in comparison. The target selected as our primary was a seaplane base on the Baltic coast at Tarnewitz, near Wismar, calling at Gustrow, Ludwiglust and Schwerin. We found no seaplanes although it was brilliant moonlight, bright enough for us to dodge high tension cables and watch our shadow to be sure one didn't become two without our noticing. Bob was keeping a very sharp lookout behind while I did some very easy map reading. However, it was not entirely a fruitless trip because Hagenow provided so many trains in its yards that we used the last burst of our cannon ammo on the water tower which showed gratifying evidence that next day's traffic would be a trifle interrupted.

On 3/4 March 1945, RAF Bomber Command sent two large forces of bombers to Germany. Some 234 aircraft were to raid the synthetic oil plant at Kamen and a further 222 aircraft would attack an aqueduct on the Dortmund–Ems canal at Ladbergen. Altogether, 100 Group dispatched sixty-one aircraft on RCM sorties at night to jam the German radar and radio networks and thus hamper the enemy flak and night-fighter

Australian and RAF crews of 192 Squadron, 100 Group in front of Halifax BIII Mathews & Co. Express Delivery Service *at Foulsham, Norfolk. Flight Lieutenant Mathews RAAF, 4th from left. Wing Commander David Donaldson CO, is to his left. Squadron Leader John Crotch is 3rd from right. On D-Day, when 100 Group aircraft jammed enemy radars and made spoof attacks on the French coast, 192 Squadron maintained a constant patrol between Cape Griz-Nez and the Cherbourg area to see if the enemy was using the centimetric band for radar, all the known enemy radars being effectively jammed. Though jamming and spoofing were crucial to the war effort, the Australians in 100 Group (462 Squadron formed at Foulsham in 1945) felt they were not hurting the enemy and insisted that they carry bombs on ops!* (John Crotch)

defences. One of the aircraft was a 192 Squadron Halifax piloted by Wing Commander Donaldson. His tail gunner was Gunnery Leader Jack Short, who had returned to Foulsham in February after a gunnery leader's course at Catfoss.

> We went out in daylight, surrounded by Lancasters of 5 Group – the 'death or glory boys', who were to punch a hole in the canal. Our lone Halifax caused a great deal of interest. They must have wondered if we had the right raid! It was a comfortable feeling though being with all these aircraft in daylight. At the target there was altostratus at 15,000 ft [4,600 metres]; bloody annoying because the searchlights silhouetted us against the cloud and we were picked up by the ack-ack. I saw three Lancs go down, one fairly close, in flames. [From these two raids, seven Lancasters were lost.] We were keyed up. Donaldson tipped the Halifax on one wing to look underneath for fighters. If suddenly your right wing crumples … but we

encountered no opposition, and we headed back to Foulsham at 10,000 ft [3,000 metres].'

That night the *Luftwaffe* mounted *Unnternehmen* (Operation) *Gisela,* an attack by 142 Ju 88Gs and almost sixty other twin-engined night-fighters on returning RAF aircraft and their airfields in eastern England. The operation, suggested by Major Heinz-Wolfgang Schnaufer *Kommmodore* of *NJG4,* the top scoring night-fighter pilot, who finished the war with 121 victories, which was to have taken place at the end of February. Details of the plan were obtained, however, and the British made it known by broadcasting the contemporary hit tune 'I Dance With Gisela Tonight' on the Allied propaganda station *Soldatensender Calais. Gisela* had therefore been postponed until the British relaxed their vigilance. However, when on 21 February 1945 the green light was given for the attack, *Oberst Generalmajor* Dietrich Peltz committed only 142 Ju 88Gs of *NJG2, 3, 4* and *5* to the *Intruder* operation; far too small a force to inflict a serious blow against RAF bombers returning from Kamen and Ladbergen. The Ju 88s penetrated the airspace over some of the 100 Group stations, Foulsham included. Jack Short recalls:

> I will always remember the WAAF girl's voice in the Foulsham tower. 'You're clear to circle and orbit at 6,000 ft [1,800 metres],' she said. Donaldson was the last back and we were the top of the stack. There were four-five more Halifaxes underneath at 500 ft [150 metres] intervals. We could see Foulsham airfield illuminated below. Donaldson started a left orbit. I suddenly saw a two-second set of tracer well beneath the aircraft, then more, in one direction. Then a ball of fire. This poor girl on the R/T screamed, '*Bandits! Bandits!*' The airfield lights were doused. She yelled out Weston Zoyland, the diversion airfield, in plain language. Then there was total silence.

Halifax BIII of 192 Squadron, which crash-landed in a field near Foulsham. (via CONAM)

The aircraft Jack Short had seen was Halifax Mk III LV955 'C' of 192 Squadron piloted by Flying Officer E. D. 'Robbie' Roberts. Roberts had taken off from RAF Foulsham at 2000 hours for a lone ELINT operation over the North Sea to search for possible navigational aids which it was thought might be associated with air-launched V-1s and their guidance to targets in the UK. The Halifax carried out its assigned task and returned to Norfolk. At about 0100 hours, the two main forces were also overflying the area. G-George arrived back over Foulsham. Robbie Roberts recalls:

> When we arrived, the airfield lighting was on and after calling the tower for permission to land I began to lose height down into the circuit when given the OK to 'pancake'. My navigation lights were on and wheels lowered. The next thing, a cry over the radio from the control tower said, 'Bandits overhead!' and the lighting went out on the ground. I hit the switch to turn off the navigation lights and turned away from the circuit.

Roberts was instructed to turn to starboard. Whilst flying at an altitude of 1,200 ft (365 metres), a Ju 88 night-fighter attacked. He continues:

> The attack appeared to come from below us. It looked like that from the tracer. The aircraft was hit and both inner engines were put out of action and the aircraft caught fire. Sergeant Ken Sutcliffe, the mid-upper gunner, reported streams of flame as the petrol leaking from the wing tanks ignited. I thought that there would be a chance for some to escape by parachute and gave the order for an emergency parachute escape, provided I could keep the aircraft under some sort of control. [Only Flying Officer R. C. Todd, the special wireless operator, was able to bale out successfully, injured.] At 1,000 ft [300 metres] I ordered all the crew back to the normal crash positions and told them to sit tight as it was too low by then to attempt any further parachute escapes. We suffered a further attack and this resulted in the extremely messy death of the wireless operator, Warrant Officer William Clementson, who was in his crash position in the cockpit, and also the disintegration of the instrument panel. I grappled with the controls and tried to maintain some sort of stability, looking for a field in which I could make a crash-landing. I can remember passing over some trees in the boundary of the field and pulling everything back in my lap in an endeavour to make a belly-landing, which apparently did come off.

G-George crash-landed in flames at Ainlies Farm, Fulmodeston, near the Mosquito fighter base at Little Snoring, setting a haystack and two huts on fire. Only two men survived, dragged clear by local people; Roberts suffered a crush-fractured spine and burns, and did not regain consciousness until two weeks later. After treatment at RAF Hospital Ely and East Grinstead, where he underwent plastic surgery under the famous Sir Archibald McIndoe and thus became a member of the famous Guinea Pig Club, was discharged from the RAF in 1947. The mid-upper gunner, Sergeant Ken Sutcliffe, survived with burns to his body and face. The navigator, Flying Officer William Darlington, the flight engineer, Sergeant John Anderson, and the air bomber, Flight

Sergeant Reginald Holmes, were found dead in the burnt-out wreckage. The aircraft was almost completely destroyed. The rear gunner, 34-year-old Sergeant Richard Grapes, was found dead with his parachute unopened, killed either by lack of altitude or enemy fire as he jumped. Jack Short accompanied his coffin to Liverpool.

All told, the *Nachtjägd* intruders shot down twenty aircraft over England, including five which crashed in Norfolk. Liberator 'B' of 223 Squadron was in the circuit at Oulton when tracer was fired at it. Although it was hit, the B-24 was able to land safely. Pilot Officer H. Bennett DFC in HB815/J, a 214 Squadron Fortress III, was about to land when he was told to go around again as his 'A' Flight Commander, Squadron Leader Bob Davies, was approaching on three engines. Bob Davies recalls:

> Our return to Oulton in the early hours of 4 March was normal, the
> individual aircraft switching on their navigation lights some time before we

Squadron Leader Bob Davies (holding Rhett, the 214 Squadron mascot) and Dick Gunton (in white shirt), 214 Squadron Engineering Officer, all smiles with gunners and RAF personnel at Oulton. On the night of 3/4 March 1945, when the Luftwaffe *mounted Operation Gisela, Gunton kicked out the spotlight on Wing Commander Roger's Humber staff car during strafing of the airfield.* (Tom Cushing Collection)

crossed the Norfolk coast. As I approached Oulton I heard control give Pilot Officer Bennett clearance to join the circuit. I called saying I was on three engines and was told to come straight in. A few moments later Bennett, who I think was on longish finals, was told to go round again as I was turning long finals and was cleared to land on runway 45. I saw Bennett climbing away, and above me, to my right. Then I saw a fairly long burst of cannon fire and his No.2 engine and wing caught fire. I lost sight of him still climbing and turning right. At this time I heard the tower say '*Bandits! Bandits!* Switch off all lights'. All airfield lights were extinguished. I had landed by now and was stationary. I switched off my navigation lights, or so I thought. However my rear gunner said, 'There is still a white light shining somewhere above me!' I told him it was impossible as both my flight engineer, Flying Officer Fitzsimmonds and I had checked all switches and they were definitely 'off'. While we started madly to check again all the switches the two of us began to feel very naked and also very panicky as we were expecting to be blown apart at any moment. I finally found the small switch which controlled the white formation light situated at the very top of the vertical stabilizer and switched it off. All ten of us only dared to breathe again when we finally found our blacked-out dispersal.

Bennett's Fortress had been shot down by 27-year-old *Leutnant* Arnold Döring of *X/NJG3* from Jever. Döring was a very experienced fighter pilot who before joining the night-fighter arm in the summer of 1943 had already completed 348 operational sorties as a bomber pilot in *KG53* and *KG55*. He had seen action during the Battles of France and Britain and in the Russian campaign, where he destroyed ten russian aircraft in the air flying an He 111 before claiming a further eight aircraft destroyed as a Wilde Sau pilot in *JG300* and three more night victories in *NJG2* and *NJG3*. Döring wrote of his experiences on the night of the *Gisela* operation:

Some 150–200 British bombers have flown into the *Reich*, released their loads on Münster and we join the returning stream over the North Sea, whilst flying at a height of less than 50 metres [160 ft], which should fool the enemy radar defences. We are heading for the peninsula of Flamborough Head, our sector to penetrate the British mainland. This is the same route that the returning bombers belonging to the British 100 Bomber Group are taking, in the area NW of Hull. We are ordered to keep absolute radio silence, the Tommy should not notice anything. Neither are we allowed to engage any *Viermots* [four-engined bombers] in combat over the North Sea, as we must succeed in totally surprising them.

Shortly before we arrive over the coast, we climb to a height of some 1,800 metres [6,0000 ft] and throw out bundles of *Düppel* [*Window*] to counter the AI of the Mosquitoes. I cross the coast a little to the north of Flamborough Head, over the small harbour town of Scarborough and watch how in this penetration zone an aircraft is hit by the flak hosing up and crashing in flames. I also observe a lot of fires from aircraft crash-landing on the enormous emergency landing ground, which is used by damaged *Viermots* that are not allowed to touch down on their regular dromes to avoid the danger of these aircraft blocking the runways. This once more proves that the true losses of the Tommies are bigger than one can assess in Germany from the wreckage of shot-down machines on the Continent.

Walter Hoyer, my *Funker*, makes notes of a series of *Abschuss*, so that we can confirm the times of claims on our return. We identify a row of airfields on which bombs are dropped and see a lot of aircraft being shot out of the sky. Lines of tracer hiss down into targets on the ground, as we are ordered not to bring back home a single bullet from our frontal guns.

I descend steeply to some 600 metres [1,900 ft] and as I approach two illuminated airfields they both switch off. Three others are still in operation, on the ground red lamps flash the night intruder-warning signal 'R for Raider'. Yet many *Viermots* are still flying around with all navigation lights on.

This drome flashes its identification 'DH' in white capital letters, the landing system is a Drem system, and over the airfield it is a frantic affair. I position myself beneath a *Viermot* with all his navigation lights on. It is a B-17 as I can see from its wide tailplane. I aim a burst from my oblique cannons into the fuel tanks, the fuselage and wings. The bomber starts to burn. The fires in its fuselage flicker up and then become fainter. The crew probably switches on the fire extinguishers. On the edge of the Drem system, the *Viermot* crashes hard in a pile of dust and smoke but without a fire. We clearly see it in the bright moonlight as we fly low and away over the wreckage.

Despite the fact that we fly very low, the navigation lights of a bomber even flash past beneath me. As I am not familiar with the surroundings and the moon disappears behind a bank of clouds, I let this *Viermot* escape and attack another one on its final approach. I destroy this Lancaster with my oblique cannons; it immediately bursts into a bright fire and crashes in an enormous sheet of flames."

Low on fuel Döring landed at Nordholz after a sortie lasting over five hours.

Bob Davies concludes:

'The night, and the fright, were not yet over. As my Hillman pick-up was parked at dispersal, I drove with my flight engineer to the still fiercely burning wreck which must have roughly impacted in a flying position. The fuselage (or what was left of it) had broken off aft of the radio room and also aft of the beam gun position. I could not believe any of the crew had survived but both waist gunners, Sergeant Alastair McDermid and Warrant Officer R. W. Church, had 'walked' from the blazing inferno. They had been taken to sick quarters where I spoke briefly to them.

Don Prutton of 223 Squadron adds:

The intruder, which we learned later was a Junkers Ju 88, then did a sharp turn and sent a few rounds in the direction of Flying Control [a cannon shell penetrated a safe near a wall behind which Dick Gunton, 214 Squadron Engineering Officer, was sheltering] before all the lights on the airfield were switched off. The Commanding Officer, who was in the tower, had left his Humber staff car outside with the spotlight on; a zealous airman immediately kicked it in but his prompt action was not greatly appreciated by the 'old man'.

The 'zealous airman' was Dick Gunton who, unable to find the off switch, had resorted to swift action. Gunton related the events next morning at the Cushing household at the Old Hall, Thursford. Eight-year-old Tom listened avidly to the family friend who at Christmas had taken him in his pride and joy, a red MG sports coupé, to see *Holiday Inn* at a Norwich cinema. Gunton, who hurt his foot kicking in the glass because 'it was tougher than expected' confided that he did it because the beam was shining on his beloved MG and he did not want it shot to bits by the Ju 88! Don Prutton concludes: 'Aircraft still airborne were diverted to another airfield, but were followed by the Junkers 88. He inflicted some more damage before being chased off by our fighters. We heard later that he was shot down somewhere in the north of England.'

Mosquito XIX MM610/H of 169 Squadron flown by Squadron Leader V. J. Fenwick and Flying Officer J. W. Pierce, who were returning from a bomber support sortie to Kamen, was shot down and crashed at The Avenue, Buxton, Norfolk. Both crew were killed. Dutch Holland and Bob Young had just landed at Snoring from an air-interception training exercise, left their fully armed Mosquito on its dispersal hard standing, parked their gear in the 515 Squadron hut and were sauntering back up the lane towards the messes. Dutch Holland recalls:

> There were several returning aircraft in the vicinity all making very familiar noises when we noticed that one was being followed by an aircraft with a distinctly unfamiliar note. I had just time to say to Bob, 'By God it's a Jerry!' when a stream of tracer streaked across and, as they were only at about 1,500 ft [460 metres], [we] could see the flicker of strikes. The stricken aircraft had its landing lights on ready for joining the circuit and was naturally not expecting any trouble. The lights went into a descending curve out of sight behind the trees. No flak, no fire.

Halifax III NA107/T of 171 Squadron, piloted by Squadron Leader P. C. Procter, the B Flight Commander, was brought down by a Ju 88 while heading for North Creake at 3,000 ft (900 metres) on returning from a *Mandrel* sortie. It crashed at Walnut Tree Farm, South Lopham, after the crew of eight parachuted out at around 1,000 ft (300 metres). Warrant Officer A. P. Richards, the mid-upper gunner, sustained a broken ankle while the flight engineer, Flight Sergeant H. Laking, 'apparently under the impression that there was no hope of survival, and anxious to save time and money in transportation', glided into a cemetery!

Altogether, thirty-three Ju 88G night intruders were lost during Gisela. Five *Luftwaffe* aircraft crashed on British soil and eight others were reported missing. Three crews perished in crashes on German territory, six baled out because of lack of fuel and eleven crashed on landing. In a poor return, the intruders shot down twenty-four aircraft –

thirteen Halifaxes, nine Lancasters, a Mosquito and the one B-17. Five of these crashed in Norfolk. Holland concludes:

> As a result of these incursions, a system of stand-by night-fighters dispersed over several adjoining airfields was set up with crews already in the aircraft, engines warmed up ready to respond to any repeat performance. We also did stand-by patrols when the main force was returning if not on ops ourselves. However, no further trade came our way when we were ready for them, but our own vigilance was redoubled when we ourselves came back into the circuit. Minimum exposure of airfield lighting became the rule and navigation lights were, for a time, not used. This in itself involved a certain amount of risk owing to the small distance separating airfields in East Anglia. There were twenty airfields north of a line between Norwich and King's Lynn and most were involved in night operations. The circuits alternated left and right so that they meshed like the gears of an enormous watch. Some of the intruders were caught by home-defence night-fighters, mostly to those fitted with Mk X AI (SCR 720).

CHAPTER XIII

Ashes to Ashes

No, it won't start because it's over-rich. And the burning smell is from one of my beautiful new starter-armatures, due to you keeping your thumb on the starter button far too long – Sir.

During early March 1945, *Luftwaffe* intruders made brief but damaging reappearance over eastern England and many Mosquito crews talked confidently of getting more victories. (During the month 100 Group Mosquitoes shot down

239 Squadron personnel outside their crew room at West Raynham. L–R: At the rear, Squadron CO, Wing Commander W. F. Gibb DSO DFC (who on 5/6 March 1945 with Flying Officer R. C. Kendall DFC destroyed two Ju 88s at Nurenberg to add to their Bf 110 and Fw 190 claims during February); unknown, Dicky Da Costa; Warrant Officer Tanner (obscured and wearing dark glasses); Flight Sergeant Briggs; Flight Lieutenant Wimbush; and Warrant Officer 'Chalky' White. Front row, L–R: unknown; Squadron Leader Holderness (who, with Flight Lieutenant W Rowley, destroyed a Bf 110 on the night of 7/8 February); Peter Poirette and an unknown Australian. (Graham 'Chalky' White)

thirteen aircraft.) At West Raynham, the nights went by with excitement at fever pitch because 239 Squadron was chasing its fiftieth victory. The first two, both Ju 88s, occurred on the night of 5/6 March, and both are credited to Wing Commander Walter Frame Gibb DSO DFC, the Commanding Officer, and Flying Officer R. C. 'Killer' Kendall DFC. They made quite sure of their claim to the fiftieth by destroying two Ju 88s. The first, Ju 88G-6 Wrk Nr 622319 C9+GA of *Stab/NJG5* flown by *Oberstleutnant* Walter Borchers, crashed near Altenburg, 16 miles [25 km] north-west of Chemnitz. *Borchers*, a *Ritterkreuzträger* (29 October 1944) and *Kommodore* of *NJG5*, a fifty-nine-victory ace, of which sixteen had been scored by day and forty-three by night, and his radar operator, *Leutnant* Friedrich Reul, were killed. The second Ju 88 to fall to Gibb's guns was Ju 88G-6 Wrk Nr 622318 C9+NL of *III/NJG5*, which also crashed near Chemnitz. *Unteroffiziers* Hans Dorminger, the pilot, Max Bartsch and Friedrich Rullman and *Obergefreiter* Franz Wohlschloegelwere killed. Gibb and Kendall's return was particularly memorable for two treasured lines. On climbing unhurriedly out of the aircraft, Killer Kendall seemed quite unmoved by the noisy throng that greeted him, and was heard to remark in acid tones, 'I still say it's a bloody awful set.' The wing commander was more verbose and his delight as he described how he had accounted for both his victims was glorious to see. 'But why,' he asked in conclusion, 'why do I always hit them in the port engine?'

March produced rich pickings for the Mosquito *Intruders*. On 6/7 March Flying Officer S. J. Bartlam and Flying Officer A. A. Harvey of 515 Squadron destroyed a Ju 52 and damaged two other enemy aircraft on the ground at Greifswald and Barth airfields during a *Freelance* low-level *Intruder* patrol of the Baltic coast in support of an attack by 336 aircraft of 5 Group on Sassnitz. At Greifswald, Bartlam and Harvey attacked north to south, and many strikes were seen on the Ju 52, an unidentified aircraft and a tractor. Bartlam pulled out of his dive at 400 ft (120 metres) and flew on to Barth, where a second aircraft was damaged. The lights at *Stalag Luft I* at Barth were doused during the main attack by the heavies and again when Bartlam and Harvey attacked the airfield. It must have been a tonic for the POWs at the infamous camp.

On 7/8 March a heavy bombing raid on Dessau destroyed the first two prototypes of the Ju 88G-7 high-performance night-fighter *Moskitojäger* (Mosquito destroyer). Flying Officer Lewis Heath and Flight Sergeant Jack Thompson of 23 Squadron enjoyed a fruitful patrol. Heath wrote:

> Mosquito took off from Little Snoring at 2044 hours and arrived in patrol area at 2225 hours and ten minutes later both Burg and Stendal lit up A/F flarepath and perimeter lights. Two green Verys and two flares were fired from each airfield as Mosquito approached. Mosquito continued patrol and each time the airfields were approached the green Verys and white flares were fired. At 2325 hours an enemy aircraft was observed taking off from Stendal, burning navigation and downward recognition lights. Mosquito was then about 10 miles [16 km] south of Stendal at the time, 'going through the gate', reached airfield as enemy aircraft was just airborne. Mosquito gave two two-second bursts at enemy aircraft at 600 ft [180 metres] height, $1^{1}/_{2}$ rings deflection, 250 yd range, but no strikes seen. Mosquito overshot and enemy aircraft turned port climbing rapidly making

left-hand circuit of airfield. Mosquito turned quickly inside enemy aircraft and came in astern. Enemy aircraft was still burning all lights which made recognition difficult (downward recognition light was very bright). Closing into 150 yd, same height, half-ring deflection, Mosquito fired a two-second burst. Strikes seen on port wing, root and fuselage and identified as Fw 190. Immediate flash and enemy aircraft peeled off to port from 1,200 ft [365 metres], exploding on the ground 6 miles [10 km] south of airfield three seconds later and 2330 hours. Mosquito immediately left patrol area with enemy aircraft still burning. Claim, one Fw 190 destroyed (Cat.A.1). Mosquito landed at 0117 hours.

Heath fired 200 rounds of 20-mm cannon (fifty rounds per cannon).

On the following night, Flight Lieutenant Ian Dobie and Warrant Officer C. R. 'Grimmy' Grimstone DFM of 85 Squadron destroyed a Ju 188 near Hamburg. Shortly afterwards, they were shot down by flak near Koblenz. Dobie bailed out successfully and wandered into the American lines. Grimmy Grimstone was found with his parachute open but burnt, still attached to his body within 50 yd of the wreckage.

On 12/13 March when the heavies bombed Lutzkendorf, Flight Lieutenant J.W. Welford and Flying Officer R.H. Phillips of 410 Squadron in an NFXXX, claimed a Ju 88 'probable' in the Dunkirk area. In 100 Group meanwhile, Squadron Leader Dolly Doleman and Flight Lieutenant Bunny Bunch DFC of 157 Squadron had taken off from Swannington at 1847 hours only to find that their *Gee* apparatus was unserviceable. Doleman, however, decided to carry on because,

> … we dared not change aircraft as Bunny had just given a lecture saying that *Gee* was merely an aid to navigation. We D/R'd onwards and checked position with a prang at Zweibrücken and picked up the 5 Group bombers shortly after. We escorted them uneventfully, looking for the odd airfield, but none were lit.
>
> We were investigating a small S/L line pointing from somewhere near Nuremberg to the target when contact was obtained, 6 miles [10 km] head-on 20° to port. We closed to 1,500 ft [460 metres] at a height of 10,000–11,000 ft [3,000–3,350 metres] from a violently moving target, orbiting and climbing and diving. Unfortunately all this was taking place in the darkest patch of sky over the whole of the continent. After sitting behind him in formation for about fifteen minutes we pulled up very close and identified as a Ju 88G by the square top of the fin and elevators set forward. Pulled up and target became an indistinct blur. Had a crack at that from short range even closer. Strikes were seen but impossible to say whereabouts they were. We were within minimum Mk X range and Bunny obtained his next contact about 2,000 ft [610 metres], 90° starboard. We whipped around but he must have gone down on the deck, as no further contact was obtained. Bags of blasphemy. Went on to target but no further joy, so set course base and landed base 0055 hours, brassed off to hell.

That same night American pilot Flying Officer (Second Lieutenant) R. D. S. 'Hank' Gregor and his navigator/radar operator, Flight Sergeant Frank H. Baker, were on a lone 141 Squadron ASH patrol in the Frankfurt–Mannheim area in support of the bombers attacking Zweibrücken, near Saarbrücken when they picked up a contact coming into land at Lachen airfield. Gregor planned to intersect just short of the runway when a 'flood' lit the runway and the enemy aircraft was seen. Gregor reported:

> My angle off was about 60° and range 2,000 ft [610 metres] so I opened fire at the 'silver shape' giving it one ring deflection and then spraying the area. We rapidly closed range to 100 ft [30 metres] and just as we started to pull out, the enemy aircraft exploded under our nose, illuminating the area. Almost immediately light flak, not too accurate, came up at us, and a searchlight coned us. We dodged the searchlight by turning into it and diving. Frank then yelled 'The ASH altitude line's gone, Hank', so I hooked back on the stick and we left for home. Frank saw all the lights go out after the attack.

It was 141 Squadron's final air-to-air victory of the war.

The following night, 15/16 March, Captain Eric Fossum (a Norwegian) and Flying Officer S. A. Hider of 85 Squadron closed in below a contact at 200 ft (60 metres) in the Hanover area. Hider used his night glasses and identified it as a Ju 88. Fossum dropped back to 600 ft (180 metres) astern and level, and pumped a two-second burst into the enemy machine. Strikes could be seen between the fuselage and the port engine. The Norwegian fired a second burst. This time the Junkers exploded and the port engine burst into flames. Hider, watching the dying moments through his glasses, saw one crew member bale out of the doomed machine. Fossum, however, closed in for a third burst at 600 ft (180 metres) range. He did not want any of the crew to escape. He blasted the machine again until a bright explosion appeared in the fuselage but Hider, still peering through his night glasses, saw two more crew abandon the doomed Ju 88 before the *coup de grace*. On the same night, Flight Lieutenant Jimmy Mathews and Warrant Officer Alan Penrose of 157 Squadron bagged a Ju 88 20 miles (30 km) south of Würzburg.

On 16/17 March 231 Lancasters of 1 Group and forty-six Lancasters and sixteen Mosquitoes of 8 Group attacked Nuremberg and 225 Lancasters and eleven Mosquitoes of 5 Group bombed Würzburg. Thirty aircraft were lost mainly to German night-fighters, which found the bomber stream on the way to the target. Squadron Leader D. L. Hughes and Flight Lieutenant R. H. Perks of 239 Squadron destroyed a Ju 88 flown by *Major* Werner Hoffmann (fifty-three victories) near Nuremberg. On 18/19 March Flight Lieutenant V. D. Win RNZAF and Flying Officer T. P. Ryan RNZAF of 85 Squadron destroyed a Bf 110. Wing Commander W. F. Gibb and Killer Kendall of 239 Squadron shot down an He 219 *Uhu* at Witten to take their score while with the squadron to five. *Hauptmann* Baake, the pilot and *Kommandeur* of *I/NJG1* and his radar operator, *Unteroffizier* Bettaque, baled out safely. Warrant Officer Taylor and Flight Sergeant Radford of 157 Squadron destroyed a Ju 88. *Nachtjägdgeschwader* crews had little defence against the Mosquitoes. Even their SN-2 AI band could now be jammed since several Fortresses of 214 Squadron had each been fitted with six installations of the latest development of *Piperack.*

Flight Lieutenant Geoff Liles' Fortress M-Mike *in 214 Squadron, showing to good advantage the* Piperack *(Dina II) American-developed radar-jamming device which replaced the* Monica *tail warning installation when it was found that German night fighters were able to home in on* Monica *transmissions from up to 45 miles (70 km) away. Behind can be seen another BIII with plastic H2S nose radome (fitted to all 214 Squadron aircraft during June–August 1944 to aid navigation).* (Geoff Liles via Murray Peden QC DFC)

Advances by the Allied armies made most of the month's operations comparatively deep penetrations, and it was not easy to confuse the German plotters once the main forces had passed the early stages of their routes over enemy territory. This problem was overcome in the latter part of the month by splitting the *Window* force, and by operating the *Mandrel* aircraft in the double role of *Mandrel* and *Window*. By these means, and with the co-operation of the American 492nd Bomb Group, it was possible to make several feint attacks simultaneously on widely separated areas. The supporting fighters of 100 Group could do little about enemy fighters which occasionally got into the stream and shot down a number of bombers, because they were flying well away from the bomber stream owing to the difficulty of operating AI in the midst of the *Window* and bomber echoes. It became clear that AI Mk X could be used for close escort provided the Mosquitoes flew above the bombers where the H2S and *Window* interference was least. It was decided to try again a close escort of the stream, and it was hoped that with experience the crews would become better able to operate among *Window* and bomber echoes. The first close escort of the bomber stream was carried out in March.

Bomber Command's tactics of deception and radio counter-measures had reached a fine perfection – just how fine can be assessed from one typical night operation on 20/21 March when no less than three feint attacks took place in support of the main force attack on the synthetic oil refinery at Bohlen, just south of Leipzig, by 235 Lancasters and Mosquitoes. The *Window* force left the main stream soon after crossing the front line and made for Kassel, which was bombed. Further on, when closer to the true target, another *Window* force broke off and bombed Halle. The third feint force was provided by the *Mandrel* screen which, after the passage of the heavies, re-formed into a *Window* force and attacked Frankfurt with flares.

The main force's zero hour was set at 0340 hrs on the 21st. Almost simultaneously, 166 Lancasters headed for the oilfield at Hemmingstedt in Schleswig-Holstein, far to the north of the first target. This force's attack was to commence at 0430 and together with the other attack involved Bomber Command's main effort. In the meantime, the evening's diversions began with a large-scale nuisance raid on Berlin: thirty-five Mosquitoes of the Pathfinder force bombed the city, beginning at 2114 hrs.

Just after 0100 hrs the main Bohlen force crossed the English Channel on a south-easterly heading, while a few miles to the south a feinting formation, comprising sixty-four Lancasters and Halifaxes from training units crossed the Channel on an almost parallel course. It was here that the complications for the German radar operators began, for by 0205 an 80 mile (130 km) long *Mandrel* screen comprising seven pairs of Halifaxes from 171 and 199 Squadrons was in position over northern France, throwing up a wall of radar jamming through which the German early-warning radar could not see. Shortly after crossing the coast of France, the Bohlen force split into two streams; hidden behind the *Mandrel* screen forty-one Lancasters broke away and headed off to the north-east, and these were to cause considerable difficulties for the Germans.

While the bomber formations were still approaching the German frontier, fourteen Mosquito fighter-bombers of 23 and 515 Squadrons were fanning out in ones and twos, and making for the airfields the German night-fighter force was expected to use that night. Once there, they orbited overhead for hours on end, dropping clusters of incendiaries and firing at anything that moved.

At 0300 the training aircraft, which had by now almost reached the German frontier near Strasbourg, turned about and went home, their work done. At the same time, the two formations making their separate ways to the Bohlen refinery burst through the *Mandrel* jamming screen. Seven Liberators of 223 Squadron and four Halifaxes of 171 Squadron went five minutes – about 18 miles (29 km) ahead of the larger Bohlen force, laying out a dense cloud of *Window* which effectively hid the bombers following them. Once over the Rhine, the more southerly of the two streams of bombers turned north-east straight towards Kassel. So far, there was no way in which the German fighter controller could tell the real target for the night. In fact, at the time the bomber forces crossed the German frontier, the German fighter controller of the Central Rhine defence area, *Major* Rüppel, seriously underestimated the strength of the two approaching formations: he thought each force involved about thirty aircraft, and both might well be *Window* feints. As the reports from the ground observation posts began to come in, however, it became clear that the southernmost of the two was much larger than he had estimated. No amount of jamming could conceal the roar of 800 aircraft engines.

Also successful that night were Flight Lieutenant G. C. Chapman and Flight Sergeant Jimmy Stockley of 85 Squadron who took off from Swannington at 0145 hours in their Mosquito XXX on a high-level escort of bombers to Bohlen. While *en route* to patrol a *Perfectos* contact was obtained at 0255 hours just after passing Hamm at 12 miles (19 km) range and 12,000 ft (3,650 metres). Chapman wrote later:

> Range was closed to 1 mile [1.5 km] but no AI contact was obtained, and the range started to increase again. So, deciding that the contact must be below we did a hard diving turn to port, down to 9,000 ft [2,750 metres] and finally, D/F'd on to the target's course at 7 miles [11 km] range. We closed

in to 6 miles [10 km] range and an AI contact was obtained at six o'clock. The target was climbing and we closed in rapidly and obtained a visual at 900 ft [270 metres], height 13,000 ft [3,000 metres]. The target was still climbing straight ahead and was identified with the night glasses as an Me 110. It had a pale blue light between the starboard nacelle and fuselage. I closed in to 600 ft [180 metres] and pulled up to dead astern when the Hun started to turn to port. I gave it a ¹/₂-ring deflection and a three-second burst, whereupon the enemy aircraft exploded in the port engine in a very satisfactory manner, with debris flying back. It exploded on the ground at 0305 hours 25–30 miles [40–50 km] NW of Kassel. All this excitement was too much for the *Perfectos*, which went u/s unfortunately, so we set course for the rendezvous with the bomber stream.

They reached the bomber stream at 0322 hours. Their patrol was uneventful until the stream left the target at 0400 hours. Chapman continued:

I noticed to port and 15 miles [24 km] south a ball of yellowish flame take off and climb very rapidly (Plauen airfield). I thought it was a flare or a V-2 (a little out of position) until it started emitting a meteor tail several hundred feet long. We turned port towards it, and lost height to 7,000 ft [2,100 metres], that being the height of this phenomenon as far as I could judge, and continued watching. It travelled in a north-west direction very fast and suddenly to our astonishment fired off some RPs [rocket projectiles], four single and one pair, in the general direction of the departing bomber stream. We were pretty amazed at all this and decided that it must be an Me 163. I continued turning port and got behind it. It was vectoring 275° by this time and doing about 260 IAS and using the AI to check range we closed in to 1,000 ft [300 metres] and visually identified a twin-engined aircraft with rocket apparatus slung under the fuselage – an He 219. [The He 219 V14 Uhu carried a BMW 109-003 turbojet, used in the He 162 Salamander programme, below the fuselage]. Considerable quantities of flames and sparks were flying back preventing me from identifying the tail unit, so I decided to open fire at that range. I gave it several longish bursts as two of the cannon had stoppages and was gratified to see an explosion take place somewhere in the fuselage and debris fly back. The enemy aircraft nosed straight down through the patchy cloud and exploded on the ground with a tremendous glare.

Chapman and Stockley landed back at Swannington at 0652 hours to claim a Bf 110 and an He 219 destroyed. The He 219V-14 Wrk Nr 190014, of *III/ NJG1* was flown by *Oberleutnant* Heinz Oloff, *Staffelkapitan, III/NJG1*.

On 24/25 March, Pilot Officer F. X. A. Huls and Flying Officer Joe Kinet of 515 Squadron flew a night *Ranger* to the Stendal area. Their presence caused consternation. Or did it? The flarepath was lit and doused three times but was identified as Buch landing ground, classified as a dummy in the Intelligence Section's 'List of Airfields, Vol. 1 Germany' back at Snoring. Huls and Kinet dropped two flares and went in at

500 ft (150 metres) to spot three Fw 190s dispersed at the runway threshold. Both men were convinced the dummy landing ground was being used as an airfield and Huls climbed to 1,500 ft (460 metres) and picked out one of the Fw 190s, which he gave a long burst of cannon fire before pulling out at 500 ft (150 metres). The Fw 190 began to burn fiercely and emit a column of smoke. Huls levelled out and the AA defences opened up but they were well clear before any hits could be registered. Not content with their night's work, on their way home they dropped forty 4 lb (1.8 kg) incendiary bombs on the east–west flarepath at Hustedt airfield north of Celle which was lit up, and caused fires on the south side of the flarepath.

Meanwhile, Flying Officer E. W. 'Bunny' Adams and Flight Sergeant Frank A. Widdicombe, who had damaged a Ju 88 the previous month, really went to town on their night *Ranger* to the Munich area after a refuelling stop at Juvincourt. They made three low runs over Erding airfield and on the third their shells overshot and struck a hangar but a line of at least six aircraft were seen in the south-west corner. Adams and Widdicombe attacked from north to south and sprayed the entire line. The second aircraft exploded and disintegrated and this was claimed 'destroyed', with four claimed as 'damaged'.

On 30/31 March Dutch Holland and Bob Young were assigned to another anti-flak job.

Holland reports:

> As it was not at such a great distance, 'there would be time to look for a bit more trouble elsewhere.'
>
> Then mine-laying was to be carried out in the Weser between Bremen and Bremerhaven, so we were expecting to run into some pretty hot opposition. As it turned out, it proved to be a somewhat tame affair with nothing like the reaction we had provoked up the Oslo Fjord.
>
> As a secondary operation we had elected to poke our nose in at Nordholz, a few miles further north near Cuxhaven. Our briefing maps had been pretty specific about aircraft parking stands in among the trees on the north side of the field. It was easy enough to find after having detoured out to sea round Bremerhaven and looked pretty bare of any game. But we had some flares and incendiaries on board. The flares were dropped first over the middle of the field and showed that nothing had been carelessly left out in the open. So, try the coverts next and see what we could draw from them. The incendiaries were duly laid in a string across the shubbery on the north side and, OHO, what have we here?
>
> In amongst the parking bays, several twin-engine aircraft without propellers and no reflections from their noses. More than likely Me 262s. This is where the handiness of the Mosquito comes in because a lot has got to be done before the fires go out. Steeply round for a low run with a short burst, which hits a trifle short but just time to correct and cover the pens with strikes. Round for another run and by this time the gun crews, probably a trifle out of breath, have got to their posts and are answering back. But this is too good to miss, so back for a couple more runs by which time there is a confused cloud of smoke and fire. We reckon we have done enough to

claim one Me 262 destroyed and two damaged, and head for home once more. And on the way out we see an odd thing, a submarine flying a balloon. We don't know whose it is, so refrain from attacking and do not call attention to it until debriefing. My guess is that it was an Allied submarine with an aerial raised by the balloon for signals monitoring.

Somewhere in Holland, flying at about 1,000 ft [300 metres] we were startled to see a V-2 rise off its pad about a mile [1.5 km] in front of us. I slipped off the safety catch but it rose at an unbelievable rate into the clouds at about 2,000 ft [610 metres], lighting up the whole sky in a weird flickering brilliant violet glow. We couldn't trace the pad but made a note of the map references so that someone could come and have a look in daylight; but some of the sites were mobile. I have also been near to being on the receiving end of those beasties and the sudden arrival has a shocking effect, much worse than the ones you hear coming.

Although late in the European war, higher authority was viewing with increasing interest the importance of the *Mandrel* and *Window* feint forces. In April, the *Mandrel* squadrons, 171 and 199, were authorized to increase their strength by four more aircraft each, and on several occasions a small force, usually twenty to twenty-four heavy bombers, was allocated from either 4 or 7 Group to support the *Window* force. Mosquito PRXVIs replaced the Mk IVs in 192 Squadron; their aircraft had been fitted with *Dina* and *Piperack* jamming equipment earlier that year. The Liberators of 223 Squadron were also to be replaced by new Fortresses, the old and worn B-24s having shown themselves to be too slow to keep up with the British bombers. Later in the month, with the front line beginning to advance further into Germany, the *Mandrel* screen formation was discarded. These aircraft flew with the bombers on three occasions, and the Mosquitoes' targets became more and more distant.

On 1/2 April 1945, four 515 Squadron Mosquitoes took part in a night *Ranger* operation in the Munich and Augsburg–Ingolstadt areas from their forward base at Juvincourt. Howard Kelsey and Smithy Smith stooged around many airfields in the Munich area but found no fighters and failed to make any ASH contacts. Kelsey attacked a factory with incendiary bombs and caused terrific explosions and a large fire. Bunny Adams and Frank Widdicombe attacked seven Bf 109s on the ground at Erding with cannon fire and damaged one before attacking Lechfeld airfield, causing fires and explosions. Leipheim airfield was attacked by Squadron Leader John Penny and Flying Officer Whitfield, and Lieutenant E. J. van Heerden SAAF and Flying Officer J. W. Robson. The South African and his navigator were killed when their Mosquito was shot down by an AA battery manned by Hitler Youth. Penny proceeded to Neuburg where he found nothing. Returning to Leipheim, he bombed the dispersals with incendiary bombs and attacked and damaged a truck at Ertingen before turning for home.

Operations were flown even further afield, to the Czech border, as Dutch Holland recalls:

Several main force attacks were made on points where there were railway concentrations in order to disorganize the movement of troops from the eastern front. In support of one of these we were assigned to patrol the airfield at Plauen, which is pretty near the Czech border. As it happened, the winds took advantage of the $2\frac{1}{2}$ hours to target to increase and get round to the south. I couldn't claim with confidence that we had located our assigned airfield because a large marshalling yard, which appeared beneath us made us think that we were at Pilsen. There was a great deal of activity and it seemed a good idea to illuminate the scene a little better. There were, we thought, a flare and incendiaries in the fuselage bay, but dropping these from 500 ft [150 metres] gave us a considerable surprise. The flare turned out to be a 250 lb [113 kg] bomb with contact fuse but fortunately splinters and debris passed us by. The incendiaries proved more true to form. (In fact the load had been changed after the briefing.) At the least we certainly made a hole in the tracks and carried on the good work by damaging some of the locos and rolling stock with cannon fire.

Having more or less established our position (as we thought), it was then necessary to think about the rather long trek home. Shortly after this, an area of scattered conflagrations to starboard of our track led us to make a tentative identification of Leipzig, which had been the main force target. This meant that it was Chemnitz and not Pilsen which we had treated in such cavalier fashion and we were making both much more northing than we wished and slow progress over the ground. After about another hour it was becoming apparent that our fuel state would need careful management. In view of the increased and adverse wind it seemed best to keep at a fairly low altitude and pull back the revs a bit. Much later, the north German islands began to drift past aggravatingly slowly. It now looked as though we might have a problem and some nice calculations began to occupy the fingers of both hands. It would be very much touch and go. Fifty miles [80 km] out, the gauges were pretty near their marks. A mayday from here should get us a clear run through the Norfolk anti-Diver belt. This would ensure a straight descending run into the first airfield that could receive us – Coltishall. The fuel pressure warning lights were on during the approach and the touch of the wheels on the asphalt was accompanied by the exaltation we had been delaying for the last five minutes. As we turned off the runway the engines stopped.

On 3/4 April, eight Mosquitoes of 157 Squadron made a Spoof raid on Berlin in support of 8 Group Mosquitoes. Over the Big City, Flight Lieutenant J. H. Leland was coned by the searchlights and an Me 262, seeing its chance, made four attacks on the Mosquito. Two strikes were recorded on Leland's engines but he escaped his pursuer after spinning his aircraft and heading flat out for friendly territory.

On 4/5 April, 141 Squadron dispatched its first Mosquito XXX sortie when three joined twelve from 239 Squadron in a bomber support operation for the heavies attacking synthetic oil plants in southern Germany. Squadron Leader Tim Woodman and Flight Lieutenant Neville, who were serving at BSDU, destroyed a Bf 109 west of Magdeburg (Woodman's seventh confirmed victory of the war). This same night, Flight Lieutenant C. W. 'Topsy' Turner and 20-year-old Flight Sergeant George 'Jock' Honeyman from Edinburgh, both of 'A' Flight in 85 Squadron, took off from

*NFXXXs of 157 Squadron from Swannington over the Norfolk countryside. NFXXXs began to equip
157 Squadron in February 1945.* (Richard Doleman)

Swannington at 2238 hours for a high-level escort of the *Window* force. Escort was only
a loose term because in the dark it was not possible to fly any kind of formation over
long distances. Turner and Honeyman were new boys who had joined the squadron in
November when they were somewhat dazzled by the arrays of 'gongs' worn by aces such
as Burbridge and Skelton (DSO* and DFC* each) and A. I. 'Ginger' Owen and
McAllister (DFC* DFM). These crews finished the war with twenty-one and fifteen
victories respectively. They flew their freshman operation on the night of 29 December
1944 and would fly seventeen together on the Mosquito. It was Turner's first tour as a
pilot. He had been a gunner on Hampdens and had been shot down twice.

Turner piloted the Mosquito on a course of 090°. On crossing into enemy territory at
the Dutch coast, they began their climb to their tasked height of 20,000 ft (6,100 metres).
After nearly two hours, they reached their patrol area north-west of Magdeburg. All the
time Honeyman was scanning the AI and all the other interception aids. Their Mosquito
was equipped with Mk X radar, which he considered

> ... probably the best AI of WW2 ... It could be operated down to circuit
> height of 1,000–1,500 ft [300–460 metres]. In addition, there were two

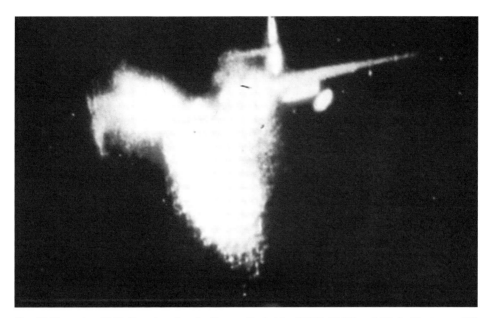

On 4/5 November 1944, Squadron Leader Branse Burbridge DSO* DFC* and Flight Lieutenant Bill Skelton DSO* DFC* of 85 Squadron shot down three Ju 88s and this Bf 110 of II/NJG *1 north of Hangelar airfield. The Messerschmitt crashed into the Rhine at 2150 hours, killing pilot* Oberleutnant *Ernst Ranze, although radar operator* Obergefreiter *Karl-Heinz Bendfeld and the gunner baled out safely. Burbridge and Skelton finished the war as the top-scoring night-fighter team in the RAF, with twenty-one aircraft destroyed, two probables, one damaged and three V-1s also destroyed.*

additional displays. *Perfectos,* a small diameter cathode ray tube fitted in the AI visor, displayed enemy IFF transmissions. Only left or right indications were given but the transmitting aircraft could be detected at a much greater range than was possible using AI, which relied on the echo from the fighter aircraft's own transmission. *Monica,* fitted at the bottom of the instrument panel, showed on its display aircraft coming from behind from a range of 1–2 miles [1.5–3 km]. Every day the Y-Service provided the enemy colours of the day and we carried similar cartridges for the Very pistols, to try to confuse enemy Bofors fire which was usually encountered on *Intruder* sorties at low level over enemy airfields. The only navigational aid was *Gee,* which could only be received as far as Holland because of enemy jamming. From there it was DR based on a detailed flight plan.

At approximately 2238 hours Jock Honeyman picked up an AI contact and immediately began his commentary to Topsy who had a visual range of only 800–1,000 yd, depending on moonlight condition.

Contact $3\frac{1}{4}$ miles (5.6 km), 200. Starboard, crossing starboard to port … Turn port … Go down. Range now two miles (3 km), 100. Starboard – harder port. Target now 12 o'clock, 5° above, 1 mile (1.5 km). Level off, ease the turn. Now steady; 800 yd 12 o'clock, 15° above; 600 yd, 12 o'clock 150 above – throttle back; 12 o'clock, 20°, minimum range – hold that speed. Can't you see him?'

Topsy called 'Visual.' He opened up the throttles and slowly closed in on a gently weaving target, adjusting his gunsight and switching on his camera-gun. At 100 yd, there was no Type F response (an infrared telescope which could pick up a light source fitted under the tail of RAF bombers but invisible to the naked eye because the light was covered by a black shield, known as Type Z). Using night binoculars, the target was identified from underneath as a Ju 188. Topsy dropped back to 200 yd to open fire when a black object, possibly a single-engined fighter, whistled across their bows at about 100 ft (30 metres). Both men ducked smartly. Turner recalls: 'After multiple curses and bags of brow mopping, we saw our quarry still ahead and I opened fire from 200 yd astern with 5° deflection, obtaining strikes on the port engine. Two more short bursts made the Hun burn nicely. It spun and crashed, burning fiercely on the ground, west of Magdeburg.' At 0130 hours C-Charlie landed back at Swannington after four hours, forty minutes in the air. This was their one and only kill of the war.

On 9/10 April Wing Commander Kelsey DFC*, the Commanding Officer of 515 Squadron, and Flight Lieutenant Edward M. 'Smithy' Smith DFC DFM flew an *Intruder* to Lübeck, a night-fighter base that was still active. Smith recalls:

> After a while we spotted a Ju 88 taking off in dark conditions and had difficulty keeping it in radar contact and slowing down sufficiently to keep behind it. The Ju 88 was climbing very hard (probably with flaps). However, it was shot at and we saw several strikes. (After the war I was with 85 Squadron at Tangmere and visited Lübeck and whilst there I was told there was somewhere about, the remnants of a Ju 88 from the appropriate time.) After that all was quiet and we headed off towards Hamburg. I spotted an aircraft coming in behind us. We feinted to the right then circled hard to port, coming in behind him in part moonlight. We had no trouble in shooting the Ju 188 down. We continued over Hamburg and dropped the *Intruder* load of two 500 lb [227 kg] HE and 160 incendiaries.

This was Howard Kelsey's fourth victory in 100 Group and his seventh overall, plus four aircraft destroyed on the ground and one 'probable'.) Air-to-air victories were now few and far between but on the night of 13/14 April Flight Lieutenant Vaughan and Sergeant MacKinnon returned triumphant. Vaughan wrote:

> We planned to cross the enemy coast at Westerhever at 2320 hours then proceed to a point 20 miles [30 km] SW of Kiel, which was the target for the main bomber force. We had originally intended to cover the bomber route out from the target area to the enemy coastline for a period of thirty-five minutes. We were then aiming to do a freelance patrol in the Luneburg area. After being on patrol for forty minutes we were still getting groups of bomber contacts. As there was apparent ground activity with searchlights and ground flashes on the bomber route which were definitely not gun flashes but some sort of indicating aid to the Hun night-fighters, we decided to continue patrolling the same area. However, this area quietened down considerably and after many alterations of height etc, on patrol, at 2020 hours, height 18,000 ft [5,500 metres], just when our time limit on patrol had expired, my navigator obtained a crossing starboard to port contact at 5 miles [8 km] range 35° above. We chased our target in a port turn on to a southerly vector with the range rapidly reducing to 9,000 ft [2,750 metres]

and the target losing height at a rather low air speed, 220–230 IAS. The target kept up a continuous weave but settled down at about 10,000 ft [3,000 metres]. We closed range to 1,000 ft [300 metres] but experienced difficulty in getting behind him owing to his weaving activities. I got a visual on a pale blue light. But the aircraft did a peel-off to port and range went out to 5,000 ft [1,500 metres]. We followed on AI, which incidentally was very ropey, in turns. Again we closed on the hard-weaving target. I got fleeting visuals on bright exhausts at one stage, at about 2,000 ft [610 metres] range, but still could not get comfortably settled astern. Three times we closed in to 1,000 ft [300 metres], the target peeling off on every occasion. The blue light was visible on most of these occasions from just astern but I was unable to follow visually owing to the target's activities.

We could identify target as a twin-engined aircraft on our very few opportunities. On one occasion, my navigator confirmed this with night glasses. On the third occasion that we closed range to 1,000 ft [300 metres], the target, to me anyway, appeared to catch fire underneath the fuselage. I got my navigator's head out of the box to confirm this and very quickly and brightly he yelled, 'That's his jet', which jolted me out of my fire theory very quickly. The target again started one of his routine turns and I immediately pushed the throttles fully open +12 and already using 28,000 revs, and gave a half-second deflection shot on his jet at about 900 ft [270 metres] range. However, this burst produced no strikes, so I got dead astern in the turn and at 700 ft [210 metres] range, fired another burst, which caused a large explosion and strikes on his starboard side. I gave him another burst for luck and another explosion appeared on the port side and the E/A burned from wing tip to wing tip, going down in a spin to starboard and hit the deck at 0031 hours. From its general appearance and behaviour, particularly the two exhausts of a jet we consider this A/C was an He 219, and we claim it as destroyed. We then set course for base. No *Perfectos* throughout patrol. The Hun did not seem to have any tail warning device, but was apparently carrying out the usual evasive action'. Claim: one He. 219 destroyed. A/c landed Swannington 0211 hours.

There were definite signs that the end of the war could be in sight but as Dutch Holland of 515 Squadron recalls:

Wing Commander Kelsey and 100 Group between them seemed determined that we should not become bored during its last throes. On 15/16 April Schleissheim, the airfield at Munich, was selected for special attention, probably because it was a likely transit point for German staff movements now that Allied armies were closing in from east and west. Be that as it may, it was supposed to have been a co-ordinated attack but I do not recall it as having been a particularly well-planned operation. We had the usual feeling that it was Bob and I alone against the Third Reich. In the absence of any general target illumination we used our own incendiaries to light up the area round the airfield buildings. Incidentally, it's a hell of a long way to Munich and we just took it for granted that we would find the place. That we did so without any great difficulty is a credit to Bob. Features on the airfield were recognizable from the photos we had studied at briefing. The object of the exercise being to create mayhem, we used our 20 mm guns on the airfield buildings, concentrating on the control tower which cannot have been too pleasant for its occupants.

After this little gesture, we climbed to about 2,000 ft [610 metres] and flew round Munich trailing our coat, looking for anything that might turn up. Having left behind the light flak at low level which had been hardly enough to mention, it was noticeable that the heavy guns undoubtedly disposed round the city did not seem over-concerned with one or two relatively innocuous Mosquitoes droning around, even though we might have been pathfinders. They probably couldn't set their fuses for that level. We once flew at about 2,000 ft [610 metres] right across the Ruhr (accidentally) without a shot being fired. Bob said it was because they couldn't believe that a hostile aircraft would do anything so stupid. There might have been balloons but the thought didn't occur to us at the time.

While over the northern purlieus of Munich, Bob picked up a contact on our level, range about 1 mile [1.5 km] and out to our right. Having turned sharply towards the supposed position of the bogey (it could have of course been one of our own aircraft), a light came into view which was evidently on the aircraft we were tracking. It was not difficult to get into a position behind it but we came near to running into it as it was evidently doing very much less than our 240 mph [380 kph]. A wide S-turn brought us back behind it and although our speed was very much reduced, we were still too near and closing too fast. As we passed beneath, the fixed landing gear of a Ju 52 could be seen distinctly but the white light made it almost impossible to pick out any other features against the moonless sky. It seemed to he doing about 120 mph [190 kph] in a slow turn round an airfield beacon, probably in a holding orbit until things had settled down at Schleissheim.

It didn't take too long to decide that although it was a transport aircraft and might be unarmed (some did carry defensive armament) there was no doubt in our minds that the chance that it could be carrying top brass or war material meant that it must be attacked. The next approach brought us into firing position and a burst of 20 mm was aimed at each of the wing engines. As we passed, it had already begun a descending turn and there appeared to be fire in the wing engines. We did not see it again and the trace disappeared from our radar.

515 had more casualties than any other squadron in 100 Group. I suppose there was a tendency to avoid dwelling on the fact if someone 'got the chop'. It just seems that it didn't happen very often and most of our particular mates came through OK.

There remained one more task before hostilities ceased in the wide-ranging activities of 515 Squadron. On 14/15 April it and 23 Squadron flew the first Mosquito Master Bomber sorties in 100 Group, dropping green TIs and orchestrating attacks by eighteen Mosquitoes of 141 and 169 Squadrons which carried a new, even more sinister form of aerial bomb for the first time, going under the code-name *Firebash*.

CHAPTER XIV

Firebash

The fires are grey; no star no sign
Winks from the breathing darkness of the carrier
Where the pilot circles for his wingman; where,
Gliding above the cities' shells, a stubborn eye
Among the embers of the nations, achingly
Tracing the circles of that worn, unchanging No -
The lives' long war, lost war – the pilot sleeps.

'The Dead Wingman' by Randall Jarrell

The quaint English locomotive steamed through the enchanting Norfolk countryside, tugging its carriages behind it. In one of the first-class compartments, Winnie Winn DFC, 141 Squadron Commanding Officer, *en route* to his station at West Raynham, sat opposite a USAAF officer. They were alone in the compartment and were soon in animated conversation, the American exchanging pointers on the daylight air war, and Winn extolling the merits of night bombing. During the course of the conversation the American told Winn that the 8th Air Force intended to drop napalm gel (petrol thickened with a compound made from aluminium, naphthenic and palmitie acids – hence 'napalm' – to which white phosphorous was added for ignition) on enemy installations. Winn was excited at the prospect of using this lethal weapon on enemy airfields. Before the day was out, the dynamic RAF officer had obtained permission to use his squadron to drop the gel in Mosquito 100 gal (450 litre) drop tanks, providing he could obtain his own supplies.

Winn made a call to the 8th Air Force and 40 gal (180 litre) and 50 gal (225 litre) drums of napalm gel soon began arriving at West Raynham, courtesy of the Americans. At first armourers pumped it into drop tanks using hand pumps but then the Americans obliged with petrol-driven mechanical pumps and the operation became much easier. Armourer LAC Johnny Claxton, at that time one of the longest-serving members of 141 Squadron's groundcrews, recalls that a 1 lb (450 gram) all-way phosphorous fuse was fitted in each tank to ignite the napalm gel on impact. The fuze was called all-way because no matter how the tank fell the fuze would ignite the contents.

In the afternoon of 6 April, Wing Commander Winn carried out the first of three trials of types of napalm gel when he flew low and parallel with the main No. 1 runway and dropped 100 gal (450 litre) drop tanks on the grass. These trials caused enormous interest and the station and aircrew crowded in the control tower while the groundcrews climbed on to the roofs of the hangars in order to get a better view of the explosions. It was decided that the crews who would drop napalm gel required no additional training because they had carried out enough low-level attacks with bombs or cannon over many months; no special tactics were to be employed. Enthusiasm and keenness to get on the night's programme reached a fever pitch. When six aircraft were asked for, a dozen were offered – and accepted! Petrol and range was reduced so that each Mosquito could carry two 100 gal (450 litre) drop tanks but, even so, they would have to land at Juvincourt, Melsbroek or Mannheim. No one was unhappy about this arrangement as it offered the possibility of being stranded on the Continent for days!

Napalm gel came in three different consistencies – thick, medium and thin. Winnie Winn carried out two further trials over West Raynham's grass expanses, on 12 and 13 April, in front of large audiences. As a result of the trials, it was discovered that the thick gel failed to ignite.

The following night, 14/15 April, eighteen Mosquito VIs and XXXs were dispatched from West Raynham. Twelve were from 141 Squadron and six from 239 Squadron, some of which were detailed to provide support for the 512 bombers attacking Potsdam just outside Berlin. This was the first time the Big City had been attacked by heavies since March 1944, although Mosquito bombers had continually attacked it. Seven Mosquitoes of 141 Squadron flew high-level Mk X AI patrols in support of the Potsdam raid but also covered the remaining five 141 Mosquitoes which would carry out the first napalm gel *Firebash* raid on night-fighter airfields at Neuruppin near Potsdam and Jüterborg near Berlin.

Winnie Winn and R. A. W. Scott in a Mk VI led the formation of five aircraft to Brussels/Melsbroek for refuelling before setting course for the Berlin area where they were to be supported by bomb- and incendiary-carrying Mosquitoes of 23 Squadron which also supplied the 'Noload' leader, the Master Bomber, for the Neuruppin raid. Master of Ceremonies, Squadron Leader H. V. Hopkins, provided 'excellent support' and Winn dropped his canisters from 800 ft (240 metres). He was followed by Flying Officers R. W. A. Marriott and N. Barber and W. P. Rimer and H. B. Farnfield. All six napalm bombs exploded near the hangars and engulfed the airfield in flame and smoke. A row of six buildings burned merrily and lit up the night sky as all three Mosquitoes, unburdened now, returned to strafe the airfield with cannon fire. Red tracer every fifth shell zeroed in on buildings and bowsers, one of which exploded in a huge flash of flame near a hangar. Rimer and Farnfield strafed the hapless base three times from 2,000 ft (610 metres) to 500 ft (150 metres) in all, helped in no small measure by TIs dropped just south-east of the airfield by the Master Bomber.

At Jüterbog Flight Lieutenant M. W. Huggins, the Master of Ceremonies, and Flying Officer C. G. Stow, in a 515 Squadron 'Sollock' aircraft (Master Bomber), was unable to help much and no TIs were seen to drop which scattered over about a 10 mile (16 km) area. Ron Brearley and John Sheldon and Flight Lieutenant E. B. Drew and Flying Officer A. H. Williams thundered low over the German countryside and had to toss their napalm bombs on the estimated position of the airfield. One of Brearley's drop tanks hung up so he dropped the port tank containing 50 gal (225 litres) of napalm gel from 300 ft (90 metres) and headed west. (Returning with a napalm gel tank still attached was, as one could imagine, problematic. On a later *Firebash* operation one tank that would not release over the target fell off on the West Raynham runway on the aircraft's return. These hang-ups occurred because of deposits of napalm on the release unit, and at the joint between the tank and the mainplanes.) Drew meanwhile, was forced to climb to 5,000 ft (1,500 metres) and position on *Gee,* following the failure of the TIs and flares, before he dropped down to 1,000 ft (300 metres) and roared over the base with the two 100 gal (450 litre) drop tanks ready to rain death and destruction. The two firebombs exploded among rows of buildings in the north-west corner of the airfield and were still burning thirteen minutes later as he twice strafed buildings amid light and inaccurate flak. All five fire-bomber Mosquitoes landed back at Melsbroek for refuelling before returning to West Raynham, no doubt highly delighted with their night's work.

On 17 April Johnnie Bridekirk and Terry Glasheen, a universally popular Australian crew crashed when taking off from Brussels/Melsbroek airfield in the early hours of the morning. The Mosquito went up in flames, and those who saw the crash say that they never expected the crew to escape with their lives. However, Terry Glasheen put up a magnificent show by dragging his pilot clear of the flames, and there is no doubt that his level-headedness and courage prevented a terrible tragedy. Terry Glasheen was back on the squadron within a comparatively few days but Johnny Bridekirk suffered extensive burns and was condemned to many weary weeks in hospital.

The second *Firebash* raid by 141 Squadron was flown on 17/18 April. Bomber Command was also abroad at night, with attacks by 5 Group on railway yards at Cham, Germany. Five 141 Squadron Mosquitoes, each armed with 100 gal (450 litre) napalm gel drop tanks, and led by Wing Commander Winnie Winn, were to head for Schleissheim airfield just north of Munich, after a refuelling stop at St Dizier. However, after landing at St Dizier, Winn was delayed with refuelling problems when petrol had to be brought 60 miles (100 km) by road. He decided that by the time they got off and found the target they would be unable to see the markers, and opted for an attack on Munchen instead. However, a bad storm front scrubbed this option and he and Scott were forced to return to England.

The three remaining napalm-armed Mosquito crews battled through solid cloud and violent thunderstorms to Schleissheim but Rimer and Farnfield were forced to abort after losing *Gee.* After vainly trying to climb above the thick cloud, Squadron Leader Thatcher was also forced to abandon the mission. Another crew, Flying Officer J. C. Barton and Sergeant L. Berlin, fought their way through the storm front and hurled their napalm bombs among airfield buildings, then, obtaining permission from the 23 Squadron Master Bomber, strafed the airfield on a return low-level run. Roy Brearley and John Sheldon climbed to 10,000 ft (3,000 metres) to escape the worst of the weather, and diving down on pinpoints provided by 'Noload' they added fuel to the flames with their two napalm bombs. They fell among two hangars and exploded. They called up the Master Bomber before returning and strafing hangars, buildings and rolling stock, then exiting the area to allow 23 Squadron to add their bombs and incendiaries to the conflagration.

Meanwhile, Mosquitoes of 85 Squadron patrolled Schleissheim and Firstenfeldbrück airfields. Wing Commander Davison, 85 Squadron Commanding Officer since Wing Commander K. 'Gon' Gonsalves had been posted in January, destroyed a Ju 88 in the Munich area using *Perfectos.* On the following night, 18/19 April 1945 seven 141 Squadron Mosquitoes each carrying two 100 gal (450 litre) drop tanks filled with napalm, eight from of 169 Squadron at Great Massingham, four Mosquito IVs of 23 Squadron and four of 515 Squadron from Little Snoring, and one 141 Squadron aircraft for high-level Mk X AI patrol over the target, flew to the forward base at Juvincourt in

France for a *Firebash* raid on Munich/Neubiberg airfield. The eight Mosquitoes from 23 and 515 Squadrons and the eight from 169 Squadron were to drop flares and HE on Munich/Neubiberg with 141 adding to the destruction.

The raid was in full swing when 141 Squadron, led once more by Winn, arrived at Munich/Neubiberg with their napalm loads. Flight Lieutenant Drew and Pilot Officer A. H. Williams were ready to commence their low-level bomb run at 700 ft (210 metres) but had to wait twenty-five minutes before they could take their turn. To add insult to injury, one of their fire-bombs refused to release. Drew climbed to 7,000 ft (2,100 metres) and tried to shake it loose and finally got it safely away just north of Munich. On the instructions of 'Noload Leader', the master bomber, Warrant Officer Ronald G. Dawson and Flying Officer Charles P. D. Childs, an all New Zealand crew in Winball 7, went in for their fire-bombing run. The 24-year-old pilot and his 32-year-old navigator/radar operator had joined 141 Squadron on 22 January and this was their tenth operation. It was also the last. As they hurtled into the attack they heard in their headphones the Master Bomber's warning of accurate light flak but pressed bravely on. Just as they reached their drop point Winball 7 was hit by flak. The New Zealanders' Mosquito appeared to climb and some ten seconds later crashed in flames near an *autobahn* north-west of the airfield. One of the tanks seemed to ricochet into the air and fall back into the burning pyre. They were the last casualties on 141 Squadron in the war.

On 19/20 April, three squadrons of Mosquitoes flew a napalm raid against Flensburg airfield on the Danish border. Six Mosquito Mk VIs of 515 Squadron marked the target with green TIs and flares, and dropped incendiaries and 500 lb (227 kg) HE bombs. The Commanding Officer of 515 Squadron, Howard Kelsey, with Smithy Smith, was master bomber. Three Mosquito VIs of 169 Squadron took off from Great Massingham and flew to West Raynham to load up with napalm tanks for their first napalm attack. The same aircraft also carried two 500 lb (227 kg) bombs beneath their wings. No. 141 Squadron was unable to carry bombs on its Mk XXX Mosquitoes as well as napalm tanks because they did not have bomb racks or the release mechanisms fitted in the bomb bay behind the cannons. For the same reason, 169 Squadron were unable to use their Mk XIX Mosquitoes. The attack was very successful, with good work by the Master Bomber. Flensburg was plastered and strafed from end to end, and smoke and flame made observation of the final result difficult. Count Bernadotte, the head of the Swedish Red Cross was at this time using the airfield to fly back and forth between Sweden and Germany for secret negotiations with Heinrich Himmler, who hoped to extract a separate surrender. The count and his chauffeur narrowly escaped death during the attack.

Also on the night of 19/20 April Flight Lieutenant Howard DFC and Flying Officer Clay DFC of BSDU at Swanton Morley were on a patrol to southern Denmark and the Island of Fyn airfields in a Mosquito XXX and they returned triumphant as Howard recalled:

Aircraft BSDU/B was airborne Swanton Morley 2043 hours to carry out a low-level patrol of South Denmark and airfields on the Island of Fyn. The aircraft was equipped with Mk X AI, *Serrate* IVA and *Wolf*. Landfall was made at 2204 hours, height 15,000 ft [460 metres], from there, height was lost to Bogense where we arrived at 2216 hours, height 3,000 ft [900 metres]. A patrol of the Fyn Island was carried out for an hour, during which time only one airfield was observed at Boldringe. At 2305 hours an attack parallel to the runway was made on a dispersed barrack site with two bursts of two seconds each. Strikes were seen. The airfield was not lit and no flak was experienced. Many small convoys were seen on roads. At 2316 hours course was set from the island at 2,000 ft [610 metres]. At 2324 hours a Mk X contact crossing starboard to port, range 4 miles [6.5 km] and above, our height being 2,000 ft [610 metres]. We turned behind the contact at 5,000 ft [1,500 metres] range when a visual was obtained on an aircraft heading on a course of 175°. A Ju 88 was identified with the aid of glasses at 1,500 ft [460 metres] range, height 3,000 ft [900 metres], speed 240 IAS. A short burst from dead astern at 250 yd, which caused the outer half of the port wing to fall away. The E/A rolled on its back, hit the ground at 2328 hours, spread over a wide area and caused a large number of small fires. Course was set for base, crossing out at Farne at 2340 hours, and landed at base 0104 hours.

Howard fired 200 rounds (fifty each gun) of 20 mm on the sortie.

Further napalm gel attacks were carried out on 22/23 April. Jägel was attacked by Mosquito XXXs of 141 Squadron, three Mosquitoes of 169 Squadron and four Mosquitoes of 515 Squadron, led by Master Bomber Squadron Leader J. H. Penny and Flying Officer J. H. Whitfield, who dropped green TIs and incendiaries. Flak greeted them and a 141 Squadron Mosquito flown by Flight Lieutenant G. M. Barrowman and Warrant Officer H. S. Griffiths suffered severe damage in the starboard wing and inner fuel tank. They returned to England hugging the German and Dutch coasts, keeping the Friesians in sight to port, and landed safely at Woodbridge. Five Mosquitoes of 23 Squadron with napalm tanks, and five Mosquitoes of 23 Squadron with Squadron Leader H. V. Hopkins as Master Bomber, bombed Westerland airfield on Sylt. Hopkins, aware that his TIs would not be seen because of the thick cloud over the target, instructed the Deputy Master Bomber to drop incendiaries.

By 23 April the British Second Army had arrived opposite Hamburg and on the next day its advanced units were on the west bank of the Elbe ready for the last thrust to Lübeck and Kiel. On 23 April, as part of the support operation for the ground troops, five Mosquitoes of 23 Squadron flew to Melsbroek with six napalm Mosquitoes of 141 Squadron led by Wing Commander Winnie Winn, refuelled and crossed to Lübeck. That night they plastered the airfield with HE, incendiaries and firebombs under the direction of Master Bomber Squadron Leader D. I. Griffiths of 23 Squadron. The whole attack took just ten minutes; the airfield was left burning and devastated. All aircraft returned safely despite light, accurate flak put up by the defenders. That same night thirty Mosquitoes and seven Lancasters dropped leaflets over eight POW camps. The war was drawing to a close and the morale of the men behind the wire soared, while at home some worried that there would be no more opportunities to fly their Mosquitoes in anger.

On 24/25 April six Mosquitoes of 141 Squadron carried out a napalm attack on Munich/Neubiberg airfield again. The 515 Squadron Master Bomber, Squadron Leader J. H. Penny and Flying Officer J. H. Whitfield, again marked for them; other 515 Squadron aircraft flew support. During the patrol Flight Lieutenant J. Davis and Flying Officer B. R. Cronin claimed eight enemy aircraft damaged on the ground during their six strafing and bombing runs with two 500 lb (227 kg) and eighty 5 lb (2.3 kg) incendiaries over Kaufbeuren airfield. The aircraft were in the moon shadow of the hangar and positive identification was therefore impossible. A fire broke out in the hangar and could be seen through the open doors. Meanwhile, at Neubiberg, Squadron Leader Harry White DFC** and Flight Lieutenant Mike Allen DFC** also claimed the destruction of a single-engined enemy aircraft on the ground; it was also the last recorded victory for 141 Squadron in the war. White and Allen dropped their napalm bombs with the safety pins still in but they exploded on impact and caused 'a good fire'. They landed at their forward base at Juvincourt, an area they had patrolled in Beaufighters from August 1943.

On 25 April special permission was granted for a single Halifax of 192 Squadron, with a full bomb load, to join 359 Lancasters on a raid on the SS barracks and Hitler's bunker at the Eagle's Nest. On 26 April the British Army took Bremen. On 25/26 April the *Firebash* Mosquitoes attacked Munich/Reim airfield while four Mosquitoes of 515 Squadron with Lieutenant W. Barton SAAF as Master Bomber, attacked Landsberg. Mosquitoes of 169 Squadron also took part in the raid on Landsberg. Flying Officer J. K. 'Sport' Rogers, navigator to Flight Lieutenant Phil Kelshall recalls:

> For this operation we flew to RAF Oulton where our drop tanks were filled with napalm. We returned to Massingham where the aircraft, a Mosquito VI (224) was armed with two 500 lb [227 kg] bombs and cannons loaded with ammo. In the afternoon we flew to Juvincourt where we refuelled and waited for nightfall – the operation took place in moonlight, so navigation was easy. We flew at low level and made initial rendezvous with all the other aircraft at the north end of the Ammer Lake and checked in with Master Bomber.
>
> At the agreed time made by the Master Bomber we made rendezvous over the airfield. We had all been assigned a call sign in numerical order. At the appropriate time, the Master Bomber called in the first aircraft to drop napalm tanks – calling '01 clear' as it dropped its tanks – and then at ten second intervals the remainder of the aircraft followed to drop their napalm tanks. This routine was adopted to avoid collision over the target area, which in this raid were the hangars and adjacent aircraft parking areas, which had been previously illuminated with flares and target markers. Also in attendance were anti-flak aircraft to suppress the flak. Having dropped the napalm, we returned to orbit the airfield and when the last aircraft had completed its drop of napalm, the master bomber called for the 500 lb [227 kg] bombs to be dropped in the same sequence as before. Having completed the bomb-drop and again returned to orbit, the Master Bomber called for cannon fire, again in the same sequence – the target area was a mass of flame by this time and the cannons were used to spray the area in the pass over the target. This completed the operation and we returned to Juvincourt -elapsed time three hours forty minutes – where we stayed the night and returned to Massingham the next day.

On 26 April another consignment of 100 gal (450 litre) drop tanks arrived at West Raynham. Word spread quickly that a final *Firebash* fling was in the offing. On 2 May, the British Second Army having crossed the Elbe now moved on to Lübeck and units of the British 6th Airborne Division reached Wismar on the Baltic and made contact with the Russian army. The war was all over bar the shouting but Dutch Holland in 515 Squadron wrote: 'May 2nd and still, as far as we were concerned, there was no let up in the determination to break the regime that had been our mortal enemy for so long. Crusaderish? It was a pretty general feeling among aircrews at that time now that the end was in sight. With only five days to go before VE Day 515 undertook just one more very hairy job.'

Large convoys of ships were now assembling at Kiel on the Baltic, and it was feared that they were to transport German troops to Norway to continue the fight from there. It was decided therefore that Mosquitoes of Bomber Command should attack Kiel on 2/3 May and this would be the very last operation of the war for Bomber Command. Some 126 Mosquitoes from 8 Group would follow in the wake of sixteen Mosquitoes of 8 Group. Thirty-seven Mosquitoes of 23, 169, 141 and 515 Squadrons in 100 Group would make attacks on airfields at Flensburg, Hohn, Westerland/Sylt and Schleswig/Jägel. Hohn and Flensburg airfields would be bombed with napalm and incendiaries directed by a master bomber. Support for the night's operations would be provided by twenty-one *Mandrel/Window* sorties by 199 Squadron Halifaxes while eleven Fortresses of 214 Squadron and nine B-17s/B-24s of 223 Squadron would fly *Window*/jamming sorties over the Kiel area. At Foulsham ten Halifaxes of 462 Squadron would carry out a Spoof operation with *Window* and bombs against Flensburg while some of the nineteen Halifaxes of 192 Squadron carried out a radio search in the area. Others dropped *Window* and TIs, and some also carried eight 500 lb (227 kg) bombs. Five Mosquitoes of 192 Squadron were also engaged in radio frequency work.

At North Creake Air Vice Marshal Addy Addison was present during the take-off of thirty-eight aircraft of the southern *Window* force including eighteen Halifaxes from 171 Squadron and ten from 199 Squadron, also heading for Kiel on *Mandrel/Window* operations. He expressed his satisfaction at the size of the final effort. All told, a record 106 aircraft of 100 Group took part. Eight Mosquito XXXs of 239 Squadron took off from West Raynham for high-level and low-level raids on airfields in Denmark and Germany, while six Mosquitoes of 141 Squadron were to make napalm attacks on Flensburg airfield with fourteen napalm-armed Mosquitoes attacking Hohn airfield.

Halifax III MZ971 6Y-E I'm Easy! (E-Easy) flown by Warrant Officer Jamieson RAAF of 171 Squadron at North Creake. (Bill Tiltman via Theo Boiten)

Master of Ceremonies at Flensburg would be Flying Officer E. L. Heath of 23 Squadron while the Master Bomber at Hohn was Squadron Leader D. I. Griffiths. Four Mosquitoes of 23 Squadron would drop incendiaries on Flensburg and seven more from 23 Squadron would bomb Hohn with incendiaries before the arrival of 141 Squadron's Mosquitoes. Meanwhile, 169 Squadron's Mosquitoes, plus four from 515 Squadron with Flight Lieutenant McEwan as Master Bomber and Flying Officer Barnes would raid Jägel. Four other Mosquitoes of 515 Squadron, with Wing Commander Howard Kelsey as Master Bomber, would drop incendiaries on Westerland airfield on Sylt. Dutch Holland of 515 Squadron wrote:

> Just what was brewing at the Westerland I have never been able to find out precisely. It couldn't have been that it was a particularly active night-fighter base because I don't remember any patrols being assigned there, but it was believed that suicide missions were being planned by the *Luftwaffe*, presumably against heads of state or centres of government. Whatever it was it must have been something out of the ordinary to make it necessary to try and burn up everything on it. At the briefing it was announced that a new type of bomb would be used, referred to as 'thermite'. It was a 50 gal [225 litre] cylinder carried on the wing racks. A warning was given that it would ignite on contact and great care must be exercised not to cause premature ignition. In other words 'For God's sake don't have a prang with these on board!' Each aircraft was detailed to take up an assigned position round the island at a designated time; great emphasis on the time. At a given signal the attack would commence with a bomb run by the Commanding Officer, followed by the rest at very short intervals, criss-crossing the field from different directions at height intervals of 50 ft [15 metres]. Bob and I were to come in No.3 at 150 ft [45 metres].
>
> It was still full daylight when we left Little Snoring in a loose gaggle, each making for his own pinpoint and ETA, and there was still enough light to make out the odd island as we approached Sylt. A marker was to be dropped on one of them to ensure complete synchronization at the target. All aircraft duly arrived at their stations and the minutes began to drag by. For some reason Kelsey wasn't ready to open the attack and we were acutely aware that immediately the airfield became encircled by orbiting aircraft the Jerries must have been fully alerted and dashed out to man every gun on the place. The covers were off and there was one up the spout of every weapon they possessed when the cue to start was finally given. I don't know what form the signal took, as I was too uptight to record an impression. The runs were to follow in very quick succession, a matter of seconds only, and after that each aircraft was to engage the defences.
>
> The first one in was greeted by a cone of tracer that looked like a tent of sparks flying upwards, meeting and then spreading like the poles of a teepee. Thinking to take advantage of their diverted attention I cut in at full belt to cross the airfield, heading for some large hangars clearly visible in the south-east side but by the time we were halfway, the whole shower swung in our direction. Things happened pretty fast from then on. I pressed

the release when I judged the aim about right and almost immediately as we turned sharply away the whole hangar erupted in an enormous ball of fire out of the roof, doors and windows. I couldn't help hoping even at that moment that there was nobody in it but all else was driven from our minds by a sharp BONK in the tail, at which the aircraft began to vibrate violently and the stick to try and shake itself out of my hand. (The cause of the vibration was that the starboard elevator had been shot through at the spar and the resulting overbalance was causing a flutter. It was gradually coming adrift and just lasted out the return to Snoring.)

Clearly this was no time to think about giving supporting fire, which turned out to be about as dangerous from risk of collision as from flak. So we excused ourselves and informed the assembled host that we had been hit and were pulling out. Still at about 100 ft [30 metres] we turned seawards and immediately found ourselves flying horizontally down the beams of a battery of searchlights. If they did shoot anything further in our direction we were heartily glad not to see any tracer, probably on account of the brightness of the lights. There was a bank of mist offshore a mile or two and the shadows of our aircraft in several discs of light were plain to see on its surface. Anything in the way of violent evasive action was out of the question and the minute it took to reach cover seemed like an hour. Losing all visual references on entering the mist then rendered us dependent on instruments which were all snaking about so much that only the artificial horizon could be seen at all clearly. However, taking stock and realizing that apart from whatever was causing the alarming vibration, all else seemed to be more or less in order, we found that by reducing speed down to about 150 mph [240 kph) it was possible to gain a little height and think about a course for home. Bob, I may say, appeared to remain unperturbed throughout apart from impolite observations about the parentage of some anti-aircraft personnel.

Warrant Officer Les Turner, who made the trip with his navigator and Flight Lieutenant Jimmy Wheldon, recalls:

By now I had enough of destruction and, while I could see the surrounding buildings, I decided to drop the napalm on the airfield. The war was obviously not going to last much longer. The opposition was quite intense and as I followed Flying Officer Keith Miller (later to become famous as an Australian Test cricketer) the light flak aimed at him was passing worryingly close to us. One of Keith's drop-tanks hung up and slewed him to starboard. But for this he reckoned that he would have got caught in the flak. [Miller and Squadron Leader Wright both returned to Great Massingham with a tank hung up but landed safely. On 28 June Miller lost an engine near Bircham Newton. He extinguished the fire and put down at Great Massingham where he overshot and crashed. He and his navigator were unhurt. Immediately afterwards. Miller jumped into his car, and headed for London where he proceeded to score 56 not out at Lords!] As it was we regrettably lost one of our crews – such a waste so near the end.

During the napalm gel attack on Jägel, Flying Officer Robert Catterall DFC and Flight Sergeant Donald Joshua Beadle of 169 Squadron were killed when their Mosquito was shot down by flak. Flight Sergeant John Beeching, a pilot in the squadron, who was on leave at the time but learned the details later, wrote: 'The commander of the German flak battery who shot the aircraft down later wrote to Catterall's mother saying that had he known that the end of the war was only two days' away he would not have opened fire, which is all right to say, but as our blokes were dropping Napalm I cannot imagine anyone standing by to watch that!

During a run on Westerland, a Mosquito of 515 Squadron flown by Flight Lieutanant Johnson and Flying Officer Thomason was hit but the pilot landed safely at Woodbridge on one engine. Two Halifaxes from 199 Squadron each with eight men on board and carrying four 500 lb (227 kg) bombs and large quantities of *Window*, probably collided while on their bomb runs, and they crashed at Meimersdorf, just south of Kiel. They were the last Bomber Command aircraft to be lost on operations in the war. Only Pilot Officer Les H. Currell, pilot of RG375/R who baled out with slight leg injuries, and his rear gunner Flight Sergeant R. 'Jock' Hunter, survived, while aboard RG373/T piloted by Flight Lieutenant William E. Brooks, only Pilot Officer K. N. Crane, the rear gunner, survived.

On the afternoon of 6 May Flight Sergeants Williams and Rhoden crashed on a cross-country training flight at Devil's Dyke (Spitalgate) near Brighton. Both men were killed. They were 169 Squadron's final casualties of the war. With Hitler dead and the European war over, celebrations got into full swing before crews began training for the Japanese war, were demobbed or transferred to other duties in the service. Dutch Holland recalls:

> There followed three weeks of flights to observe bomb damage in Germany and a few practice flights before 515 broke up and we took our aircraft up to Silloth and left them forlornly standing in a row. That flight doesn't appear in my logbook. While the House of Commons was being told on the afternoon of the 7th that cessation of hostilities was imminent, they may have heard a Mossie go over at 500 ft [150 metres] and if they or the milkman whose horse gave him a bit of trouble at Sudbury Hill wondered who was the lunatic up there – well, now they know.

Geoff Liles, a Fortress pilot in 214 Squadron, says:

> On VE-Day minus one, I approached Wing Commander Bowes for his permission to take my groundcrew on a round trip of 'Happy Valley' to show them the results of their labours in keeping the kites flying. This was approved and actually resulted in the two of us flying at low level and in very loose formation, crammed full with sightseers. It was something that I don't think any of us will ever forget.

Les Turner adds.

> On the day before VE Day we did a sightseeing tour covering Aachen, Cologne, Düsseldorf, the Möhne Dam, Dortmund and Duisburg. The

destruction was appalling and a sense of the terrible waste hung over a number of us over the Victory celebration days. We repeated the trip a week later – it was for the benefit of groundcrews who had, of course, seen nothing of this. We did some desultory flying throughout June and I last flew a Mosquito on 17 July 1945. One of my duties on 169 Squadron was to collect, on his return from POW release, Pilot Officer (then Flying Officer) Miller, who had the successes in May 1944 and had subsequently been shot down. I flew the Oxford very carefully. The responsibility of getting him back safely seemed very great indeed. My total flying time on Mosquitoes was 350 hours, the majority at night.

Dutch Holland concludes:

> May 9th dawned bright and clear with only one drawback: I was orderly officer and I was awakened by a sergeant of RAF Police standing beside my bed staring straight ahead through the peak of his cap announcing that it was believed that an officer from Little Snoring had made off with the Union Jack which had been flying at the King's Lynn Steam Laundry and if it was returned, no more would be said. If the sergeant would give me a few minutes I would join him in the search for said item. He dutifully departed and as I was hoisting myself out of the pit, noticed that my bed had for a quilt a very large Union Jack. It was quite a night.

Squadron Leader John Crotch was specially chosen to fly Air Commodore Rory Chisholm on 21 May and Air Vice-Marshal Addison on 28 May, to Schleswig and return in Halifax IIIs. From 25 June to 7 July 1945 Exercise Post-Mortem was carried out to evaluate the effectiveness of RAF jamming and Spoof operations on the German early-warning radar system. Simulated attacks were made by aircraft from four RAF groups including 100 Group, the early-warning radar being manned by American and British personnel on this occasion. Post-Mortem proved conclusively that the countermeasures had been a great success.

On 5 July John Crotch flew Brigadier General W. R. Peck, the commander of the US Second Air Division at Ketteringham Hall, Norfolk, to Denmark to inspect the underground fighter headquarters at Grove and see the tests at Schleswig, returning on 7 July. Meanwhile, on 25 June Tim Woodman flew to Germany and Denmark with Flight Lieutenants Neville and Bridges.

> At Grove I was walking back across the airfield after inspecting some of their aircraft when I passed four *Luftwaffe* airwomen in white shirts and grey skirts. Typical Frauleins. They stood smartly to attention but looked pretty boot-faced at having lost the war. 'OK sweethearts,' I said. 'Your time will come again.' How right I was.
>
> But what disasters they must have gone home to.

APPENDIX I

100 (SD) Group Order of Battle

Sqdn	Aircraft	1st Op in 100 Group	Base
192	Mosquito BIV/BXVI/ Wellington BIII, Halifax /V Mosquito II	December 1943	Foulsham
141	Beaufighter VI Mosquito II/VI/XXX	December 1943	West Raynham
239	Mosquito II/VI/XXX	20 January 1944	West Raynham
515	Mosquito II/VI	3 March 1944	Little Snoring Great Massingham
169	Mosquito II/VI/XIX	20 January 1944	Little Snoring
214	Fortress II/III	20/21 April 1944	Sculthorpe/Oulton
199	Stirling III/ Halifax III	1 May 1944	North Creake
157	Mosquito XIX/XXX	May 1944	Swannington
85	Mosquito XII/XVII	5/6 June 1944	Swannington
23	Mosquito VI	5/6 July 1944	Little Snoring
223	Liberator VI/ Fortress II/III	cSept 1944	Oulton
171	Stirling II/ Halifax III	15 Sept 1944	North Creake
462 (RAAF)	Halifax III	13 March 1945	Foulsham

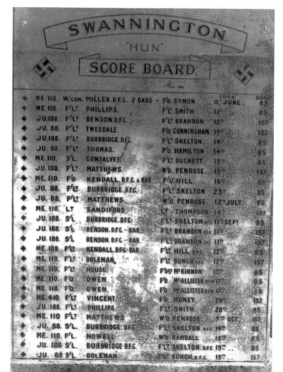

Associated Units: 25(F); 101(8); 141(F); 151(F); 264(F); 307(F) 406(F); 410(F); 456(F); The Defiant Flight; 605(F); 1692 BSTU (formerly 1692 Flight) 1694 Flight; 1699 Flight; Bomber Support Development Unit and The '*Window*' Research Section.

The Swannington 'Hun' scoreboard which once graced a wall at the Norfolk airfield and which is now on permanent display in the 100 Group Memorial room at the City of Norwich Aviation Museum. (Author)

APPENDIX II

100 Group Fighter Air-to-Air Victories

Date	Type Serial SQN Enemy A/C Details	Pilot-Navigator/Radar Op
23/24.12.43	Beaufighter VIF V8744 141 Sqn Ju 88 nr. Düren	F/L H. C. Kelsey DFC-P/O E. M. Smith DFM. Ju 88 of *4/NJG1.* Oblt Finster, pilot, KIA. Radio operator WIA and the gunner both baled out.
28/29.1.44	II HJ941 'X' 141 Bf 109 nr Berlin	F/O H. E. White DFC-F/O M. S. Allen DFC
28/29.1.44	II HJ644 239 Sqn Bf 110 near Berlin	F/O N. Munro-F/O A. R. Hurley
30/31.1.44	II HJ712 'R' 141 Sqn Bf 110 near Berlin	F/L G. J. Rice-F/O J. G. Rogerson
30/31.1.44	II HJ711 'P' 169 Sqn Bf 110 Brandenburg area	S/L J.A.H. Cooper-F/L R. D. Connolly. Bf 110G-4 Wrk Nr 740081 D5+LB of *Stab III/NJG3,* which crashed at Werneuchen, 20 km E of Berlin. Oblt. Karl Loeffelmaan, pilot KIA. Fw. Karl Bareiss, radar op and Ofw. Oscar Bickert, both WIA, baled out.
5/6.2.44	II HJ707 'B' 169 Sqn Bf 110 North Sea off England	P/O W. H. Miller-P/O F. C. Bone
15/16.2.44	II DZ726 'Z' 141 Sqn He 177 Berlin	F/O H. E. White-F/O M. Allen
20/21.2.44	II DZ270 239 Sqn Bf 110 near Stuttgart	F/O T. Knight-F/O D. P. Doyle
25/26.2.44	II DZ254 'P' 169 Sqn Bf 110 SW Mannheim	F/L R. G. Woodman-F/O P. Kemmis
5.3.44	VI 515 He 177 Bretigny? Melun	W/C E. F. F. Lambert DFC-F/L E. W. M. Morgan DFM. He 177A-3 Wrk.Nr. 332214 5J+RL of *3./KG100* cr. near Châteaudun/France. Lt. Wilhelm Werner (pilot); Uffz. Kolemann Schoegl (WOp); Uffz. Gustav Birkebmaier (Flt. Eng); Uffz. Alfred Zwieselsberger (AG); Uffz. Josef Kerres (AG) all KIA.
18/19.3.44	II HJ710 'T' 141 Sqn 2 x Ju 88 near Frankfurt	F/O H. E. White DFC-F/O M. S. Allen DFC
18/19.3.44	II DZ761 'C' 141 Sqn Ju 88 near Frankfurt	F/O J. C. N. Forshaw-P/O F. S. Folley. Ju 88C-6 Wrk.Nr. 750014 R4+CS of *8./NJG2,* shot down by Mosquito of 141 Squadron, cr. at Arheilgen near Darmstadt, 25 km S of Frankfurt. Ofw. Otto Müller (pilot); Ogefr. Erhard Schimsal (radar op); Gefr. Gunter Hanke (AG) all KIA.
22/23.3.44	II 239 Sqn Bf 110 Frankfurt	S/L E. W. Kinchin-F/L D. Sellers
24/25.3.44	II DD717 'M' 141 Sqn Fw 190 Berlin	F/L H. C. Kelsey DFC*-F/O E. M. Smith DFC DFM
30/31.3.44	II DZ661 239 Sqn Ju 88 Nuremberg	F/Sgt J. Campbell DFM-F/Sgt R. Phillips. Ju 88C-6 Wrk.Nr. 360272 D5+ of *4./NJG3,* cr. 10 km SW of Bayreuth. Oblt. Ruprecht Panzer (pilot); radar op & AG baled out safely.
11/12.4.44	II DZ263 239 Sqn Do 217 Aachen	S/L N. E. Reeves DFC*-W/O A. A. O'Leary DFC** DFM
18/19.4.44	II DD799 169 Sqn Bf 110 Compiègne	F/O R. G. Woodman-F/O P. Kemmis
20/21.4.44	II DD732 'S' 141 Sqn Do 217 N of Paris	F/L H. E. White DFC*-F/L M. S. Allen DFC*. Either Do 217N-1 Wrk Nr 51517 of *5/NJG4,* which cr. near Meulan N of Paris. Ofw. Karl Kaiser, pilot WIA, and Uffz. Johannes Nagel, radar op WIA, baled out; Gefr. Sigmund Zinser (AG) KIA or Do 217E-5 Wrk.Nr. 5558 6N+EP of *6./KG100,* crash place u/k. Fw. Heinz Fernau (pilot), Hptm. Willi Scholl (observer), Uffz. Josef Bach (WOp), Ofw. Fritz Wagner (Flt. Eng), all MIA.
20/21.4.44	II 169 Sqn Bf 110 Ruhr	F/L G. D. Cremer-F/O B. C. Farrell
22/23.4.44	II W4085 169 Sqn Bf 110 Bonn area	F/L R. G. Woodman-F/O P. Kemmis
22/23.4.44	II W4076 169 Sqn Bf 110 Köln	P/O W. H. Miller-P/O F.C. Bone
23/24.4.44	II HJ712 'R' 141 Sqn Fw 190 Flensburg	F/L G. J. Rice-P/O R. S. Mallett
26.4.44	VI 515 Sqn UEA Gilze a/f	S/L H. B. Martin DSO DFC -F/O J. W. Smith
26.4.44	VI 515 Sqn UEA Le Culot a/f	W/O T. S. Ecclestone-F/Sgt J. H. Shimmon
26.4.44	VI 515 Sqn UEA Brussels Evere	" "
26/27.4.44	II W4078 239 Sqn Bf 110 Essen	F/O W. R. Breithaupt-F/O J. A. Kennedy DFM
27/28.4.44	II W4076 169 Sqn Bf 110 SE of Strasbourg	P/O P. L. Johnson-P/O M. Hopkins
27/28.4.44	II 239 Sqn Bf 110/Ju 88 Montzon-Aulnoye	Montzon-Aulnoye F/O R. Depper-F/O G. C. Follis
27/28.4.44	II DD622 239 Sqn Bf 110	S/L N. E. Reeves DFC*-W/O A. A. O'Leary DFC** DFM

8/9.5.44	II DD709 169 Sqn Bf 110 Braine-Ie-Comte	S/L R. G. Woodman DFC-F/O P. Kemmis. Bf 110 of *I./NJG4* crewed by Lt. Wolfgang Martstaller and his radar operator/air gunner who had taken off from Florennes at 0300 hrs shot down Lancaster ND587 of 405 Squadron before their combat with Woodman. The Bf 110 belly-landed in a field. Martstaller was KIA in a crash at St. Trond aerodrome in August 1944.
10/11.5.44	II W4078 239 Sqn Bf 110 Near Courtrai	F/O V. Bridges DFC-F/Sgt D. G. Webb DFM. Bf 110 3C+F1 Wrk Nr 740179 of *I./NJG4,* which cr. at Ellezelles, Belgium. Oblt. Heinrich Schulenberg, pilot and Ofw. Hermann Meyer, radar operator, baled out near Flobeq. Meyer was wounded and badly concussed and spent 3 weeks in hospital and 4 more weeks at home.
11/12.5.44	II DZ726 'Z' 141 Sqn Ju 88 N of Amiens	F/L H. E. White DFC*-F/L M. S. Allen DFC*
11/12.5.44	II DZ240 'H' 141 Sqn Ju 88 SW of Brussels	F/L L. J. G. LeBoutte-F/O R. S. Mallett. Ju 88 of *6./NJG2.* Wilhelm Simonsohn, pilot, Uffz. Franz Holzer, flight engineer and Uffz. Günther Gottwick, wireless operator-air gunner all baled out. A/c cr. near Mechlen, north east of Brussels.
12/13.5.44	II W4078 239 Sqn Bf 110 Hasselt-Louvain	F/O W. R. Breithaupt-F/O J. A. Kennedy DFM
12/13.5.44	II W4092 239 Sqn Ju 88 Belgium	F/O V. Bridges DFC-F/Sgt D. G. Webb DFM. Ju 88C-6 Wrk Nr 750922 D5+ of *5./NJG3* cr. at Hoogcruts nr. Maastricht. Uffz. Josef Polzer, Ogefr Hans Klünder, radar op, KIA. Gefr. Hans Becker (AG) WIA.
15/16.5.44	II DZ748 169 Sqn Bf 110/2 x Ju 88 Cuxhaven area	P/O W. H. Miller-P/O F.C. Bone
22/23.5.44	II DZ309 239 Sqn Bf 110 Dortmund	F/L D. L. Hughes-F/O R. H. Perks
22/23.5.44	II 169 Sqn Bf 110 Groningen area	W/C N. B. R. Bromley OBE-F/L P. V. Truscott. Bf 110G-4 Wrk Nr 720050 D5+ of *3.NJG3* cr. at Hoogeveen S of Groningen. Fw. Franz Müllebner (FF), Uffz. Alfons Josten (radar op); Gefr. Karl Rademacher (AG) all WIA & baled out.
24/25.5.44	II DZ265 239 Sqn Bf 110 Aachen	F/L D. J. Raby DFC-F/Sgt S. J. Flint DFM
24/25.5.44	II DZ309 239 Sqn Bf 110 Aachen	F/L D. L. Hughes-F/O R. H. Perks Bf 110G-4 Wrk Nr 730106 2Z+AR of *7./NJG6* poss. shot down by either of these two crews at 0230 hrs in forest between Zweifall & Mulartshuette SE of Aachen. Oblt. Helmut Schulte (FF) baled out, Uffz. Georg Sandvoss (radar op) KIA, Uffz. Hans Fischer (AG) baled out. Bf 110G-4 Wrk.Nr. 720387 2Z+HR of *7./NJG6,* poss. shot down by Raby/Flint or Hughes/Perks, cr. at 0235 hrs at the Wesertalsperre near Dipen, S of Aachen. Crew: Uffz. Oskar Voelkel (pilot); Uffz. Karl Hautzenberger (radar op); Uffz. Günther Boehxne (AG) all baled out.
24/25.5.44	II DZ297 239 Sqn Ju 88 15m ESE of Bonn	F/O W. R. Breithaupt-F/O J. A. Kennedy DFM
27/28.5.44	II DD622 239 Sqn Bf 110F Aachen	S/L N. E. Reeves DFC*-P/O A. A. O'Leary DFC** DFM. Bf 110F Wrk.Nr. 140032 G9+CR of *7./NJG1* cr. at Spannum in Friesland Province/Neth. at 0115 hrs. Uffz. Joachim Tank (pilot, 26), slightly wounded. Uffz. Günther Schroeder (radar op, 19) & Uffz. Heinz Elwers (AG, 24), KIA.
27/28.5.44	II HJ941 'X' 141 Sqn Bf 109 W of Aachen	F/L H. E. White DFC*-F/L M. S. Allen DFC*
31.5/1.6.44	II DZ297 239 Sqn Bf 110 Near Trappes	F/O V. Bridges DFC-F/Sgt D. C. Webb DFM
31.5/1.6.44	II DZ256 'U' 239 Sqn Bf 110 West of Paris	F/L D. Welfare -F/O D. B. Bellis
1/2 6.44	II DZ265 239 Sqn Bf 110 Northern France	F/L T. L. Wright-P/O L. Ambery
5/6.6.44	II DD789 239 Sqn Ju 88 off Friesians	F/O W. R. Breithaupt-F/O J. A. Kennedy DFM. Ju 88 G-1 Wrk.Nr. 710454 of *5./NJG3,* cr. 20 km N of Spiekeroog. Uffz. Willi Hammerschmitt (pilot), Uffz. Friedrich Becker (radar op) and Fw. Johannes Kuhrt (AG) all KIA.
5/6.6.44	II DZ256 'U' 239 Sqn Bf 110 North of Aachen	F/L D. Welfare-F/O D. B. Bellis. Poss. Bf 110 Wrk.Nr. 440272 G9+NS of *8./NJG1* shot down at great height, cr. at 0054 hrs on Northern beach of Schiermonnikoog. Uffz. Adolf Stuermer (22), pilot, KIA; Uffz. Ludwig Serwein (21) Radar Op MIA; Gefr. Otto Morath (23) AG, KIA.
8/9.6.44	II DD741 169 Sqn Do 217 Paris area	W/C N. B. R. Bromley OBE-F/L P. V. Truscott. Poss. Do 217K-3 Wrk.Nr. 4742 6N+OR of *Stab III./KG100* claimed in Paris area but crash-place u/k. Oblt. Oskar Schmidtke (pilot); Uffz. Karl Schneider (Observer); Uffz. Helmuth Klinski (WOp); Uffz. Werner Konzett (Flt. Eng), all MIA.
8/9.6.44	II DD303 'E' 141 Sqn UEA Rennes	F/O A. C. Gallacher DFC-W/O G. McLean DFC
11/12.6.44	II DZ256 'U' 239 Sqn Bf 110 North of Paris	F/L D. Welfare-F/O D. B. Bellis

11/12.6.44	XIX MM642 'R' 85 Sqn Bf 110 10m NE Melum a/f	W/C C. M. Miller DFC**-F/O R. O. Symon
12/13.6.44	XIX MM630 'E' 157 Sqn Ju 188 Fôret De Compiègne	F/L J. G. Benson DFC-F/L L. Brandon DFC
12/13.6.44	XIX 85 Sqn Bf 110 near Paris	F/L M. Phillips-F/L D. Smith
13/14.6.44	II DZ254 'P' 169 Sqn Ju 88 Near Paris	W/O L. W. Turner-F/Sgt F. Francis
14/15.6.44	II DZ240 'H' 141 Sqn Me 410 North of Lille	W/O H. W. Welham-W/O E. J. Hollis
14/15.6.44	XIX MM671 'C' 157 Sqn Ju 88 Near Juvincourt	F/L J. Tweedale -F/O L. I. Cunningham
14/15.6.44	XIX 'Y' 85 Sqn Ju 188 SW Nivelles	F/L B. A. Burbridge DFC-F/L F. S. Skelton DFC. Ju 188 flown by Major Wilhelm Herget, *Kommandeur I./NJG4*. By the end of the war 58 of the 73 victories Herget gained were at night.
14/15.6.44	XIX 'J' 85 Sqn Ju 88 near Creil	F/L H. B. Thomas-P/O C. B. Hamilton
15/16.6.44	XIX 'C' 85 Sqn Bf 110 St Trond a/f	S/L F. S. Gonsalves-F/L B. Duckett. Bf 110 Wrk.Nr. 5664 G9+IZ of *12./NG1*, cr. 9 km W of Tongres (between St. Trond and Maastricht). Uffz. Heinz Bärwolf (pilot, injured, bailed out); Uffz. Fischer (WOp/Radar op) baled out. Ogfr. Edmund Kirsch (23, AG) KIA.
15/16.6.44	XIX MM671 'C' 157 Sqn Ju 88 Creil-Beauvais	F/L J O. Mathews-W/O A. Penrose
16/17.6.44	II W4076 169 Sqn Ju 88 Pas de Calais	F/O W. H. Miller-F/O F. Bone. Poss. Ju 88 Wrk.Nr. 710590 of *1./NJG2* cr. in Pas de Cancale/France. Hptm. Herbert Lorenz (pilot), Fw. Rudolf Scheuermann (radar op.) and Flg. Harry Huth (AG) all KIA.
17/18.6.44	XIX 85 Sqn Bf 110 Eindhoven	F/O P. S. Kendall DFC*-F/L C. R. Hill. Bf 110 of *NJG1* shot down at 0230 hrs & cr. at Soesterberg airfield. Müller & 2(?) others KIA.
17/18.6.44	II W4092 239 Sqn Ju 88 Near Eindhoven	F/O G. F. Poulton-F/O A. J. Neville. Ju 88G-1 Werke Nr 710866 R4+NS of *8./NJG2* which crashed at Volkel airfield. Lt. Harald Machleidt (pilot) (k). Uffz. Kurt Marth (radar op) WIA, Gefr. Max Rinnerthaler (AG) KIA.
21/22.6.44	II DZ2950 239 Sqn He 177 Ruhr	F/O R. Depper-F/O R. G. C. FoIlis
21.6.44	VI PZ203 'X' 515 Sqn Bf 110F	S/L P. W. Rabone DFC-F/O F. C. H. Johns. Bf 110G Wrk Nr 440076G9+NS of *8./NJG1*, which had just taken off from Eelde a/f, shot down at 1519 hrs. Uffz. Herbert Beyer (21) pilot, Uffz. Hans Petersmann (21) radar op, & Ogfr. Franz Riedel (20) AG, all KIA.
23/24.6.44	XIX 'Y' 85 Sqn Ju 88	F/L B. A. Burbridge DFC-F/L F.S. Skelton DFC
24/25.6.44	II DD759 'R' 239 Sqn Ju 88 Paris-Amiens	F/L D. Welfare-F/O D. B. BeIIis
27/28.6.44	II HJ911 'A' 141 Sqn Ju 88 Cambrai	S/L G. J. Rice-F/O J. G. Rogerson
27/28.6.44	DZ240 'H' 141 Sqn Ju 88 S of Tilburg	W/O H. Welham-W/O E. Hollis. Poss. Ju 88G-1 Wrk.Nr 710455 of *4./NJG3*, cr. at Arendonk/Belgium. Uffz. Eügen Wilfert (pilot), KIA; Ogefr. Karl Martin (radar op.), KIA; Gefr. Rudolf Scherbaum (AG), KIA.
27/28.6.44	II DD759 'R' 239 Sqn Me 410 E of Paris	F/L D. Welfare-F/O D. B. BeIIis
27/28.6.44	II 239 Sqn Fw 190 Near Brussels	W/C P. M. J. Evans-F/O R. H. Perks DFC
27/28.6.44	II DD749 239 Sqn Ju 88 Near Brussels	F/L D. R. Howard-F/O F. A. W Clay
27/28.6.44	VI PZ188 'J' 515 Sqn Ju 88 Eindhoven	P/O C. W. Chown RCAF-F/Sgt D. G. N. Veitch. Ju 88 Wrk Nr. 300651 B3+LT of *9./NJG54* during landing approach at Welschap (after a mine-laying operation in the invasion area) at 0213 hrs. The Ju 88 crashed into a house, killing 3 children and Uffz. Gotthard Seehaber, pilot, Gefr. Kurt Voelker, Ogefr. Walter Oldenbruch & Ogefr. Hermann Patzel.
28/29.6.44	VI NT150 169 Sqn Bf 110 nr Mucke	P/O H. Reed-F/O S. Watts
30.6.44	VI PZ203 'X' 515 Sqn He 111 Jagel/Schleswig	S/L P. W. Rabone DFC-F/O F. C. H. Johns
30.6.44	VI PZ188 'J' 515 Sqn Ju 34	P/O C. W. Chown RCAF-F/Sgt D. G. N. Veitch
30.6/1.7.44	VI DZ265 239 Sqn Ju 88 Le Havre	F/L C. J. Raby DFC-F/Sgt S. J. Flint DFC Probably Ju 88 Wrk.Nr. 711114 of *5./NJG2*. Cr. SE of Dieppe/France. Uffz. Erich Pollmer WIA. Other crew details u/k.
4/5.7.44	II DZ298 239 Sqn Bf 110 NW Paris	S/L N. E. Reeves DFC* - P/O A. A. O'Leary DFC** DFM
4/5.7.44	VI PZ163 'C' 515 Sqn Ju 88 Near Coulommiers	W/O R. E. Preston-F/Sgt F. Verity
4/5.7.44	II DD725 'G' 141 Sqn Me 410 Near Orleans	F/L J. D. Peterkin-F/O R. Murphy
4/5.7.44	II 169 Sqn Bf 110 Villeneuve	F/L J .S. Fifield-F/O F. Staziker
5/6.7.44	II DZ298 239 Sqn Bf 110 near Paris	S/L N. E. Reeves DFC*-W/O A. A. O'Leary DFC** DFM
5/6.7.44	VI NT121 169 Sqn Ju 88 South of Paris	F/O P. G. Bailey-F/O J. O. Murphy. Ju 88 Wrk.Nr. 751065 R4+ of *5./NJG2*, cr. near Chartres/France. Ofw. Fritz Farrherr (pilot) KIA; Gefr. Josef Schmid (Radar op) WIA baled out; Ogefr. Heinz Boehme (AG) KIA.
5/6.7.44	II W4097 239 Sqn 2 x Bf 110 Paris	S/L J. S. Booth DFC*-F/O K. Dear DFC. Bf 110G-4 110028

		C9+HK of *2./NJG5*, which crashed near Compiègne, is believed to be one of the two aircraft shot down by Booth and Dear. Lt. Joachim Hanss, pilot and Fw. Kurt Stein, *bordschütz*, were killed. Ufzz. Wolfgang Wehrhan, radar operator, was wounded.
7/8.7 44	II HJ911 'A' 141 Sqn Bf 110 NW of Amiens	S/L G. J. Rice-F/O J. G. Rogerson. Poss. Bf 110G-4 Wrk.Nr. 730006 D5+ of *2./NJG3* cr. 5 km W of Chièvres/Belgium. Pilot u/k & Gefr. Richard Reiff WIA, baled out. Ogefr. Edmund Hejduck KIA.
7/8.7.44	II DD789 239 Sqn Fw 190 Pas de Calais	W/C P. M. J. Evans-F/L T. R. Carpenter
7/8.7.44	II DZ29S8 239 Sqn Bf 110 Near Charleroi	F/L V. Bridges DFC-F/Sgt D. G. Webb DFM
10.7.44	VI PZ188 'J' 515 Sqn Ju 88 Zwishilnahner a/f	F/O R. A. Adams-P/O F. H. Ruffle) shared
10.7.44	VI PZ420 'O' 515 Sqn	F/O D. W. O. Wood-F/O K. Bruton) shared
12/13.7.44	XIX TA401 'D' 157 Sqn Ju 88 SE Étampes	F/L J. O. Mathews-W/O A. Penrose
14.7.44	VI RS993 'T' 515 Sqn Ju 34 Stralsund, NE Ger.	F/L A. E. Callard-F/Sgt E. D. Townsley
14/15.7.44	XIX 157 Sqn Bf 110 20m NE Juvincourt	Lt Sandiford RNVR-Lt Thompson RNVR (anti *Diver*)
14/15.7.44	VI NT112 'M' 169 Sqn Bf 109 Auderbelck	W/O L. W. Turner-F/Sgt F. Francis
20/21.7.44	VI NT113 169 Sqn Bf 110G-4 near Courtrai	W/C N. B. R. Bromley OBE-F/L R Truscott DFC. Bf 110G-4 Wrk Nr 730218 G9+EZ of *12./NJG1* cr. near Moll, Belgium. Ofw. Karl-Heinz Scherfling (25) pilot, a *Ritterkreuztraeger* since 8 April 1944 & who had 33 night victories, KIA. Fw Herbert Winkler, (31, AG), Fw. Herbert Scholz (25, radar op), baled out seriously injured. Fw. Herbert Winkler (31, AG) KIA.
20/21.7.44	VI NT146 169 Sqn Ju 88	Homburg area P/O H. Reed-F/O S. Watts
20/21.7.44	VI NTl21 169 Sqn Bf 110 Courtrai	F/L J. S. Fifield-F/O F. Staziker
23/24.7.44	II HJ710 'T' 141 Sqn Ju 88 SW of Beauvais	P/O I. D. Gregory-P/O D. H. Stephens. Poss. Bf 110G-4 Wrk.Nr. 730117 G9+GR of *7./NJG1*, shot down by Mosquito NF at 0125 hrs, cr. 5 km N of Deelen a/f. Lt. Josef Hettlich (pilot); Fw. Johann Treiber (WOp/Radar Op.) both slightly injured & baled out. AG also baled out. Or, Bf 110 Wrk.Nr. 441083 G9+OR of *III./NJG1* or *7./NJG1*, shot down by Mosquito NF' at 0147 hrs during landing at Leeuwarden a/f, cr. at Rijperkerk N of Leeuwarden. Hptm. Siegfried Jandrey (30, pilot) & Uffz. Johann Stahl (25, Radar op) KIA. Uffz. Anton Herger (24, AG) injured.
23/24.7.44	VI NS997 'C' 169 Sqn Bf 110G-4 near Kiel	F/L R. J. Dix-F/O A. J. Salmon. Bf 110G-4 Wrk Nr 730036 G9+ER of *7./NJG1* was shot down at very low level around midnight. The 110 cr. near Balk in Friesland Province, Holland. Fw. Heinrich-Karl Lahmann (25, pilot) & Uffz Günther Bouda (21 AG) both baled out. Uffz. Willi Huxsohl (21, radar op) KIA.
23/24.7.44	II DZ661 239 Sqn Bf 110 Kiel	F/O N. Veale-F/O R. D. Comyn. At 0125 hrs Bf 110G-4 730117 G9+GR of *7./NJG1* was shot down N of Deelen airfield. Lt Josef Hettlich, pilot, Fw Johann Treiber (RO) and the air gunner all baled out safely.
25/26.7.44	VI RS961 'H' 515 Me 410 Knocke, Belgium	S/L H. B. Martin DSO DFC-F/O J. W. Smith
25/26.7.44	VI PZ178 23 Sqn UEA Laon Pouvron	F/L D. J. Griffiths-F/Sgt S. F. Smith
28/29.7.44	II HJ712 'R' 141 2 x Ju 88 Metz/Neufchâteau	F/L H. E. White DFC*-F/L M. S. Allen DFC*
28/29.7.44	II HJ741 'Y' 141 Sqn Ju 88 Metz area	P/O I. D. Gregory-P/O D. H. Stephens. Ju 88G-1 Wrk.Nr. 713649 R4+KT of *9./NJG2*, possibly shot down by Mosquito of 141 Sqn (White & Allen or Gregory/Stephens), cr. 20 km SSW of Toul, France. Hptm. August Speckmann (pilot), KIA; Ofw. Arthur Boos (radar op) WIA. Ofw. Wilhelm Berg (Flt Eng) & Uffz. Otto Brueggenkamp (AG) both KIA.
8/9.8.44	II DZ256 'U' 239 Sqn Fw 190 St Quentin	F/L D. Welfare-F/O .B. BeIlis
8/9.8.44	II 239 Sqn Bf 109 N France	F/L D. J. Raby DFC-F/Sgt S. J. Flint DFM
8/9.8.44	VI NT156 'Y' 169 Sqn Fw 190 E Abbeville	F/L R. G. Woodman DFC-F/L P. Kemmis
10/11.8.44	VI NT176 'H' 169 Sqn Bf 109 Over Dijon	F/O W. H. Miller DFC-F/O F. C. Bone DFC
12/13.8.44	VI NT173 169 Sqn He 219 nr Aachen	F/O W. H. Miller DFC-F/O F. C. Bone DFC
16/17.8.44	VI HB213 'G' 141 Sqn Bf 110 Ringkobing Fjord	W/O E. A. Lampkin-F/Sgt B. J. Wallnutt
26/27.8.44	VI NT146 'T' 169 Sqn Ju 88 near Bremen	W/O L. W. Turner-F/Sgt F. Francis. Ju 88G-1 Wrk.Nr. 710542 D5+BR of *7./NJG.* cr. nr Mulsum 42 km E of Bremen. Lt. Achim Woeste (pilot), KIA. Uffz. Heinz Thippe, WIA, baled out. Gefr. Karl Walkenberger, WIA, baled out. Uffz. Anton Albrecht KIA.
29/30.8.44	II W4097 239 Sqn Ju 88 near Stettin	F/L D. L. Hughes-F/L R. H. Perks
6/7.9.44	VI PZ338 'A' 515 Sqn Bf 109 Odder, Denmark	W/C F. F. Lambert DFC -F/O R. J. Lake AFC
11/12.9.44	XIX 'Y' 85 Sqn Ju 188 Baltic Sea	S/L B. A. Burbridge DFC-F/L F. S. Skelton DFC

11/12.9.44	VI HR180 'B' 141 Sqn Bf 110 SW of Mannheim	F/L P. A. Bates-P/O W. G. Cadman
11/12.9.44	XIX MM630 'E' 157 Sqn 2 x Ju 188 Zeeland	S/L J. G. Benson DFC-F/L L. Brandon DFC
11/12.9.44	XIX 'A' 85 Sqn Bf 109G Limburg area	F/L P. S. Kendall DFC*-F/L C R. Hill DFC*
12/13.9.44	XIX MM643 'F' 157 Sqn Bf 110 Frankfurt	F/L R. D. Doleman-F/L D. C. Bunch DFC
12/13 9.44	II 239 Sqn Bf 110 Ranschhack	F/O W. R. Breithaupt DFC-F/O J. A. Kennedy DFC DFM
13/14.9.44	XIX 'D' 85 Sqn Bf 110 nr Koblenz	F/L W. House-F/Sgt R. D. McKinnon. Bf 110G-4 Wrk.Nr.440384 G9+EN of *5./NJG1 which took off* from Düsseldorf A/F at 2234 hrs cr. at Birresborn in the Eiffel at 2335 hrs. Oblt. Gottfried Hanneck, pilot, baled out WIA. Uffz. Thdch Sacher (radar op) & Uffz. Willi Wurschitz (radar op/AG) both KIA.
17/18.9.44	XIX 'J' 85 Sqn 2 x Bf 110	F/O A. J. Owen-F/O J. S. V. McAllister DFM. Bf 110 G-4 Wrk.Nr. 740358 G9+MY of *11./NJG1* cr. E of Arnhem/Holland. Uffz. Walter Sjuts KIA; Uffz. Herbert Schmidt KIA; Uffz. Ernst Fischer KIA. Bf 110G-4 Wrk.Nr. 740757 G9+GZ of *12./NJG1* cr. E of Arnhem/Holland. Uffz. Heinz Gesse, Uffz. Josef Kaschub & Ogefr. Josef Limberg all KIA.
26/27.9.44	VI PZ301 'N' 515 Sqn He 111 Zellhausen a/f	S/L H. F. Morley-F/Sgt R. A. Fidler
28/29.9.44	XIX 'Y' 85 Sqn Ju 188	F/L M. Phillips-F/L D. Smith
28/29.9.44	XVII HK357 25 Sqn 2 x He 111H22 over N Sea	W/C L. J. C. Mitchell-F/L D. L. Cox
29/30.9.44	XIX 157 Sqn Me 410 *(Prob)* 10m ESE Yarmouth	F/L Vincent-F/O Money
6/7.10.44	VI NT234 'W' 141 Sqn Ju 88 S of Leeuwarden	F/L A. C. Gallacher DFC-P/O D. McLean DFC. Ju 88G-1 Wrk.Nr. 710639 D5+EV of *10./NJG3* cr. near Groningen. Oblt. Walter Briegleb (pilot) WIA; Fw. Paul Kowalewski (radar op) KIA; Uffz. Brandt (Flt. Eng) WIA; Uffz. Bräunlich (AG) WIA.
7/8.10.44	XIX MM671 'C' 157 Sqn Bf 110 W of Neumünster	F/L J. O. Mathews DFC-W/O A. Penrose DFC
8.10.44	VI PZ181 'E' 515 Sqn Bf 109 Eggebek, Denmark	F/L F. T. L'Amie-F/O J. W. Smith
11.10.44	II DZ256 'U' 239 Sqn Seaplane Tristed	F/L D. Welfare DFC-F/O D. B. Bellis DFC (on the water)
14/15.10.44	XIX 'Y' 85 Sqn 2 x Ju 88G Gütersloh a/f	S/L B. A. Burbridge DFC*-F/L F. S. Skelton DFC*
14/15.10.44	VI PZ245 239 Sqn Fw 190 Meland	F/L D. R. Howard-F/O F. A. W. Clay
15/16.10.44	XIX 'D' 85 Sqn Bf 110	F/L C. K. Nowell-W/O Randall
19/20.10.44	XXX NT250 'Y' 141 Sqn Ju 88 SE of Karlsruhe	F/L G. D. Bates-F/O D. W. Field. Poss. Ju 88G-1 Wrk.Nr. 712312 2Z+EB of *I./NJG6*, which cr. at Vaihirgen/Marksdorf ENE of Pforzheim/Germany. Oblt. Wilhelm Engel (pilot) WIA; radar op safe.
19/20.10.44	VI PZ175 'H' 141 Sqn Ju 88 NW of Nuremberg	F/O J. C. Barton-F/Sgt R. A. Kinnear
19/20.10.44	XIX TA404 'M' 157 Sqn Ju 88 nr Mannheim	S/L R. D. Doleman DFC-F/L D. C. Bunch DFC. Poss. Ju 88G-1 Wrk.Nr. 714510 2Z+CM of *4./NJG6*, which cr. at Murrhardt, SE of Heilbronn/Germany. Uffz. Georg Haberer (pilot) & Uffz. Ernst Dressel (radar op) both KIA.
19/20.10.44	XIX 'Y' 85 Sqn Ju 188 Metz	S/L B. A. Burbridge DFC*-F/L F. S. Skelton DFC*
19/20.10.44	VI PZ275 239 Sqn Bf 110 Strasbourg	W/O P. C. Falconer-F/Sgt W. C. Armour
28/29.10.44	II PZ245 239 Sqn He 111 Dummer Lake	F/L D. R. Howard-F/O F. A. W. Clay
29.10.44	VI PZ344 'E' 515 Sqn Fw 190+Ju W34	F/L P. T. L'Amie-F/O J. W. Smith
29 10.44	VI PZ217 'K' 515 Sqn Bf 110	P/O T. A. Groves-F/Sgt R. B. Dockeray
1/2.11.44	XIX 'R' 85 Sqn Ju 88 20m S Mülhouse	F/O A. J. Owen-F/O J. S. V. McAllister
4/5.11.44	XIX TA401 'D' 157 Sqn Bf 110 Osnabrück	W/G K. H. P. Beauchamp-P/O Money
4/5.11.44	II 239 Sqn Bf 110 Bochum	F/O J. N. W. Young-F/O R. H. Siddons
4/5.11.44	XIX TA401 'D' 85 Sqn Bf 110 Bochum	S/L R. G. Woodman DFC-F/O A. F. Witt
4/5.11.44	XIX 'Y' 85 Sqn Ju 88G 30m S. Bonn	S/L B. A. Burbridge DSO DFC*-F/O P. S. Skelton DSO DFC* Ju 88 5m SE Bonn Bf 110 N of Hangelar Bf 110 of *II./NJG1* which crashed into the River Rhine nr Hangelar airfield at 2150 hrs. Oblt. Ernst Runze, pilot, KIA. Ogefr. Karl-Heinz Bendfield, radar operator, and air gunner baled out. Ju 88 N of Hangelar
4/5.11.44	XIX 'B' 85 Sqn Ju 88 S E Bielefeld	F/O A. J. Owen-F/O J. S. V. McAllister DFM Bf 110 of *II./NFG1*, shot down by Mosquito NF at 1900 hrs at 20,000 ft. Uffz. Gustav Sario (pilot) injured & baled out; Uffz. Heinrich Conrads (radar op) & Ogefr. Roman Talarowski (AG) both KIA. Bf 110G-4 Wrk.Nr. 440648 G9+PS of *8./NJG1* possibly shot down by Mosquito NF, cr. at Bersenbrueck, 30 km N. of Osnabrück/Germany. Fw. Willi Ruge (pilot) WIA, baled out; Uffz. Helmut Kreibohm (radar op) & Ogefr. Anton Weiss (AG) both KIA. Bf 110 Wrk.Nr. 730272 G9+E2 of *IV./NJG1* shot down by Mosquito NF SW of Wezel/Germany. Lt. Heinz

Rolland (26, pilot, 15 night victories); Fw. Heinz Krüger (25, WOp/Radar Op); Uffz. Karl Berger (22, AG) all KIA.

6/7.11.44	XIX 'N' 85 Sqn Ju l88	S/L F. S. Gonsalves-F/L B. Duckett
6/7.11.44	XXX 'Y' 85 Sqn Bf 110 S Bonn a/f	F/O B. R. Keele DFC-F/O H. Wright
6/7.11.44	XIX 'A' 85 Sqn Ju 88 (prob)	Capt T. Weisteen RNWAF
6/7.11.44	XIX TA391 'N' 157 Sqn Ju 188 (prob) Osn/Minden	F/O H. P. Kelway-Sgt Bell
6/7.11.44	XIX TA404 'M' 157 Sqn Bf 110 S of Koblenz	S/L R. D. Doleman DFC-F/L D. C. Bunch DFC
6/7.11.44	II DD789 239 Sqn Ju 188 Osnabrück	F/O G. E. Jameson-F/O L. Ambery
10/11.11.44	XIX TA402 'F' 157 Sqn Ju 88 Frankfurt-Koblenz	S/L J. G. Benson DFC*-F/L L. Brandon DFC*
10/11.11.44	XXX PZ247 169 Sqn Ju 188 NE Germany	S/L R. G. Woodman DFC-F/O A. F. Witt
11/12.11.44	XIX MM671157 Sqn Ju 88 (Prob) Bonn	F/O J. O. Mathews DFC-W/O A. Penrose DFC. Ju 88 Wrk.Nr. 712268 of 1./NJG4, cr. near Giessen/Germany. Pilot and radar op baled out. Gefr. Alfred Graefer (AG) KIA.
11/12.11.44	XIX 'B' 85 Sqn Fw 190 30m SE Hamburg	F/O A. J. Owen-F/O J. S. V. McAllister DFM
21/22.11.44	XIX 'N' 85 Sqn Bf 110 Near Würzburg	S/L B. A. Burbridge DSO DFC*F/L F. S. Skelton DSO DFC* & Ju 88 Over Bonn
30.11.44	VI HR242 169 Sqn He 177 Liegnitz	W/C H. C. Kelsey DFC*-F/O E. M. Smith DFC DFM (on the ground)
30.11/1.12.44	XIX 85 Sqn Ju 88	S/L F. S. Gonsalves-F/L B. Duckett
30.11/1.12.44	XIX 157 Sqn Ju 188 5030N 0920E	F/O R. J. V. Smythe-F/O Waters
2/3.12.44	XIX 'A' 85 Sqn Bf 110	Capt T. Weisteen RNWAF. Bf 110G-4 Wrk.Nr. 180382 of 12./NJG4 took off Bonninghardt at 2047 hrs, cr. at 2145 hrs near Lippborg (near Hamm/Germany). Lt. Heinz-Joachim Schlage (pilot) safe. Fiebig & Uffz. Kundmüller KIA.
2/3.12.44	XIX 157 Sqn Ju 88 Osnabruck	F/L W. Taylor-F/O Edwards. Poss. Ju 88 Wrk.Nr. 714819 3C+WL of 3./NJG4, which cr. at Rheine. Ofhr. Erhard Pfisterhammer (pilot) WIA; Uffz. Wolfgang Sode (radar op) WIA; AG u/k probably safe.
4/5.12.44	XIX MM671 'C' 157 Sqn Ju 88 Dortmund a/f	F/L J. O. Mathews DFC-W/O A. Penrose DFC
4/5.12.44	XIX 157 Sqn Bf 110 Limburg	F/L W. Taylor-F/O Edwards
4/5.12.44	XXX 'C' 85 Sqn 2 x Bf 110 Germesheim	F/L R. T Goucher-F/L C. H. Bulloch
4/5.12.44	XXX 'B' 85 Sqn Bf 110 50m ENE Heilbronn	Capt S. Heglund DFC-F/O R.O. Symon
4/5.12.44	XXX 'H' 85 Sqn Ju 88 nr Krefeld	F/O A. J. Owen-F/O J. S. V. McAllister DFM. Prob. Ju 88G-1 Wrk.Nr. 714152 of 6./NJG4 (85 Squadron's 100th victory), which cr. nr Krefeld/Germany. Uffz. Wilhelm Schlutter (pilot) WIA; Uffz. Friedrich Heerwagen (radar op) & Gefr. Friedrich Herbeck (AG) both KIA.
6/7.12.44	XXX 'O' 85 Sqn Bf 110 West of Münster	F/O E. R. Hedgecoe DFC-F/Sgt J. R. Whitham. Poss. Bf 110G-4 Wrk.Nr. 140078 G9+HZ of 12./NJG1, shot down by Mosquito & cr. 10 km NW of Münster-Handorf/Germany. Hptm. Hans-Heinz Augenstein Knight's Cross 9.6.44 (St.Kpt 12./NJG1, 46 night victories, of which 45 were four-engined RAF bombers) KIA. Fw. Gunther Steins (radar op) KIA; Uffz. Kurt Schmidt (AG) WIA, baled out.
6/7.12.44	XIX MM671 'C' 157 Sqn Bf 110 Near Limburg	F/L J. O. Mathews DFC-W/O A. Penrose DFC Ju 88 15m SW Giessen
6/7.12.44	XIX TA404 'M' 157 Sqn Bf 110 Giessen	S/L R. D. Doleman DFC-F/L D. C. Bunch DFC
6/7.12.44	XIX MM638 'G' BSDU Bf 110 W of Giessen	S/L N. E. Reeves DSO DFC*-F/O M. Phillips
12/13.12.44	XIX 'A'? 85 Sqn Ju 88	Capt E. P. Fossum-F/O S. A. Hider
12/13.12.44	XXX 'O' 85 Sqn 2 x Bf 110 20m S Hagen/Essen	F/L E. R. Hedgecoe DFC- F/Sgt J. R. Whitham (with FIU)
12/13.12.44	XXX 'Z' 85 Sqn Ju 88 Gütersloh a/f	S/L B. A. Burbridge DSO DFC**-F/L F. S. Skelton DSO DFC**. Ju 88G-1 Wrk Nr. 714530 of 6./NJG4, cr. at Gütersloh airfield. Uffz. Heinrich Brune, pilot, Uffz Emil Hoftharth, radar op & Uffz. Wolfgang Rautert (AG) all KIA. Bf 110 2m W of Essen
17/18.12.44	XIX MM627 'H' 157 Sqn Bf 110 5112N 0635E	W/O D. A. Taylor-F/Sgt Radford
17/18.12.44	XIX MM653 'L' 157 Sqn Bf 110	F/Sgt J. Leigh
17/18.12.44	XXX 'J' 85 Sqn Bf 110 40m from Ûlm	F/L R. T. Goucher-F/L C. H. Bullock
18/19.12.44	XIX MM640 'I' 157 Sqn He 219 Osnabrück area	F/L W. Taylor-F/O J. N. Edwards. Poss. He 219A-0 Wrk Nr 190229 G9+GH of I./NJG1. Uffz. Scheuerlein (pilot) baled out, Uffz. Günther Heinze (radar op) KIA. Taylor and Edwards were killed on 22/23 December trying to land at Swannington.
21/22.12.44	XIX TA401 'D' 157 Sqn Ju 88 N of Frankfurt	W/C K. H. P. Beauchamp DSO DFC-F/L L. Scholefield
22/23.12.44	XXX 'B' 85 Sqn 2 x Ju 88+Bf 110 Saarbrücken area	F/O A. J. Owen-F/O J. S. V. McAllister DFM. Ju 88 Wrk.Nr. 621441 2Z+HK of 2./NJG6 cr. at Larxistuhl/Germany. Ofw. Max Hausser (pilot) KIA; Ofw. Fritz Steube (radar op) KIA; Fw.

Ernst Beisswenger (AG) WIA. Ju 88G-6 Wrk.Nr. 621436 2Z+DC of *II./NJG6* cr. at Lebach, N of Saarbrücken/Germany. Uffz. Werner Karau, aircrew function unknown, KIA; 2 others safe?

22/23.12.44	XXX 'P' 85 Sqn Bf 110 Koblenz-Gütersloh	S/L B. Burbridge DSO*DFC*-F/O F. S. Skelton DSO*DFC*
22/23.12.44	XIX TA404 'M' 157 Sqn Ju 88 5m W Limburg	S/L R. D. Doleman DFC-F/L D. C. Bunch DFC
23/24.12.44	XXX 157 Sqn Ju 88 Near Koblenz	F/L R. J. V. Smythe-F/O Waters
23/24.12.44	XIX 'N' 85 Sqn Bf 110 Mannheim-Mainz	F/L G. C. Chapman-F/L J. Stockley
24/25.12.44	XIX MM671 'C' 157 Sqn Ju 88G 3m SW Köln	F/L J. O. Mathews DFC-W/O A. Penrose DFC
24/25.12.44	XIX TA404 'M' 157 Sqn 2 x Bf 110 Köln/Duisburg	S/L R. D. Doleman DFC-F/L D. C. Bunch DFC. Bf 110G-4 G9+CT Wrk Nr 740162 of *9./NJG1* flown by Hptm Heinz Strüning, *Ritterkreuz mit Eichenlab* (Knight's Cross with Oak Leaves) and 56 night victories in *NJG1* & *NJG2* cr. at Bergisch Gladbach/. *Bordfunker* and *bordschütze* baled out safely. Strüning hit the tail of his Bf 110 and was killed. 2nd Bf 110 was G9+GR of *7./NJG1* which crashed nr. Soppenrade at 1922 hrs. Pilot and bordfunker inj. Gfr Wilhelm Ruffleth inj.
24/25.12.44	XIX MM676 'W' 157 Sqn Bf 110 5038N 0752E	S/L J. G. Benson DFC*-F/L L. Brandon DFC*
24/25.12.44	XXX 'A' 85 Sqn Bf 110 20m N Frankfurt	Capt S. Heglund DFC-F/O B. C. Symon
31.12/1.1.45	VI RS518 'L' 515 Sqn Ju 88 Lovns Bredning	S/L C. V. Bennett DFC-F/L R. A. Smith. Ju 88 of *4./NJG2*. Oblt. August Gyory (k). Enemy spun in and dropped into Lim Fijord.
31.12/1.1.45	XIX MT491 'E' 169 Sqn He 219 Köln area	F/L A. P. Mellows-F/L S. L. Drew (*att 85 Sqn*) He 219A-2 Wrk.Nr. 290194 G9+KL of *3./NJG1*, cr. at Schleiden, 50 km SW of Köln. Oblt. Heinz Oloff (pilot) & Fw. Helmut Fischer (radar op) both WIA & baled out.
31.12/1.1.45	VI RS507 'C' 239 Sqn Ju 88 Alhorn area	S/L J. Tweedale-F/O L. I. Cunningham
1/2.1.45	XXX 'R' 85 Sqn Ju 188 10m N of Münster	F/L R. T. Goucher-F/L C. H. Bullock. 2nd enemy was Ju 88G-6 Ju 88G 10m E of Dortmund Wrk Nr 621364 2Z+CP of *5./NJG6* which cr. at Dortmund killing Oblt. Hans Steffen, pilot, Uffz. Josef Knon, Uffz. Helmut Uttler and Uffz. Frierich Krebber.
1/2.1.45	XXX 85 Sqn Ju 88	F/O L. J. York
2/3.1.45	XXX 'N' 169 Sqn Ju 188 near Frankfurt	F/L R. G. Woodman DFC-F/L B. J. P. Simpkins DFC (*85 Sqn*)
2/3.1.45	XIX TA393 'C' 157 Sqn Ju 88 3m W Stuttgart	F/L J. O. Mathews DFC-W/O A. Penrose DFC
2/3.1.45	XXX 'X' 85 Sqn Ju 88 15m SW Ludwigshafen	S/L B. A. Burbridge DSO DFC* F/L F. S. Skelton DSO DFC*
5/6.1.45	XXX 'B' 85 Sqn Bf 110 25m N Münster	Capt S. Heglund DFC-F/O R. O. Symon
5/6.1.45	XIX TA394 'A' 157 Sqn He 219 S Hanover	S/L J. G. Benson DFC*-F/L L. Brandon DFC*. He 219A-0 Wrk.Nr. 190188 G9-CK of *2./NJG1* cr. 5 km S of Wesendorf/Germany. Ofw. Josef Stroelein (pilot) KIA. Uffz. Kenne (radar op) baled out safely.
5/6.1.45	VI RS881 'C' 515 Sqn Ju 88 Jagel a/f	F/L A. S. Briggs-F/O Rodwell. Poss. Ju 88 Wrk.Nr. 620513 R4+CD of *III./NJG2* which cr. in Denmark (at Jagel airfield?) Oblt. Bruno Heilig (pilot), Uffz. Günther Kulas (radar op), Gefr. Johann Goliasch (Flt. Eng) & Ogefr. Horst Jauernig (AG) all KIA.
14/15.1.45	XXX 'Y' 85 Sqn Ju 188 Frankfurt	F/L K. D. Vaughan-F/L R. D. MacKinnon
14/15.1.45	VI HR294 'T' 141 Sqn UEA Jüterborg	F/L B. Brearley-F/O J. Sheldon
16/17.1.45	VI RS507 'C' 239 Sqn Bf 109 Fassberg	F/L T. Smith-F/O A. Cockayne
16/17.1.45	XXX 'Y' 85 Sqn He 219 Ruhr	F/L K. D. Vaughan-F/Sgt R. D. MacKinnon. Poss. Ju 88G-1 Wrk.Nr. 710818 D5+EP of *Stab/NJG3* which cr. 3 km SE of Friedberg (N of Frankfurt). Ofw. Johann Fels (pilot), Uffz. Richard Zimmer (radar op) & Gefr. Werner Hecht (AG) all KIA.
16/17.1.45	VI HR200 'E' 141 Sqn Bf 110 Magdeburg	F/L D. H. Young-F/O J. J. Sanderson
16/17.1.45	VI HR213 'G' 141 Sqn Bf 110 SW Magdeburg	F/O R. C. Brady-F/L M. K. Webster
16/17.1.45	XIX TA446 'Q' 157 Sqn Ju 188 Fritzler	F/L A. Mackinnon-F/O Waddell
1/2.2.45	XIX 157 Sqn Bf 110 (*Prob*) Oberolm	S/L RyalI-P/O Mulroy
1/2.2.45	XXX NT309 'C' 239 Sqn Bf 110 Mannheim	W/C W. F. Gibb DFC-F/O R. C. Kendall DFC. Bf 110G-4 Wrk.Nr.730262 G9+CN of *5./NJG1*, probably shot down by Mosquito of 157 or 239 Sqn, belly-landed 2km W of Kettershausen. Oblt. Gottfried Hanneck (pilot) WIA. Fw. Pean (radio/radar op) and Uffz. Gloeckner (AG) baled out safely.
1/2.2.45	XXX NT252 169 Sqn Bf 110 Stuttgart	F/L A. P. Mellows DFC-F/L S. L. Drew DFC. Prob. Bf 110 Wrk.Nr. 730370 2Z+EL of *3./NJG6* which cr. 25 km S of Stuttgart. Oblt. Willy Rathmann (pilot), Fw. Erich Berndt (radar op) and Uffz. Alfred Obry (AG) all KIA.
2/3.2.45	XXX MV548 'Z' 85 Sqn Ju 88	W/C W. K. Davison
2/3.2.45	VI RS575 'V' 515 Sqn Ju 88 Vechta	W/C H. C. Kelsey DFC*-F/L E. M. Smith DFC DFM

7/8.2.45   XXX NT330 'P' 239 Sqn Bf 110 Ruhr   F/L A. J. Holderness-F/L W. Rowley DFC.

7/8.2.45   XXX NT361 'N' 239 Sqn Bf 110 Ruhr   F/L D. A. D. Cather DFM-F/Sgt L. J. S. Spicer DFM. Bf 110G-4 Wrk.Nr. 730322 G9+HR of *7./NJG1* cr. W of Soest (Ruhr). Fw. Heinz Amsberg (pilot) & Uffz. Matthias Dengs (radar op) both KIA. Gefr. Karl Kopperberg (AG) WIA, baled out.

13/14.2.45   XIX MM684 'H' BSDU 2 x Bf 110 Frankfurt area   F/L D. R. Howard DFC-F/L F. A. W. Clay DFC. Bf 110 Wrk.Nr. 480164 C9+ of *5./NJG5* cr. nr Bodenbach (Frankfurt area). Fw. Heinrich Schmidt (pilot), Uffz. Erich Wohlan (radar op) and Uffz. Adam Zunker (AG) all KIA.

14/15.2.45   XXX MV532 'S' 85 Sqn Ju 88 Schwabish Hall a/f   F/L F. D. Win RNZAF-F/O T. P. Ryan RNZAF

20/21.2.45   XXX NT361 'N' 239 Sqn Fw 190 Worms   W/C W. F. Gibb DFC-F/O R. C. Kendall DFC DFM

5/6.3.45   XXX NT361 'N' 239 Sqn 2xJu 88 Chemnitz/Nuremberg   W/C W. F. Gibb DFC-F/O R. C. Kendall DFC DFM. Ju 88G-6 Wrk.Nr. 622319 C9+GA of *Stab/NJG5* flown by Obstlt Walter Borchers KIA (*Kommodore NJG5*, (59 victories -16 by day, 43 by night) Knight's Cross 29.10.44 KIA. Lt. Friedrich Reul (radar op) KIA (cr. nr Altenburg 25 km NW of Chemnitz in Thuringia). Ju 88G-6 Wrk.Nr. 622318 C9+NL of *3./NJG5* cr. near Chemnitz. Uffz. H. Dorminger (FF), Uffz. Max Bartsch (BF), Ogfr. Franz Wohlschlögel (BMF); Uffz. Friedrich Rullmann (BS) all MIA.

7/8.3.45   VI 'S' 23 Sqn Fw 190 Stendahl   F/O E. L. Heath-F/Sgt J. Thompson

8/9.3.45   XXX MV555 85 Sqn Ju 188   F/L I. A. Dobie-W/O A. R. Grimstone

14/15.3.45   VI HR213 'G' 141 Sqn UEA Lachen, Germany   F/O (2/Lt) R. D. S Gregor-F/Sgt P. S. Baker

14/15.3.45   XIX TA397 'R' 157 Sqn Ju 88G Lützkendorf   S/L R. D. Doleman DSO DFC-F/L D. C. Bunch DFC

15/16.3.45   XXX NT309 85 Sqn Ju 88 Hanover area   Capt E. P. Fossum-F/O S. A. Hider

15/16.3.45   XIX TA393 'C' 157 Sqn Ju 88 20m S Würzburg   F/L J. O. Mathews DFC*-W/O A. Penrose DFC*

16/17.3.45   XXX NT330 239 Sqn Ju 188 Nuremberg   S/L D. L Hughes DFC-F/L R. H. Perks DFC. Pilot Maj Werner Hoffmann?

18/19.3.45   XXX NT364 'K' 157 Sqn Ju 88 Hanau   W/O D. Taylor-F/Sgt Radtord

18/19.3.45   XXX NT271 'M' 239 Sqn He 219 Witten   W/C W. F. Gibb DFC-F/O R. C. Kendall DFC DFM. Prob. He 219 of *NJG1* Hptm. Baake (pilot & Kommandeur *I./NJG1*) and Uffz. Bettaque (radar op) both safe.

18/19.3.45   XXX MV548 'Z' 85 Sqn Bf 110   F/L F. D. Win RNZAF-F/O T. P. Ryan RNZAF

20/21.3.45   XXX NT324 'T' 85 Sqn Bf 110+He 219V-14   F/L G. C. Chapman-F/Sgt J. Stockley. Poss. He 219V-14 Wrk.Nr. 190014 of *3./NJG1*. Oblt. Heinz Oloff (pilot & *St.Kpt. 3./NJG1*); radar op u/k.

3.4.45   XXX 239 Sqn Ju 188   S/L D. L. Hughes DFC-F/L R. H. Perks DFC

4/5.4.45   XXX NT540 'C' BSDU Bf 109 W Magdeburg   S/L R. G. Woodman DFC-F/L A. J. Neville DFC

4/5.4.45   XXX 'C' 85 Sqn Ju 188 Near Magdeburg   F/L C. W. Turner-F/Sgt G. Honeyman

7/8.4.45   XXX 'Q' 85 Sqn Fw 190 NW Mobiis   W/C K. Davison DFC-F/L D. C. Bunch DFC (85/157 Sqns)

8/9.4.45   XXX NT494 'N' 85 Sqn Ju 88 20m W Lützkendorf   F/L H. B. Thomas DFC-F/O C. B. Hamilton

9/10.4.45   VI RS575 'V' 515 Sqn Ju 188 SE Hamburg   W/C H. C. Kelsey DFC*-F/L E. M. Smith DFC DFM

10/11.4.45   XXX 239 Sqn He 111   W/C P. O. Falconer-F/Sgt W. G. Armour

13/14.4.45   XXX NT334 'S' 85 Sqn He 219 Kiel   F/L K. D. Vaughan-F/Sgt R. D. MacKinnon

14/15.4.45   XXX 239 Sqn Ju 88 Potsdam   S/L D. J. Raby DFC-F/O S. J. Flint DFM

15/16.4.45   VI PZ398 'C' 515 Sqn Ju 52/3M Nr Schleissheim   P/O L. G. Holland-F/Sgt R. Young

17/18.4.45   XXX MV557 55 Ju 88 Munich area   W/C K. Davison DFC

19/20.4.45   XXX NT276 'B' BSDU Ju 88 S Denmark   F/L D. R. Howard DFC-F/L F. A. W. Clay DFC

21.4.45   VI 23 Sqn Ju 188   W/O East-F/Sgt Eames

24/25.4.45   VI RS575 'V' 515 Sqn Do 217 6m N Libeznice   W/C H. C. Kelsey DFC*-F/L E. M. Smith DFC DFM Do 217 Prague, Czech   "   "   "

Index